Cities in Contemporary Africa

Edited by

Martin J. Murray

and

Garth A. Myers

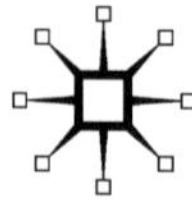

CITIES IN CONTEMPORARY AFRICA

First published in hardcover in 2006 by
PALGRAVE MACMILLAN®
in the United States—a division of St. Martin's Press LLC,
175 Fifth Avenue, New York, NY 10010.

Where this book is distributed in the UK, Europe and the rest of the world, this is by Palgrave Macmillan, a division of Macmillan Publishers Limited, registered in England, company number 785998, of Houndmills, Basingstoke, Hampshire RG21 6XS.

PALGRAVE MACMILLAN is the global academic imprint of the above companies and has companies and representatives throughout the world.

Palgrave® and Macmillan® are registered trademarks in the United States, the United Kingdom, Europe and other countries.

ISBN: 978–0–230–11664–1

Library of Congress Cataloging-in-Publication Data

Cities in contemporary Africa / edited by Martin J. Murray and Garth A. Myers.
p. cm.
Includes bibliographical references and index.
ISBN 1–4039–7035–1 (alk. paper)
1. Cities and towns—Africa. 2. City and town life—Africa. 3. Urban policy—Africa. 4. City planning—Africa. 5. Urbanization—Africa. 6. Africa—Social conditions—1960– 7. Africa—Economic conditions—1960– 8. Africa—Geography. 9. Africa—History, Local. I. Murray, Martin J. II. Myers, Garth Andrew.

HT148.A2C55 2006
307.76096—dc22 2006045227

A catalogue record of the book is available from the British Library.

This book is printed on paper suitable for recycling and made from fully managed and sustained forest sources. Logging, pulping and manufacturing processes are expected to conform to the environmental regulations of the country of origin.

Design by Newgen Imaging Systems (P) Ltd., Chennai, India.

First PALGRAVE MACMILLAN paperback edition: July 2011

10 9 8 7 6 5 4 3 2 1

Cities in Contemporary Africa

Contents

List of Illustrations vii

List of Tables ix

Acknowledgments xi

Preface xiii

Introduction: Situating Contemporary Cities in Africa 1
Garth A. Myers and Martin J. Murray

I Culture, Imagination, Space, and Place

1 Douala/Johannesburg/New York: Cityscapes Imagined 31
Dominique Malaquais

2 Internal Migration and the Escalation of Ethnic and Religious Violence in Urban Nigeria 53
Daniel Jordan Smith

3 (Re)Configuring the City: The Mapping of Places and People in Contemporary Kenyan Popular Song Texts 71
Joyce Nyairo

Photographic Essay 1: Johannesburg Fortified 95
Martin J. Murray (Text) and Juanita Malan (Photography)

4 Douala: Inventing Life in an African Necropolis 103
Basile Ndjio

II Political Economy, Work, and Livelihood

5 Economic Globalization from Below: Transnational Refugee Trade Networks in Nairobi 125
Elizabeth H. Campbell

6 Changing African Cityscapes: Regional Claims of African Labor at South African–Owned Shopping Malls 149
Darlene Miller

7 Cars Are Killing Luanda: Cronyism, Consumerism, and Other Assaults on Angola's Postwar, Capital City 173
M. Anne Pitcher with Aubrey Graham

Photographic Essay 2 Luanda, Angola 195
Aubrey Graham (Photography) and M. Anne Pitcher (Text)

8 Human Capital, Embedded Resources, and Employment for Youth in Bulawayo, Zimbabwe 201
Miriam Grant

9 Gender Relations, Bread Winning, and Family Life in Kinshasa 221
Guillaume Iyenda and David Simon

III Urban Planning, Administration, and Governance

10 South African Urbanism: Between the Modern and the Refugee Camp 241
AbdouMaliq Simone

11 Planning, Anti-Planning, and the Infrastructure Crisis Facing Metropolitan Lagos 247
Matthew Gandy

12 City Life in Zimbabwe at a Time of Fear and Loathing: Urban Planning, Urban Poverty, and Operation Murambatsvina 265
Deborah Potts

13 Social Control and Social Welfare under Neoliberalism in South African Cities: Contradictions in Free Basic Water Services 289
Greg Ruiters

Notes on Contributors 309

Index 311

List of Illustrations

Photographs

P1.1 Sutured city 98
P1.2 Retreat into fortified luxury 99
P1.3 Suburban secession 99
P1.4 Street hawkers 100
P1.5 City in ruins 101
P2.1 A mosaic of aesthetic conventions 195
P2.2 Urban comfort meets social exclusion 196
P2.3 Life in the trash lane 197
P2.4 The business of car washing 197
P2.5 From car care to shoe care 198
P2.6 Imagined mobility 199
11.1 Ebute-Metta, Lagos, 2003 250
11.2 Lagos Island, Lagos, 2003 252

Figures

9.1 Involvement of women in formal employment in Kinshasa 227
9.2 Involvement of women in informal financial networks 231

Maps

9.1 Map of Kinshasa 223
11.1 The growth of modern Lagos 249

List of Tables

7.1 Costs of selected car makes and models in Angola versus the United States (in U.S. dollars) 185
8.1 Employment phases and courses of female youth 206
8.2 Households and mentors for female youth 208
8.3 Economic pathways of male youth 211
8.4 Households and mentors for male youth 212
9.1 Evolution of Kinshasa's population 224
9.2 Involvement in Informal Activities by Gender in Kinshasa, 2001 229
12.1 Reported possible destinations: The displaced in Killarney, Bulawayo 279
12.2 Place of birth and previous residence of recent migrants to Harare in 1985, 1994, and 2001 280

Acknowledgments

We would like to acknowledge the many individuals and institutions that have made this book possible. In particular, we would like to express our gratitude to the colleagues who participated in our sessions at the snowy meetings of the African Studies Association in Washington, DC, in December 2002, where the ideas for this book first began to see the light of day. We refined our ideas at the Association of American Geographers meetings in Philadelphia (2004) and Denver (2005), as well as the African Studies Association meeting in New Orleans (2004), and we thank anyone and everyone who helped us think things through along the way. We would also like to thank all our contributors for surviving our forgetfulness, for putting up with our gentle reminders, and for persevering in what took a long time to complete. At Palgrave Macmillan Press, we would like to thank our wonderful editor, Gabriella Pearce, for her confidence in us. It was she who suggested that we undertake this project, and from start to finish she has been tireless and unflinching in her support and encouragement.

We would also like to acknowledge the sources of some of the contributions to this volume. The essays by AbdouMaliq Simone ("South African Urbanism: Between the Modern and the Refugee Camp") and Domique Maliquais ("Douala/Johannesburg/New York: Cityscapes Imagined") were originally published by the Islandla Institute (University of Cape Town) in the *Dark Roast* Occasional Papers Series. They appear here in slightly altered form. We would like to express our appreciation of the Isandla Institute, its Managing Editor Mirjam van Don, and the Editorial Collective of Edgar Pieterse, AbdouMaliq Simone, and Mirjam van Donk.

At State University of New York at Binghamton, Martin would like to thank Professor Richardo Laremont, Chair of the Department of Sociology, for his support. He would also like to express his gratitude for the support his wife Anne Pitcher, and to acknowledge ongoing conversations about cities in Africa with Mary Moran, Shaun Jacobs, Ron Amizade, Lindsay Bremner, Jenny Robinson, and Garth Myers. He wishes to thank his daughter Alida Pitcher-Murray for her boundless enthusiasm and for her patience with being dragged from Johannesburg to Maputo, and from Kampala to Luanda. She will never forget being chased by the angry elephant in Kruger National Park. Martin hopes that his two sons, Andrew and Jeremy Levine-Murray, might someday get inspired to go to Africa. With the completion of this project, perhaps now his "tribe"—the increasingly sedentary "boys of summer" (brothers Mark, Dennis, Greg, and Thomas)—will finally come to their senses, and accept that writing books is actually hard work.

Garth wishes to thank, in particular, Melanie Hepburn, Phebe and Atlee Myers, as well as Byron Caminero-Santangelo, Liz MacGonagle, Brian Daldorph, Rick Schroeder, Chris Brown, Jenny Robinson, Ben Page, Matthew Gandy, Debby Potts, Steve Pile, Michael Keith, Karen Hansen, Kathleen Sheldon, Basile Ndjio, Fred Lerise, Godwin Murunga, Makame Muhajir, Wolfgang Scholz, Angela Gray, Sarah Smiley, Noel Rasor, Iwake Masialeti, and probably a hundred other people besides who have helped with ideas or friendship through the long process of making this book. The Kansas African Studies Center, Hall Center for the Humanities, and the Departments of Geography and African & African-American Studies at the University of Kansas have provided a very comfortable and supportive home for this work for a decade, and Garth is grateful for the opportunities being there has afforded.

Preface

One of the principal goals of this book is to place cities in Africa at the center of analysis—rather than relegating them to the margins, or pushing them into the shadows. Though the contributors to this volume share a commitment to exploring aspects of urban life that are often ignored or overlooked, they are not wedded to a single perspective, paradigm, or framework of analysis. This collection of essays consists of a combination of case studies, empirically grounded vignettes, historical-geographic illustrations, and normative critiques of urban policies. The overall aim of this book is to provide a glimpse, albeit necessarily partial, into the complicated dynamics of urban life in contemporary African cities. By way of analogy, each essay represents a kind of fragmentary "snapshot" that, when pieced together, presents a *montage* that enables us to gain a genuine appreciation of the great diversity of African cities and their residents.

In seeking to expand our understanding of cities in Africa, we have tried to move tentatively toward a new kind of urban analysis—one that is receptive to a diversity of interpretive perspectives and one that is open to a variety of vantage points. We do not pretend to grasp the "true" or "objective" reality of contemporary cities in Africa. In our view, this goal is unattainable. Cities in Africa are constantly changing, evolving, and mutating entities that resist efforts seeking to capture their essence, to categorize them in accordance with preestablished classification schemes, or to freeze them into rigid molds. Though "Grand Schemes" and "Big Theories" are often helpful in reorienting thinking in ways that advance our understanding of cities and urbanization, there is the inherent danger of turning attractive, all-encompassing theoretical ideas into taken-for-granted conceptions.

We use this collection of essays to challenge a number of received wisdoms about cities in Africa. Instead of trying to fit African cities into preestablished modes of urban development, we adopt a more open-ended approach that is less concerned with identifying and measuring attributes than in grasping relationships, connections, and linkages. A great deal of the scholarly literature in urban studies starts with an ideal-typical models of normal urbanization and then proceeds to use these classificatory schemes as the benchmark with which to evaluate the progress of African cities along a continuum of expected urban development. Rather than looking at cities in Africa as embodiments of distorted urbanism, we stress their historical specificity. In other words, we seek to recover the ordinariness of these places as entities in their own right.

One of our goals was to reach into the often-overlooked world of scholarship as it is practiced in Africa to encourage as many scholars as we could get, living and working there, to contribute to this book. Our contributors come from places as far apart as Hamilton, New York, and Nairobi, Kenya; Lawrence, Kansas, and London; Oxford and Grahamstown or Johannesburg, South Africa; Cameroon, Canada, and Kinshasa. We hope that those who read these essays will find the collection as thought provoking and useful as it was challenging and gratifying for us to bring together.

Introduction: Situating Contemporary Cities in Africa

Garth A. Myers and Martin J. Murray

Introduction

The process of urbanization in sub-Saharan Africa has elicited a variety of different reactions and interpretations amongst researchers and casual observers alike. There is general consensus in the scholarly literature concerned with African cities that the accumulation of such distressing features as unregulated growth, limited opportunities for gainful employment in the formal economy, severe environmental degradation, lack of decent and affordable housing, failing and neglected infrastructure, absence of basic social services, pauperization, criminality, negligent city-management, and increasing inequalities amount to a more or less permanent condition of urban crisis of monumental proportions (Rakodi 1997; Tostensen et al. 2001). Nevertheless, there is little agreement over the root causes for the ongoing urban crisis, or what to do to reverse the situation. Whereas some attribute the urban crisis largely to explosive population growth and to adverse economic circumstances, others place the blame on corruption, or mismanagement, or the failures of municipalities to provide proper institutional and legal frameworks necessary for triggering entrepreneurial growth and development (Tostensen et al. 2001: 7, 10–11).

Though there is considerable variation in the patterns of urban growth and development, most scholarly research and writing on cities in Africa tend to overlook their differences and historical specificities and to focus instead on shared characteristics. Even a cursory review of popular outsider portrayals of African urbanism, in the form of journalism, documentary and commercial films, novels, or photography, reveals a decided preoccupation with the degraded features of city life. As a general rule, contemporary accounts and commentaries on cities in Africa have produced largely mechanistic (and simplistic) accounts of spatial incoherence, overcrowding, impoverishment, unemployment, decay, neglect, organized crime, everyday violence, inter ethnic strife, civil disorder, environmental degradation, pollution, unruly behavior, and juvenile delinquency (for views critical of this literature, see Abdoul 2005: 337–340; Ahonsi 2002: 129; Gandy 2005; Gberie 2005; Tostensen et al. 2001: 7). All too often, talk of African cities is invariably turned into a dire litany of the seemingly boundless chaos, anarchy, and disorder of everyday life (Kurtz 1998; Lewis 2005). This almost exclusive obsession with urban pathologies and enduring failures—to the exclusion of almost everything else—reduces city life in Africa to a dystopian nightmare, where the "eschatological evocation of urban apocalypse" (Gandy 2005: 38) feeds into the one-sided perceptions of those "Afro-pessimists" who suggest that cities in Africa, like Africa as a whole, are so hopelessly chaotic and disorderly that they are beyond redemption (Gberie 2005; Schwab 2002). This lopsided stress on the "uncontrolled" or "disorderly" process of urbanization in Africa dovetails with a kind of unreflective sensationalism that has long indelibly marked Africa as the "Dark Continent," where "tradition" and custom overshadow rational-legal authority, primordial "tribal" loyalties are fixed and permanent, folk beliefs triumph over good sense, and neo-patrimonial leadership goes hand-in-glove with corruption, patronage, and the widespread mismanagement of urban affairs (Abdoul 2005; Enwezor et al. 2002; Tostensen et al. 2001).

This focus on urban crisis in Africa has generated a plethora of policy recommendations aimed at promoting sustainable development and poverty alleviation. These policy recommendations are usually underpinned by what Mohamadou Abdoul calls "an epistemology of normative action" calling for remedial intervention to offset the urban crisis by filling in what cities lack. These policy recommendations for making cities in Africa more workable, sustainable, and livable—and for reversing the slide into further decay—have largely been framed through the narrow lens of the conjoined discourses of modernization and development (see Ferguson 1990). On the one hand, the pragmatic discourse of modernization has held out the promise that African urban systems can reform themselves through a heavy dose of trade liberalization, creation of an institutional and legal framework that guarantees respect for the rights of private property, deregulation of local economies, the wholesale privatization of state assets, and encouragement of entrepreneurialism and private enterprise. On the other hand, the functionalist discourse of developmentalism has called for the repair or replacement of outdated and neglected infrastructure, the creation of specialist niches (such as culture, leisure, entertainment, and tourism) to attract visitors, and the establishment of institutional support for micro-enterprises in order to make urban economies "more efficient and conducive to the generation of wealth and social dividends" (Enwezor et al. 2002: 13).

This tendency to project fluid, contingent, and historically-specific situations into ahistorical indicators of a permanent condition of failed urbanism effectively substitutes assertion for critical investigation and analysis. Though well-meaning, these curative approaches often do not take into account the complexity and heterogeneity of the urbanization process and its consequences for ordinary urban residents (Abdoul 2005: 236–237). Limiting the study of urbanization in Africa to such bleak themes as sprawling slums, inadequate social service provision, neglected infrastructure, predatory crime and random violence, personal failures, poverty and ignorance, disease, and self-destructive behavior not only leaves a great deal of room for misunderstandings, misconceptions, and even inadvertent stereotypes about African cities and their residents, but also tends to ignore the resourcefulness, inventiveness, and determination of the countless millions of ordinary people who somehow manage to successfully negotiate the perils of everyday life (Abdoul 2005; Bouillon 2002; Cheru 2002; De Boeck and Plissart 2004; Mbembe 2004; Simone 2001b; 2004; 2005a,b). The real challenge is not merely to describe the failure of cities in Africa to emulate Western models of urbanization, but to seek a deeper comprehension of why these urban agglomerations have developed the way they have. In other words, what is needed is a much more nuanced and rounded view that not only acknowledges the spatial unevenness of the urbanization process but also treats African urban residents as active agents in constructing meaningful lives for themselves rather than simply passive victims of inexorable structural processes beyond their control (Enwezor et al. 2002; Tostensen et al. 2001).

The point of departure for this book is our view that urbanization is a complex, multifaceted, and sometimes contradictory process that encompasses multiple pathways without a privileged, common end-point. To think in terms of multiple pathways is to challenge the claims to a singular urbanization process that takes place through recognizable stages along a linear path. We aim to encourage a critical engagement with new thinking about urbanization, to deviate from the conventional practice of evaluating so-called Third World cities from the fixed perspective of First World cities, and to dispense with rigid demarcation between core zones and peripheral regions of the world economy as if they somehow represent a permanent geographical fix (Smith 1996).

The bulk of the scholarly literature in urban studies has developed out of an engagement with the leading "primate" cities of Europe and North America. Despite claims of inclusiveness, conventional theories of urbanization have largely ignored cities of the "Global South," with the result that these places are largely underemphasized and undertheorized. The challenge is to differentiate between divergent paths of urbanization, and to bring cities of the Global South back in to the scholarly dialogue as objects of inquiry in their own right.

In seeking to grasp the complexity of the urban experience in Africa, it is necessary to connect ongoing processes of urbanization with the current phase of globalization. It goes without saying that there are no cities in Africa that are somehow untouched by the global, but the nature of this connection depends upon the specific conduits of transmission and the networks that mediate them. In thinking about this relationship, we should avoid the mistake of conceiving of the global and local in terms of the binary oppositions of universal and particular, macro- and micro-, and permanent and contingent. Global networks are maintained, adjusted, guarded, and configured in the local. On the one hand, the force of globalization can result in the reconfiguration and even the disappearance of localities. On the other hand, it is possible to conceive of the emergence of place-specific localities whose power is precisely a consequence of their alignments with global networks (Read 2005: 10–11).

Situating the Urban Crisis

Cities have long been structurally enmeshed in global economic and geopolitical networks, so the challenge for us is to distinguish what is distinctive about the current phase of globalization from long-term trends in urban transformation. The main cities of Africa have long played important roles in facilitating the global movement of capital and commodities, since well before the onset of formal European overrule in the late nineteenth century, continuing through the colonial era, and extending through the postindependence period. The current phase of global economic restructuring has brought about a wholesale transformation in the transnational division of labor that, in turn, has put into motion new urban dynamics on a world scale. This process of globalization has not only triggered fundamental shifts in the worldwide flows of capital, commodities, and labor, but also redefined the functional roles of cities in terms of their transnational linkages and their position in the international division of labor. On the one hand, a handful of key urban agglomerations have crystallized into so-called global (or world) cities at the apex of the world urban hierarchy. In seeking to move upward in rank order, "second-tier" cities with world-class aspirations have tried to exploit their competitive advantage in whatever fields—tourism, arts and culture, financial and producer services—that provide a niche in the competitive quest for trade and investment. On the other hand, cities with little or nothing to offer in the global marketplace have faced the dire prospect of disappearing into ruin and decay, and thereby "falling off the world map," at least in terms of connections to the world economy (Robinson 2006; Smith 1996).

This ongoing geopolitical restructuring of the world economy unleashed by globalization has also gone hand-in-hand with long-term structural trends in the worldwide patterns of urbanization. Over the past half-century, the scale of urban population growth around the world has proceeded at an unprecedented pace. As Mike Davis (2004: 5) has pointed out, cities have absorbed nearly two-thirds of the global population explosion since 1950, and the present urban population (3.2 billion) is larger than the total population of the world in 1960. The overall size of cities in the impoverished regions of the Global South has expanded at a much higher rates than those for cities in the relatively wealthy regions of the "Global North," and, in some cases, eclipsing even the most apocalyptic forecasts of Malthusian overpopulation (Davis 2004; 2005). Contrary to the hopeful visions of scholars and planners who imagine Livable and Sustainable Cities, the capacity of many of the world's megacities and other large urban agglomerations to accommodate their burgeoning populations has lagged far behind the pace of urbanization. What is perhaps most alarming about current patterns of rapid urbanization is that the population growth of the world's poorest cities has continued unabated, in spite of stagnant or declining real wages, rising prices, and skyrocketing urban unemployment. Urbanization without an accompanying economic growth has produced a kind of "perverse urbanism" where the radical decoupling of population growth from industrialization has severed whatever previous linkages existed between work-seeking urbanites and opportunities for regular, wage-paid employment (Davis 2004). The exponential growth of overcrowded and impoverished slums, shanty-towns, and informal settlements that have metastasized around many of the world's cities provides visible evidence for what some researchers have called "over-urbanization" (Gugler 1997; Rakodi 1997).

Recent trends in African urbanization have prompted some scholars to speak of the most rapidly expanding metropolises as the quintessential "shock cities" of "over-urbanization" (Knox and Marston 2003). While at the start of the twenty-first century sub-Saharan Africa remains one of the least urbanized regions in the world, cities and towns across the continent have experienced rates of population growth for the past 50 years that equal or exceed those that have taken place elsewhere (Brunn and Ziegler 2003; Rakodi 1997; Simon 1997; Stren and Halfani 2001: 478). In ways that parallel worldwide trends, the rapid pace of urbanization has taken place without accompanying economic growth. Over the past several decades, the implementation of structural adjustment programs, including trade liberalization, the relaxation of state protectionist measures, drastic cutbacks in the provision of municipal services, the reduction of tariff barriers, privatization of municipal enterprises and assets, and the elimination of subsidies has resulted in the decline in urban-based, industrial and manufacturing jobs, the casualization of labor markets, the decline in real wages, higher rates of permanent unemployment, soaring prices for basic necessities (such as food, housing, medical attention, water, and electricity), greater inequality, and the deterioration of living standards for the "poorest of the poor." As urban economies have collapsed, the kinds of social interdependency, collaboration, and cohesion that depend upon regular wage-paying work have broken down, leaving countless numbers of city residents vulnerable in the extreme (Rakodi 1997: 50, 60–61; 2002; Simone 2005b; Stren and Halfani 2001; Tostensen et al. 2001).

The globalization of economic transactions has fostered intense rivalries amongst cities seeking competitive advantage in attracting outside investment and trade. In trying to favorably position themselves in the world economy, city officials have often ploughed public resources into big-ticket tourist attractions and other showcase extravaganzas, rather than into projects aimed at poverty alleviation. In Africa and elsewhere, easy access to the global flow of ideas, information, and images has profoundly reshaped the identities of well-to-do urban residents, as their sense of belonging and social allegiances become less rooted in specific localities and more tied to global consumer culture (Bremner 2002; Mbembe 2004). With the increasing privatization of basic social services and the overall neglect of physical infrastructure, the privileged middle classes with global connections have increasingly cloistered themselves into the fortified enclaves of Western modernity that have materialized in cities all over Africa. As the propertied, the privileged, and the powerful have retreated behind the protective shield of gated residential communities, enclosed shopping malls, and other barricaded sites of luxury, the urban poor are often left to fend for themselves in urban environments that have deteriorated almost beyond repair (Bremner 2002; 2004; 2005; De Boeck 2002; De Boeck and Plissart 2004; Myers 2005; Robins 2000; Watts 1994).

At the same time that the forces of globalization have fostered increased functional interdependence and integration into the world economy, cities in Africa have experienced a retreat into localism, where specialized and particularistic interests go their own way, often bypassing official channels and fashioning their own rules of the game, in ways that are "relatively autonomous of the dynamics prevailing in the rest of the urban system" (Simone 2001a: 46–47; 2001b; 2004). As the physical and social spaces of the urban landscape have become more fragmented, disconnected, and disjointed, social collectivities of all kinds—whether grounded in religious affiliation, ethnic identification, "homeboy" or hometown connections, youth culture, criminal gangs, mutual aid, and the like—have formed, evolved, and metastasized, offering everything from solace and emotional support, protection and occasional reward, to leisure and access to opportunities.

In counteracting the blanket treatment of urban Africans as an undifferentiated mass, a range of recent studies offer a more nuanced, complex understanding of how urban affiliations operate on the ground (Anderson 2002; De Boeck and Plissart 2004; Diouf 1999; Simone 2001b; 2004). Even in cities where officials are most responsive to popular pressure from below, municipal authorities are simply unable to keep up with the demand for basic infrastructure, social services, and access to resources and opportunities. As a consequence, large numbers of urban residents have looked outside the formal economy and beyond conventional administrative channels in order to gain access to income, shelter, land, and vital social services (Stren and Halfani 2001: 474; Tripp 1992; 1997). In cities in Africa, the accumulation and reproduction of urban poverty undermines existential security and poses extraordinary challenges to the ingenuity and inventiveness of the shelter-less and the jobless. The socioeconomic survival of the poor depends upon a downward spiral of self-exploitation, an urban involution of sorts, where the competitive subdivision of already overcrowded marginal niches in the "shadow economies" of the urban milieu generates only miniscule returns, despite the extensive expenditure of time and effort (Davis 2004: 27; Lorenço-Lindell 2002; Tripp 1997).

The centrifugal forces of globalization and localization have magnified tendencies toward spatial fragmentation and social polarization. In circumstances where urban entrepreneurialism has become the new dogma of development discourse, cities in Africa have undergone a ruthless division of urban space, where cocooned islands of extreme wealth and social power are interspersed with places of deprivation and decline. Under such conditions, how do we make sense of cities in Africa? For some commentators, the collapse of physical infrastructure, the breakdown of the mechanisms fostering social collaboration, and the absence of the institutional frameworks necessary for social cohesion have led them to the inescapable conclusion that cities in Africa just "don't work." Others cling to the notion of African exceptionalism—the idea that urban development works everywhere "except Africa," because cities in Africa are intrinsically different and uniquely incapacitated (Roe 1999).

A great deal of the scholarly literature on urbanization in Africa begins—implicitly or explicitly—with normative prescriptions of how cities should ideally work. Framed in this way, Africa's sprawling metropolises typically appear as exemplary expressions of failed, distorted, or stalled urbanism—lacking the basic requirements and attributes of genuine urbanity that mark the urbanization process elsewhere. A more fruitful approach starts with the premise that cities in Africa are, as Abdoumaliq Simone (2004: 1–2) puts it, "works in progress," at one and the same time driven forward by the inventiveness of ordinary people themselves and held in place by inertia and slowness in adapting to changing circumstances. The challenge for us is to critically assess how cities in Africa actually work. In fostering a critical engagement with cities in Africa, we seek to uncover what kinds of constraints and opportunities exist and play out on the ground. This stress on provisionality enables us to conceive of cities in Africa as contingent sites where the possibilities of urban becoming are not already predetermined. In city after city, there is the appearance of vitality, where urban residents typically rely on their own resourcefulness and ingenuity to rework and make sense of their daily lives. Yet there is also the appearance of entropy and stasis, where capacities for innovative change are stalled by ruin, choked with waste, and clogged with useless objects out of place, and where "enormous creative energies have been ignored squandered, and left unused" (Simone 2004: 2). It is undoubtedly true that cities in Africa are, for the most part, distressed places in need of good governance, effective management, refurbished infrastructure, greater popular participation in local decision-making, sustainable livelihoods, and expanded opportunities for socioeconomic advancement. Yet they are more than simply manifestations of failed urbanism. Unless we move outside this diagnostic mind-set with its normative injunctions, we will be unable to discover and appreciate the historical specificity of cities in Africa—how they make themselves at the same time they are made (Simone 2004: 15–16).

As a general rule, the conventional urban studies literature conceives of cities as discrete entities—unitary objects of inquiry—that can be understood independently of location within global networks and outside their historical context. Yet cities in Africa are not just physical locations defined by their geographical boundaries, but platforms or "jumping-off" points for the realization of individual needs and collective aspirations. Cities evolve and function in relational networks, as nodal points facilitating circulation, movement, and transit. Just as we can conceive of multiple modernities, we can imagine a variety of different pathways of urbanization and divergent modalities of urban life.

THEORETICALLY SPECIFYING CITIES IN AFRICA: IDENTIFICATION AND CLASSIFICATION

What is striking about cities in Africa is their astonishing diversity and heterogeneity. Though many cities in Africa came into existence as overseas extensions of metropolitan colonial powers seeking to establish beachheads on the African continent, their subsequent growth and development did not conform to a linear logic or uniform pattern. City-building processes that took place under the dominance of European colonialism often left an indelible imprint on the original spatial layout, the built environment, and architectural styles of cities and town in Africa. Yet with the passage of time, these features have sometimes faded into obscurity or been modified beyond recognition. The diversity of cities in Africa is reflected in their dissimilar morphological forms, their distinctive social and demographic compositions, and their varying translocal linkages and connections.

Scholarly efforts to construct an ideal-typical model of the generic "African city" have failed to find a single profile that fits all cases. Anthony O'Connor (1983), for example, tried to fashion such a general scheme, but this effort quickly dissolved into a classification scheme with six possible types. His sixth category—"the hybrid city"—actually functions as a kind of catch-all for cities with multiple morphological characteristics. Over time, more and more cities in Africa seem to have acquired the characteristics of the "hybrid city."

While some of the cities that began as frontier mining towns have grown into major manufacturing and financial centers (Johannesburg), others have fallen on hard times as the mining they depended upon just petered out. The main cities of the Zambian Copperbelt, for example, conform to this pattern of de-industrialization and abandonment (Ferguson 1999). Coastal cities that were built as ports functioned as gateways to the interior (Durban, Cape Town, Mombasa, Maputo, Luanda, and Lagos). But each of these cities has its own historically specific story—there is no way to successfully lump all "port cities" in Africa into a single model either (Hoyle 1996). Still others, such as Lusaka, Nairobi, Nouakchott, Gabarone, or Lilongwe, were fashioned relatively recently, essentially as administrative centers. But again, these cities developed at different times, and were built by different powers, for different types of colonial (and postcolonial) administration.

Despite the diversity and heterogeneity of urban experiences in Africa, the scholarly literature on urban studies has generally failed to pay much attention to the pace and tempo of urbanization in Africa, or to the real differences between coastal port cities and metropolises of the interior, between commercial hubs and administrative centers, or between sprawling megacities and neglected cities that face abandonment and ruin. On balance, existing theories of urbanization provide little ground for understanding cities in Africa, other than to suggest that they are either deviations from or adaptations of a preexisting Western pattern. The tendency to view African cities purely in terms of their exceptionality and particularity (with its "exotic" overtones), or, equally important, as failed, incomplete, or deficient examples of "normal" urban development effectively diminishes their significance as objects of inquiry in their own right (Mbembe and Nuttall 2004: 348).

The difficulties that scholars often encounter in theoretically specifying cities in Africa stem from two analytic flaws. The first follows from an undue reliance upon ideal-typical models of urban development derived from identifying the salient features of key Western cities as the defining characteristics of a paradigmatic urbanism. The methodological problem with the ideal- typical approach is that it tends to generalize from a specific set of characteristics, relying on this narrow set of attributes as the standard yardstick or indicator of "normal" (or expected) urbanization everywhere (see Amin and Graham 1997: 416–417). Viewed through this frame of reference, the development of cities in Africa always appear as the outcome of flawed, distorted, or unfinished patterns of urbanization, where they lack particular attributes of genuine "cityness" (Robinson 2002). This tendency to define cities in Africa by what they lack easily falls prey to a teleological and evolutionary way of thinking that characterizes them as "not-as-yet" developed and in need of remedial intervention. By treating cities in Africa as "deviations" that lag behind or stray away from an alleged "normal" path of urbanization, they are too easily reduced to structural irrelevance, or else subjected to a kind of moralizing discourse that prescribes remedies to overcome their inadequacies and backwardness (Robinson 2006).

The second flaw arises from the continued reliance upon analytic categorizations and distinctions that were developed under specific historical and spatial conditions that may have been appropriate for an earlier epoch or time frame, but no longer carry the same relevance under contemporary circumstances. For example, the tendency in the scholarly literature to divide the world economy into the simplified spatial categories of core and peripheral areas is often accompanied by the similar temptation to draw a rigid, hard-and-fast distinction between "peripheral urbanization" that produces Third World cities, on the one hand, and "core (or metropolitan) urbanization" that produces First World cities, on the other. These "either/or" categorizations filter out the possibility of mediating or intervening conditions, precluding a more nuanced reading of urbanization as a contradictory and multilayered process of cross-fertilization, mimicry, and plagiarism. In the current phase of global capitalism, categories such as center and periphery, First World and Third World, and the *mélange* of qualities inextricably attached to them, have ceased to fully capture the actual, objective qualities of space (de Boeck 2002: 264–265). Dispensing with simple binary oppositions enables us to challenge the essentializing tendency in both the scholarly and popular literature to lump "African cities" together under the same generic rubric as instances of Third World, or peripheral urbanism. Whatever advantages such descriptive shorthand labels provide, they typically ignore the historical specificities, social complexities, myriad differences amongst cities in Africa.

In recent years, a number of urban theorists have drawn attention to the pivotal role of the current wave of globalization in fostering intensified competition amongst and between cities that aspire to "world-class" status. Much of this scholarly writing about urban rivalries has crystallized around a research agenda that has come to be known as the "global cities" paradigm (Sassen 2000). The discursive power of this global city hypothesis depends upon identifying certain key attributes of cities that function as the driving force behind the globalizing impulses in the world economy. By framing their research agenda around identifying which cities possess these stellar attributes (and with what quantities), scholars operating within this paradigmatic framework have—inadvertently it seems—triggered a competitive urge amongst city boosters to aspire to the world-class status of "global city."

Yet as is the case with all overarching paradigms, there is an inherent danger in seeking to explain too much. As a heuristic device, the global cities hypothesis has become so generalized that the substantive differences between genuine "global cities" and just "big cities" has become somewhat blurred. Taken to its extremes, the global cities paradigm has largely succumbed to a categorizing imperative, reducing scholarly research to something akin to a taxonomic exercise, where cities are classified, labeled, and assigned a place in ranked hierarchy according to the relative socioeconomic power they command in the world economy. To the extent that it focuses almost exclusively on transnational business and financial networks that link leading metropolitan centers in a ranked global hierarchy, the urban studies literature tends to ignore those cities that are economically marginal. As a consequence, these cities disappear "off the map" of global importance (Robinson 2002: 536, 546).

THE INHERENT DANGERS OF FACILE GENERALIZATIONS

If the prototype of urban development is derived primarily from looking at the histories and experiences of a few key Western cities, then the "structurally irrelevant," economically marginal, or globally inconsequential cities of Africa appear to present a kind of anomaly (Robinson 2002: 534, 536; Sassen 1994: 4, 27). Because they do not possess in equal measure the redeeming qualities of "cityness" that characterize the leading Western cities of the First World, they are classified under the rubric of Third World cities in the developing (and the still-as-yet underdeveloped) world (see Dick and Rimmer 1998; Drakakis-Smith 2000; Robinson 2002: 540; Simon 1989; Smith 1996). Interpreted through the discriminating lens of developmentalism, cities in Africa are hence identified and classified by what they lack: important global connections, good governance, adequate infrastructure, formal employment, functional and efficient transportation linkages, and the like. As a result, they are regarded as imperfect, stunted, and underdeveloped versions of what they ought to be and may some day become, that is, something that resembles the developed, modern cities of the West (Robinson 2002: 531; van der Merve 2004).

What is needed is a rethinking in urban studies away from ready-made, deductive theories seeking to generalize across cases, and toward a kind of genuine theoretical openness and flexibility that seeks through comparison and contrast to account for the historical-spatial specificity of particular cities (Robinson 2002). The fascination with grand theories whose universalizing claims are applied everywhere tends to conflate divergent processes of urban growth and development, and flatten out the rich diversity of what constitutes the urban experience. This way of thinking has effectively restricted the scope of analysis for urban studies. An alternative approach calls for looking at "ordinary cities"—that is, those cities that seem to resist inclusion in *a priori* analytic classifications and hierarchies—as distinctive objects of inquiry in their own right, thereby enabling us to see them as historically specific entities, rather than as embodiments of abstract models (Amin and Graham 1997; Dick and Rimmer 1998; Robinson 2006). Broadening the field of inquiry for urban studies in this way provides a foundation for a deeper, nuanced understanding of the diversity of urban experiences and the complexity of urbanization as it has taken place in different areas of the world.

The aim of this book is to open up new ways of understanding cities and city-making processes in Africa from a variety of different perspectives and vantage points. In doing so, we have tried to move away from conceptual frameworks and classification schemes that seek to categorize, or pigeonhole, cities into preestablished categories. We have organized this collection of essays around three broad thematic fields: (1) culture, imagination, space, and place; (2) political economy, livelihoods, and work; and (3) urban planning, administration, and governance. These three fields are loosely connected with each other, and they correspond to different approaches to studying cities. We make no claims to comprehensiveness—either in terms of geographical scope or conceptual breadth. Yet in juxtaposing this assortment of essays, we hope to illuminate some of the spectrum of scholarly writing on cities in Africa, and to engage with theoretical understandings of urbanization. Though it is impossible to fully encompass all features of city-ness in Africa, we have tried to piece together a collection of essays that express the diversity and complexity of urban experiences. These essays offer new ways of making sense of the urban experience, and, as such, they reveal blind spots and omissions in the conventional approaches to urban studies. In the following sections, we describe each of these fields in turn, taking care to stress what we consider neglected domains in contemporary scholarly debates concerned with urbanization.

Culture, Imagination, Space, and Place

Over the past several decades, the "cultural-turn" has marked a dramatic shift in scholarly interest in both the humanities and the social sciences. Recent cultural theories have argued that "culture-making" is more fluid than previously acknowledged, and more complex than the simplified evocations of difference that dominated conventional literature of the past. This stress on culture as intersubjective practice—instead of as an object possessed—enables us to investigate everyday life through the lens of contested meanings and symbolic understandings.

Culture, space, and place—in essence, cultural geography—have once again figured prominently as explanations for development in Africa (Huntington and Harrison 2000). The deployment of these themes, though, appears to be a simplistic throwback with a "pungent, late-Victorian imperial odor," wherein complexities, subtleties, and contexts in battles over identity and place are swept aside (Watts 2004: 12). Surely, the question of how we imagine the intersections of culture and space is more complicated than these grand theorists want us to think, as one look at the inflamed passions that have accelerated dramatically around those intersections in many cities of sub-Saharan Africa over the past few decades suggests. There is no doubt that the assertion of "cultural difference" has often proven to be a source of urban conflict. The bitter animosities that sometimes spill over into violent battles between Christians and Muslims in some Nigerian cities and towns, for example, provide ample evidence of the salience of religious identities as the driving force behind intracommunal strife. It is easy, but ultimately thoroughly facile, to read in these sorts of conflicts a "clash of civilizations," a conflict of "tradition against modernity," or "the cross versus the crescent" (Huntington and Harrison 2000; Mbogoni 2004; Schech and Haggis 2000).

Cultural identities and assertion of difference do not necessarily result in urban conflict. For instance, the marked growth of revivalist churches and religious sects—with their transnational connections and networks—offer meaning and hope for millions of impoverished urban residents seeking solace and comfort in a heartless world. As social gathering-places providing "redemptive moments and spaces of spiritual and social communion" (Zeleza 1999: 55), these religious sects play important roles in the associational life of urban Africans.

To a large extent, spatially constituted scripts of alleged "cultural difference" originated with the efforts of urban planners to construct urban landscapes around the principle of racial segregation. Colonial strategies of divide-and-rule left their spatial imprints on urban landscape that were at once physical markers of racial difference and symbolic signifiers of dominant and subordinate positionalities in the sociocultural order. Not only have these legacies from the past proven exceedingly difficult to erase, it is also the case that postcolonial regimes have often replicated and expanded on them, deftly using the "invented traditions" and "identity politics" of the colonial period to maintain power, privilege, and property in the cities (Schech and Haggis 2000: 143). European colonial rulers took "a multitude of African social formations with different, often particularist memories competing with each other" (Mudimbe 1994: 129), and sought to configure these into a legible grid of subordinate groups. The colonial project sought to *domesticate* differences, that is, it tried to make them appear as "natural," primordial, and "common sense" conditions of everyday life (Mbembe 2004; Mudimbe 1994). The structural impact of colonial rule cannot explain by itself "the politics of cultural difference" cities in Africa. Yet it does provide a "vital reminder to any inquiry to situate African cities today between the warp of colonialism and the woof of the post-colonial inheritors of its powers" (Myers 2005).

The "mapping of Empire" involved more than cartographic exercises in charting empty spaces, and constructing topographical surveys. It also entailed the implementation of urban planning schemes where ideas of racial segregation functioned as the principal mechanism for the physical separation and division of urban space. The cartographic imagination of European colonial rule was responsible not only for the original physical layout and division of urban space of many cities in Africa, but also helped to create much of the sense of city-ness on the continent. It was often the case that high-ranking colonial administrators assumed primary responsibility for planning and constructing colonial cities from scratch—trying to emulate Europe on the African continent (Home 1997; Myers 2003). With the establishment of colonial rule, those who practiced this dual trade gradually settled into a role Myers (2005) calls "geography *mundane*," working as "the surveying and inventory-making agents of colonial regimes."

With political independence, the failure of postcolonial regimes to implement city-building projects that substantially improved the lives of urban residents led to widespread resentment that has taken a variety of different forms (Watts 2004). Whereas the main sources of conflict in colonial cities stemmed primarily from the spatial separation between (European) colonizer and (native) colonized, the new fault lines that characterize postcolonial cities in Africa are much more complicated. These lines of cleavage have manifested themselves in a variety of ways, including the rich against the poor, long-standing residents versus newcomers, youth against elders (Diouf 1999), citizens versus immigrants (Murray 2003; Simone 2000), and those professing adherence to one religious faith against those claiming allegiance to another (Watts 1999). A great deal of innovative scholarship has focused on how urban residents have engaged in "battles over cultural identities—and the power to shape, determine, and literally *emplace* those identities" (Mitchell 2000: 11).

The contemporary force field of globalization has refracted these urban geographies in new directions that demand an imagination of the intersections of culture, space, and place that goes beyond the locality of the city. Scholarly literature on cities in Africa has increasingly explored the connections between scattered diasporic communities marooned in "foreign places" and their cities of origin located in other countries or regions of the African continent (Tambiah 2000). As patterns, migration and movement have become less fixed and unidirectional, the broad topography of interconnections, networks, and linkages for transnational African communities has expanded greatly. As struggles over legal rights for asylum-seekers, refugees, and immigrants have sharpened, questions of belonging—and the rights of citizenship—have become more problematic (Simone 2004: 119; Tambiah 2000).

A number of recent studies have sought to draw connections between the economic, political, and cultural dimensions of transnationalism and the transformation of urban space. For scholars such as Jackson et al. (2004: 1–2), "space is constitutive of transnationality in all its different forms." Transnationalism—like diaspora—cannot be understood apart from its "particular spatialities." There is great need to map the difference that spatiality makes, as well as to differentiate between forms of diaspora and transnationality. This stress on movement, flows, and circuits encourages us to look beyond the narrow confines of the geographical boundaries of urban space in order to grasp the relational networks within which cities in Africa are inextricably embedded.

Political Economy, Livelihoods, and Work

In his 1973 study of Accra, Ghana, Keith Hart (1973) first coined the term "informal economy" to distinguish self-employed individuals engaged in unenumerated, small-scale, income-generating activities from the formal sector consisting of enumerated, large-scale, capital-intensive firms operating in regulated markets. In its conventional usage, the informal economy generally refers small-scale or family ownership of enterprises operating outside of administrative regulation, characterized by ease of entry, high turnover, reliance on local resources, small-scale operations, labor-intensive and adapted technologies. Yet perhaps because of their overuse, notions such as informal economy, the informal sector, and informality have become highly elastic terms, with vague and imprecise meanings (Olmedo and Murray 2002).

The kinds of unregulated production, distribution, and service provision vary widely from city to city throughout the African continent. Likewise, the incomes they yield and the positions they occupy in relation to legal regimes and law enforcement defy simple classification. The increasing heterogeneity of those informal markets that can be found in cities in Africa has meant that not just the poor but also better-off urban residents often seek to generate income through unregulated and sometimes extra-legal activities (Hansen and Vaa 2004: 11; Simone 2001b; Tripp 1997).

Cities throughout Africa have experienced profound transformations of socioeconomic life over the past several decades. Faced with dwindling opportunities for regular wage-paying work, the unemployed and underemployed have turned to various income-generating survival strategies, including small-scale trading, barter, and part-time work. The overall decline of employment opportunities in full-time, wage-paying jobs in large-scale (state and private) enterprises has led to an explosion of new forms of irregular, casualized work in services, petty trade, and micro-enterprises (Rogerson 1998; Rogerson and Rogerson 1996; 1997; Tripp 1992).

In order to make sense of these fundamental shifts in the labor market, scholars have typically made use of an analytic distinction between what they refer to as the "formal economy" and the "informal economy." In their conventional usage, the formal economy refers to those economic activities and relations that are legally sanctioned, regulated through state oversight, and marked by full-time wage-paid employment. In contrast, the informal economy typically refers to those income-generating activities outside official legal sanction, and without state regulation and oversight of any sort (Mead 1996; Portes et al. 1989; Portes and Sassen-Koob 1987; Hart 1973; Rakowski 1994).

In the hands of neoliberal ideologues like Hernando de Soto (1989), the informal economy has assumed a kind of mythical status as the incubator of "anti-statist" entrepreneurial ingenuity, the wellspring of economic rationality, and the catalyst for economic growth. Despite its inherent weaknesses as a theoretical intervention, this neoliberal approach attracted institutional support over the years as a policy platform calling for the nurturing of microenterprises as a primary mechanism for job creation and poverty alleviation (Bromley 1990; AlSyyad 2004: 12–14).

Though terms like the informal economy, informal work, and informalization can be useful heuristic devices, these notions are notoriously slippery and imprecise when employed as conceptual tools. One tendency in the scholarly literature has been to subsume all socioeconomic activities that are unlicensed, operate with low levels of capitalization, function outside existing juridical and legal sanctions, and take place outside statutory regulative frameworks under the all-encompassing rubric of informality. Such an overarching approach tends to overlook often complex interactions between diverse socioeconomic activities and regulatory frameworks as they take place over time and space. Similarly, this failure to adequately account for the range, scope, and scale of so-called informal activities often ignores how all sorts of socioeconomic activities spillover and weave back and forth between formality and informality. Another tendency in the scholarly literature has been to uncritically conflate wholly different socioeconomic processes under the label of informality (Guyer 1995; Guyer et al. 2002; Olmedo and Murray 2002).

What is clear from investigating work and income-generating activities in African cities is that the widespread deregulation of labor markets and flexibilization of work relations has blurred the dividing line between formality and informality. In cities all across Africa, the overwhelming majority of urban residents derive all or part of their income from extra-legal socioeconomic activities outside official sanction and state regulation. These developments pose an important question: what does officially regulated, legally sanctioned employment actually mean when deregulation has become the norm? Looking at actual ways through which urban residents generate income in order to support themselves and the households to which they belong enables us to question the hermetically sealed distinction between formality and informality. The view presented here is that to maintain a hard-and-fast analytic distinct between formal and informal economies—each with their own structural logic and "rules of the game"—hinders our understanding of how the connection between work and income actually operate on the ground in urban settings in Africa today. Instead of treating these two spheres as separate zones of socioeconomic activity, it is much more fruitful to conceive of formality and informality as evolving moments along a fluid continuum of work relations, conditions of employment, and processes of competition in commodity markets (AlSyyad 2004; Olmedo and Murray 2002: 421–423). Business enterprises operating in the formal economy largely depend upon the irregular work, casual employment, and self-employed services of a vast army of others. By the same token, a vast array of microenterprises, small-scale hawkers and traders, and self-employed service-providers relies upon material goods available only through connections with business enterprises in the formal economy (Grosh and Somolekae 1996).

With formal employment in regular wage-paying work a pipe dream for most urban residents, alternative modes of income-generating activities have proliferated. Strategies of socioeconomic survival require both innovation and drastic action (De Boeck and Plissart 2004; Emizet 1998; Gombya 1994; Lugalla 1995). Where trade liberalization has opened the floodgates to cheap imports like clothing, household items, and plastics, local manufacturing has closed down, putting tens of thousands out of work. At the same time, the implementation of the neoliberal program of privatization has enabled powerful local elites to commandeer municipal assets, such as enterprises, real estate, and services, thereby enriching themselves, their allies, and their extended families. African urban residents have learned to compensate for the decline of long-term, large-scale capital investment in the built environment, the absence of functional infrastructure spreading evenly across the urban landscape, and the lack of formal employment in dependable wage- paying jobs by developing new skills, new capacities, and new specializations that enable them to survive and even prosper in the midst of seeming disorder, chaos, and constricted opportunities (Simone 2001a,b; 2004; 2005a: 1–2).

The virtual absence of regular wage-paying work for millions of urban poor has necessitated the emergence of new organizational forms of economic activity. All around the world, alternative economic systems—informal, underground, parallel, hidden, shadow, irregular, black market, unrecorded, unlicensed, or second economies—exist alongside formal, regulated, and official ones. Conventional economic analysis largely ignores these alternative forms of production, exchange, and distribution because they do not appear in official reports and statistics. Although the scale of the informal trade and markets in African cities has expanded considerably over the past several decades, little is actually known about its causes and consequences, organization, scope and scale, costs and profitability, the conditions that motivate people to participate in it, or the precise nature of its linkages with the formal economy. Such information is lacking not only because these transactions are largely unrecorded and unmeasured, but also because a great deal of these activities are covert, on the margins of the law, or plainly illegal, and thus quite difficult to investigate (MacGaffey 1991; MacGaffey and Bazenguissa-Ganga 2000; Simone 2001b).

Income-generating activities outside of the formal economy require constant vigilance, a great degree of provisionality and innovation, and continuous hedging of bets (Simone 2000; 2001a, b; 2004; 2005b). The workability of informal-sector activities typically involves a simultaneous narrowing of social fields and a wider dispersion of economic processes over larger territorial space. In other words, the success of informal economic activities depends, on the one hand, upon extending lateral networks, maintaining social connections, and securing membership in trading groups that are tightly drawn, typically along religious, ethnic, and cultural lines, and, on the other hand, upon intricate social arrangements that are increasingly transnational in nature, involving wider circuits of cross-border trade that take advantage of disparate exchange rates, customs regulations, and prices, and that are sometimes cunning and ruthless in their operational practices (Rogerson 1997; 1998; Rogerson and Rogerson 1996; 1997).

Looking at informality in African cities enables us to explore the intricate and subtle ways that internal cultural mechanisms, such as ethnic, religious, and racial identities, operate in concert with social forces to determine the choices that long-time residents and newcomers alike make in order to ensure their livelihoods. Focusing attention on the visible cultural surfaces of everyday life can yield insights into the rhythms, patterns, and social practices that characterize the survivalist ethos in the city, but these alone cannot capture underlying (and out-of-sight) social mechanisms that govern the movements of people and goods across vast distances. In the conventional literature, urban informality is frequently miscast as a peripheral, exceptional, or dysfunctional kind of desperate socioeconomic activity, subordinated to survivalist logic and relegated to the spatial margins of the city. Yet instead of treating it as a euphemism for urban marginality, or as an expression of "failed" modernity or truncated development, informality is properly understood as a central feature of contemporary cities in Africa, a place-making process that actively creates a different kind of urban dynamism. It is characterized by the continual restlessness of its participants, neither "here" nor "there," a never-ending process in constant motion. It is a fluid zone of opportunity, operating at great scale and reach, which ironically depends upon instability, where such structural unevenness as fluctuations in supply and demand and price differentials across territories provide chances to take advantage of unequal exchange (see Lorenço-Lindell 2002; Peberdy and Rogerson 2000; Portes 1994).

A great deal of informal entrepreneurship in African cities depends upon socially intensive labor, or the ability to mobilize, regulate, and manipulate different social networks. Thus, entrepreneurs typically stay close to the action to observe the ebb and flow of daily transactions, and to position themselves favorably in a nexus of information. The most successful cultivate patronage in order to command the loyalty of subordinates. In contrast, many small traders with limited resources and flexibility seek to actively foster the illusion of entrepreneurial accomplishment through the visible display of the conventional signs of financial success. For example, aspiring entrepreneurs often dress in expensive clothes with designer labels, and wear all sorts of fancy accessories like gold watches and jewelry. This aggressive assertion of elegance and polish enables them to accentuate their urbanity and cosmopolitanism. By participating in this elaborately staged performance of concealment and masquerade, these fledgling entrepreneurs create the impression of their business prowess. This visible impersonation of entrepreneurial success, or what MacGaffey and Bazenguissa-Ganga (2000: 3–4) have called the "cult of appearance," produces a useful tactical ambiguity in business negotiations, where individuals are never quite sure with whom they are dealing, and the true extent of their capabilities and connections. In this way, the dramaturgical "presentation of self"—through clothing, mannerisms, style of speech—sometimes becomes a kind of theatrical production, or an elaborate masquerade (Hansen and Vaa 2004; Simone 2000).

Governance, Administration, and Planning

Scholarly writing on contemporary cities in Africa has tended to focus on the unruly and disorderly features of urban development (Rakodi 2002). In part, this portrayal of African cities as places that have descended into chaos because of the collapse of effective governance, the absence of workable infrastructure, and the lack of services stems from an uncritical acceptance of a normative ideal derived from the European and North American perceptions about what a "good city" should look like and how it should function (Swilling 1997). Urban planners, international experts, and high-paid consultants look at unregulated and sprawling urban agglomerations, rapid demographic growth, mixed land use, unsanitary living conditions, broken-down infrastructure, and they see urban chaos and disorder. Municipal authorities have reacted to the perception of uncontrolled urban growth by attempting to impose a modicum of "order" on towns and cities. In seeking to secure urban environments conducive to efficient enterprise and good governance, they have tried to institute politico-administrative systems for urban management and to regulate urban land use (Halfani 1996; Rakodi 2002: 46, 67–68; Vaa 2000).

Following in the footsteps of neoliberal urban reforms instigated elsewhere, cities in Africa have experienced a profound transformation over the past several decades in the form and function of local governance. This shift from old-style local governmental action (with its formal and hierarchical bureaucratic organization and commandist pretensions) to emergent forms of urban governance has involved the introduction of new types of competition- based, enterprise policies and the increased participation of business coalitions in local decision-making. The adoption of new modes of urban governance has led to a significant hollowing out and reduction of municipal functions and responsibilities, including relegating to city agencies the truncated role of providing increasingly weak regulatory and coordinating roles for the private- and voluntary-sector delivery of services, and the transfer of the mandate for economic and social policy formulation to a mixture of quasi-autonomous, nongovernmental agencies (NGOs). Borrowing from the neoliberal model of the contract state, municipal authorities in African cities have become more entrepreneurial in outlook and orientation, undertaking various "off-loading," "downsizing," and "rightsizing" initiatives, including the privatization of public utilities and other city assets, the outsourcing and subcontracting of services, the whittling down of the size and scale of the public sector workforce, and the creation of public–private partnerships to manage city assets and attract new investment.

Yet for the most part, city officials have met with limited success in promoting "orderly" urban development, in regulating private entrepreneurship and land use, and in "outlawing systems and practices regarded as unsuitable and undesirable" (Rakodi 2002: 67). Patronage politics, exit strategies, and noncompliance with regulatory rules have filled the void.

By promoting entrepreneurial solutions to the problems of long-term urban malaise in African cities, neoliberal modes of urban governance hold out the promise of renewal and rejuvenation. Yet ironically, as Simone has noted with regard to Douala, the emergence of a freewheeling entrepreneurial culture has contributed to the fragmentation of the urban landscape, where the formation of separate domains militates against the development of a collective responsibility for improving social life "beyond an entrenched insularity" (Simone 2005b: 214).

Over the past several decades, the animating powers of multiparty participation in policy debates, electoral contests, and public dialogue have provided urban politics in African cities with a visible and audible vibrancy that was largely absent (or forced underground) during periodic periods of autocratic one-party rule. Over the past several decades, state management and administrative control over the public aspects of associational life of urban African residents has loosened. In cities all over Africa, a whole range of social actors, including NGOs, and a reawakened popular press, television, and radio have rushed to fill the void, reenergizing what had become a somewhat moribund civil society. What has complicated matters is that Western donor countries and international financial institutions have championed their own neoliberal version of civil society, stressing multiparty parliamentary democracy, privatization of municipal assets, outsourcing of service provision, and urban entrepreneurship. For the most part, the implementation of these policy proposals has both weakened the capacities of municipalities to underwrite the provision of requisite social services, respond to infrastructural collapse, and provide for decent and affordable housing for the urban poor, and strengthened the hand of the urban rich.

The rural–urban cleavage in African politics sometimes manifests itself in situations where political parties that have drawn their electoral support from rural areas have tenuously held office in cities. In contrast, "oppositional" political parties and social movements have often cultivated the loyalties of impoverished residents of slums, informal housing projects, and squatter settlements. Popular mobilization in cities has sometimes led to multiparty elections, but urban protests have also produced a kind of stasis that has undermined the capacities of municipalities to function as the organ of the public good.

Urban policymakers like to speak of "good governance." While the use of this term is notoriously slippery, advocates of neoliberal modes of urban governance usually combine calls for weakening the powers of municipalities to unilaterally manage cities with pleas for strengthening the organs of civil society that buy into the normative doctrine of urban entrepreneurialism (Griffin 2001; Hyden and Mugabe 1999: 33). Whereas neoliberal prescriptions often do little more than advocate less municipal regulation, intervention, and oversight (Drakakis-Smith 1997: 815), urban policymakers typically associate "good governance" with public–private partnerships and the rhetoric of "stake-holder" decision-making (Mercer 2003).

Yet critics charge that the implementation of "good governance" measures often leads not to democratization but to "the disempowerment of local authorities and local communities alike" (Beall et al. 2002: 65). Abrahamsen (2000: 50), for example, maintains that, in the hands of doctrinaire neoliberal urbanists, "good governance" is an empty abstraction, or a rhetorical device, that effectively reproduces what she terms an *exclusionary democracy* in African cities. Exclusionary democracies "allow for political competition but cannot incorporate or respond to the demands of the majority in any meaningful way" (Abrahamsen 2000: xiv). Critics such as Abrahamsen (2000: xiv) and others (Nabudere 2000: 23) also contend that international lending agencies, like the World Bank, have utilized a "one-size-fits-all" agenda for "good governance" to promote the penetration of global capital Africa.

In large numbers of cities in Africa, a significant proportion of urban residents live in self-built shelters in unauthorized and unserviced settlements. Extralegal housing and unregistered economic activities constitute the "informal city" (Hansen and Vaa 2004). In most African cities, there is a widening gap between the construction of new housing units with access to basic urban infrastructure in authorized locations and the rapid influx of newcomers to the city in search of shelter. As a consequence of the shortfall of formal housing, large numbers of urban residents are forced to find accommodation in self-built shelter in unauthorized and unserviced settlements, often on the fringes of the metropolis. For the most part, municipalities in Africa inherited and have subsequently maintained (colonial-era) legal and regulatory frameworks for planned urban development that were designed to contain settlement rather than to deal with rapid growth. Even if blatantly repressive regulations were abolished at political independence, municipalities typically retained such regulatory mechanisms as zoning laws, building codes, and land-use standards (Kamette II 2001; Mabogunje 1994; Robinson 1997). These regulations have restricted the construction of affordable housing. In order to circumvent existing building codes, poor residents have constructed shelter in unauthorized sites, often at great distances from the historic urban core. The construction of illegal or extralegal shelter typically takes three forms. The first is illegal occupation of land that infringes on established property rights (whether communal or private). The second is illegal or clandestine subdivision of land to accommodate increased numbers of housing units in contravention of existing planning regulations. The third is construction or use of shelter without official permission or in violation of building codes (Hansen 1997; Hansen and Vaa 2004: 8–9; Mitullah and Kibwana 1998).

Limited access to financial resources has meant that municipalities have been unable to meet the demands of low-income households for land, formal housing, and basic urban services (Amis 1996; Amis and Lloyd 1990; Durand-Lasserve 1998: 236; Gandy 2005). Under circumstances where privatization of housing markets takes place without the construction of low-cost residential accommodation for less-affluent urban residents, large numbers of urban dwellers are forced to live in self-built shelter without official authorization and often outside the law. In many cities originally planned by British colonial authorities, patterns of urban residence have remained highly polarized, formerly along lines of strict racial segregation and more recently along class lines. As a result, the search for affordable accommodation often pushes the poor onto the metropolitan fringe, where basic infrastructure and social amenities are virtually nonexistent. Under circumstances where available land for residential accommodation is in short supply, the struggle for access to affordable housing has often led to extreme overcrowding in existing residential areas and informal settlements where newcomers squeeze into subdivided plots and rented rooms (Potts and Mutambirwa 1991).

Whatever large-scale capital investment that has taken place in cities has remained largey concentrated in commercial undertakings, tourist-related enterprises, and finance, rather than in industrial undertakings and manufacturing. These kinds of capital investments have resulted in new patterns of spatial segregation, particularly the displacement of small-scale trading and service activities from urban centers to locations on the periphery, thereby yielding space for new tourist hotels, enclosed shopping malls, and fancy retail boutiques and eateries. Violent confrontations between municipal authorities and informal traders over the commercial use of public space have taken place with predictable regularity in many African cities. City officials have frequently sought to remove street vendors, itinerant traders, and idle youth from the central city, using city bylaws to criminalize their activities and justifying their heavy-handed actions by claiming that they disrupt established business enterprises and retail stores (Hansen and Vaa 2004: 12–13).

REFERENCES

Abdoul, M. 2005. "Urban Development and Urban Informalities: Pikene, Senegal," in A. Simone and A. Abouhani (eds.). *Urban Africa: Changing Contours of Survival in the City.* London: Zed Books, pp. 234–260.

Abrahamsen, R. 2000. *Disciplining Democracy: Development Discourse and Good Governance in Africa.* London: Zed Books.

Ahonsi, B. 2002. "Popular Shaping of Metropolitan Forms and Processes in Nigeria: Glimpses and Interpretations from an Informed Lagosian," in O. Enwezor et al. (eds.). *Under Siege: Four African Cities. Freetown, Johannesburg, Kinshasa, Lagos* (Documenta 11, Platform 4). Ostiledern-Ruit, Germany: Hatje Cantz, pp. 129–151.

AlSyyad, N. 2004. "Urban Informality as a 'New' Way of Life," in N. AlSayyad and A. Roy (eds.). *Urban Informality: Transnational Perspectives from the Middle East, Latin America, and South Asia.* New York: Lexington Books, pp. 7–30.

Amin, A. and S. Graham. 1997. "The Ordinary City," *Transactions of the Institute of British Geographers* [NS] 22 (4): 411–429.

Amis, P. 1996. "Long-Run Trends in Nairobi's Informal Housing Market," *Third World Planning Review* 18 (3): 271–285.

Amis, P. and P. Lloyd (eds.). 1990. *Housing Africa's Poor.* Manchester: Manchester University Press.

Anderson, D. 2002. "Vigilantes, Violence and the Politics of Public Order in Kenya," *African Affairs* (101): 531–555.

Beall, J., O. Crankshaw, and S. Parnell. 2002. *Uniting a Divided City: Governance and Social Exclusion in Johannesburg.* London: Earthscan.

Bouillon, A. 2002. "Between Euphemism and Informalism: Inventing the City," in O. Enwezor et al. (eds.). *Under Siege: Four African Cities. Freetown, Johannesburg,*

Kinshasa, Lagos, Documenta 11, Platform 4. Ostiledern-Ruit, Germany: Hatje Cantz, pp. 81–98.

Bremner, L. 2002. "Closure, Simulation, and 'Making Do' in the Contemporary Johannesburg Landscape," in O. Enwezor et al. (eds.). *Under Siege: Four African Cities. Freetown, Johannesburg, Kinshasa, Lagos, Documenta 11, Platform 4.* Ostiledern-Ruit, Germany: Hatje Cantz, pp. 153–172.

Bremner, L. 2004. "Bounded Spaces: Demographic Anxieties in Post-Apartheid Johannesburg," *Social Identities* 10 (4): 455–468.

Bremner, L. 2005. "Remaking Johannesburg," in S. Read, J. Rosemann, and J. van Eldijk (eds.). *Future City.* London and New York: Spon Press, pp. 32–47.

Bromley, R. 1990. "A New Path to Development? The Significance and Impact of Hernando de Soto's Ideas on Underdevelopment, Production, and Reproduction," *Economic Geography* 66 (4): 328–348.

Brunn, S. and R. Ziegler. 2003. *Cities of the World: World Regional Urban Development*, 3rd edition. New York: Harper Collins.

Cheru, F. 2002. *African Renaissance: Roadmaps to the Challenge of Globalization.* London: Zed Books.

Davis, M. 2004. "Planet of Slums: Urban Involution and the Informal Proletariat," *New Left Review* 26 [NS]: 5–34.

Davis, M. 2005. *Planet of Slums.* New York and London: Verso.

de Boeck, F. 2002. "Kinshasa: Tales of the 'Invisible City' and the Second World," in O. Enwezor et al. (eds.). *Under Siege: Four African Cities Freetown, Johannesburg, Kinshasa, Lagos.* Ostfildern-Ruit, Germany: Hatje Cantz, pp. 243–286.

de Boeck, F. and M.-F. Plissart. 2004. *Kinshasa: Tales of the Invisible City.* Ludion: Royal Museum for Central Africa, Tervuren.

de Soto, H. 1989. *The Other Path: The Invisible Revolution in the Third World.* New York: Harper & Row.

Dick, H. W. and P. J. Rimmer. 1998. "Beyond the Third-World City: The New Urban Geography of Southeast Asia," *Urban Studies* 35 (12): 2303–2321.

Diouf, M. 1999. "Urban Youth and Senegalese Politics: Dakar 1988–1994," in J. Holston (ed.). *Cities and Citizenship.* Durham and London: Duke University Press, pp. 42–66.

Drakakis-Smith, D. 1997. "Third World Cities: Sustainable Urban Development III: Basic Needs and Human Rights," *Urban Studies* 34: 797–823.

Drakakis-Smith, D. 2000. *Third World Cities*, 2nd edition. London: Routledge.

Durand-Lasserve, A. 1998. "Law and Urban Change in Developing Countries: Trends and Issues," in Edésio Fernandes and Ann Varley (eds.). *Illegal Cities: Law and Urban Change in Developing Countries.* London and New York: Zed Press, pp. 233–287.

Emizet, K. 1998. "Confronting the Apex of the State: The Growth of the Unofficial Economy in the Congo," *African Studies Review* 41 (1): 99–137.

Enwezor, O. et al. 2002. "Introduction," in O. Enwezor et al. (eds.). *Under Siege: Four African Cities. Freetown, Johannesburg, Kinshasa, Lagos* (Documenta 11, Platform 4). Ostiledern-Ruit, Germany: Hatje Cantz, pp 13–22.

Ferguson, J. 1990. *The Anti-Politics Machine; "Development," Depoliticization, and Bureaucratic Power in Lesotho.* Cambridge: Cambridge University Press.

Gandy, M. 2005. "Learning from Lagos," *New Left Review* (33): 36–52.

Gberie, L. 2005. "Review Article: Africa: The Troubled Continent," *African Affairs* 104 (415): 337–342.

Gombya, C. 1994 "Eating Cities: Urban Management and Markets in Kampala," *Cities* 11 (2): 86–94.

Griffin, A. 2001. "The Promotion of Sustainable Cities," in M. Freire and R. Stren (eds.). *The Challenge of Urban Government: Policies and Practices.* Washington, DC: The World Bank, pp. 63–72.

Grosh, B. and G. Somolekae. 1996. "Mighty Oaks from Little Acorns: Can Micro-Enterprise Serve as the Seedbed of Industrialisation?" *World Development* 24 (12): 1879–1890.

Gugler, J. 1997. "Over-Urbanization Reconsidered," in Josef Gugler (ed.). *Cities in the Developing World: Issues, Theory and Policy.* Oxford and New York: Oxford University Press, pp. 114–123.

Guyer, J. 1995. "Introduction: The Currency Interface and its Dynamics," in J. Guyer (ed.). *Money Matters: Instability, Values, and Social Payments in the Modern History of West African Communities.* Portsmouth, NH and London: Heinemann and James Currey, pp. 1–33.

Guyer, J., L. Denzer, and A. Agbaje (eds.). 2002. *Money Struggles and City Life: Devaluation in Ibadan and other Urban Centers in Southern Nigeria, 1986-1996.* Portsmouth, NH: Heinemann.

Halfani, M. 1996. "The Challenge of Urban Governance in East Africa: Responding to an Unrelenting Crisis," in Patricia McCarney (ed.). *Cities and Governance: New Directions in Latin America, Asia, and Africa.* Toronto: Centre for Urban and Community Studies, University of Toronto, pp. 183–203.

Hansen, K. T. 1997, *Keeping House in Lusaka.* New York: Columbia University Press.

Hansen, K. T. and M. Vaa. 2004. "Introduction," in K. T. Hansen and M. Vaa (eds.). *Reconsidering Informality: Perspectives from Urban Africa.* Uppsala, Sweden: Nordiska Afrikainstitutet, pp. 7–24.

Hart, K. 1973, "Informal Income Opportunities and Urban Employment in Ghana," *The Journal of Modern African Studies* 11(1): 61–89.

Home, R. 1997. *Of Planting and Planning: The Making of British Colonial Cities.* London: Spon.

Hoyle, B. 1996. *Cityports, Coastal Zones, and Regional Change: International Perspectives on Planning and Management.* New York: Wiley.

Huntington, S. and E. Harrison. 2000. *Culture Matters: How Values Shape Human Progress.* Cambridge: Harvard University Press.

Hyden, G. and J. Mugabe. 1999. "Governance and Sustainable Development in Africa: The Search for Economic and Political Renewal," in J. Mugabe (ed.). *Governing the Environment: Political Change and Natural Resources Management in Eastern and Southern Africa.* Nairobi: ACTS Press, pp. 29–38.

Jackson, P., P. Crang, and C. Dwyer. 2004. "Introduction: the Spaces of Transnationality," in P. Jackson, P. Crang, and C. Dwyer (eds.). *Transnational Spaces.* London: Routledge, pp. 1–23.

Kamette II, A. 2001. "Civil Society, Housing and Urban Governance: The Case of Urban Housing Co-operatives in Zimbabwe," in Arne Tostensen, Inge Tvedten, and Mariken Vaa (eds.). *Associational Life in African Cities: Popular Responses to the Urban Crisis.* Stockholm: Nordiska Afrikaininstitutet, pp. 162–179.

Knox, P. and S. Marston. 2003. *Places and Regions in Global Context: Human Geography.* Upper Saddle River, NJ: Prentice Hall.

Kurtz, R. 1998. *Urban Obsessions, Urban Fears: The Postcolonial Kenyan Novel.* Trenton, NJ: Africa World Press.

Lewis, J. 2005. " 'It's a Jungle Out There': Townlife in Modern Africa," *African Affairs* 104 (414): 137–139.

Lorenço-Lindell, I. 2002. *Walking the Tight Rope: Informal Livelihoods and Social Networks in a West African City.* Stockholm: Stockholm University, Department of Human Geography, Stockholm Studies in Human Geography 9. [Distributed by Almqvist & Wiksell International.]

Lugalla, J. 1995. *Adjustment and Poverty in Tanzania.* Munster, Germany: Lit Verlag.

Mabogunje, A. 1994. "Urban Land and Urban Management Policies in Sub-Saharan Africa," *Urban Perspectives* (4): 27–42.

MacGaffey, J. 1991. *The Real Economy of Zaire: The Contribution of Smuggling and Other Unofficial Activities to National Wealth.* Philadelphia: University of Pennsylvania Press.

MacGaffey, J. and R. Bazenguissa-Ganga. 2000. *Congo-Paris: Transnational Traders on the Margins of the Law.* Oxford: James Currey; and Bloomington: Indiana University Press.

Mbembe, A. 2004. "Aesthetics of Superfluity," *Public Culture* 16 (3): 373–475.

Mbembe, A. and S. Nuttall. 2004. "Riting the World from an African Metropolis," *Public Culture* 16 (1): 347–372.

Mbogoni, L. 2004. *The Cross versus the Crescent: Religion and Politics in Tanzania from the 1880s to the 1990s.* Dar es Salaam: Mkuki na Nyota Publishers.

Mead, D. 1996. "The Informal Sector Elephant," *World Development* 24 (10): 1611–1619.

Mercer, C. 2003. "Performing Partnership: Civil Society and the Illusions of Good Governance in Tanzania," *Political Geography* 22: 741–763.

Mitchell, D. 2000. *Cultural Geography: A Critical Introduction.* Malden, MA: Blackwell.

Mitullah, W. and K. Kibwana. 1998. "A Tale of Two Cities: Policy, Law, and Illegal Settlements in Kenya," in E. Fernandes and A. Varley (eds.). *Illegal Cities: Law and Urban Change in Developing Countries.* London and New York: Zed Press.

Mudimbe, V. Y. 1994. *The Idea of Africa*, Bloomington, IN: Indiana University Press.

Murray, M. 2003. "Alien Strangers in our Midst: The Foreign Dreaded Invasion and 'Fortress South Africa," *Canadian Journal of African Studies* 37 (2–3): 440–466.

Myers, G. 2003. *Verandahs of Power: Colonialism and Space in Urban Africa.* Syracuse, NY: Syracuse University Press.

Myers, G. 2005. *Disposable Cities: Garbage, Governance and Sustainable Development in Urban Africa.* Aldershot: Ashgate.

Nabudere, D. 2000. *Globalisation and the Post-Colonial African State.* Harare: SAPES Books.

O'Connor, A. 1983. *The African City.* London: Hutchinson University Library for Africa.

Olmedo, C. and M. Murray. 2002. "The Formalization of Informal/Precarious Labor in Contemporary Argentina," *International Sociology* 17 (3): 421–443.

Peberdy, S. and C. Rogerson. 2000. "Transnationalism and Non-South African Entrepreneurs in South Africa's Small, Medium and Micro-Enterprise (SMME) Economy," *Canadian Journal of African Studies* 34 (1): 20–40.

Portes, A. 1994. "The Informal Economy and Its Paradoxes," in N. Smelser and R. Swedberg (eds.). *The Handbook of Economic Sociology.* Princeton, NJ: Princeton University Press, pp. 426–450.

Portes, A. and S. Sassen-Koob. 1987. "Making It Underground: Comparative Material on the Informal Sector in Western Market Economies," *American Journal of Sociology* 93 (1): 30–61

Portes, A., M. Castells, and L. Benton. 1989. "The Policy Implications of Informality," in A. Portes, M. Castells, and L. Benton (eds.). *The Informal Economy: Studies in Advanced and Less Developed Countries.* Baltimore: The Johns Hopkins University Press, pp. 298–311.

Potts, D. and C. C. Mutambirwa. 1991. "High-Density Housing in Harare: Commodification and Overcrowding," *Third World Planning Review* 13 (1): 1–55.

Rakodi, C. (ed.). 1997. "Global Forces, Urban Change, and Urban Management in Africa," in Carole Rakodi (ed.). *The Urban Challenge in Africa: Growth and Management of Its Largest Cities.* Tokyo: United Nations University Press.

Rakodi, C. 2002. "Order and Disorder in African Cities: Governance, Politics, and Urban Land Development Processes," in O. Enwezor et al. (eds.). *Under Siege: Four African Cities. Freetown, Johannesburg, Kinshasa, Lagos, Documenta 11, Platform 4.* Ostiledern-Ruit, Germany: Hatje Cantz, pp. 45–80.

Rakowski, C. 1994. "The Informal Sector Debate, Part 2: 1984–1993," in C. Rakowski (ed.). *Contrapunto: The Informal Sector Debate in Latin America.* Albany: State University of New York Press, pp. 31–50.

Read, S. 2005. "The Form of the Future," in S. Read, J. Rosemann, and J. van Eldijk (eds.). *Future City.* London and New York: Spon Press, pp. 3–17.

Robins, S. 2000. "City Sites," in S. Nuttall and C.-A. Michel (eds.). *Senses of Culture: South African Cultural Studies.* Oxford and Cape Town: Oxford University Press, pp. 408–425.

Robinson, J. 1997. "The Geopolitics of South African Cities: States, Citizens, Territories," *Political Geography* 16(5): 365–386.

Robinson, J. 2002. "Global and World Cities: A View from Off the Map," *International Journal of Urban and Regional Research* 26 (3): 531–554.

Robinson, J. 2006. *Ordinary Cities: Between Modernity and Development.* London: Routledge.

Roe, E. 1999. *Except-Africa: Remaking Development, Rethinking Power.* New Brunswick, NJ: Transaction Publishers.

Rogerson, C. M. 1997. "International Migration, Immigrant Entrepreneurs and South Africa's Small Enterprise Economy," *Migration Policy Series*, No. 3. Cape Town: Southern African Migration Project.

Rogerson, C. M. 1998. " 'Formidable Entrepreneurs': The Role of Foreigners in the Gauteng SMME Economy," *Urban Forum* [Johannesburg] 9 (1): 143–153.

Rogerson, C. M. and J. M. Rogerson. 1996. "The Metropolis as Incubator: Small-Scale Enterprise Development in Johannesburg," *GeoJournal* 39 (1): 33–40.

Rogerson, C. M. and J. M. Rogerson. 1997. "The Changing Post-*Apartheid* City: Emergent Black-Owned Small Enterprises in Johannesburg," *Urban Studies* 34: 85–103.

Sassen, S. 1994. *Cities in a World Economy.* London: Pine Forge Press.

Sassen, S. 2000. *Global Cities: New York, London, Tokyo*, 2nd edition. Princeton: Princeton University Press.

Schech, S. and J. Haggis. 2000. *Culture and Development: A Critical Introduction.* Malden, MA: Blackwell.

Schwab, P. 2002. *Africa: A Continent Self-Destructs.* New York: Palgrave Macmillan.

Simon, D. 1989. "Colonial Cities, Postcolonial Africa and the World Economy: A Reinterpretation," *International Journal of Urban and Regional Research* 13 (1): 68–91.

Simon, D. 1997. "Urbanization, Globalization, and Economic Crisis in Africa," in C. Rakodi (ed.). *The Urban Challenge in Africa: Growth and Management of its Largest Cities.* Tokyo: United Nations University Press.

Simone, A. M. 2000. "Going South: African Immigrants in Johannesburg," in S. Nuttall and C.-A. Michael (eds.). *Senses of Culture: South African Cultural Studies.* Cape Town: Oxford University Press, pp. 426–442.

Simone, A. M. 2001a. "Between Ghetto and Globe: Remaking Urban Life in Africa," in A. Tostensen, I. Tvedten, and M. Vaa (eds.). *Associational Life in African Cities: Popular Responses to the Urban Crisis.* Stockholm: Nordiska Afrikainstitutet, pp. 46–63.

Simone, A. M. 2001b. "Straddling the Divides: Remaking Associational Life in the Informal City," *International Journal of Urban and Regional Research* 25 (1): 102–117.

Simone, A. M. 2004. *For the City Yet to Come: Changing African Life in Four Cities.* Durham and London: Duke University Press.

Simone, A. M. 2005a. "Introduction: Urban Processes and Change," in A. M. Simone and A. Abouhani (eds.). *Urban Africa: Changing Contours of Survival in the City.* London: Zed Books, pp.1–26.

Simone, A. M. 2005b. "Local Navigation in Douala," in S. Read, J. Rosemann, and J. van Eldijk (eds.). *Future City.* London and New York: Spon Press, pp. 212–227.

Smith, D. 1996. *Third World Cities in Global Perspective: The Political Economy of Uneven Urbanization.* Boulder, CO: Westview Press.

Stren, R. and M. Halfani, 2001. "The Cities of Sub-Saharan Africa: From Dependency to Marginality," in R. Paddison (ed.). *Handbook of Urban Studies.* Thousand Oaks, CA: Sage, pp. 466–485.

Swilling, M. 1997.*Governing African Cities.* Johannesburg: Witwaters and University Press.

Tambiah, S. 2000. "Transnational Movements, Diaspora, and Multiple Modernities," *Daedalus* 129 (1): 163–169.

Tostensen, A., I. Tvedten, and M. Vaa. 2001. "The Urban Crisis, Governance and Associational Life," in Arne Tostensen, Inge Tvedten, and Mariken Vaa (eds.). *Associational Life in African Cities: Popular Responses to the Urban Crisis.* Stockholm: Nordiska Afrikaininstitutet, pp. 7–26.

Tripp, A. M. 1992. "Local Organizations, Participation and the State in Urban Tanzania," in Goran Hyden and Michael Bratton (eds.). *Governance and Politics in Africa.* Boulder, CO: Lynne Riener, pp. 221–241.

Tripp, A. M. 1997. *Changing the Rules: The Politics of Liberalization and the Urban Informal Economy in Tanzania.* Berkeley and Los Angeles: University of California Press.

Watts, M. 1994. "Development II: The Privatization of Everything?" *Progress in Human Geography* 18 (3): 371–384.

Watts, M. 1999. "Islamic Modernities? Citizenship, Civil Society and Islamicism in a Nigerian City," in J. Holston (ed.). *Cities and Citizenship.* Durham and London: Duke University Press, pp. 67–102.

Watts, M. 2004. "Antinomies of Community: Some Thoughts on Geography, Resources and Empire," *Transactions, Institute of British Geographers* 29 (2): 195–216.

Vaa, M. 2000. "Housing Policy after Political Transition: The Case of Bamako," *Environment and Urbanization* 12 (1): 27–34.

van der Merve, I. 2004. "The Global Cities of Sub-Saharan Africa: Fact or Fiction?" *Urban Forum* 15 (1): 36–47.

Zeleza, P. 1999. "The Spatial Economy of Structural Adjustment in African Cities," in P. Zeleza and E. Kalipeni (eds.). *Sacred Spaces and Public Quarrels: African Cultural and Economic Landscapes.* Trenton, NJ: Africa World Press, pp. 43–71.

I

Culture, Imagination, Space, and Place

In seeking to make sense of cities, metaphors of flows, circuits, and networks have often replaced the conventional language of hierarchies, places, and boundaries (Simonsen 2004). Cities are not only material places defined by physical boundaries but also platforms in wider circuits of movement and staging areas for global flows. Besides their morphological form, their built environment, and their physical infrastructure, cities also consist of an imaginary dimension through which urban residents define themselves and give meaning to their daily lives. Just as Walter Benjamin interpreted urban modernity through an examination of decaying ruins of cities, and Robert Venturi looked at urban image through vernacular architecture, it is possible to make use of such *genres* as fiction writing, documentary filmmaking, autobiographical reminisces, along with such performative acts as music, art, and plays, to reflect upon the experience of urban living (Askew 2002).

The essays in part 1 address a central paradox that shapes the understanding of African cities, namely, their inherent dynamism, improvisation, and mutability, on the one side, and decay, obsolescence, and stasis, on the other. The intersection of the global and the local has produced hybrid spaces where clarity, coherence, and consistency have become not much more than a pipe dream.

For many residents of African cities, fixed places have utility only as diasporic spaces, that is, as points of departure, or launching pads, facilitating movement to somewhere else. In looking at cities like Douala as temporary staging areas for travel to somewhere else, Dominique Malaquais captures the unsettled quality of urban living in contemporary Africa. In describing a painted image found on a barber stand in Douala that depicts an imaginary urban skyline roughly resembling New York City as her point of departure, she argues that places such as Douala, Johannesburg, Kinshasa, and Lagos are significantly less invested in ideas of locality than cities such as London or Paris. For her, movement—voyages real or imagined—gives meaning and substance to urban life in African cities today where the production of new forms of urbanity involves the transgression of barriers, borders, and boundaries.

In addressing the connection between migration and the escalation of ethnic and religious violence in Nigerian cities, Daniel Smith brings us face to face with the headlines of the day in a case study dealing with Igbo migrants in Kano.

Smith argues that the patterns of internal migration are central to the causative forces in the upsurge in this urban violence, adding a nuanced understanding of the "circuitry" of migratory life for Igbos in the north of the country. He carefully retraces the history of conflicts in Kano over both ethnic and religious issues, stretching back into the colonial era, and through the importance of memories of the Biafra war for Igbos in Kano. It is the dynamic circulation of ideas of us and them, Smith shows, that have made contemporary conflicts so unsettling and potentially destabilizing, particularly in the ways that stories of violence in the north magnify when they move to the southeast, to Igboland. Smith's long-standing ethnographic interests in both semirural Igboland and in Kano enable him to connect the circuits with a considerable depth of understanding and empathy.

Urban residents invest even the most regulated urban space with meaning, memory, and desire. Drawing upon the work of such theorists as Michel Foucault, Edward Said, and Michel de Certeau, Joyce Nyairo uses the lyrics of popular songs to investigate the symbiotic relationship between cultural forms and urban space. In supporting her claim that urban space is a product of the creative imagination, she lays particular stress on the power of popular music to shape and transform urban identities. Like other expressions of popular culture, these songs are syncretic blends, or hybrid creations, that combine recognized markers of Western modernity with local idiom and cultural references. Nyairo is less concerned with the question of whether or not the mimickry and appropriation of American hip hop music amounts to a dilution or enrichment of local popular culture than in understanding how the lyrics of these songs reverberate locally by taking on a life of their own. In their lyrics, these popular songs conjure up imaginary figures—*matatu* [taxi] drivers, thugs and criminals, desperate youth, ambitious and talented musicians, and urban newcomers—who inhabit the marginal spaces of the cityscape. Brought to life in the dance halls and music venues of the slum areas of Nairobi, these ordinary people project the class anger and resentment of slum dwellers and at the same time convey a message of hope for a better future.

Fiction writers, filmmakers, photographers, literary critics, and others have exposed us to the view of the city as text, a perspective that calls for reading the city as a conglomeration of signs. Despite its popularity in current cultural and postmodernist approaches to urban studies, this trope of the city as sign has a remarkably long and resilient history that has moved back and forth between the pictorial, visual, and image-related portrayals of urban life to the written texts that range from storytelling and fictionalized accounts, to statistics and graphs.

Photographic images are a visual language that tell stories in pictures rather than words. Visual depictions are never just innocent illustrations. They are the material representations of "fields of force" frozen in historical time. In assembling this series of photographs, Martin Murray tries to provide a visual record of the evolving shape of the built environment of post-*Apartheid* Johannesburg. Working together with photographer Juanita Malan, he uses these pictorial images of the urban landscape as a photo *montage* that provides a partial glimpse of urban fragmentation and social exclusion. These assembled photographs represent a kind of documentary exercise that records the steady encroachment of fear on the built environment of Johannesburg.

In his investigation of the imaginative dimension of city living in Douala, Basile Ndjio uses a very lively imagination of his own to articulate what he terms a necropolis. Anticipating the potential connectivity with Afro-pessimism or anti-urbanism that will come to mind, Ndjio immediately distances his chapter from that negativity. Instead, he is at pains to show the creativity by which death comes alive in Douala, comes to have a life of its own. To be sure, tragedy, violence, disease, horror, and anxiety dominate people's everyday existence. Yet Ndjio sees a "living-dead" strategizing that enables vast numbers of urban Cameroonians to cope with, and in some cases thrive off, the necropolis. It is hard to ignore the anger in Ndjio's voice from years of researching and surviving this "disabling city" and its "infrastructure of lack" amidst an array of authoritarian state tactics. He does not shirk away from showing that "living in the necropolis entails making death one's intimate," in fairly graphic terms. Yet, drawing on popular cartoons, popular songs, and his own experiences and research, Ndjio also suggests the myriad ways—some indeed that appear quite bizarre at first pass—by which Douala's residents seek to turn a necropolis into what he terms a hedonopolis, a city of life and celebration. By blending the imaginary with the "real," he provides an account that might be read as fiction—indeed a truth stranger than fiction.

In bringing these pieces together in this part, we seek to draw attention to the many ways in which the overlapping of culture, imagination, space, and place help express the heterogeneous realities of contemporary cities in Africa. Conflict and creativity, despair and dynamism, appear and reappear side by side and seemingly as part of one another in cities across the continent, but in distinct ways for each place and time. Not even entire books could hope to encompass culture, imagination, space, or place in cities in Africa now, or in the past, or in the future. Rather, these chapters are signposts and snapshot forays into a sea of extraordinary experiences that are symptomatic of city-ness in contemporary Africa.

REFERENCES

Askew, K. 2002. *Performing the Nation: Swahili Music and Cultural Politics in Tanzania*. Chicago: University of Chicago Press.

Simonsen, K. 2004. "Networks, Flows, and Fluids—Reimagining Spatial Analysis?" *Environment and Planning A* 36 (8): 1333–1340.

1

Douala/Johannesburg/New York: Cityscapes Imagined

Dominique Malaquais

> The capability to imagine . . . worlds is now itself a globalized phenomenon.
> (Appadurai 1999: 8)

Thinking Cities: First Words

Consider an image, a panel, painted in acrylic on wood, on the side of a barber's stand. Such stands are a mainstay of cities in West and Central Africa. Here, a man can get his hair cut and shaped. Here too, people gather, discuss current events, politics, sports, the shape and state of the city. On structures of this kind, painted images of people and places are common: celebrities from the president to Osama bin Laden and Mickey Mouse and sites the owner has inhabited, visited, or dreams of knowing. This particular stand shows a city skyline, pictured at dusk, flat against a reddening sky, a sun setting in the distance; several buildings loom, their facades in shadow. The structure with this image is in Douala. It is located in a neighborhood called Nylon, so named for its propensity to flood (water pools there, as it does when spilled on synthetic fabric). Nylon is a neighborhood typical of Douala in many respects: grossly underserved in terms of formal infrastructure, formal housing, formal job markets; the majority of inhabitants are in flux, in transit from or to another place, inside or outside Cameroon, in voyages real and imagined.

I propose to use the image on this barber stand to think, broadly, about definitions of the term "city." My focus is African cities. One caveat, however: I am far from convinced that it is possible—or even reasonable—to speak of African cities as constituting a category on their own. It would be significantly more productive to discuss cities more generally, with given African cities as starting points, prototypes for an emerging, global form of urbanity. (What "global" might be taken to mean in this context, I return to by and by.) The types of urban centers scholars have tended to think of as normative—so-called First World, Euro-American cities—I contend, are in fact nothing of the kind. Far more normative, or in any event more useful as points of reference, if only because they are infinitely more numerous, are cities outside the industrialized "North."[1]

If we can agree that cities in Southeast Asia, sub-Saharan Africa, or the Indian Ocean offer as valid a set of spaces from which to initiate a discussion of the urban condition today as do those of Western Europe and North America, it seems fair to argue that a reconceptualization of the city is in order. Douala, after all, though it undoubtedly shares certain features with London, is very different from its sister on the Thames; the two are far less alike than are London and Paris, or Barcelona and New York.[2] What, then, do we mean—what precisely are we referencing, when we use the term "city"? An initial set of answers might involve a rethinking of notions of place and boundary.

Douala, I propose—like Lagos or Kinshasa—as an urban center is significantly less invested in ideas of locality than cities such as London or Paris.[3] This is not to say that "placeness," that is, conceptions of the city as an entity bounded in space, is absent here. Like most cities, Douala is a locus of histories, pasts, and, for some of its inhabitants at least, rootedness; children are born there, loved ones are buried in its cemeteries, life stories unfold on its streets. At the same time, however, it is a site of infinite porosity. The appearance and demographic makeup of its neighborhoods is constantly shifting.[4] Only its colonial core-cum-formal business district, Bonanjo, seems, at first glance, relatively untouched by such shifts, by a propensity for change so common in other districts that it is best described as a daily occurrence. Every day, boundaries—physical, social, interpersonal—are dismantled and reconstituted, rethought and constructed anew (or not), often, as AbdouMaliq Simone has shown (2002a), in accordance with rules, or for reasons, that defy ready classification. Radical alterations, microscopic to the eye perhaps, but socially, politically, economically fundamental, are par for the course, in ways arguably less common in urban centers such as London and New York. The city's edges are in constant flux as well, expanding and, on occasion, shrinking virtually overnight. So too is—and to this I shall return shortly, for it is my principal concern here—the city's identity as a node, a place one chooses to be "in." Douala, I propose in these pages, is a city defined above all by mobility. Passage—in, through, beyond—in active refusal of closure, of boundedness, is one of its primary characteristics.

Recent studies of globalization have begun to challenge notions of place and boundedness, notably in relation to the idea of the nation-state and its borders (Appadurai 1996, 1999; Mbembe 1999; Pieterse 2004; Roitman 2004; Sassen 1999; *inter alia*). In discussions of cities too the relevance of these notions has been queried (see, notably, Sassen 2001). In the latter context, however, the focus has tended to be on what Saskia Sassen terms "global cities": urban centers typified by strong concentrations of capital and infrastructure—sophisticated financial instruments, banking institutions, transport, electronic and telecommunications networks that support a significant volume of traffic with like centers, over vast distances mitigated by the instantaneity of cyber-exchanges (Sassen 1999). Fundamental to their study, indeed to their very identification as sites worthy of investigation, is their imbrication in what many agree are two key features of globalization, namely the collapse of space and the concomitant collapse of time made possible by the advent of the digital age and the availability of increasingly streamlined high-speed transport (Augé 1992; Pieterse 2004; Shami 1999). The fact nonetheless remains that many cities of the "South" are unevenly affected by such phenomena. For the overwhelming majority of their inhabitants, both time and space, thoroughly *un*-collapsed, remain very real, tangible in the extreme. Indeed, it might be argued that, in certain respects, they are exacerbated by the availability of images (on the Internet, via satellite TV) showing far away places most know they will never see. (Shortly, I shall contradict myself on this point, but contradictions are integral to the contemporary urban condition in such places as sub-Saharan Africa. They belong to the world of "disjunctive flows" theorized by Appadurai (1996), which, he has shown, are both characteristic and productive of globalization, the latter in ways that can prove extraordinarily creative.[5])

If "global cities" are the stuff of instantaneity and distances collapsed into near-nothingness, what is to be made of cities like Douala or Lagos, where travel from one point to another can take hours and typically involves stops and starts the duration of which cannot be anticipated? Where the Internet, beholden to an electricity grid at very best uncertain, is subject to innumerable failures? Where 1960s jets rust on the tarmac of airports bereft of the most elementary security procedures and the business of negotiating one's exit from customs can take as long as the flight from a country thousands of kilometers away? As Mbembe (1999) has argued regarding such regions as the Chad Basin, it will hardly do to call such spaces "marginal." Forty percent of Africa's inhabitants—320 million people—live in cities akin to Douala (Enwezor et al. 2002: 15); given such numbers and the urban explosion they represent notions of "marginality" seem inapposite, not to say racist.[6] This is all the more so as the cities in question are staging areas for remarkable cultural innovation, not least in the international art world, a point masterfully brought to the fore by such recent exhibitions as "The Short Century" (2001) and "Dokumenta 11" (2002). Nor will it do to define these cities as "not yet" or "in the process of becoming" global. Such permutations, rooted in the teleologies of Modernist discourse, are plainly Eurocentric and, for this (and other) reasons, largely useless.[7] Many neo-Marxist analyses present problems as well. Clearly, economic globalization, in its present form, is a source of sharp inequities, the overwhelming burden of which is shouldered by "Third World" city-dwelling populations. Yet discussions that focus on these aspects alone, articulating (as do certain right-wing approaches as well—e.g., Kaplan 2001) a vision of cities fundamentally beyond the reach of anything positive globalization might have to offer, vastly oversimplify complex states of affair. Still more problematic, they deny agency to the "Third World" citizens in whose defense they rise.[8]

WHAT THEN?

In cities like Douala, movement may be curtailed—stopped dead in its tracks, even—by dysfunctional traffic patterns and crumbling infrastructure, resulting in an urban experience characterized by near-intractable boundedness. Nevertheless, this does not mean that other, radically different, experiences of the city are impossible. In fact, wholly contradictory ones are common. Mired though they may be in *embouteillages* ("traffic jams")—"bottled in" is the literal translation—Doualais frequently know more about cities and city dwellers half a world away than do their infinitely more mobile Euro-American counterparts in New York or London. An inhabitant of Nylon is likely to be much more curious about, and better versed in, the ways of streets and spaces far removed from his own than a high-ranking functionary or the founder of the Douala stock exchange, for whom such "otherwheres" are ordinary. In the face of immobility, ideas and ideals of mobility are deployed, to ends as creative as they are unpredictable. If, as has been widely theorized, a key aspect of globalization is vastly increased knowledge of the world, throughout the world, then Douala is beyond a doubt a city of the global age. For significant numbers of Doualais, such knowledge is a platform for action, within and (far) beyond the city. In this setting, the imagination plays a fundamental role. Conjurings of mobility—mobilities imagined, acted upon or not, attempted, thwarted, and launched over and over again—are the driving force of the city. They shape the ways in which it is thought, lived, and daily transformed.

Better suited to my argument here may be the French *imaginaire* rather than the term "imagination." *Imaginaire* encompasses both the act of imagining and that which is imagined, the sum total of what can, or might, be imagined of a given place, person, or idea.[9] Central to its articulation is the idea of "the possible." Contemporary Douala, I would suggest, is a place of the *imaginaire*, brought into being—made—by the aspirations of its inhabitants to what is conceivable, to what (and where) they and it *might be*. This is not a matter of the intangible, though the invisible unquestionably plays a significant role here (Geschiere 1997; Séraphin 2000). Fuelled by possibilities of becoming, Doualais bring into being tangibly new, and different, identities, objects, and spaces. Of course this is true, to some degree, of all people everywhere. Nevertheless, in Douala, Kinshasa, Lagos, such processes are so prevalent, so fundamental a part of everyday life, that they must be seen as constitutive. They are an integral part of the architecture of the city, a building block in the most literal sense.

IMAGE-"IN"-ING CITIES

First and foremost among these processes, most vital of the city's motors, are mobilities imagined over vast spans of space, the ability to "see" (and to see oneself in) otherwheres far away. Consider, once again, the image with which we started. Below the skyline, outside the frame of the image itself, are three words, painted in eye-catching blue and orange script: "New York City." Let us suppose for now that, as these words suggest, the skyline depicted is (or is meant to be) that of New York. Self-evidently, this is a very particular view of the "Big Apple." Most Euro- and African Americans, it seems fair to say, would not represent New York as it appears here: as a city where some 50 percent of the buildings are mosques or, in any event, with a strong affinity to Islam. (Part curve, part spine, the lettering below the image brings to mind features of Arabic script, adding to a sense of things Islamic in the scene depicted.) The presence of palm trees, framing the skyline to the far left and right, seems also less than typical. The view pictured, however, is not a simple figment of the painter's imagination, for it includes two elements that suggest a real knowledge of the city. First, slightly off center and to the viewer's left, is a building whose profile most New Yorkers know well: the Citicorp Center, Midtown Manhattan's high-Modernist architectural anchor, with its distinctive slanted roof. Second, further to the left, is a high-rise equipped with a quintessentially New York appendage: a water reservoir. (Faced in brick or stone, such structures—squat and often less than aesthetic—appear atop most apartment buildings; less expensive to construct than an entire additional floor, they extend upward from the building's roof, which, in the process, acquires a stocky, truncated profile.)

I have spent many hours wandering about New York in search of vantage points to glimpse such views of the city's skyline. I am not suggesting that there is a place from which New York City looks—photographically—like the image considered here. On the other hand, this *kind* of view, dominated by mosque architecture or by a profile of the Citicorp Center, is possible. Two particular vantage points are of interest in this regard and one noteworthy thing about them is both are places of transit, spaces one moves through on one's way from one place to another. One is the Van Wyk Expressway, leading from Kennedy Airport to Manhattan. The other is the Tri-Borough Bridge, which one crosses, en route to Manhattan, when coming from Kennedy and LaGuardia Airports. On the Van Wyk, some seven minutes after leaving the airport, one is struck, on the passenger side of the car, taxi, or bus in which one is riding, by a distinctly Islamic architectural form: the profile of a dome-topped building identified in bold letters, quite similar to those seen below the Nylon skyline, as the "Headquarters of the Al-Khoei Benevolent Foundation." This structure, together with a cluster of mid-rise buildings at its side, is the first hint of a monumental skyline one encounters after leaving Kennedy Airport. From the second vantage point, the Tri-Borough, particularly at sundown, the first view of Manhattan, with the Citicorp at center, is quite similar to that depicted on the Nylon barber stand.

What might the relevance of this be? It seems likely that the panel's painter has visited New York. Although one might argue that vistas highlighting the Citicorp Center at nightfall are the stuff of postcards, one or several of which the artist might have seen outside New York, the same is not true of structures akin to the Al-Khoei headquarters or the reservoir-capped buildings he depicts.[10] This, however, strikes me as less noteworthy than the particular vision of the city the painter proposes: a vision of New York as a place one is approaching from elsewhere—transiting toward—rather than a place one is *in*; so too, by logical inference (and to this I will return), a place one will eventually be transiting away from (by car, by bus, by plane).

In terms of myths prevalent in the United States about foreign desires concerning the American city—desires to settle, to make America home—the foregoing is striking. The goal of staying, it seems to me, is very much absent from this picture. The focus here is on coming and going, going and coming. Transit to and fro—the voyage to and from the place depicted—is not only foregrounded: it trumps the place itself. This, in turn, I find interesting because it speaks, in ways at once very concrete and metaphorical, to one of the primary characteristics of a place like Douala.

In Nylon, as in most quarters of Cameroon's economic capital, the matter of coming and going is paramount. Virtually every conversation leads, at some point, to a discussion of leaving. Dreams of elsewhere are everywhere. On the subject of such dreams, AbdouMaliq Simone quotes a man named Malam.[11] The subject is New Bell, a quarter of Douala similar in many ways to Nylon:

> We in New Bell always seem to imagine ourselves somewhere else. While we don't necessarily want to leave, we behave as if we already have. This affects us in various ways. On the one hand, those who are neighbors, who share this street, sometimes act as if they don't see what is going on. The life around them doesn't impact them because they are not really here; they are living their dream. As a result, people are freer to do what they want to do. On the other hand, because so many people are in so many other places in their minds, this becomes their only common point of view; and so they can't really ask each other for anything, can't rely on one another, because no one has a sense of what others are really experiencing. Also, it means that things are sped up: the children have already left the house and gone somewhere else; the father is already old, the mother is already old. The normal rhythm of growing up, of dying, of leaving and coming back is all collapsed into a single note that everyone sings. And so no one listens. It is a way of living everywhere and nowhere at the same time. (Simone 2002b)

Whether Malam's somewhat pessimistic attitude to the effects of this phenomenon is warranted is a matter for debate.[12] The situation he describes, that is, living here, everywhere, and nowhere at once, nonetheless seems characteristic of much of the city. Transit, the distances between places, the experiences and the time spent getting there and back, the itineraries followed in doing so, routes often improvised or un-anticipated, commonly take precedence over places where one stops, where the body stands still. This is so on multiple levels. Within the city, the absence of a regular public transport system means that the business of moving about occupies the better part of people's days and nights. A similar state of affairs obtains within the country more broadly; movement between the city and the capital, Yaoundé, smaller urban centers and *le village*—places where one sells things, looks for work, goes to bury kin—accounts for significant chunks of daily life. Most consuming of all is movement beyond the city and the country: travel between Douala and cities abroad, in Africa and elsewhere. For so many, in Douala as in other cities of the continent, movement of this kind has become so common that it is something of a cliché to say that Africa, today, is a continent on the move.

Such movement, constant, back, forth, back again, and crisscrossing vast expanses of space, has a tangible impact on readings of African cities by those who inhabit them. This is underscored by life stories, tales told by men and women of transit between and through cities, over thousands of kilometers. A rich body of such tales chronicles the experience of moving between Douala and Johannesburg. Over the past two years, I have had occasion to speak with many Doualais who undertook such journeys. Most of those kind enough to share their experiences with me live today in Hillbrow and Yeoville, neighborhoods of inner-city Johannesburg that, since the fall of Apartheid, have become magnets for intra-African migration. Characterized by near-total neglect on the part of city and private interests, over the past ten years they have morphed into overcrowded, insalubrious, and (in Hillbrow's case in particular) extraordinarily dangerous places for foreign Africans to live in. The great majority of those with whom I have spoken were living in New Bell and Nylon when they left Douala. Most abandoned these spaces for those of Johannesburg in the hope of finding work there or, in more general terms, opportunities—the means, financial, instrumental, psychological, to change their lives.

One aspect of these stories strikes me as fundamental. My interlocutors' views of both Douala and Johannesburg are marked not so much by the cities themselves as by the experience of travel between them. A majority of the people with whom I have had occasion to discuss such matters spent months or even years in the process of moving from one city to the other. One man left by bus via Equatorial Guinea.[13] From there, he traveled to Gabon, mostly on foot. Then came Brazzaville. He was on his way to Kinshasa, where he planned to stow away in a boat sailing south. But there was no moving beyond Brazza, which, at the time, was mired in a hugely destructive civil war. For sixteen months he remained there, caught in the crossfire of militias—Zulu, Cobra, Ninja—named after cultures and places, lands and ideas, countries and continents away. When the guns fell silent, he made his way, through DRC, to Angola, where again he was waylaid, this time by a love affair that may or may not have involved a marriage. Disentangled from a relationship he did not wish to pursue, he proceeded to Namibia, where an attempted passage into South Africa failed. This prompted a redirection into Zimbabwe, which failed as well. From there, the traveler returned to Namibia, where he lost everything to a passer who reneged on getting him across the border. Eventually, a good Samaritan, a truck driver, got him across, depositing him on the edges of Cape Town. There, for months, home became a refugee camp. Previously, the camp had been a mental asylum. A few inmates remained on the premises, forgotten he surmises. The first experiences he recalls of South Africa were of negotiating the space between inside and outside, leaving and entering the camp anew. The guards, it appears, could not tell the refugees from the insane because they shared no common language with either group.

The story this man tells is by no means exceptional. The overwhelming majority of the people with whom I have spoken followed similarly circuitous routes. And not a few doubled back, most or all of the way, one, two, even three times, after having been caught, racketed, deported, or otherwise waylaid at various border crossings. For some, such stops, starts, and doublings back produced precisely the kinds of change they sought. One traveler, turned back after a violent encounter with soldiers on the southern fringes of Congo, made his way to Gabon, where he settled in Libreville; in time, he entered politics there. As such careers, in Africa as elsewhere, are commonly shortlived, three to four years later, he left. Still, he had experienced things in Libreville, accumulated knowledge and means, which might well have been beyond his reach in Douala. Another Doualais remained for a year in Luanda. There, he bought a bakery from a Senegalese man who, if memory serves, was on his way to Southeast Asia.[14] The acquisition proved a mistake, as the bakery was a poor investment. With his business crumbling about him, the new owner did the only reasonable thing. With the many sacks of flour still in his possession, for weeks he fed the expatriate community of Doualais moving through Luanda. In so doing, he built friendships, networks, and ties, which, a year and more later, proved of immense use in Johannesburg, where several of those whom he had fed found him again.

Many who tell these stories have no intention of staying in South Africa, which adds in significant ways to the focus on transit that typifies both their tales of travel and the experiences of urban life these suggest. Many are already planning to move on.[15] North America and Southeast Asia are the destinations most often mentioned. The plan to move on, however, is often several years old. For a great number, every day is an exercise in trying to accumulate the funds necessary to begin the next journey. A sense of movement always incipient structures their daily lives. This is underscored by the very names of spaces many occupy, typically in the interstices—geographical, legal, financial—of the inner city. A case in point is a squat known as *l'Ambassade* ("The Embassy"), run by a Cameroonian in Johannesburg.[16] Many see as the best approach a movement back and forth between Douala and Johannesburg, the business of daily life taking place not in one city or in the other, but in both at the same time, in neither and, most saliently, in between.

Such approaches to cities and movement are not a Cameroonian phenomenon per se. I doubt that they are specifically African, either. Similar states of affair, I imagine, obtain in many Asian, Eastern European, and Middle Eastern cities. What this suggests, among other things, is that classical definitions of the city are very much in need of *re*-definition. For a majority of the earth's inhabitants, it seems clear, the city is not by any means an entity bounded in space, nor even one bounded in time, as Malam's statement on New Bell suggests. In very real ways, it is always, for a huge number of its people, several places simultaneously: places that it will or might be, places that have been previously seen or that will be seen in the future and—again, saliently—the spaces, experiences, and time of travel between and through these places.

To propose, by way of definition, that the city, in many parts of the world, is radically delocalized, gets in part at what this signifies concretely. Still, it is not quite enough. The definition is inadequate because notions of de-localization—a mainstay of globalization theory (Augé 1992; Pieterse 2004; Sassen 1999)—call on models developed to articulate the realities (or aspirations) of a highly specific minority: a high-speed, Internet, videoconferencing, jet propelled "First World," which, we have seen, bears little relation to the daily experiences of the majority of people. The notion of de-localization is problematic also because—like ideas of the translocal, dear to globalization theorists as well—it is predicated on the preeminence of locality. Places bounded in space, localities, structure the translocal; without them, there is no "trans." How does this relate to places like Nylon and New Bell, for many of whose inhabitants, it seems fair to say, the "trans" takes precedence over the spaces it is intended to bridge?

The skyline in the Nylon barber stand is a richly textured account of what such precedence might mean. The city depicted is peculiarly static. It is noticeably without people. Two figures do appear, both facing the viewer, but neither is located within the frame of the picture proper. Both are in the form of a truncated head and bust; they are haircut models, images clients can look at to see what kinds of haircut the barber offers. From a narrative point of view, there is no direct link between the skyline and the models. Scale, perspective, and a clear-cut border, that is, a painted frame surrounding the skyline, separate them.[17] The models are emphatically not in the city depicted. Dark, devoid of people, this city is not a place in which life is lived, not, at any rate, in the artist's estimate. If the models in the foreground, both of whom make insistent eye contact with the viewer, are any indication, it is a space lived, physically, *behind*. The skyline, from their standpoint, reads almost like a landscape glimpsed in a rearview mirror. The positioning of the two busts in relation to the scene behind them, as well as the space between the models, brings to mind a driver and the passenger at his side. The two men appear to be motoring away from the city, leaving it in their wake, empty and shrouded in darkness.

From this stems a distinct sense of space lived in the process of leaving or, if one focuses, rather, on the skyline itself, moving toward. Process, movement— whether in approach or departure—rather than being "in" defines the place depicted.[18]

Whether in approach or departure, New York is not alone here. Other cities are being glimpsed as well. This is suggested by two of the buildings that make up the skyline. The first, a large domed structure to the viewer's left, brings to mind the mosque of Aya Sophia, in Istanbul.[19] Right of center (again, from the viewer's perspective), a second building appears, whose form seems to draw on a number of structures at once. Third from the far right, it is capped by a needle-like extension, jutting up into space. For most U.S.-based viewers, this construction recalls the Sears Tower, in Chicago. For others, different prototypes may come to mind, among these the Djingeray Mosque of Timbuktu and the Carlton Tower, in Johannesburg. Echoes of Johannesburg also are present in the skyline as a whole, not so much in terms of form as of the scene's "feel," or atmosphere. The painter's handling of the sky, his articulation of a color-saturated, almost tangible dusk against which buildings appear massive, yet at the same time peculiarly flat, bears a strong resemblance to photographic views of the City of Gold's Central Business District, images readily available on the Internet and in countless postcards and tourist brochures.[20]

From this accumulation of city referents emerges a skyline that reads almost like an archaeology of architectural forms, one in which structures and landscapes have been built into and upon one another, giving rise to a profoundly hybrid space.[21] One is faced, here, with a vision of the city as a manner of palimpsest. Yet, unlike a palimpsest proper, the image we see does not foreground any one form: erasures are absent, giving way instead to a series of superimpositions in which all referents are equal and coeval.[22] Two further analogies come to mind, which might help put in words the sense of a city evoked by the painted skyline. One is Freud's "mystic writing pad," as rethought by Derrida and, in his wake, theoreticians of hypertext and virtual reality. The other is a type of talisman in use throughout vast swathes of Islamic West Africa.

Freud's mystic writing pad is a child's toy. It is in two parts: a thick waxen tablet and superimposed plastic sheet. With a pencil, a stylus, or any hard-tipped object, shapes or words can be drawn on the plastic. These do not appear on the sheet itself but through it, in the form of dark traces, on the tablet beneath it. When one lifts the plastic, however, the traces disappear, as on a blackboard whose chalk markings have been erased. For Freud, the act of sketching, lifting, erasing, and starting anew functions as a metaphor for basic cognitive processes. It is "analogous to the way the psychic system which receives sense impression from the outside world remains unmarked by those impressions which pass through it to a deeper layer where they are recorded as unconscious memory. Thus, 'the appearance and disappearance of the writing' is similar to 'the flickering-up and passing-away of consciousness in the process of perception.' "[23]

If, for Freud, the mystic writing pad is a metaphor, for Derrida it is a concrete model. Perception, for the French philosopher, "really is a kind of writing machine like the Mystic Writing Pad":

> Derrida . . . notes . . . that the marks on the pad are not visible due to the stylus leaving a deposit on the sheet of plastic (in the manner of a pen, ink and paper). The marks only become visible because of the contact the wax has on the reverse side of the sheet . . . This is also the case in perception. None of us, Derrida claims, apprehend the world directly, but only retrospectively; our sense of that which is beyond ourselves is the product of previous memories, previous writings. (Derrida 1980: 224)

Derrida's rereading of Freud can be reworked, here, to articulate the sense of a city brought to the fore by the painted skyline. The Nylon panel suggests an apprehension of the world that is the product not only of previous memories, or experiences, but also of future and possible ones. A useful analogy is that of hypertext.[24] In such a text, other words, images, and ideas are always already present. They are an integral part of the text as it appears to the reader, yet prefigure the text's future, ways in which it can (or is likely to) be experienced by the reader thereafter. Still, the hypertext analogy is insufficient. Like the palimpsest and the mystic writing pad (whether Freud's or Derrida's), hypertext does not offer an experience in which multiple, superimposed ideas, images, or realities can be apprehended *at the same time*. To access other words and forms—other worlds—it is necessary to click on one or several links, a process that causes signs and images previously in the viewer's line of sight to disappear. One can only experience such a text as a series of strata, never as one landscape, with all (or even most) of its components in view simultaneously. This results in an experience palpably different from that prompted by the Nylon skyline.

A fourth, and final, analogy may serve us best: that of the talisman. As previously noted, it is a type of object in wide use throughout Muslim (and Muslim-inspired) Africa (Bravman 1984; Prussin 1985). The object is a leather pouch, typically worn on the body. Created by a religious practitioner or a specialist affiliated to a spiritually endowed caste (for instance, in the Bamana region of Mali, a *nyamakala*), the pouch contains words. These may be Q'ranic verses or (as again in the Bamana area) strings of signs drawn from an esoteric alphabet. The words are placed in the pouch in one of two ways. They may be scripted on a piece of paper or parchment, which is then inserted into the pouch, or—and this is the technique that strikes me as most interesting for present purposes—applied to a piece of paper or a tablet, which is then washed clean, resulting in a mixture of ink and water that is poured in (or on) to the pouch, where it fuses with the talisman's leather. By this latter means, further words can be added to the pouch, in time and as circumstances may require. The words within, and the ideas to which these allude, mystically charged, impact the owner's experiences and perceptions. All, no matter how many or how diverse, are always present with the wearer; they are an integral part of his/her apprehension of the world, which actively shapes his (or her) present and possible futures. In this sense, the talisman is very much like the Nylon skyline: it is a locus for, and gives tangible expression to, multiple possibilities—of time, space, and being.

What, then, is the city in the skyline? New York? Timbuktu? Chicago? Istanbul? Johannesburg? Each one, it seems, and, as a result, none. In all likelihood, it is many other cities, too. It may, in fact, be Douala, as Douala might (or could) be seen from and en route to other cities, and in transit to still others. In this sense, the painted skyline might be seen to function itself as a talisman: *pars pro toto* for the dream of other lives in other cities, some or all of which might be(come) Douala herself.[25]

(RE)THINKING ARCHITECTURE

If we suppose that the city is Douala, we are faced with the need to redefine not only what the term "city" may signify, but also the meaning of "architecture." This is all the more pressing as what architecture is, or should be understood to be, in cities like Douala is a matter of some contention. Although this seems to have escaped most architects and all too many architectural historians, among anthropologists and sociologists it is now agreed that the study of architecture should include the unplanned, the temporary, the recycled (see, notably, Agier 1999). What is less generally agreed upon—what has yet to be seriously examined as an object of architecture and a legitimate subject for its practitioners and students—are buildings that are not physically there, in other words, imagined structures, edifices that exist only (or mostly) as rumor.[26] The inclusion of these in discussions of the architecture and the life of cities, all cities, opens up a variety of perspectives, new ways of conceptualizing spaces, sites, and the ways people live in them. In reflecting on urban centers like Douala, where, I have argued, the *imaginaire* plays a constitutive role, it is vital.

Structures of this kind, that is, buildings said but not shown to exist, have as powerful an impact as edifices present and tangible and, arguably, just as much presence. They also have a very real history. Architectural rumor has played a central role in the articulation of urban centers, political orders and movements, and ideas elaborated in response to these. This has been so in a wide variety of geographical and historical contexts. A case in point is Washington, DC. The U.S. capital is the site of widely rumored, alternative maps, a grid of Masonic meaning that the architect L'Enfant and his patrons are said to have built into the plan of the city. These maps, rumor has it, make it possible for Washington to be read and navigated in multiple, radically different ways at one and the same time. The sheer power of this rumor is underscored by the well over two thousand Internet sites it crowds, a number of which, it might be noted, were visited regularly by Timothy McVeigh, to whom we owe one of the great attacks of recent date on the idea of official architecture and its role in bringing the *polis* into being.[27]

In African cities, architectures of rumor have a rich history. The postcolonial period offers a number of significant examples.[28] In Kinshasa under Mobuto Sese Seko and in Douala too, in the reign of present president Paul Biya, rumor has affected in powerful ways the meaning of and attitude toward individual buildings as well as entire spaces within the city. So striking was one instance in Kinshasa, in the early days of Zaire, that it makes its way into tales told of the city by none other than Norman Mailer. In 1974, Mailer traveled to Kinshasa to attend the "Rumble in the Jungle," the boxing match in which Muhammad Ali famously wrested from George Forman the title of heavyweight champion of the world. Shortly before the arrival of the boxers and the phalanxes of trainers, reporters, celebrities, and groupies following in their wake, a small crime wave swept the city's nicer quarters. Four Europeans were said to have died at the hands of Kinois bandits. Stateside, alarm bells rang: was this African city really one that one could visit? Where (and *what*), after all, was Zaire, a country whose very name—"Zare?" "Ziare?"—many of the would-be travelers were having trouble pronouncing. Such worries were a matter of considerable concern for Mobutu who, by hosting the much anticipated event, sought to put his Zaire on the map of African countries attractive to Western moneyed interests. Under the circumstances, architectural rumor served the dictator magnificently.

In preparation for the match, he had erected a massive stadium. Shortly, tales of horror concerning the structure began spreading through the city, encouraged, likely, by Mobutu's redoubtable secret services. The building's underbelly, rumor had it, contained torture chambers awash in blood. To make his crime-fighting intentions clear, Mobutu had arranged for the arrest of 100 criminals, chosen at random; none were ever seen again. All, it was widely believed, had disappeared into the bowels of the stadium, where they had been ruthlessly slaughtered. Above ground, on the stadium's stage, before a world audience whose TV viewing of the match was assisted by GMT-friendly scheduling, BB King, James Brown, and their dancing girls spread the message of one world united under Mobutu; below, a hell of his creation lurked. Were the dungeons real? Did they in fact exist? To this day, no one knows. In the end, it may not matter: rumor and the profound, justified, fear it elicited made the killing grounds a fact of life in mid-1970s Kinshasa. Not only did they bring to a halt violence against Europeans; they also strengthened and, in so doing, perpetuated the reign of terror Mobutu and his Western backers imposed for decades on the people of Congo.[29]

Fifteen years later, as Mobutu's reign was winding down to what would shortly prove an end as unglamorous as it was anticlimactic, architectural rumor continued to play a vital role. In 1989, while at work in the Pende region of what was then still Zaire, art historian Zoe Strother encountered insistent rumors concerning the sprawling, marble-clad palace the dictator had built for himself in the village of his birth, Gbadolite.[30] In this palace, it was widely recounted, stood a chamber host to dreadful secrets. Mobutu, it was reported, had given stern directives to his wife, the twin of his official mistress (a public relations coup of some genius in a region where many see twins as sacred beings): she could go anywhere she wanted in the palace, save this one room. Those who have read "Bluebeard" know the rest: the lady, of course, defied her husband's orders. In the chamber, she found not corpses but a statue, standing on a pedestal. As she looked on, the statue began to dance. She had stumbled on the secret of her husband's success: he was un-attackable because his soul resided not in his body but in the figure on the pedestal, locked away from the sight of all but its owner. Horrified, she fled. Running from the building, she made her way to her limousine, which brought her to the airport and thence to her private jet, in which she flew to Rome. She was on her way to the Vatican, home to the one earthly being whose spiritual powers outweighed her husband's. Photographs of Mme. Mobutu, widely shown in the press, and, thereafter, of the Mobutu couple, in the Italian city (a reconciliation, perhaps?) added fuel to the fire. Was the chamber real? Who could know? And who would be so foolhardy as to deny its existence outright, in a country done such apocalyptic violence for so long by one man and his helpmates in the "West"?

In urban Cameroon, architectural rumor is a powerful force. Spaces built and un-built alike are its focus. One structure, a hulking tower, stands near the administrative center of Yaoundé. Unfinished, it remained for years gathering soot and grime, after its construction was brought to a halt by the staggering economic crisis of the mid-1980s and 1990s. For well over a decade, it served as a refuge for thieves and for the homeless. It acquired a fearsome reputation as a place of danger and death. In the final years of the century, just as the Biya regime was beginning to see the end of the tunnel in which it had nearly met its demise, rumors began emerging of training sessions held there for members of an elite corps created by the government to maintain itself in power, by extreme violence if necessary.

Under the reign of a president in place for 20 years despite stringent opposition and for whom massive crackdowns, assassinations, and torture have long been tools of the trade, such rumors had a chilling effect on the city. In 2000–2001, Douala became a place for remarkable architectures of the *imaginaire*. Following what was presented in the press, both local and foreign, as a sharp rise in urban crime, the government created a paramilitary unit known as *Commandement opérationnel* (CO). Ostensibly, the CO's purpose was to render the city safe. Its presence, in fact, had more to do with the need, for Biya and his clique, to bring to heel a growing number of young urban dwellers who, in the wake of a failed 1990s movement to institute genuine political pluralism and in the face of disastrous living and work conditions, were proving alarmingly difficult for those in power to control. Within six months of its creation, the CO had perpetrated no fewer than 500 extra-judicial executions; six months later, the number had doubled, drawing the very public attention of the city's highest prelate, Cardinal Christian Tumi, himself. During this time, Douala had become a city under siege, its streets barred by countless police and army checkpoints, entire neighborhoods held hostage and hundreds of young people arrested nightly. Torture was rampant, disappearances legion. Faced with a staggering death toll, the people of Douala took to the streets. Massive protests pitted thousands of inhabitants against the forces of the CO, chiefly in a neighborhood called Bépanda, which, in one night of violent arrests, had lost nine of its young people. In these and other clashes, Doualais were forced to acquire forms of knowledge about their city that, once deployed, proved profoundly destabilizing for those at the helm. In places such as Bépanda, not ordinarily used to such things, ways of escaping the armed forces were borrowed from districts long subject to intense police harassment. One such quarter is Makéa, at the heart of New Bell, arguably the economic capital's toughest neighborhood. There, people fleeing the law have long made use of narrow alleys called *mapan*, barely wide enough for a grown man to slide through, escape routes that meander through the unpaved spaces of Makéa, past and often through private courtyards and dwellings. Adapted for use in Bépanda, the *mapan* system altered the ways in which the neighborhood's inhabitants had for years apprehended their streets. New approaches to moving through the city were superimposed onto others, notably the use of cell phones, a recent introduction to Douala, which proved of considerable assistance, for individuals and entire crowds, in outflanking the CO. Also of key importance were alternative cartographies of the city, born of the violence visited upon Doualais during this period. Rumors of mass graves, most of which existed, but whose exact location few could pinpoint absolutely, led to the elaboration of multiple, overlapping, contradictory maps of the city, complete with renaming of important sites, plazas, and streets, to accommodate a growing sense of the urban landscape as a place in which the otherworld (many of its denizens unburied) had been loosed onto the world of the living.[31]

Starting in 2001, if traditional indicators are to be believed, Cameroon's overall economic situation began to improve. Investments from abroad, notably South Africa, ushered in by renewed interest in the country on the part of the IMF and World Bank, have had a positive effect on its standing in the international community. For the majority of Camerounais, however, there has been little or no change. In Douala, this has resulted in a variety of phenomena, not least a pervasive disgust with what seems to many an intractable situation. Striking for observers interested in alternative approaches to, or readings of, globalization—what Jean-François Bayart and others have termed *la globalisation par le bas*—are rumors about Douala's new stock exchange. Inaugurated with great fanfare in 2002, in an elegantly refurbished building of Akwa, the city's oldest commercial neighborhood, the exchange has yet to produce a single trade. In large part, the responsibility for this lies with the government, which has been riven, on this as on many questions, by internal bickering and turf battles. For ordinary Doualais, the new headquarters of the exchange are a subject of considerable cynicism. Indeed, for many, the exchange might as well not exist. Headed though it is by a dynamic and outspoken director, *la bourse de Douala* seems to them no more real than the several, de-centralized universities the government created in the 1990s, following student protests it violently repressed—Potemkin institutions where one would be hard put to attend a class, let alone obtain a diploma worth more than the paper it was printed on.

Such architectures of the *imaginaire* are not the stuff of buildings and spaces alone. Infrastructure—means of getting from here to there—is subject also to elaborations of this kind. Here, an example from Lagos might be given. In an essay entitled "The Visible and the Invisible: Remaking Cities in Africa" (2002a), Simone mentions a catastrophe in 2002 in which many people drowned. Fleeing a disaster zone, entire neighborhoods, most of whose inhabitants could not swim, took to the Isolo Canal, trying to make their way to safety over a carpet of water hyacinths on the surface of the canal. Some 2,000 people died as the vegetation, failing to bear their weight, opened huge gaps into the water below. One could look at this episode as an instance of misplaced belief, or hope, gone tragically disappointed; indeed, many have. But there is more to the event than at first meets the eye. The failed hyacinth bridge—a rumor of infrastructure—I would argue, belongs squarely to the realm of architecture. That it was made of transient materials and that it failed because it proved to be more rumor than tangible fact makes it no less fundamental a building block in the lived experience of the city. By the same token, the maps of Douala produced and used to imagine, tell, and navigate the city in 2000 and 2001 stand as a fundamental fact in the understanding of Douala as an architectural ensemble. So too the itineraries mapped and remapped by so many Doualais in moving back and forth across thousands of kilometers and countless borders: these too become techniques in the production of architectural space.

I do not wish to suggest by this that the *imaginaire* and its architectures are a lone solution, a means in and of themselves of resolving the crises faced by so many cities of the subcontinent. Romanticizing such constructions of the mind leads nowhere: clearly, water hyacinth bridges are not a viable alternative to bridges made of wood, cement, or steel. Like related structures in Douala and Kinshasa, they nonetheless represent something that is painfully absent from much official discourse, whether by municipal and government authorities or international "lending" institutions, namely a capacity to imagine what the city could be. Implicit in these imaginaries is a critique of the city and its leaders and a conceptualization of what they both might offer, a vision for the urban where it is most needed, by those whom it most concerns. Simply put, a hyacinth bridge may not be the solution, but its production, in the *imaginaire* of a community, signals what should be there in the way of infrastructure and gives a sense of what form this might take. It stems from a lived knowledge of the character of the city and a study of its needs, which is a textbook definition of the term "urbanism."[32] We shall return to this matter shortly. For now, suffice it to say that the privileging of such knowledge, by practitioners and students of architecture alike, is a must.

CITYSCAPES AND KNOWLEDGESCAPES: WORDS BY WAY OF A CONCLUSION

In terms of contemporary theorizations, the approaches I propose to the city in these pages find, perhaps, the most resonance in Dear and Leclerc's (2003: 10) concept of the "postborder city." As they define it, the postborder city is a place characterized by "hybridity" and "cosmopolitanism." The latter they identify as "neither European nor class conscious, but instead . . . primarily grounded in an immigrant, diasporic experience of transnational crossings" (6). "Cosmopolitanism's postmodern geographies," they state, "do not uphold historic structures of power and knowledge, but daily reinvent new pathways for living, for personal and collective visions, and for sharing knowledge; in so doing, they give rise to "new mental and material cartographies that proclaim our collective futures" (1), "alternative [mappings that] must continually be recast and contested" (10). The city of which Dear and Leclerc (14) speak is also a locus for producing path-breaking art, "a new cultural aesthetic being . . . manufactured from the archaeologies of past and emerging identities."

In many ways, this view of the city echoes the Douala(s) considered here. There is one key distinction, however. Dear and Leclerc's model in articulating the concept of the postborder is a city (or cities) astride a physical boundary, specifically, the emerging, transborder metropolitan area made up of Tijuana and Mexicali, San Diego, and Los Angeles, to which they give the evocative name of Bajalta California. The distinction, for Douala is located squarely within the borders of a single country, would be little more than theoretical were it not that the city the authors describe differs in significant ways from the city I, at least, have encountered in Douala. The presence of (and focus by the writers) on a border results in a reading of the city that, even as it seeks to dispel them, tends to reify binary oppositions: Mexico/United States, tradition/modernity, rural/urban, past/present, family/strangers. Such dichotomous constructs are fundamental to their analysis, which situates the city in the interstices between these dualisms—in the "limen" (Dear and Leclerc 2003:10), a "third space," "the gap between two worlds." This is not, I believe, a problem of theorization, though certainly other types of approach would be possible; rather, I suspect, it reflects a very real condition of the urban space under consideration. I am struck, in this regard, by the resonance Dear and Leclerc's analysis finds in de Boeck's work on Kinshasa, a city poised itself on a border.[33]

The dichotomies Dear, Leclerc, and de Boeck posit as building blocks or, more properly, as barriers—borders—that are transgressed in the production of new forms of urbanity in Bajalta California and Kinshasa respectively are very much present in Douala as well. A number are addressed by Séraphin in his study, *Vivre à Douala* (2000). There is, however, more. That a significant number of Doualais (Kinois, Lagosians, and so on) are in dialogue with multiple otherwheres half a world away results in strikingly different conditions. Transit, whether real or imagined, in such settings, becomes so fundamental a factor in the experience of urban life as to overshadow many others. Movement, in a sense, becomes place. Cities become city-scapes—scapes, that is, in the sense that Appadurai conceives of the term: constructs born of and giving rise to incessant, overlapping flows.[34] How to theorize this is, to say the least, a challenge. Augé's otherwise fascinating analysis of spaces of transit as "non places" (1992) proves inadequate here.[35] Notions of liminality are problematic as well: if a man of 25 has spent five years—a full fifth of his life—in transit, is it reasonable to speak of his years on the road as time spent in limen? What beginning and end points—what binaries—might we adduce to define the in-between spaces to which such language confines him? How to say the process, the idea, the dream of moving, when movement itself is not the goal ultimately sought? How to render in words the sensations evoked by the Nylon skyline?

Still, the challenge must be met. Essays such as this are relevant only insofar as they might offer platforms for a productive, tangible rethinking of the city. It is not enough to speak or write of the *imaginaire*, to identify and analyze it: it must be given leave to speak for itself. From the processes of moving, thinking, and planning movement, so fundamental to urban centers like Douala today, stem extraordinarily rich bodies of knowledge—about cities, peoples, and geographies, political and economic systems, societies, cultures, and art forms. The futures of a Douala, a Kinshasa, a Lagos, if these cities are to offer their inhabitants conditions less dramatic than exist for most today, rests on harnessing such knowledge. The challenge for those whose tomorrows may lie in the balance is to create the networks, home-grown, yet extending beyond the local, to share this knowledge.[36] For, in the sharing, its potential is staggering.

NOTES

1. This suggestion—that in discussions of cities worldwide, we start by looking at cities in Africa or the "south" more generally rather than at their "northern" counterparts—differs from another, related suggestion by Enwezor et al. (2002: 14) to which I fully subscribe: that we eschew notions of *the* African city, a concept entirely too broad and reductive.
2. Clearly, there are many differences between London and Paris, Barcelona and New York. It is not my intention to elide these. Limitations of space, however, and the focus of this essay on cities in Africa may result, as here, in what a specialist of European or North American cities is likely to see as over-generalization.
3. Here too there is a risk of over-generalization. I base this comparison on numerous exchanges with colleagues at work in Lagos and Kinshasa, notably Filip de Boeck, Ch. Didier Gondola, Brian Larkin, Ruth Marshall-Fratani, and AbdouMaliq Simone. I hasten to say, however, that I myself have not lived or conducted research in either of these cities.
4. Here, I echo Appadurai: "This is not to say that there are no relatively stable communities and networks of kinship, friendship, work, and leisure, as well as birth, residence, and other filial forms. But it is to say that the warp of these stabilities is everywhere shot through with the woof of human motion . . ." (1996: 33–34).
5. "The new global cultural economy," Appadurai writes, "has to be seen as a complex, overlapping, disjunctive order." Constitutive of this order, he proposes, are flows—of people, media, technologies, modes of financing, and ideas—that crisscross the globe, overlapping, reinforcing, and contradicting one another, giving rise, in the process, to multiple, coeval worlds or, in the words of Saskia Sassen, to multiple spatialities and temporalities (Appadurai 1996: 32–33; Sassen 1999: 260).
6. Whereas the populations of Mexico City and New Delhi quadrupled between 1950 and 1985, over the same period those of Lagos and Kinshasa grew sevenfold (Enwezor et al. 2002: 15). Douala has grown by similar leaps and bounds (see Mainet 1986 and Séraphin 2000). At this point, estimates of its population vary from 1.5 to 4 million, with the latter most likely closer to the actual total.
7. Such analyses are mere extensions of those that see Africa, whether urban or rural, as a place likely never to be "modern." For a disappointing stance in this vein, from a writer usually ahead of his time see Lefebvre (1991: 123). A pithy critique of this approach is found in de Boeck (2002: 264 ff).
8. Such parallels between "left" and "right" approaches to the effects of globalization are usefully though in a rather different context outlined in Parker (1998).

9. Appadurai defines *l'imaginaire* as "a constructed landscape of collective aspirations" (1996: 32).
10. As the overwhelming majority of sign painters in Douala are men, I use a male pronoun in referring to the artist, but the possibility that the painter is a woman should not be discounted.
11. "Malam" is a pseudonym, the professional name chosen by Simone's interlocutor, an artist of considerable talent (see note 13) called Isaac Essoua Essoua.
12. Malam's stance might be attributed, in part, to who he is: a brilliant artist who has decided to stay in Douala despite the fact that, in Europe or the United States, he would likely lead a far more comfortable life. His choice parallels that of several other artists of his generation, notably members of a collective by the name of Cercle Kapsiki, whose members have all elected to live in Douala because they feel a responsibility—ethical, creative—to the often very poor communities in which they grew up. But such choices are not, or in any event are significantly less, open to young people who depend for their livelihood on employment that is increasingly difficult to obtain.
13. Neither this man nor any of the other people whose accounts of travel from Douala to Johannesburg I consider hereafter are identified. This is so for obvious reasons: most of them are in South Africa illegally or, where this is not the case, because it is so difficult to be a foreign African in South Africa today, they do not wish to draw undue attention to themselves. Pseudonyms would, of course, have been possible, but to use them would obscure the experiences of exclusion and alienation many African immigrants describe as an everyday experience in the Rainbow Nation today. All of the Doualaises whose experiences in transit I allude to in this essay are men. This should not be taken to mean that women do not play a significant role in this context. Several Doualaises have agreed to speak with me of their travels; some of their accounts share important similarities with those by men that I discuss. It seems to me, however, that there remains much to be done in teasing out differences between men's and women's accounts of migration; indeed, there may well be a need to theorize profoundly gendered cartographies of the movement between cities. My research in this regard is at too incipient a stage, however, to make such theorizations possible. Many more conversations are necessary, in both Johannesburg and Douala, and significantly more reading. Under the circumstances, and as I have had occasion to speak with more men than women, I prefer to limit myself here to men's accounts.
14. I invoke memory, here, with a specific purpose. The memory to which I allude is both my own and that of the story's teller. It will not do to speak of the itineraries described here as "facts"—precise mappings of travel over time and space. The types of stories discussed here, like most stories, are subject to change in the telling and retelling both by the speaker and the writer. They are shaped, some of their details highlighted, and others, if not necessarily elided, given shorter shrift. They are shaped, also, by other speakers. Some of the people who have spoken to me of their travels have done so in private. Others have come together as groups, in which contexts it is not uncommon for stories to meld into one another, for one teller's memories to bleed into another's and vice versa. This is particularly true as such tales reflect the experiences of so many people and are in the process of becoming a genre, a type of oral literature subject to its own internal dynamics. Central to these dynamics is conversation among Doualais living in Hillbrow and Yeoville, notably in two bars, both located in Yeoville, one a drinking place-cum-small restaurant and pool hall, the other more like a local *shebeen*. The writer's existence, as well, impacts on these dynamics; with every request to hear stories, with every conversation she

initiates, in one of these bars or elsewhere in the city, she participates in the construction of a genre of stories. This, in turn, shapes the types of details foregrounded by the tellers and the modes of telling they favor.

15. Carlos Monsiváis encounters similar intentions—the ever-present plan to move on, sometimes before one has even arrived—in discussions with city dwellers transiting between Central and North America: "If we are going to stay, let's try to leave as soon as possible"; "When I arrived at the border I brought with me a desire to leave soon." "These days," Monsiváis writes, ". . . the city as a totality, as a concept is escaping from the traditional idea of a city and becom[ing] instead an anxiety to populate city-space without the intention of staying" (2003: 34, 35).
16. Here again, stories and genres intersect. I have heard of *l'Ambassade* from one teller and read of it too in a text, part novel, part document, entitled *Finding Mr. Madini*, a heart-wrenching book on homelessness, exile, and illegality in Johannesburg, authored by a collective of writers known as The Great African Spider Writers, under the direction of a writer named Jonathan Morgan (2000).
17. One is put in mind, here, of portraits taken by urban photographers in West Africa in the 1950s and 1960s: images in which the sitters appear against a painted background figuring a city, street, or interior. Though an effort at *trompe-l'oeuil* has been made in some cases, more often than not it is clear and meant to be so that the backdrop is just that: a stage set.
18. An extraordinary photograph by Stanley Greene (2003) offers, in a sense, a reverse image of that described here. In Greene's picture, a camera looks through a windshield at a road in Chechnya; the car is motoring toward people—likely refugees—who are walking away from a landscape stark and empty of other inhabitants.
19. I am indebted to Jason Rosen for this observation.
20. Such images, it is interesting to note, in view of the suggestion made here that the city, as depicted by the artist, is one glimpsed in transit rather than a place in which one spends time, are commonly associated with warnings not to linger in the Johannesburg CBD. The overwhelming majority of travel agencies offering tours of South Africa, on whose websites such images can be found, avoid Johannesburg. Following arrival at Jan Smuts Airport, travelers are commonly housed in airport hotels and, following at best a bus tour of the city, in which they glimpse a picture-postcard view of the CBD—typically at sunset—are shuttled away from "the murder capital of the world," toward the primitivized spaces of various Kwas (Kwa Ndebele, Kwa Zulu-Natal): wilderness zones where they can encounter other kinds of "wildlife" and, finally, in a much-touted "return to civilization," the quaint vineyards and Dutch-inspired houses of the Western Cape.
21. I pattern my use of the term "archaeology," here, on Foucault's. I mean by it a form of layering, in which strata of knowledge, ideas, forms come together to form a whole, the components of which, while they can, at least in theory, be distinguished from one another, are not, in fact, distinct.
22. The idea of the city as palimpsest is explored, with considerable poetry, by de Boeck (2002), regarding Kinshasa. The vision I propose here differs from his, however, in that it stresses above all the coeval nature of the city's many parts. De Boeck's analysis looks at meetings and meldings of past and present, inside and outside, center and periphery. Though such an approach certainly offers a rich palette of ideas for the study of Douala, it seems less apposite for consideration of the painted skyline and, more generally, the idea of the city with which we are concerned. What is striking here is the complete absence of "before" and "after," "either" and "or." The city depicted is all of the places it references at the same time and, most importantly, in equal measure.

23. See C. Keep, T. McLaughlin, and R. Palmar. "The Electronic Labyrinth." <http:// www.iath.virginia.edu/elab/hfl0257.html>. Quotations from Freud here are from the *Standard Edition of the Complete Psychological Works of Sigmund Freud*, English translation (1953, 1974), Vol. XIX: 230.
24. The parallel I draw between Freud and Derrida's mystic writing pads, on the one hand, and hypertext, on the other, is suggested by Keep et al. My approach to hypertext, however, differs significantly from theirs.
25. The picture I propose that the painter offers of the city is, in key ways, an inverse of that which Italo Calvino proffers in his *Le citta invisibili* (1993). In this book, Marco Polo regales Emperor Kublai Khan with tales of the many cities he has visited; in time, however, it turns out that each of the places Marco Polo is describing is, in fact, one place: Venice. All cities are one. The Nylon panel suggests otherwise. Here, one city is all others.
26. Some treatments of the subject do exist: Burden 1999; Harbison 1994; and Thomsen 1994 are cases in point. None of these texts, however, consider in any depth the political implications of such rumored forms. All three, further, focus on buildings and sites imagined by "great thinkers"—da Vinci, Boullée, Verne, Finsterlin, Orwell, and so on. The architectural imaginings of "ordinary" city dwellers have little or no place in their pages, a factor that renders these three works less useful, for present purposes, than one might have hoped.
27. A number of other examples of rumored buildings and sites in the United States could be adduced. I have written elsewhere of some of these, among which the Denver International Airport, whose lower levels are said to house a vast underground city, concerning which much is written on the Internet and which are a subject of fascination for conspiracy theorists (Malaquais 2002: 21–23).
28. For an overview of examples from the precolonial and colonial periods, see Malaquais (2002:13 ff.).
29. Mailer discusses these rumors and their effect in a documentary on the Rumble in the Jungle entitled "When We Were Kings," directed by Taylor Hackford and Leon Gast (DasFilms 1996). On his return from Kinshasa, he published a book on the match and his experiences in Zaire, *The Fight* (1975).
30. Personal communication, New York, April 2000.
31. For a fuller treatment of the CO, its raison-d'être and its effects on the architectural *imaginaire* of Douala, see Malaquais (2003). For still other impacts of the CO on the city, see Simone 2002a:37 ff. An evocative theorization of such conceptual maps of the city as are adduced here appears, in a very different context, in Dear and Leclerc (2003:6 ff.).
32. For purposes of comparison, see the definition given for "urbanism" in Harper Collins's *College English Dictionary*. A rethinking of "urbanism" as the province of those who have a firsthand, lived experience of the city at its most difficult, as a "science" as much of their domain as that of professionals, most of whom do not have such lived experience, might offer the beginning of an answer to architect Rem Koolhaas's much touted question: "Whatever happened to urbanism?" (Koolhaas 2000).
33. See, in particular, de Boeck's (2002) study of Kinshasa as a space of the in-between, wherein multiple dichotomies reflect one another as in a series of mirrors.
34. Appadurai, we have seen, speaks of "disjunctive flows"; these, he says, are a product of and actively shape globalization. Among these flows, or "landscapes," he writes, are "ethnoscapes" (flows of people), "mediascapes" (flows of media), "technoscapes" (technology flows), "financescape" (flows of finance or modes of financing), and "ideoscapes" (flows of ideas and ideologies). "The suffix—*scape*," he explains, "allows

us to point to the fluid, irregular shapes of these landscapes . . . These terms with the common suffix—*scape* also indicate that these are not objectively given relations that look the same from every angle of vision but, rather, that they are deeply perspectival constructs, inflected by the historical, linguistic, and political situatedness of different . . . actors" (1996: 33).

35. Whether such spaces of transit, even in the most high-tech of contexts, are really "non-places" is, in any event, a subject for debate. A person without a "home," living or seeking to do so in an airport—the quintessential "non-place" for Augé (1992)—might well take issue with this.
36. Here, Simone's suggestion (2002a) that networks of people, rather than structures such as bridges, are the most productive forms of infrastructure at work in many parts of African cities today, is particularly helpful.

References

Agier, M. 1999. *l'Invention de la Ville: Banlieues, Townships, Invasions et Favelas.* Paris: Editions des Archives Contemporaines.

Appadurai, A. 1996. *Modernity at Large: Cultural Dimensions of Globalization.* Minneapolis: University of Minnesota Press.

Appadurai, A. 1999. "Grassroots Globalization and the Research Imagination," in A. Appadurai ed. *Globalization.* Durham and London: Duke University Press, pp. 1–21.

Augé, M. 1992. *Non-Lieux: Introduction à une Anthropologie de la Supermodernité.* Paris: Seuil.

de Boeck, F. 2002. "Kinshasa: Tales of the 'Invisible City' and the Second World," in O. Enwezor et al. (eds.). *Under Siege: Four African Cities. Freetown, Johannesburg, Kinshasa, Lagos.* Kassel: Hatje Cantz, pp. 243–28.

Bravman, R. 1984. *African Islam.* Washington, DC: Smithsonian Institution Press.

Burden, E. 1999. *Visionary Architecture: Unbuilt Works of the Imagination.* New York: McGraw-Hill.

Calvino, I. 1993. *Le Citta Invisibili.* Milan: Arnoldo Mondadori.

Dear, M. and Leclerc G. 2003. "The Postborder Condition: Art and Urbanism in Bajalta California," in M. Dear and G. Leclerc (eds.). *Postborder City: Cultural Spaces of Bajalta California.* New York: Routledge, pp. 1–30.

Derrida, J. 1980. *Writing and Difference.* Trans. A. Bass. Chicago and London: University of Chicago Press.

Enwezor, O. et al. 2002. "Introduction," in O. Enwezor et al. (eds.). *Under Siege: Four African Cities. Freetown, Johannesburg, Kinshasa, Lagos.* Kassel: Hatje Cantz, pp. 13–20.

Freud, S. 1999. *Complete Psychological Works of Sigmund Freud Standard Edition,* Vol. XIX. Ed. J. Strachey. New York: W.W. Norton & Company.

Geschiere, P. 1997. *The Modernity of Witchcraft: Politics and the Occult in Postcolonial Africa.* Trans. J. Roitman. Richmond: University of Virginia Press.

Greene, S. 2003. *Open Wound: Chechnya 1994–2001.* London: Trolley Press.

Harbison, N. 1994. *The Built, the Unbuilt and the Unbuildable. In Pursuit of Architectural Meaning.* Cambridge: M.I.T. Press.

Kaplan, R. 2001. *The Coming Anarchy: Shattering the Dreams of the Post Cold War.* New York: Knopf.

Koolhaas, R. 2000. "Whatever Happened to Urbanism?" in M. Miles, T. Hall, and I. Borden (eds.). *The City Cultures Reader.* New York: Routledge, pp. 327–329.

Lefebvre, H. 1991. *The Production of Space.* Trans. D. Nicholson-Smith. London: Blackwell Publishers.

Mailer, N. 1975. *The Fight.* [1st ed.] Boston: Little, Brown.
Mainet, G. 2001. *Douala: Croissance et servitudes.* Paris: Harmattan.
Malaquais, D. 2002. *Architecture, Pouvoir et Dissidence au Cameroun.* Paris: Karthala.
Malaquais, D. 2003. "Blood/Money," *Chimurenga* Vol. 3.
Mbembe, A. 1999. "At the Edge of the World: Boundaries, Territoriality, and Sovereignty in Africa," in A. Appadurai (ed.). *Globalization.* Durham and London: Duke University Press, pp. 22–51.
Monsiváis, C. 2003. "Where Are You Going to Be Worthier? The Border and the Postborder," in M. Dear and G. Leclerc (eds.). *Postborder City: Cultural Spaces of Bajalta California.* New York: Routledge, pp. 33–45.
Morgan, J. and the Great African Spider Writers. 2000. *Finding Mr. Madini.* Cape Town: David Philip Publishers.
Parker, M. 1998. "Nostalgia and Mass Culture: McDonaldization and Cultural Elitism," in M. Alfino, J. Caputo, and R. Wynyard (eds.). *McDonaldization Revisited: Critical Essays on Consumer Culture.* Westport, CT: Praeger, pp. 1–18.
Pieterse, J. Nederveen. 2004. *Globalization & Culture: Global Mélange.* Lanham, Boulder, New York, and Oxford: Rowman & Littlefield Publishers.
Prussin, L. 1985. *Hatumere: Islamic Design in Africa.* Los Angeles, Berkeley, and London: University of California Press.
Roitman, J. 2004. *Objects of the Economy and the Language of Politics.* Princeton: Princeton University Press.
Sassen, S. 1999. "Spatialities and Temporalities of the Global," in A. Appadurai (ed.). *Globalization.* Durham and London: Duke University Press, pp. 260–278.
Sassen, S. 2001. *The Global City.* Princeton: Princeton University Press.
Séraphin, G. 2000. *Vivre à Douala, l'Imaginaire et l'Action dans une Ville Africaine en Crise.* Paris: Harmattan.
Shami, S. 1999. "Prehistories of Globalization: Circassian Identity in Motion," in A. Appadurai (ed.). *Globalization.* Durham and London: Duke University Press, pp. 220–250.
Simone, A. 2002a. "The Visible and Invisible: Remaking Cities in Africa", in O. Enwezor et al. (eds.). *Under Siege: Four African Cities. Freetown, Johannesburg, Kinshasa, Lagos.* Kassel: Hatje Cantz, pp. 23–44.
Simone, A. 2002b. "Reaching Larger Worlds: Negotiating the Complexities of Social Connectedness in Douala." Unpublished paper.
Thomsen, C. 1994. *Visionary Architecture: From Babylon to Virtual Reality.* Munich and New York: Prestel.

2

Internal Migration and the Escalation of Ethnic and Religious Violence in Urban Nigeria

Daniel Jordan Smith

Introduction

In 1999, Nigeria inaugurated its first civilian government in sixteen years. Expectations for the return to democracy ran high, and Nigerians hoped that an elected government would help lift the country from two decades of decline. More than six years after the transition, disappointment is widespread, as democracy has failed to deliver the desired economic dividends, and the popular perception is that the country continues to lurch from one crisis to another. Poverty, inequality, and unemployment remain pervasive, and people's sense of economic uncertainty is exacerbated by feelings of physical insecurity heightened by rising levels of violent crime and repeated outbreaks of what is characterized in the local media as "urban communal violence."[1] Urban communal violence has killed literally thousands of people in Nigeria's major cities in the past six years. Most often, the clashes involve bands of young men who attack each other using machetes, knives, stones, and (increasingly) guns. Even more worrisome to ordinary citizens, violence seems to be ever more frequently targeted at the homes, businesses, and places of worship of opposing groups. Characteristically, the disputes are described as ethnically or religiously motivated. The ethnic and religious dimensions are often intertwined, as clashes commonly involve populations that are divided by both religious affiliation and ethnic identity.

Because these conflicts occur in cities, and frequently pit "natives" against "migrants" or "hosts" against "strangers," this phenomenon of urban violence is deeply entangled with the prevalence and processes of internal migration. Using a case study of predominately Christian Igbo-speaking people from southeastern Nigeria who have migrated to Kano, the largest city in heavily Islamic Hausa-speaking northern Nigeria, I argue that internal migration is integral to the production and reproduction of ethnic and religious identities, and that the circuitry characteristic of these migration networks contributes significantly to the escalation of violence in local conflicts, creating national crises that threaten to splinter Nigeria along ethnic and religious lines. The case of Igbo migrants in Kano is particularly significant and illustrative, because violence between Hausa-speaking Kano residents and Igbo migrants evokes collective memories of past conflicts. Beginning with clashes between Igbo migrants and local Hausa residents before independence in the 1950s, climaxing in the massive violence and thousands of deaths that occurred prior to Nigeria's civil war from 1967 to 1970, reemerging in major religious riots in the 1990s, and continuing in current conflicts over the imposition of Sharia law in northern Nigeria, Kano has been a flashpoint and an important symbol for over 50 years for both southern Christians and northern Muslims. Although instances of communal violence in Kano, and in many other Nigerian cities, are typically portrayed as the outcome of ethnic and religious tension, produced by long-standing identities that are accentuated by the proximities of urban life, the escalation and potentially explosive nature of these conflicts must be situated in the context of internal migration. Minor local disputes with little or no macro-political significance are magnified and inflamed into national ethnic and religious issues through the amplifying circuitry of Nigeria's migration networks.

I do not mean to suggest that ideas about ethnic and religious difference emerge only through processes of migration. But I do argue and try to show that the growing tendency for groups in Nigeria to characterize heightened tensions and conflict in religious and ethnic terms, and the apparent merging of ethnic and religious identity, can only be fully explained by taking into account the effects of internal migration.[2] Relations between host communities and migrants unfold in a particular political, economic, and cultural context, with each group bringing already existing identities and preconceptions about the other to the relationship. But these ideas are not fixed, and the dynamics of the relationship between hosts and migrants have important consequences for the production of identity, the meanings attributed to conflicts, and the trajectories of violence that emerge. The ongoing relations between migrants and hosts, and between migrants and their communities of origin serve to circulate ideas about ethnicity, religion, and "us" versus "them" across Nigeria.

The idea that ethnic identity is, as Barth (1969) and others have suggested, more about boundaries between groups than the cultural content within the boundaries, makes it clear why relations between migrants and their hosts are so central in broader processes of identity construction. In situations of migration, boundaries are both blurred and contested, and recreated and strengthened. For Igbos, the experiences of migrants in Kano are defining elements in the very conception of ethnic and religious identity—produced and diffused through internal migration and the social-institutional circuits that connect migrants to their places of origin. Similarly, the Muslim Hausa-speaking Kano "natives," who are the city's host population, define and identify themselves partly in relationship to migrant "others."[3] While these processes of boundary maintenance and identity construction occur in the micro-dynamics of everyday interactions between locals and migrants, often producing disputes, explaining the escalation of these conflicts into large-scale violence perceived as national crises requires understanding the highly charged circuitry of internal migration.

TWO SETTINGS IN NIGERIA'S INTERNAL MIGRATION CIRCUITRY

The migration circuitry that links places and people in Nigeria is vast and complex. Most rural communities in the Igbo southeast, for example, send migrants to literally dozens of cities and towns across the country. People move back and forth not only between rural place of origin and urban place of destination, but between cities and towns, along lines that are similarly grounded in kinship and community of origin. In addition, within cities of destination, migrants rely extensively on ties to people of common places of origin (Chukwuezi 2001; Smock 1971; Wolpe 1974). The grid of connections between Igbo rural communities and Nigeria's cities, between cities and towns, and within urban areas, is complicated, intertwining, and dense. To illustrate how these migration circuits work, to explain the key role they play in producing and reinforcing ethnic and religious identity, and to show how they contribute to the intercommunal urban violence that sometimes erupts, I focus on one Igbo community and its migrants in Kano.

The two settings I have been working in are the semirural community of Ubakala, located in Abia State, in the Igbo heartland in southeastern Nigeria, and the area of Kano known as *Sabon Gari*, or strangers' quarters, where the vast majority of the Igbo population in Kano resides (Anthony 2002; Paden 1973). These two settings are representative of much larger populations and more widespread phenomena. Ubakala is very much like most other rural communities in the Igbo heartland in terms of its almost ubiquitous Christianity and its high levels of rural–urban out-migration. Kano is very much like many other cities in northern Nigeria, particularly in the far north, in the sense that it is predominately Islamic, Hausa-speaking, and home to a large population of southern migrants.

However, Kano is perhaps more dramatic than other northern Nigerian Islamic cities in the degree to which it separates and marks off its southern Christian migrants, thereby accentuating polarities along the lines of religion and ethnicity. Though Kano may be more extreme than some other northern cities in its patterns of polarization, it is particularly important for understanding the national scene. Kano's importance is due both to the fact that it is the largest and, in many respects, the most politically significant city in the north, and to the fact that relations between religions (Islam and Christianity) and ethnicities (in this case, Hausa and Igbo) in Kano are symbolic in the minds of Igbos and Hausas throughout Nigeria of the way in which religion and ethnicity structure social relations of power in the country (Anthony 2002). In other words, even if levels of differentiation and tension along ethnic and religious lines are more intense in Kano than in some other northern cities, its prominent place in producing shared understandings of ethnicity, religion, identity, and political interests across Nigeria make it especially important to study and understand.

Ubakala

Ubakala has a population of approximately 20,000 people in 11 villages spread across roughly 24 square miles. Though still significantly rural in character, the community bears the influence of being just eight miles outside the town of Umuahia, the capital of Abia State. By the standards of much of sub-Saharan Africa, Ubakala would be considered relatively "developed." In terms of infrastructure, the community has half a dozen primary schools, two secondary schools, a government health center, a large marketplace, a police barracks, and a post office. Most houses have cement walls and floors and metal roofs, and many are wired for electricity (though it is only sporadically supplied). People have easy access to public transportation and relatively good roads link the community with nearby towns and cities. Young people dress in blue jeans and T-shirts as often as they wear more traditional Igbo dress. Radios are common household possessions, and though most people do not own TVs or VCRs, nearly everyone knows someone who does. But local people definitely think of themselves as poor. They want much more.

Hoe agriculture and small-scale trade dominate the local economy, though many people are employed in nearby Umuahia. Igbos, including those in Ubakala, are almost universally Christian, with people belonging in large numbers to Catholic, Protestant, and Pentecostal congregations. Social organization is characterized by patrilineal descent, patrilocal residence, lineage exogamy, strong affinal networks, and a large number of important crosscutting forms of local association such as age-grades, secret societies, and village development unions.

In Ubakala, as in most Igbo communities, huge proportions of people migrate to and live in Nigeria's many cities and towns. Approximately 95 percent of men and 75 percent of women resident in Ubakala and surveyed during fieldwork in 2001 had lived more than one year in a city or town, and more than three out of four adults had at least one relative living in Lagos, Nigeria's megacity. At any given time, at least half of adults who consider Ubakala "home" have migrated and live elsewhere. Migrants' ties and obligations to their extended families and communities of origin create what Sara Berry (1985) has called "extended communities." Indeed, though levels of out-migration are high in Ubakala, a crucial feature of this out-migration is its circulatory nature. Most people who move out come back, either for temporary visits or longer-term resettlement (Gugler 1971; 1991). When they migrate, Igbos maintain strong links to their villages and reproduce many of the social structural forms of their natal communities in town (Ahanotu 1982; Chukwuezi 2001; Gugler and Flanagan 1978).

Sabon Gari, Kano

Kano and Ubakala are strikingly different worlds, and not simply because Ubakala is a rural community whereas Kano is a city of several million people. The most profound differences are cultural. By bus it is about a fifteen-hour journey from Ubakala to Kano. Culturally, one feels as if one has passed from one kind of civilization to another. From my perspective, it is hard to overstate the degree of difference. The weather, the pace of life, the architecture, the modes of dress, the food, the language, and, of course, the religion are all completely different. Moving from Ubakala to big southern cities like Port Harcourt or Lagos can be a significant adjustment for rural Igbos, but these are adjustments to changes in scale, with southern cities feeling, at least to some extent, like a more crowded, intense version of the familiar. Migration to Kano, and to the north in general, would appear to require adaptation to a whole other way of life.

But, in fact, one of the most significant features of Igbo migrant life in Kano is the degree to which southerners reproduce the social institutions and cultural practices of their place of origin (and Igbos are, by almost every estimate, the largest group of southern and Christian migrants in Kano, and in most cities in the north). Though there are certainly significant individual exceptions (e.g., the very rare cases of Igbo migrants who convert to Islam (Anthony 2000)), the most striking aspects of Igbo social life in Kano are the continuities with life in the southeast. The extent of these continuities is particularly easy to note in Kano, and is perhaps even more extensive in Kano than in some other northern cities, because of the enclaved residential structure wherein the vast majority of Igbo migrants live in *Sabon Gari*. Walking through the old walled city of Kano (where very few Igbos reside) with its narrow paths and still surviving mud architecture, one feels as if one has entered an ancient and very Islamic civilization. Devout Muslims pray five times a day at ubiquitous mosques. Men dress in gowns that evoke images of North Africa. Many women generally stay in their family compounds and rarely move about in public space. The spoken language is, almost without exception, Hausa. A few thousand yards away, in *Sabon Gari*, one feels almost as if one could be in any southern Nigerian city. Churches are ubiquitous, women buy and sell in the market, people wear Western styles of dress, beer is sold in restaurants and hotels, and one hears multiple languages, including Igbo, English, and Nigerian pidgin English.

Igbos in Kano are primarily traders and business people. They dominate many sectors in the vast local markets, including motor vehicle spare parts, pharmaceuticals, cosmetics, electronics, and imported textiles. In addition, Igbos manage and staff numerous local hotels and countless taverns, bars, and restaurants. Significant numbers of Igbos are still coming to Kano, even though discourses back east represent the city negatively. No one knows how many Igbo migrants live in Kano, or anywhere else in Nigeria for that matter. Ethnicity is such a politically charged category that it was not asked about in the last census in 1991. The 1963 census, the only other one conducted in postindependence Nigeria, counted more than 10,000 Igbos in and around Kano (*Kano State Statistical Yearbook* 1972). Recent estimates are that Kano and its environs are home to at least 40,000–50,000 Igbo migrants (Anthony 2002), but these numbers are likely to be significant underestimates, and they certainly rise and fall in response to economic conditions and perceptions of political security. Most estimates suggest that at least several hundred thousand Igbo migrants live and work in northern Nigeria. The vast majority of these migrants are connected in social organizational circuits reinforced by a sense of shared place of origin, but also increasingly experienced as a larger ethno-religious identity.

The degree to which Igbo communities extend and reproduce local social institutions and patterns across vast geographical and cultural space is one of the most profound and significant aspects of Igbo social organization (Smith 1999; 2004a; Uchendu 1965). In each city across Nigeria, migrants from Ubakala maintain a branch of the Ubakala Improvement Union (the formal name of the community development association), and in bigger cities like Kano each of the 11 villages of Ubakala may have a branch of its own development union. These urban branches of community development unions serve as vehicles to bring migrants together in the city and assure their continued involvement in the politics, economics, and cultural life in their places of origin. In Kano, and indeed in every city in Nigeria, Ubakala migrants meet the first Sunday afternoon of every month with co-villagers and the second Sunday afternoon of every month with the wider Ubakala community. Through these meetings migrants contribute to development projects in the village, pay dues that support the transport home for burial of those who die in the city, build consensus on issues in Ubakala for which migrant input is frequently sought (such as the selection of village and community leaders, development priorities, etc.), and organize to assist new migrants to find work or accommodation. Also, through these meetings people keep track of who is traveling home to the east. People routinely send remittances or messages to Ubakala through fellow migrants.

It is hard to overstate how seriously Igbo migrants take the obligation of participation in these organizations. Among Ubakala Igbos in Kano, about 90 percent of migrants participate, and nonmembership is viewed as tantamount to rejecting one's identity.[4] This is not unique to Ubakala. Every Igbo community organizes its migrants in this way (Chukwuezi 2001; Gugler 1991; Smock 1971). The reproduction of these social structural forms provides a sense of community and continuity, but it also extends the obligations of kinship across the Nigerian political and economic landscape. A native of Ubakala in Kano will seek the help of kinsmen just as easily as he/she would at home—perhaps more easily because of the mutually recognized need for help in a distant place and because the physical and cultural distance from home actually serves to reduce the social distance that might separate individuals in the village.

The extent to which contemporary politics in much of sub-Saharan Africa is connected to the construction of ethnic identities that run through social networks rooted in place of origin has received considerable scholarly attention (Bayart 1993; Chabal and Daloz 1999; Geschiere and Gugler 1998). The importance of rural–urban ties has been documented not only for Igbos (Gugler 1991), but also for other groups in Nigeria (Aronson 1971; Berry 1989; Trager 2001) and sub-Saharan Africa (Geschiere 1982; Lentz 1995; Setel 1999; Woods 1994). However, relatively little work has explored how the circuitry of internal migration is central in the very reproduction of ethnic identity (see Cohen 1969), and, more specifically, how, in contemporary Nigeria, the production of ethnicity incorporates religious identity and contributes to the escalation of local conflicts into national crises.

Biafra, Kano, and Ethno-Religious Identity

It is impossible to tell the story of Igbo ethnicity, explain the growing role of religion in shaping Igbos' sense of their place in Nigerian society, or understand the way in which violence is intertwined with these ideas, without discussing Nigeria's civil war, during which Igbos attempted to secede from Nigeria and create the independent state of Biafra. The history of Igbo migration to Kano, events in Kano and other parts of the north that led up to the declaration of Biafran independence, and the experiences of Igbo migrants in Kano over the past 35 years since the defeat of Biafra have played a particularly important role in the history of how Igbos conceptualize their ethnicity (Anthony 2002; Nnoli 1995). Interpretations of contemporary violence are shaped by this history.

Among Igbo people, the widespread African identification with "home" was intensified by the experience of civil war. From 1967 to 1970, following bloody reprisals against Igbos living throughout northern Nigeria in the wake of an Igbo-dominated military coup, the people of southeastern Nigeria sought to secede from Nigeria and create their own state, called Biafra (Harneit-Sievers et al. 1997; Kirk-Greene 1971; Post and Vickers 1973). In the aftermath of Biafra, during which as many as a million Igbos were killed or starved to death, Igbo people lost property, buildings, and land. Today in Igboland, it is considered imperative to build one's first home in the village and foolish to build outside Igboland before building "at home." I often heard Igbos alluding to Biafra and saying they would not make the same mistakes again—meaning that they would not completely invest their livelihoods elsewhere because only "home" was truly safe. Igbo people are acutely aware that they must depend upon having strong kinship-based social networks of obligation and alliance to survive and succeed in Nigeria (Smith 2001; 2004a). Although the importance of "having people" is widespread in sub-Saharan Africa (Guyer 1993; 1995), the historical legacy of Biafra has made this perception particularly powerful among Igbos.

The experience of Igbo migrants in Kano in the months leading up to Biafra holds a particularly salient place in collective memory (Anthony 2002; Harneit-Sievers et al. 1997). Prior to Biafra, thousands of Igbo migrants lived in Kano, dominating certain sectors of trade and working as teachers, civil servants, and in numerous technical and professional positions. Igbos held economic and social positions in Kano far disproportionate to their numbers. Their dominance of certain sectors of professional and economic life in Kano was rooted in British colonial policies, including a longer history of Western education in the southeast than in the north (Anthony 2002). The Igbos' social and economic position in Kano, combined with cultural and religious differences, created tensions between migrants and their Muslim Hausa-speaking hosts. In the months preceding Biafra, a series of coups brought ethnic and regional political conflicts to new heights and in several incidents hundreds of Igbos were killed by Hausa-speaking rioters (Anthony 2002; Kirk-Greene 1971; Paden 1971). These killings, still described today by Igbos as pogroms, occurred across cities in northern Nigeria, but because Kano had northern Nigeria's largest Igbo population the impact of anti-Igbo riots in Kano reverberated mostly widely. In the run up to the declaration of Biafran independence, virtually all Igbos fled Kano and other northern Nigerian cities for their southeastern homeland, and along the way many thousands were killed by mobs and by Hausa-speaking soldiers (Anthony 2002).[5]

In the aftermath of the war, won by a Nigerian army dominated by Hausa-speaking soldiers, the federal government made significant efforts to encourage Igbos to return to Kano and other places throughout Nigeria where they had lived before Biafra (Anthony 2002). Indeed, the movement of Igbos back to Kano resumed within months after the war, and by the end of the 1970s, Kano's Igbo population reached or surpassed its prewar levels (Anthony 2002). Equally interesting, Igbos report that they were largely welcomed back by their Hausa hosts, albeit with a very different power dynamic characterizing postwar interethnic relations.[6] Whereas before the war it was Hausa discourse that spoke of Igbo domination, in the aftermath it is Igbo discourse that has focused on Igbo marginalization.

Prior to, during, and immediately after Biafra, differences in religion certainly formed an important part of the constellation of characteristics that separated Igbo migrants and their Hausa hosts in Kano. But it was not always the dominant difference, and indeed in the riots that characterized the prelude to Biafra, Hausa-speaking rioters specifically targeted Igbos, leaving other southern Christian ethnic groups mostly undisturbed. In contrast, in the past 10–15 years, conflicts between migrants and Kano natives have been perceived as religious in nature. Major riots in 1991 were sparked by Christians' invitation of a well-known European evangelist to speak in Kano. Riots in 1995 followed the beheading by Muslim youths of the young Igbo man accused of desecrating the Koran by using a page as toilet paper.

Religious Politics, Sharia, and Ethnic Polarization

Certainly the return to civilian rule has contributed to the resurgence of ethnicity and the rise of religion as polarizing political forces in Nigeria, as politicians have sought to exploit popular sentiments for their own ends, but also as people have felt freer to express their beliefs and vent their dissatisfactions with Nigeria's insecure political economy. In Igboland, for the first time since the war, one hears renewed calls for Igbo separatism, albeit not wholeheartedly supported by the masses.[7] In 2001, a commission created by the federal government with the aim of national reconciliation after more than 15 years of military rule, modeled loosely after the Truth and Reconciliation Commission in South Africa, heard calls from Igbos for reparations for the atrocities committed against them prior to, during, and after Biafra. Along with numerous accounts of human rights violations since 1966, stories of massacres in Kano were retold and relived. In these twenty-first-century narratives, complaints of persecution based on ethnicity have incorporated references to religion in ways that were uncommon just a couple decades ago. Many Igbos share a sense, symbolized and exacerbated by the recent experiences of migrants in Kano, that religion has become inseparable from ethnicity in social relations of power in Nigeria.

Without a doubt, the strongest contemporary symbol of the divide between Nigeria's mostly Islamic north and its mostly Christian south is the practice of Islamic Sharia law, introduced in much of northern Nigeria since the return to democracy in 1999. In northern states that have adopted Sharia law, political leaders argue that democracy and decentralization entitle them to govern under laws that are locally supported and culturally appropriate.[8] Critics, especially southern Christian critics, charge that politicians have utilized Sharia as a political weapon, purposely exploiting religion for political ends and pandering to the worst of people's prejudices.

Islam in northern Nigeria is by no means a monolithic entity. Many different traditions and brotherhoods are represented and considerable debate takes place within Nigerian Muslim society about religious doctrine, including Sharia law. I do not think it is possible to accurately estimate the extent of popular support for Sharia law among Nigerian Muslims, but clearly such support is considerable in Kano, where hundreds of thousands of people publicly celebrated its official introduction. Though much of the international focus on the introduction of Sharia law in Nigeria has centered on a few celebrated cases of punishments that global human rights watch groups charge violate individual rights, among non-Muslims in Nigeria most of the debate has been about the degree to which Sharia is being applied to, or is adversely affecting, the lives of Christians who reside in the north.[9]

When I first began working in Kano in 2001, Igbos recounted numerous instances of perceived injustices inflicted upon them, in their interpretation, because of Sharia law. People escorted me to churches they said were burned by bands of Muslim vigilantes. Attacks and counterattacks on mosques and churches are by far the most egregious symbols of offense in both Christian and Islamic communities. The burning of the opposing group's religious institutions typically occurs at the climax of violence that has escalated for a number of complicated reasons. Christian migrants in Kano almost always retaliate for perceived aggression and sometimes attack mosques in areas of the city where the number of Christians is high. In addition to burned churches, Igbos showed me many businesses (mostly bars and hotels—many of which operate as brothels) that were reportedly attacked, ransacked, and, in some cases, burned by Muslim vigilantes.

Not long before my arrival in Kano in June 2001, a spate of ethno- religious violence had erupted in the city. In the Nigerian press (which, it must be acknowledged, is dominated by southerners and Christians), and in accounts of the violence I heard from Igbo informants in the southeast and in Kano, the violence allegedly began when young Muslim vigilantes confronted some young female Igbo secondary school students who were returning home from taking their university entrance exams. The girls were reportedly challenged for not covering their heads (one of the requirements of Islam), and the ensuing skirmish allegedly resulted in the death of at least one of the students. Word of this incident spread and led to widespread violence in Kano between Christian Igbo migrants and mostly Hausa-speaking Islamic youths. An unknown number of people were killed (some reports said dozens), but in the stories that Igbos told me afterward, they viewed this clash as a successful demonstration of their ability to defend themselves, their businesses, and *Sabon Gari*. People described the degree to which the Igbo community had armed itself with automatic weapons and told me proudly that at the height of the most recent conflict "no Hausa man could be found alive in *Sabon Gari*." But despite this "successful" defense of their small section of Kano, Igbos still felt very insecure about their position in the city—their economic lives depended on coexistence and commerce with the much larger Hausa-speaking Islamic city.

MIGRANT CIRCUITRY AND SYMBOLIC STORIES OF ETHNO-RELIGIOUS VIOLENCE

The same summer, I spent several weeks in Ubakala, talking to the kin of the migrants I was studying in Kano. The incident of the schoolgirl(s) killed in Kano had circulated widely in the east through the media, but especially in the stories and rumors disseminated in the social networks that connect migrants and their places of origin. In the aftermath of the Kano killings and the resulting riots, smaller clashes occurred in the eastern cities of Aba and Owerri, where significant numbers of northern Hausa migrants reside. Just as Igbos dominate market sectors such as motor vehicle spare parts, pharmaceuticals, and electronics in northern cities, Hausas dominate the trade in cattle, kola nuts, and currency exchange in southern cities. It is common that when violence erupts in one region of the country it is followed by retaliatory attacks in another region.[10] Conflicts in Kano and other northern cities that are perceived as attacks on Igbos and Christians are avenged by violence directed against Hausas and Muslims in the east.

Through interviews and participant observation in both Kano and Ubakala in the weeks following the 2001 violence, I was able to document some of the ways in which migration circuitry contributes to ethnic and religious polarization, and the resulting escalation of violence. In *Sabon Gari* it was difficult to discern anything that resembled an objective and coherent account of the initial killing and the ensuing violence. Stories varied dramatically. By the time I discussed the same events with people in Ubakala, the accounts were almost unrecognizable, exaggerated in ways that both inflated the extent of violence in Kano and embellished its ethnic and religious significance.

By most accounts in Kano, the extent of bloodshed in this particular set of events was much less than in some of the previous riots; a fact most Igbos attributed to their preparedness—having armed themselves with guns that deterred Hausa incursions into *Sabon Gari*. However, when I interviewed one of the top Igbo leaders in Kano, he suggested that good relations between the Igbo leadership and the emir of Kano (the traditional political and religious leader of the local Hausa population) had staved off escalating violence. Although he also made reference to the Igbos' increased armament, he suggested that negotiations between Igbo and Hausa leaders had prevented full-fledged rioting and wider intercommunal conflict. Indeed, by his estimation, the actual violence was minimal. Although ordinary Igbos attributed the relative smaller scale of the violence to their resolve and armament rather than to their leaders' diplomatic relationships with the emir, it was generally agreed in Kano that the worst kind of "crisis," experienced several times in the past decade, had been averted.

Back home in the east things sounded much worse. My friends and informants in Ubakala, who knew I had just returned from several weeks in Kano, had many questions about the situation there. They told me stories of the versions of events that they had heard, which clearly blew things out of proportion. For example, a teacher in a local primary school, who has several cousins residing in Kano, said that half a dozen schoolgirls had been killed, and he added that in the ensuing violence a pregnant Christian woman had had her fetus cut from her belly by a Muslim mob. This was an archetypal (and I think apocryphal) story

I heard frequently from Igbos in past descriptions of ethno-religious conflicts in the north. Hausas and Muslims were routinely portrayed as barbaric in their violence. Such stories provided justification for unprovoked attacks against Muslims in the Hausa quarters of Igbo cities in the southeast. Indeed, several people I spoke with in Ubakala suggested that the level of retaliation and revenge against Hausas in Aba and Owerri was insufficient.

That such exaggerations and rumors contribute to the justification and escalation of ethnic and religious violence is not surprising. I have spent enough time with both Igbo migrants in Kano and Hausa migrants in Owerri to know that there is plenty of innocence and plenty of culpability on both sides, and that the role of rumors in the symbolic creation of "us" versus "them," enabling and rationalizing violence, is powerful in both communities. What I want to emphasize here is the important role that the circuitry of migrant networks plays in exacerbating and expanding local conflicts into what are popularly perceived as large-scale national crises. Undoubtedly, media accounts disseminate knowledge about intercommunal conflicts in Nigeria. However, my research in Ubakala, and among Ubakala migrants in Kano, suggests that networks of communication between migrants produce a personalized brand of truth value. Further, even when migrants are not, in fact, the sources of information, the very existence of "extended communities" contributes significantly to both the intensification of ethnic and religious identities and to the rationale for the expansion of violence. Regardless of where people actually learn about communal violence in Kano (or in other cities of destination), back home people commonly tell the stories of their knowledge with references to kin who are actually living in these destinations. Accounts routinely include prefaces such as "my in-law in Kano said . . . ," or "my neighbor's brother told us . . . ." The personalization of these stories creates both a certainty about truth value and a level of emotional investment that are fundamental to understanding the production of violence around issues of ethnic and religious identity.

I remember vividly the particular case of the Igbo man in Kano who was killed for allegedly wiping himself after defecation using a page from the Koran. He was reportedly beheaded by an angry mob of young Muslims and his severed head was placed on a pole and paraded around the city. That incident occurred when I was conducting dissertation fieldwork from 1995 to 1997 and was widely discussed in Ubakala and throughout Igboland. The execution, beheading, and parading of the head were well documented in the media, but whether the man actually wiped himself with a page of the Koran, and whether this was an intentional act were impossible to uncover. Regardless, the symbolic power of the alleged act in the Muslim community was evident and triggered a response that drew on deeper historical resentments about Igbo economic domination of certain sectors of the economy. In Christian Igboland the incident was represented as an example of Hausa and Islamic barbarity, with Hausa ethnicity, the Muslim religion, and barbarism merging into one category.

As I indicated above, the immediate causes of major instances of urban communal violence are often impossible to untangle, in part, no doubt, because the parties involved interpret events so differently. But some stories emerge that become symbolic in the minds of the actors (and in the collective consciousness of wider Nigerian society) of the issues at stake in these clashes. Though it would be misguided to view any of these stories as "true," I believe they are important as symbolic statements about the nature of truth to the people involved. For example, the story of the schoolgirls who had just taken their university entrance exam being (allegedly) killed for not covering their heads is all the more symbolically powerful to Igbos because of the imagery of formal education. Igbos (and southern Christians more generally) see and represent themselves as more "progressive," "enlightened," and "civilized" than northern Muslims. A schoolgirl completing her university entrance exam epitomizes such progressiveness. Whether or not the story of the immediate cause of that particular clash in Kano is true, the resonance of the story for an Igbo audience is predictable.

Central to my argument is the importance of the mechanisms by which such stories move across cultural and geographical boundaries. The circuitries of migrant communication perpetuate and solidify symbolically the economic, social, and cultural ties that link communities and their urban migrants. Stories of violence circulated through migrant networks personalize the truth of "us" versus "them" accounts. These stories do not in themselves explain the strength of people's ties to place of origin and the salience of ethnicity and religious affiliation in the context of internal migration, but they illustrate the degree to which rural and urban communities (and, indeed, different urban communities) remain linked in contemporary Nigeria. Further, they demonstrate that, in many ways, the roots of urban communal violence are grounded in a "politics of belonging" (Geschiere and Gugler 1998) that undergirds social and demographic processes in Nigeria. Central to this "politics of belonging" are shared notions of ethnic and religious identity that have associations with place—associations that are both the result of and put to productive (and destructive) use in processes of internal migration.

INTERNAL MIGRATION, VIGILANTISM, AND ETHNO-RELIGIOUS VIOLENCE

Any account of urban communal violence in contemporary Nigeria would be incomplete without some mention of the rise of vigilantism, and of the ways in which organized vigilante groups have become the means through which larger political, ethnic, and religious interest groups inflict violence on their perceived enemies. Vigilantism typically targets cultural "others," and in Nigeria's cities such "others" are frequently migrants. The rise of vigilantism and the stories of vigilante actions that circulate across geographical boundaries contribute to the solidifying of ethno-religious identities and resulting antagonisms.

Organized vigilantism in Nigeria's major cities has emerged dramatically since the transition to civilian rule in 1999. In each of the major regions of the country—the north, the southwest, and the southeast—large vigilante groups have been organized and operate in the main cities. These vigilante groups ostensibly operate to prevent violent crime and rid urban neighborhoods of the gangs of armed robbers that have increasingly terrorized urban communities. Indeed, groups such as the Bakassi Boys in the southeast, The O'odua People's Congress in Lagos in the southwest, and various pro-Sharia "militias" in the north have garnered significant mass public support for their efforts to stamp out armed robbery and other violent crimes (Gore and Pratten 2003). However, the techniques used by these vigilante groups, including arbitrary arrest, torture, and extra-judicial public executions have been documented and condemned by human rights groups in Nigeria and abroad (Human Rights Watch 2002). In addition, over the past several years in Nigeria, I have read numerous media accounts and heard increasing numbers of stories from friends and informants alleging that these vigilante groups are being used by political elites to foment unrest that serves their interests and persecute political opponents. No doubt the rise of organized vigilantism has dangerous and potentially destabilizing consequences for Nigeria's nascent democracy, the fabric of civil society, and the conduct of justice.

Though practices of torture and extra-judicial executions—what Nigerians call "jungle" or "street" justice—are worrying from a human rights perspective, what interests me in the context of this chapter is the way in which stories about the work of these vigilante groups move across Nigeria through the social networks that connect rural villages and urban migrant communities. The actions of these groups, and the discourses that surround them, serve to promote a connection in public consciousness between ethnicity and religion. As the violence perpetrated by these vigilante groups is recast from the killing of criminals to the rooting out of ethnic and religious "others" (most often, in Nigerian urban contexts, migrants), the potential scale of this violence becomes much greater, the ability to rationalize it much stronger, and the line between violent crime, vigilantism, and urban communal violence becomes almost imperceptible. Criminals, vigilantes, and ethnic militias seem to blend together, with identities dependent on the particular events and on who is doing the interpreting.

By far the biggest eruption of Christian–Muslim violence in Nigeria since the return to democracy in 1999 began in the northern city of Kaduna in February 2000. Though the specific events that led to the initial violence are almost impossible to untangle, the resulting clashes killed thousands of people in Kaduna in just a few days and sparked related clashes and retaliatory attacks in many other cities. Many, if not most, of the Christians killed in Kaduna were Igbo migrants and my Igbo informants in the east recounted stories of the resulting violence against the migrant Islamic Hausa communities in eastern cities as track-trailer loads of Igbo corpses arrived in the city of Aba in the days after the violence in Kaduna. As part of the retaliation, many Hausas were killed and their businesses burned in the towns of Aba and Owerri. The ransacking and burning of the Hausa areas in Aba and Owerri and the killing of Hausa migrants in these cities was, by all accounts I heard, carried out directly by the Bakassi Boys, the main vigilante group in the southeast (Harnischfeger 2003; Smith 2004b). Although Nigeria's human rights groups and many individual Igbos expressed concern over the involvement of the Bakassi Boys in ethnic and religious strife, their role as defenders of Igbo ethnicity and, by extension, of Christianity (since the Igbos killed in Kaduna were purportedly killed for being Christian) served to increase their popularity, even as it raised troubling questions about the extent to which they are controlled and manipulated by politicians (Smith 2004b).

In Kano, the pro-Sharia vigilante groups (like the vigilante groups elsewhere, made up almost entirely of male youths between the ages of 15 and 30) are positioned in similarly ambiguous ways between vigilante group, ethnic militia, and criminal gang, seeming to be all three at different moments and depending upon one's position and perspective. Igbos in *Sabon Gari* attribute many instances of urban communal violence to the instigation of these "vigilantes." Many Igbos told me, in moments of reflection, that it was the Muslim youths (sometimes referred to as *yan dabas*) and their political patrons who created the problems between Igbos and Hausas—though at other moments, in other conversations, all Hausas and Muslims were painted in the same broad (and negative) strokes. That vigilante groups in urban Nigeria are manipulated by politicians seems clear; that their role in combating violent crime has become conflated with their role as defenders of and prosecutors for the ethnic and religious identities they represent is also evident. More complicated is the way in which the actions of these violent groups are interpreted and represented in popular consciousness. As discourses about ethnicity, religion, and violence circulate between cities, and between rural and urban areas, the strength and divisiveness of identities rooted in place of origin, but increasingly overlaid with a religious dimension, become all the more powerful. In the process, the distinction between violent crime (arguably rooted in poverty) and communal violence (seen as rooted in identity) becomes obscured—or, perhaps more accurately, the connections between the two disappear from view. As Nigerians increasingly interpret crime and injustice in ethnic and religious terms, it becomes more difficult to address the political and economic roots of inequality and injustice.

CONCLUSION

Few Nigerians would disagree that urban communal violence is a problem and the vast majority of people would like to live peacefully, without crime, violence, and ethnic and religious conflict. Yet the experiences of migrants in Nigeria's cities, and the stories that circulate between cities and in Nigeria's many thousands of rural sending communities—stories about crime, violence, and conflicts between people of different ethnicities and religions—create popular support for the very violence that people lament. The political importance of ethnic identity in Nigeria, and the grafting of religious identity onto ethnic identity that seems to be occurring ever more rapidly, can only be understood in the context of internal migration, by recognizing the degree to which identity in Nigeria is produced across places through the human relationships that connect them. The strength of rural–urban ties—people's attachments to and instrumental reliance of networks of kin and "home people"—is both productive of and reproduced by the experiences of ethnic and religious divisions in urban areas.

Admittedly, my account of the role of internal migration in the production of ethnic and religious identity is partial in that it has focused on the experience of one ethnic group, and, indeed, on members of that ethnic group who have migrated to a particular destination. But I contend that the example of Igbos in Kano represents a wider phenomenon, wherein the ties between migrants and their place of origin and the circulation of knowledge (and rumors) about the experience of living amongst other peoples serve to produce and reproduce a sense of ethnic and religious identity. The idea that ethnic identity is produced in relationship to an "other" is by no means new (Barth 1969), but the degree to which this process is facilitated through migration has not been thoroughly examined. In addition, the emergence of religious affiliation as a marker of ethnic identity among Igbos and Hausas in Nigeria can only be adequately explained by taking into account the historical and contemporary effects of migration. Although migration and the intermingling of people from different regions, language areas, cultural traditions, and religions offers some hope for promoting tolerance, the current trend in Nigeria seems to be increasing ethnic tension, exacerbated by the rise of religious difference as a marker of ethnic identity.[11] Unfortunately, the casting of violence and its discontents in ethnic and religious terms prevents Nigerians from focusing on the material and political roots of inequality.

NOTES

1. "Urban communal violence" is typically distinguished from more random violent crime that is conceived of as the work of individuals or gangs whose purposes are purely criminal and unrelated to ethnic or religious affiliation. However, the lines between violent crime and communal violence can become blurred, as in the case of emerging vigilantism, which I describe further below.
2. For example, "Igboness" is increasingly equated with Christianity and "Hausaness" is typically equated with Islam.
3. Within Kano's Hausa-speaking "host" population there are also significant divisions, including some that include a native–stranger dimension; however, these divisions are beyond the scope of this chapter (Paden 1973).
4. As part of my research in Kano, I identified and interviewed 121 Ubakala migrant households; only 10 were not active members of hometown associations.
5. There has also been much documented violence of Igbos against Hausas, and even many Igbos admit that some of the violence directed against Igbos in the north was exacerbated by the sense that Igbos exploited the local population through their positions of economic dominance prior to the civil war. I do not mean to underplay the extent of Igbo participation in prewar violence, or to suggest that one side or the other deserves more "blame." But there seems to be no doubt that in the months immediately preceding the war, Igbos in the north were particularly targeted, and this memory continues to influence Igbo interpretations of postwar interethnic and interreligious violence in the north, especially in Kano.
6. Igbos' experience in Kano is contrasted, in Igbo discourse, with the way they were treated by their nearer non–Igbo neighbors in places such as Port Harcourt.
7. Most prominent in this regard is the Movement for the Actualization of the Sovereign State of Biafra (MASSOB), which has organized various demonstrations, produced its own literature, and regularly run afoul of the federal government.
8. Currently 12 of Nigeria's 36 states (all in the north) have officially adopted Sharia law.
9. Arguably, the focus on the human rights abuses associated with Sharia law in northern Nigeria has been exaggerated relative to the extent of abuses that have actually occurred. For example, none of the women sentenced to death by stoning for committing adultery has ever actually been killed. Furthermore, during the period that the consequences of Sharia law garnered so much Western media attention, many hundreds of people were being killed in extra-judicial executions by vigilante groups in southeastern Nigeria (see Human Rights Watch 2002; Smith 2004b).

10. For example, communal violence in Yelwa in Plateau State in 2004, in which clashes between Christian "indigenes" and Muslim "settlers" resulted in hundreds of deaths, was followed by riots and retaliatory killings in Kano (see Human Rights Watch 2005).
11. Certainly polarization of "us" and "them" is not the only outcome of internal migration. Even in Kano there are experiences and voices of accommodation and mutual appreciation.

REFERENCES

Ahanotu, Austin. 1982. The Role of Ethnic Unions in the Development of Southern Nigeria: 1916–1966, in B. I. Obichere (ed.). *Studies in Southern Nigerian History.* London: Frank Cass.

Anthony, Douglas. 2000. " 'Islam Does Not Belong to Them': Ethnic and Religious Identities among Male Igbo Converts in Hausaland," *Africa* 70 (3): 422–441.

Anthony, Douglas. 2002. *Poison and Medicine: Ethnicity, Power and Violence in a Nigerian City, 1966 to 1986.* Portsmouth, NH: Heinemann.

Aronson, Dan. 1971. "Ijebu Yoruba Urban–Rural Relationships and Class Formation," *Canadian Journal of African Studies* 5 (3): 263–279.

Barth, Fredrik. 1969. Introduction. *Ethnic Groups and Their Boundaries.* Boston: Little, Brown, pp. 9–38.

Bayart, Jean-Francois. 1993. *The State in Africa: The Politics of the Belly.* London: Longman.

Berry, Sara. 1985. *Fathers Work for Their Sons: Accumulation, Mobility and Class Formation in an Extended Yoruba Community.* Berkeley: University of California Press.

Berry, Sara. 1989. "Social Institutions and Access to Resources," *Africa* 59 (1): 41–55.

Chabal, Patrick and Jean-Pascal Daloz. 1999. *Africa Works: Disorder as Political Instrument.* Oxford: James Currey for the International African Institute.

Chukwuezi, Barth. 2001. "Through Thick and Thin: Igbo Rural–Urban Circularity, Identity and Investment," *Journal of Contemporary African Studies* 19 (1): 55–66.

Cohen, Abner. 1969. *Custom and Politics in Urban Africa: A Study of Hausa Migrants in Yoruba Towns.* Berkeley: University of California Press.

Geschiere, Peter. 1982. *Village Communities and the State: Changing Relations among the Maka of Southeastern Cameroun.* London: Kegan Paul.

Geschiere, Peter and Josef Gugler. 1998. "The Urban–Rural Connection: Changing Issues of Belonging and Identification," *Africa* 68 (3): 309–319.

Gore, Charles and David Pratten. 2003. "The Politics of Plunder: The Rhetorics of Order and Disorder in Southern Nigeria," *African Affairs* 102: 211–240.

Gugler, Josef. 1971. "Life in a Dual System: Eastern Nigerians in Town, 1961," *Cahiers d'Etudes Africaines* 11: 400–421.

Gugler, Josef. 1991. "Life in a Dual System Revisited: Urban–Rural Ties in Enugu, Nigeria, 1961–1987," *World Development* 19 (5): 399–409.

Gugler, Josef and William Flanagan. 1978. *Urbanization and Social Change in West Africa.* Cambridge: Cambridge University Press.

Guyer, Jane. 1993. "Wealth in People and Self-Realization in Equatorial Africa," *Man* 28: 243–265.

Guyer, Jane. 1995. "Wealth in People, Wealth in Knowledge—Introduction," *Journal of African History* 36 (1): 83–90.

Harneit-Sievers, Axel, Jones Ahazuem, and Sydney Emezue. 1997. *A Social History of the Nigerian Civil War: Perspectives from Below.* Hamburg: Lit Verlag.

Harnischfeger, Johannes. 2003. "The Bakassi Boys: Fighting Crime in Nigeria," *The Journal of Modern African Studies* 41 (1): 23–49.

Human Rights Watch. 2002. *The Bakassi Boys: The Legitimization of Murder and Torture*, Vol. 14, No. 5(a). New York: Human Rights Watch.

Human Rights Watch. 2005. *Revenge in the Name of Religion: The Cycle of Violence in Plateau and Kano States*, Vol. 17, No. 8(a). New York: Human Rights Watch.

Kano State Statistical Yearbook. 1972. Kano: Military Governor's Office.

Kirk-Greene, Anthony. 1971. *Crisis and Conflict in Nigeria*. London: Oxford University Press.

Lentz, Carola. 1995. " 'Unity for Development': Youth Associations in Northwestern Ghana," *Africa* 65 (3): 395–429.

Nnoli, Okwudiba. 1995. *Ethnicity and Development in Nigeria*. Brookfield: Ashgate.

Paden, John. 1971. "Communal Competition, Conflict and Violence in Kano," in Robert Melson and Howard Wolpe (eds.). *Nigeria: Modernization and the Politics of Communalism*. East Lansing: Michigan State University Press.

Paden, John. 1973. *Religion and Political Culture in Kano*. Berkeley: University of California Press.

Post, Ken and Michael Vickers (eds.). 1973. *Structure and Conflict in Nigeria, 1960–1966*. London: Heinemann.

Setel, Philip. 1999. *A Plague of Paradoxes: AIDS, Culture and Demography in Northern Tanzania*. Chicago: University of Chicago Press.

Smith, Daniel Jordan. 1999. "Having People: Fertility, Family, and Modernity in Igbo-Speaking Nigeria." Ph.D. dissertation. Emory University.

Smith, Daniel Jordan. 2001. "Kinship and Corruption in Contemporary Nigeria," *Ethnos* 66 (3): 344–364.

Smith, Daniel Jordan. 2004a. "Contradictions in Nigeria's Fertility Transition: The Burdens and Benefits of Having People," *Population and Development Review* 30 (2): 221–238.

Smith, Daniel Jordan. 2004b. "The Bakassi Boys: Vigilantism, Violence and Political Imagination in Nigeria," *Cultural Anthropology* 19 (3): 429–455.

Smock, Audrey. 1971. *Ibo Politics: The Role of Ethnic Unions in Eastern Nigeria*. Cambridge: Harvard University Press.

Trager, Lilian. 2001. *Yoruba Hometowns: Community, Identity and Development in Nigeria*. Boulder, CO: Lynne Rienner.

Uchendu, Victor. 1965. *The Igbo of Southeastern Nigeria*. Fort Worth, TX: Holt, Reinhart and Winston.

Wolpe, Howard. 1974. *Urban Politics in Nigeria: A Study of Port Harcourt*. Berkeley: University of California Press.

Woods, Dwayne. 1994. "Elites, Ethnicity and 'Hometown' Associations in the Cote d'Ivoire: An Historical Analysis of State–Society Links," *Africa* 64 (4): 465–483.

3

(Re)Configuring the City: The Mapping of Places and People in Contemporary Kenyan Popular Song Texts

Joyce Nyairo

Introduction

A significant share of the popular music created by youthful urban groups in Kenya over the last ten years generates various discourses of the capital city, Nairobi. My analysis of some of this output proceeds by showing how the relationship between cultural forms, such as music, and places is symbiotic. Places help to shape cultural forms and cultural forms are in turn crucial in mediating our understandings of spaces and places (Connell and Gibson 2003).[1] My arguments are premised upon theoretical ideas of geographers and cultural theorists who view urban space as a product of social and cultural engineering to the extent that people shape the places around them, just as much as places themselves influence social behavior and cultural practice. This study of the geography of Kenyan popular music focuses on song lyrics and treats them as texts that comprise a "configuration of signs that is coherently interpretable by [a] community of users" (Hanks 1989: 95). In order to fully exploit the levels of meaning in popular music, song-texts must be seen as more than the themes that are carried in song lyrics (Fabian 1998; Graham 1989). They need to be read within various contexts and alongside paratextual elements such as group names, album titles, the visual images on album sleeves, liner notes, and music videos. In seeking to outline how all these aspects of song-texts either mention, suggest, or otherwise construct places, I deliberately extend Julia Kristeva's (1980) concept, and take "intertextuality" to mean the various senses in which one text refers to others. Therefore, I trace the sources of the textual referents embedded in a song, and debate the ways in which they inform its sense of place. And as Simon Gikandi (2000) has urged, I work toward outlining the historical specificity of these referents so that we can appreciate the cultural depth of the works under study.

The bulk of my arguments are centered on three contemporary Kenyan popular songs—"4 in 1" (1999), "*Wasee Githurai*" (2002), and "Mona Lisa"

(2002).[2] I use these song-texts to illustrate the artists' portrayal of the novel ways in which postcolonial Africans have inhabited the city of Nairobi increasingly privileging local genius and the marginal spaces of Eastlands. In the process the architectural plans and other official discourses of the city have gradually been overturned. This reconfiguring of the city has been achieved through what de Certeau (1993: 156) terms the "surreptitious creativities" on the margins, creativities that contain powerful legitimating practices of new urban existences. Thus I show how the once middle-class residential estate Buru Buru is disparaged and conceived in opposition to the slums of the Industrial Area, which Ndarlin P posits as places of hidden pleasures. In "Mona Lisa" by Deux Vultures, the pleasures of Mama Ngina Street in the city center are threatened by the obtrusive presence of street beggars. Beyond tracing the spatial and sociohistorical contexts surrounding these poeticized locations, I demonstrate "the literary strategies through which the said locality is evoked" (Clifford 1992: 97). For instance, we see the hyperbolic efficacy of Ndarlin P's polyphonic discourses and the effect of the gleeful repetition of the place name Githurai in "*Wasee Githurai.*" Further, I delineate the characters that are sketched into the places the artists sing about, showing them to be ubiquitous as well as functional in the key ways that they inject specific identities onto the places that they frequent or inhabit. Ultimately, I emphasize the spatial senses in which Kenyan popular music succeeds in defining and shaping urban class differentiations in postcolonial Kenya.

Theorizing Space

> Space was treated as the dead, the fixed, the undialectical, the immobile. Time on the contrary was richness, fecundity, life, dialectic.
>
> (Foucault 1980: 70)

My analysis of the (re)presentations of place in contemporary Kenyan song lyrics is guided by Michel Foucault's (1980) intermittent commitment to a resituating of geography, of spatial terms, in the "archaeology of knowledge." It is also premised on Edward Said's (1995) formulation of "Orientalism," which articulates the notion of invented geographies as part of a system of dominance. Though consciously committed to historicism, Foucault nonetheless embraces the idea of a critical practice that will henceforth project space, just as much as time, as key to the mediation of human existence. A spatial epistemology necessarily proceeds by recognizing that space, like time, exists freely in nature. The ways in which we fill up space are a matter of our own designs and consciousness, in the same way that we purposefully sketch out time with demarcations, details, and events. In other words, and as Edward Soja (1989: 136) would have it, we daily engage in "the social production of space and the restless formation and reformation of geographical landscapes." Whether we speak of the formation of national, provincial, regional, or council boundaries, or we focus on the building of cities, highways, agricultural research stations, or beach resorts, the fact is that we are consciously intervening in the perception and creation of space:

> A group of people living on a few acres of land will set up boundaries between their land and its immediate surroundings and the territory beyond, which they call

> "the land of the barbarians." In other words, this universal practice of designating in one's mind a familiar space which is "ours" and an unfamiliar space beyond "ours" which is "theirs" is a way of making geographical distinctions that *can* be entirely arbitrary. (Said 1995: 54)

Our making of places and peoples is guided by rational as well as emotional processes. In the case of the West's formulation of the Orient, unbalanced and overambitious spatial imagination led to the smothering of a whole variety of social, linguistic, political, and historical realities. This resulted in the creation of staid and static portrayals of the whole area labeled "Orient," reducing it to a site of the exotic, the despotic, sensuous, cruel, and so on. Said's study calls attention to the need to carefully limit the area under study, and also to inject approaches other than the purely geographical in the understanding of peoples. Humanity endows spaces with certain values and attributes to these places key functions, experiences, and connotations (Bachelard 1964). Edward Said (1995: 55) says: "(s)pace acquires emotional and even rational sense by a kind of poetic process, whereby the vacant or anonymous reaches of distance are converted into meaning for us here." Said's approach of anchoring spatial imagination within other critical approaches, such as poetics, is echoed by both Foucault and Soja who are quick to point out that the injection of spatial consciousness into critical theory should not, for one, result in the denial of history. In actual fact, Soja (1989: 137) urges a critical practice that will bear the "triple dialectic of space, time, and social being." This way, the whole notion of an African modernity will be more usefully problematized, not solely as an intrusion on and destruction of tradition, but as a complex reordering of the ways in which time and space relate. If the African city has hitherto been perceived as the seamless product of Western influences introduced in the wake of colonialism, we might more usefully begin to see the interaction between ethnic elements and global practices as the more accurate identity of the African city (Robins 2000). We would also then begin to appreciate the extent to which urban influences permeate the countryside increasingly calling for a redefinition of what we term rural areas.

An examination of spatial imagination in the postcolonial African city cannot escape a concern with relations of power. Indeed, Foucault argues, "(t)he spatialising description of discursive realities gives on to the analysis of related effects of power" (Foucault 1980: 70–71). Just as Said demonstrates the colonial design that in a sense necessitated "Orientalism," so too must we pay attention to the reasons why, and the ways in which spaces are ordered and how they thereby reflect relations of inequality—landed owner/squatter, indigene/foreigner, insider/outsider, oppressor/oppressed. Inequalities of this kind will find resonance in spatial policies of segregated neighborhoods whose effect is the validation of racial and/or economic differences. But we need to look out for the instances in which spatial zoning does not strictly adhere to the set boundaries or policies. In this regard Foucault develops the notion of "heterotopias." He describes them as "those singular spaces to be found in some given social spaces whose functions are different or even the opposite of others." This idea of heterotopias greatly illumines a study of the political economy of space and dramatizes the indelible tie between space, social relations, and discourses of power.

In "Walking the City," Michel de Certeau applies Foucault's approach of tying space to power relations and examines the city as a construct of power. De Certeau looks at city bylaws, plans, architectural designs, and concept cities as part of the official discourses of the city space and, therefore, as key components in the exercising of power. Within these official discourses of the city, however, there lie many other practices of urban existence that defy laid down structures and that contain powerful legitimating practices of the "surreptitious creativities" (de Certeau 1998: 156) that proliferate on the margins. My own reading of the way lyrics document places, adopts de Certeau's thinking and moves away from notions of the ideal(ized) city to seek instead understandings of (alter)native urban practices. The deterioration of city structures and planning cannot, therefore, be viewed in negative terms that reside in the designs of official power structures. Instead, the idea is to concentrate on unearthing the life that is lived in the gaps between official practice/discourse; in the "everyday practices of lived space, of the disquieting familiarity of the city" (de Certeau 1993: 157). In other words, the focus is on "the city in a cultural context" (Agnew et al. 1984) and on dramatizing the human agency that lends the city its subaltern rhythm and tempo. Reading the city in this way necessitates that one pays attention to modes of movement through the streets and neighborhoods. How people move through locations—whether they walk or drive for instance, or they stick to named streets, or alternatively, create their own walkways—is critical to the ways in which they can impact upon it. It is, as de Certeau says, an indicator of whether people spatialize the city or are simply flattened and totalized by it.

What Foucault, Soja, Said, and de Certeau help us to appreciate is the fact that geographical space is as much of a manmade entity as history. But equally important, these scholars bring into clear focus the fact that there are many indicators that must be probed in seeking to understand the ways in which people shape places. Filling out both space and time is in part achieved by cultural engagement, and popular music makes soundtracks, it helps to map and define place, just as it marks and documents time. The geography of popular music that I am interested in therefore, is first, a question of examining the places that popular music talks about, and the ways in which it represents those places (Rose 1994). How a place is referred to in a song will not only tell us plenty about the people who live there, it will also affect the ways in which those very people relate to and live in that place. As a fundamentally performative act, music creates a dialogue between people and places even when it merely ascribes meaning and significance to bare landscapes and quotidian experiences. Equally important, music evokes memory and nostalgia over places and events (Nyairo 2005a,b; Nyairo and Ogude 2003; 2005). Talking of the sense of a place as Steven Feld (1996: 91) reminds us actually entails not just seeing it and possibly smelling it; it is also fundamentally about coming to recognize the sounds associated with that place. Acoustic experience of a place is therefore one way in which a song text can echo or represent a place (Finnegan 1989; Olson 1998). In the songs that I deal with, this acoustic experience is relayed through injecting the everyday sounds of a city street onto the dialogue and themes in the song-text.

NAIROBI: "GREEN CITY IN THE SUN"

Throughout the 1990s and into the millennium, the "Green City in the Sun" has been a cosmopolitan city hosting a varied mix of indigenous ethnic groups, including those of either Asian or European descent.[3] But in this mix lies a history of colonial segregation that has today been replaced by spatial zoning that is based on socioeconomic difference.[4] The racially mixed expatriate crowd resides in the northern part of the city—Gigiri, Spring Valley, Runda, and Muthaiga. A growing corpus of upper-middle-class Africans have found their way into areas in the west that the colonialists had reserved for Europeans—Karen, Kileleshwa, Lavington, Loresho. But there are many who continue to reside in Eastlands, the area of the town that the colonialists had designated for Africans. In some instances one finds that the patterns of settlement in these areas replicate the kind of ethnic zoning that colonial policy engendered.[5] This is particularly true of the ethnic character of the Eastleigh neighborhood that is so overwhelmingly dominated by Somalis. For the most part, social recreation is similarly zoned. Expatriates and well to do locals, including the fifth-generation Kenyan whites who live in the Kareng'ata zone, find their leisure in shopping malls such as Sarit Centre in Westlands and Village Market in Gigiri.[6] At the obvious level their cultural life bears virtually no contact with the residents of Nairobi's Eastlands or the lower-middle-income Africans and Asians who live in South B, South C, and Nairobi West. However, one fascinating aspect of the recreational life of Nairobi has to do with the ways in which cultural branding and to a smaller extent zoning sometimes takes place within one specific venue. This is true of the Carnivore Simba Salon, a club and restaurant off Nairobi's Lang'ata Road. As the name suggests, the restaurant specializes in a meat cuisine that even includes wild game. This is particularly popular with Nairobi's upper classes whose youth might also frequent the club to listen to visiting international artists such as Shaggy (December 2000) and Sean Paul (April 2004). Carnivore's marketing strategy is in part pegged on genre categorization of musical appreciation. Bangra nights on Friday pull in a predominantly Indian clientele. A mature and fairly sophisticated racially mixed crowd graces the Jazz nights. The Sunday evening Soul Nites are dominated by other varieties including Rock and Reggae nights. Another sense in which the Carnivore achieves cultural zoning is in their fashioning of what have come to be known as "ethnic nights." On a *Mugiithi* night for instance, the club hosts popular Gikuyu artists such as Mike Rua and his one-man guitar.[7] Patrons seem familiar with a repertoire of, say, 20 songs that are interpreted to constitute contemporary Gikuyu ethnic identity. Along with this music the club will also offer Gikuyu cuisine and the adverts in the local newspapers will encourage patrons to attend the function clad in traditional Gikuyu dress.

Through Star Search contests and the launching of albums from a varied corpus of Kenyan artists the Carnivore has been instrumental in the significant boom in both the production and consumption of Kenyan music that the country began to experience in the mid-1990s. This boom came after close to 20 years of decline and stagnation in the local music industry (Wallis and Malm 1984: 92–93; Stapleton and May 1989: 272–273).[8] Local producer Tedd

Josiah's compilation albums *Kenyan the First Chapter* (1998) and *Kenyan the Second Chapter* (1999) grew out of his conscious decision to showcase local talent. He wanted to pioneer a new moment, "an awakening," in the Kenyan music industry.[9] The inclusion of Ndarlin P's "4 in 1" on the second album indicates that the song offers a representative sample of the novel emergent trends that Josiah has been promoting.[10] More importantly for the concerns of this analysis, "4 in 1" is a very good example of the way sounds become representative of places.

David Samper (2004: 43) is right when he observes that Kenyan rappers are using ethnic languages as a "revalorisation of the past" and to "add an African flavor to rap." Indeed, the resonance of Ndarlin P's art comes from his ability to mimic the polyethnic nation by rapping in Kiswahili that is spoken in three different accents (Kamba, Kalenjin, Indian) in addition to employing five distinctly different languages—Kiswahili, English, Sheng, Kamba, and Gĩkũyũ.[11] Perhaps the song's title is a reference to its multilingual composition. It could further be read as a metaphor for the unity in diversity that is a much sought after ideal in the polyethnic and multiracial postcolonial Kenya. One could also argue that the title, "4 in 1," refers to the four different identities that Ndarlin P performs in the song. There is the combative *matatu* driver,[12] the inquisitive Asian, a rapper, "a gee from the west side, Nailovi" (a rap master purportedly from Nairobi's Westside),[13] and Ndarlin P himself, posing as an ardent suitor.

At the onset, "4 in 1" reconstructs the geography of Nairobi's Eastlands through a menacing *matatu* crew. The crew encounters an inquisitive Asian trader: "*kijana wewe nani na unataka nini, ebeshte wewe nani unakaa kama jambazi*"(young man who are you and what do you want, my friend who are you, you look like a rogue). The answer comes through a graphic spatial invocation of the driver's daily contact with the city's marginalized Eastlands suburbs: "mimi driver wa Umoja kule Kayole pamoja na Komarock" (I am a (*matatu)* driver plying the route between Umoja, Kayole and Komarock). Umoja and Kayole are low-income high-density residential estates within Embakasi constituency in northeast Nairobi. Umoja was a site and service USAID-sponsored Nairobi City Council project started in 1974. The developers put up the infrastructure, namely roads, sewer, street lighting, water, and electric power. In addition, they built a kitchen and bathroom/toilet for each unit leaving each allottee (most of whom were lower-level civil servants) to complete the house in his/her own time, along the lines of a project-designated plan, by adding a sitting room and two bedrooms. But because allottees hired artisans of dubious qualifications, and because supervision and inspection were compromised, and later, utterly overlooked owing to tensions between the city engineer and the project manager, Umoja lost its designed uniformity. It took on eclectic designs, sizes, and quality according to the whims and abilities of the allottees. For one, many residential units double up as commercial premises.

Kayole was completed in the 1980s and provides another example of a housing project that, from the onset, steered away from the original plans to take on a shape and character that has been dictated by the owners of the housing units and their needs. Komarock, which is within the same

Embakasi constituency, was completed in 1991. It was a turnkey mortgage housing scheme, meaning that occupants received a fully completed unit developed by Kenya Building Society, a subsidiary of the Housing Finance Company of Kenya Limited. But much as Komarock was intended to be a middle-class, medium-density estate, since its inception, it has fallen prey to numerous unplanned extensions in contravention of all the planning, designs, and city bylaws, thus resulting in "illegal densification" (Ochieng 2001: 1).

Ndarlin P's reference to all these places in "4 in 1" builds up an image of a zooming camera. It defies the places even as it names them since the act of driving through the neighborhoods is at once also an act of distancing as well as of engagement. It is a statement about transience, a scanning movement over the space that refuses to connect with the places or furnish us with detail. In essence, the driver makes a statement of denial as well as affiliation, he knows these urban spaces, identifies with them through the nature of his work even though he may not be domiciled there. In Kenya, *matatu* drivers belong to what has come to be known as the *jua kali*, or informal sector, in which the government has hardly formulated policy guidelines, let alone provided incentives that would streamline practice.[14] Again, the failure of local authorities to provide efficient transport networks to the city's later-day housing schemes long created a commercial lacuna that has been readily filled in by private enterprise.

Each of the neighborhoods referred to in "4 in 1" lies in the greater Eastlands residential area of Nairobi comprising, in the main, estates that were built in the 1970s, the 1980s, and 1990s as turnkey mortgage company estates and some as site and service projects with International funding. In a temporal sense, these neighborhoods take on a secondary existence within the city. They came into being at a time when the services provided by the local authority—the Nairobi City Council—had deteriorated badly on account of petty competitive politics and graft.[15] To this extent, the "spatial legacies" (Robins 2000: 409) in these latter-day estates are metonyms of disorder, need, and neglect.[16] Many of these estates lack basic facilities such as street lighting, paved pathways, recreational spaces, refuse disposal, and other social services. Security is bad and organized surveillance by the police is erratic and unreliable. No distinctions are made between residential zones and commercial ones, all flow into one another in a seamless stream of haphazard land-use. Looked at in terms of urban practice (Agnew et al. 1984; de Certeau 1993; de Certeau et al. 1998), these neighborhoods are the hallmark of (alter)native enterprise, reflecting much local ingenuity and improvisation. Kenneth King (1996: 50) describes the altering of architectural plans in the new "middle-class" residential areas of Eastlands thus:

> It would appear that one of the commonest forms of housing is not that actually owned by the low or lower-middle income occupant (for whom these schemes were intended) but is rather the barrack-to-rent blocks which have been built informally, but which are organized to take 6–12 one-room renters . . . they illustrate a very different face of jua kali to be found in the city. A kind of middle-class self-help that finds expression in the phrase: "We're all jua kali these days!"

The informal nature of the protagonist's job in "4 in1" is therefore reenacted in the areas he daily traverses where the dominant architectural scheme speaks of *jua kali*—informality, bold self-help initiatives, and an utter lack of official or institutional support. As the lyrics drive us through these neighborhoods, the emphasis may be on the speed of the wheezing *matatu*. Detailed graphic images of the neighborhood are blurred into a continuous flow of built-up environment that speaks with familiarity to the driver even as he avoids prolonged engagement with it.

In the third verse however, the protagonist's gaze lingers on two residential areas—Buru Buru and Mukuru (wa Njenga):

Nie ndigikuhenia
ati "gwitu ni Buru Buru"
nyumete ghetto noma
iria ya inda
ya Mukuru
Next Sunday thaa inyanya
we oka gutware ghetto,
nyumbaini cia mafati
nginya uigwii ukenete
ni ndire na mbeca cia kugura
ati bhajia
guku chips na karanga
hot dog kana pizza
ngugutwara
market imwe funny
nginya umake
turie chips cia kobole
na githeri gia kobole
. . . na maembe ma kobole[17]

I won't cheat you
saying "I come from Buru Buru"
I come from a troubled slum
the Industrial Area one,
Mukuru
Next Sunday at two o'clock
you come I take you to the slums
to house made of iron sheets
and you will be happy
I don't have money to buy
things like bhajia,
chicken and fried meat
hot dog or even pizza
I will take you
to an ingenious market
and you'll be shocked
we will eat chips for five shillings
and maize and beans for five bob
and mangoes at five shillings.

At this point, it is interesting to note how the protagonist as ardent suitor introduces himself to his amorata through a passionate identification of his home. And both his person and his home are, of necessity, identified by a negation of Nairobi's more affluent neighborhoods: "*Nie ndigikuhenia ati 'gwitu ni Buru Buru'* " (I won't cheat you that I am from Buru Buru). Significant too is the fact that this negation is uttered by way of a disdainful sneer, witnessed in the mocking tone of childish mimicry that is meant to imitate the snobbish ways of those from the middle-class quarters of Buru Buru.[18] This mimicry rules out the possibility of interpreting the suitor's negation of Buru Buru as an instance of his being apologetic or even ashamed of his own background. Actually, the mocking tone lends pride of place, and even a measure of authority, to the next line when he unequivocally declares that he comes from a "ghetto."

The derisive attitude to Buru Buru that we hear in "4 in 1" arises from multiple sociohistorical nuances that are based on the design of the segregated city that I outlined at the start of this section. Although Eastlands was meant for Africans, all of whom belonged to the low-income socioeconomic strata, the postcolonial economy has overturned previous zoning and created interesting heterotopias within Eastlands. Frank Furedi (1973) traces the history of "native" occupation of the city of Nairobi.[19] He underlines that the growth of haphazard African settlements arose from the steady marginalization of Africans in towns, and, as Roger Kurtz (1998: 78) also shows, from the widely held view that Africans were merely temporary residents of the city. It was not until 1939, Kurtz (1998: 79) points out, that a "deliberate policy of government paternalism" was designed and "the first housing projects for Africans in Ziwani, Kaloleni, and Pumwani," all confined to Eastlands, were started. Even then, the infamous pass laws strictly controlled the movement of Africans to the city. After independence in 1963, and all through the 1970s, Eastlands broadly comprised two parts: one was the planned and government developed sector, for instance, Ofafa, Jericho, Jerusalem, Shauri Moyo, Ziwani, Mbotela, Kaloleni, Pumwani, and the other estates that today make up Makadara constituency; the other was the then small, unplanned, and undeveloped area of informal settlement around Mathare, which in later years was to grow exponentially to become the sprawling slum that it is today.

In the 1960s and early 1970s, the developed part of Nairobi stopped, on the Eastern side, just short of the grassland plains where Buru Buru was later constructed. Chronologically, Kimathi (1969), Harambee (1973), and Buru Buru (1975) estates were the first middle-income residential areas to be sited in this part of Nairobi; an area that was previously reserved for low-income groups and which correspondingly carried small dwelling units, with shared compounds and sometimes even shared ablutions. Buru Buru Estate is bounded to the immediate south by Jogoo Road and still further south by a long stretch of Railway land followed by the Industrial Area. To the southwest is the low-income cum slum neighborhood of Makadara Estate, and to Buru Buru's west, in fact adjacent to Buru Buru Phase 3, lie Jericho, Lumumba (low-income), and the middle-income Harambee Estate. Further afield to the north and northeast are low-income Kariobangi and Dandora estates. To the east Buru Buru is bordered by the Outer Ring Road. This arterial road, and the ones that jut out of it such as Jogoo Road, Juja Road, and Kangundo Road, takes one through perhaps the widest collection of low-income and informal settlement areas in East Africa.[20] Not surprisingly, the more plentiful and comparatively spacious rooms, the enclosed compounds, and the provisions for car-parks in Kimathi, Harambee, and Buru Buru estates have always stood out amidst the smaller and crowded holdings that previously defined the Eastlands area. This (dis)location makes these estates, particularly the vast Buru Buru, stand out like iconoclasms, Foucault's insulated heterotopias. And although middle-class estates (Doonholm, Fedha, Avenue, Tena, Continental) have since proliferated along Outer Ring Road, Buru Buru still remains the primary index for middle-class disjuncture in Eastlands. Its residents have had to live with the Sheng label for middle-class snobbery and for the elite—*mababie*—regularly being touted at them by their less privileged neighbours.[21] It is this same disparaging reference to elite urbanites that we hear Ndarlin P the suitor making just before his derisive negation of Buru Buru: "*nie ndiri kabarbie ta kambuyu puff* daddy, *no tikwenda gwakwa ni mbeca atari* daddy" (I am not elite like that old man Puff Daddy, but it isn't my fault, it is just that my father has no money).[22]

It is all of these sociohistorical contexts of disjuncture, dramatic architectural contrasts, class tensions, and neighborhood rivalries that coalesce around "4 in 1" 's sneered disclaimer on Buru Buru. It is a disclaimer aimed at shunning perceived middle-class pretensions while at the same time vaguely concealing the dreams and desires of low-income and slum dwellers whose signifier of material success is a residence in Buru Buru. But it is also true that there is palpable pride and appropriation in the protagonists declaration of his origins in Mukuru (wa Njenga) slums, next to the city's Industrial Area.[23] Mukuru wa Njenga is one of the many informal settlements that have strategically mushroomed around Nairobi's Industrial Area, sheltering a large reservoir of unskilled and semiskilled workers as well as innumerable job-seekers. The other slums in the vicinity are: Kayaba, Kisii Village, Fuata Nyayo, Sinai, Langa Langa, Mariguini, kwa Reuben, Kahirira, and Commercial. In the 1960s, Mukuru was the Nairobi City Council garbage dump, and since slum shelters are largely built from waste material, the site easily lent itself to informal settlement. This history of informal settlement reverberates with new import when one takes cognizance of the etymology of the word *mukuru*. It is a Gikuyu word meaning "a ditch," and there is a commonplace idiomatic phrase—*gukira mukuru wa thina* (to cross the poverty line). In the case of Mukuru wa Njenga slums, the leap across to Industrial Area and on to the coveted Buru Buru is supposed to be the turning point, it rarely ever comes though and the hopefuls invariably crossover into the slum, into a designated poverty zone.

As the ardent suitor in "4 in 1" imagines a weekend date with Njeri, one cannot help noticing the lack of geometrical symmetry, the haphazard structural layout in the sites of the proposed outing. He imagines guiding his intended past shanty houses built of iron sheets and on to a low-budget food outlet. With pride and a vaguely disguised claim to authenticity, he shows off the socioeconomic activities of the slum—earthy food outlets offering ethnic cuisine. The emphasis is on the simplicity, the humble cost of the indigenous menu in contrast to the pretentious "pizzas and hot dogs" from the high-class outlets far away from the slums. The song echoes a definite preoccupation with food. In verse one, there is the bag of *mahindi* (maize) that the driver solicits from the Asian, then in verse two, there is talk of the street smart Kavindu whose lucky catch of a white man guarantees her a meal of rice. Ultimately in verse three, we listen to the lengthy menu of the ghetto market's cuisine. This preoccupation with food can very well be read as an amplification of the hunger and desire that defines existence in marginal locations. It is a hunger in material terms, but also in psychosocial terms; a desire to gain entry and advance, or even just the desire to be recognized and accepted on one's terms. The imaging of these desires reveals some slippage in the song's reconfiguring of marginal spaces since it works within officially defined discourses of slums as sites of perpetual need and longing.

The shrillness of the desire for recognition and space is apparent in the dominant motif of contest along which "4 in 1" is structured. There are three key sites of contest. First, there is the rapper's boast in the Introduction:

Wakati tunasema si(si) ni wanoma	when we say we are troublesome
Sio kusema tuko na homa	it doesn't mean we have a flu

Mimi siwezi kutwangana ati niku s(h)oot	I can't fight if it means I shoot you
Nikusomoa rungu	I'll remove my knobkerrie
na kutandika kichwa,	hit your head
Mpaka unatoa nundu	until you have a bump

We got stuff that is hundred times nicer than the bestis
Yoo! Even Tupac Mashakur and S(h)aquille Onyi
Including Osam Bin wa madeni knows this

The promise of lyrical prowess is heard in the structuring of witty rhymes and puns. The humor is advanced further by the naivety of the protagonist who necessarily interprets a rapping contest to mean physical combat. To dramatize his mastery over internationally famous hip-hop stars such as Tupac Shakur and legendary basketball star, Shaquille Oneal, the multifaced Ndarlin P invokes international terrorist Osama Bin Laden to authenticate his claim to lyrical prowess, a prowess that then becomes the subject of the song's chorus.

In verse one, we see a continuation of verbal eloquence when the inquisitive Asian engages the protagonist, as a *matatu* driver, in a heated exchange of insults. The exchange ends when the driver issues the treat of a physical beating: "*naweza kukuchana hivyo wacha tukanana*" (I can beat you up so you'd better stop hurling insults). Lastly, there is the romantic contest, and as Ndarlin P tries to win Njeri's heart, he tears apart perceived rivals in the neighborhood by continually referring to them as cowards and weaklings who can even be beaten up by a girl ("*no kihurwo ni muiritu*"). In the staging of all these contests Ndarlin P, in his various subaltern identities, is always framed as the only credible victor. The motif of contest, and particularly the resort to physical violence, echoes very succinctly age-old attitudes and tensions between *mababie* and *ulolo*, the youths from lower-income Eastlands. In these neighborhoods, challenges are invariably met and resolved through combat, and Eastlands has actually produced virtually all of Kenya's finest boxers.[24]

Much as "4 in 1" rings with many official discourses of subaltern existence, it does nonetheless inject many moments of the untold and often ignored aspects of life on the margins. Key to this display of the banal is the promise of romance between Njeri and Ndarlin P. In essence, the romance template upon which this geography of Nairobi is written is twofold. It is about Njeri whose heart the driver turned suitor is trying to win, and it is also about the idyllic rewriting of the slum that he makes. Based on the commonplace notions of the slum as a site of abject hunger, privation, and violence, romantic love might be imagined to be hopelessly at variance with the space in question. But in both of the instances of romance in "4 in 1," there is the determined effort to escape marginality, to refute the official city discourses of socioeconomically challenged spaces, places of fear, abject poverty, and utter misery. In their place, the song projects images of innovative provision of basic services, education of a different kind, relaxation, and romantic love. Much of the power of this song comes from its consistent application of a comic tone. Defying the emotive anger that normally governs rap, and ironically subverting the contest motif structuring the song, "4 in 1" resituates marginal spaces in the popular imagination through humor. It succeeds through the conviction with which it evokes lived experience in Nairobi's marginalized spaces as something that is real, that has its quotidian and even bright moments. These are shown to be places where people laugh and cry, and from which comic relief can be generated, to offer respite from the uptight pretensions and social vertigo induced by the middle class.

Walking the Margins versus Walking the City

Nominees at the seventh Kora All Africa Music Awards, Googs and Vinnie Banton (Moffat Omari and Vincent Ihaji), captured the attention of Kenyans through their audacious, almost radical, privileging of the margins of the city as a major site of fun and recreation. "*Wasee Githurai*," which is featured in the *Ogopa 1* (2002) album, remained a dancehall hit for much of 2002 and effectively asserted the place of peri-urban youth in Nairobi's entertainment circuits. Full of pride of place and origins the artists effusively sing:

Na wasee tumetoka Githurai	People we come from Githurai
Twa come kukupa rhymes zingine dry	We come to bring you great rap
Tuki fry mpaka MCs kama jai, mpaka rapper	We beat MCs like Jai, even rappers
Ikiwa zimeshika sema	If (our rhymes) are good, say
"my, oh my"	"my, oh my"
Come together we can do this together	
Take your time we're staying here forever	
Ona [see] *Mr. Lenny, Mr. Googs, Vinnie Banton*	
Hepi na mabeshte kule chini Githurai	Having fun with friends down in Githurai

Githurai is a fast-growing informal, middle- to low-income peri-urban settlement, 16 kilometers east of the city center and adjacent to the sprawling Eastlands. Since it lies on the margins of the city it carries all of the advantages of the lower land rates and cheaper standard of living connected to peri-urban areas. The proximity to Eastlands gives Githurai a typically urban culture that is accentuated by all the spontaneity of low-income settlements. It has a patchwork mix of commercial enterprises and residential dwellings. Many of these are precarious looking high-rise flats, as high as six stories, and none of them with elevators. The staircases are invariably narrow, structurally questionable, and very poorly lit. Nearly one out of every four shops is a bar and the smell of the patrons' favorite staple, *nyama choma* (roast meat), competes with the putrid stench from overflowing garbage heaps scattered on the untarmaced potholed roads. Goats and chicken scavenge round these heaps of waste and along the numerous alleys. Sometimes these animals choke on the carelessly disposed plastic bags that are a ubiquitous feature of the Githurai landscape. The area teems with the violence and insecurity that is alluded to in "*Wasee Githurai*" and graphically portrayed in its music video. Githurai is shown to be polluted by a gun culture and by the degeneration of its youth into alcohol, desperation, and violent crime:[25]

I say something going wrong in our world
People take something serious so pleasurable
And lots of guns, and guns forever gone
Are we living so high that we see nothing at all?

Clearly, and as the music video dramatizes, the specter of violence constantly hangs over the song's deep commitment to the pursuit of pleasure in Githurai. Images of neighborhood graffiti, idle youth, guns, and wildly driven *matatus*, ferrying passengers to Githurai, dominate the music video. Shots of the novel TV aerials that are designed by *jua kali* artisans to aid TV reception in this area further help to typify the Githurai and Zimmerman skyline.[26] In fact, it is possible to argue that the partying and jubilation of "*hepi na mabeshte kule chini Githurai*" (having fun with friends down in Githurai) is merely an interlude in a life of serious threats and grave moral pressures. The song attempts to subvert the recurring images of violence and insecurity by invoking a rather stark sexual grammar as one of the pockets of imagined leisure that permeate this space:

Whose got the biggest	
appetite for Kenyan ladies?	
Madame hu vaa thongs	Girls wear thongs
wakijua they'*re wearing tighties*	when they know they're wearing tight skirts
Madame hu vaa shorts,	Girls wear shorts
silky skirts with no high heels	
Ni [its] *Mr Googs*	

But there are material restrictions that persistently stand in the way of all these objects of desire, so that seeing or imagining them is one thing, but having them quite the other:

Stupid MCs are still asking Githurai beshtes [friends]	
What you thinking boys, Googs afford this?	
That's, that's that's a lie.	
I'm a simple crazy guy toka kule [from] *Githurai*	
And if I had the dough	
Ninge kuwa nime buy fries	I would have bought chips
Au sio [isn't it] *Mr. Sly?*	

Let us for a moment compare the moments of fear and economic deprivation expressed here with the images from "*Ninanoki*" (2002) by Nameless, a song from and about the more upmarket locations of the city's Southlands and Westlands.[27] A reading of "*Ninanoki*" reveals that in the more affluent neighborhoods of the city recreation has a different flavor.[28] Here Friday nights are filled with nothing but mindless dance and sexual lust:

It's a Friday night	
Eh nyinyi mabeshte twende tu katike	Hey, friends lets go out and dance

If you like to dance,	
well then here's your chance	
sisi wa Nairobi tunapenda hepi . . .	we Nairobians love fun
it is in the air, it is everywhere,	
makes you feel like removing your underwear	
Ogopa DJs, wacha kudelay	Ogopa DJs, stop the delay
Sisi tumefika	we have arrived
sasa tutawika.	Now we will scream (reign).

And the chorus begs the question "*kaĩ mũtaraigwa wega mũkĩna? mũkũina kaĩ mũtaraigwa wega, wega?* (don't you feel excited as you dance, as you dance aren't you excited?). This atmosphere of jubilation, is not, as in the case of both "4 in 1" and "*Wasee Githurai*" crowded by anxious thoughts of deprivation. In "*Ninanoki*" there is uninterrupted preoccupation with personal gratification, at both a social and a sexual level.

One of the strengths of "*Wasee Githurai*" comes from the way it constantly seeks alternatives out of this quagmire of need and insecurity that is so endemic of life in marginal spaces:

For real hapa Kenya,	Truly, here in Kenya
msee, stori huwanga hivi	man, this is the story
Shika shika mic karibu MCs	Grab a microphone, invite MCs
jenga CV	build a CV (repertoire)
Believe me, this just had to be on TV	
And other radio stations	
They wanna play my CDs	
Excuse me Mr. Joe	
You really don't have to pay me	
Just air my song	
And let, let it, let it play.	

Rather than wallow in disappointment and desire, the protagonists reveal a street smartness, a keen understanding of the way the Kenyan socioeconomic fabric, and not just life in marginal Githurai, functions. It is difficult not to read the parallels the song creates between, on the one hand, the fame and excitement of a career in music and, on the other, the ugly prospects of an emerging gun culture. As in the case of "*Unbwogable*" by Gidi Gidi Maji Maji musical engagement is suggested as a site of freedom, a legitimate way to seek recognition and come away from the margins of despair (Nyairo and Ogude 2005). The pitfalls of the music industry in Kenya are intimated in the lyrics of "*Wasee Githurai.*" Artists seldom get their dues from hustling DJs who are steeped in payola scandals. The majority of media houses, clubs, and hotels never live up to their royalty obligations to the Music Copyright Society of Kenya and, by extension, to the artists. In effect, and as the lyrics of "*Wasee Githurai*" intimate, the engagement with music pays not in monetary terms, but more in terms of opening new spaces of expression. Disorder and violence are quotidian aspects of life in Githurai. This is true whether one is talking of the patterns of land use, the crime and insecurity, or the shortchanging and hustling that confronts those who seek alternative forms of expression. Within this space, freedom can never be "a permanent state of grace" (Fabian 1998: 21). It can only come in moments such as those that Vinnie Googs and Banton enjoyed when their song dominated Kenyan airwaves and was nominated for a continental award. The residents of Githurai shared in this success and momentarily felt duly recognized as part of the city's fame and emergent urban culture. Looking at the song's opening chorus, it is clear that women's appreciation is key to contemporary notions of success and is perhaps even the biggest reward for acquiring fame.

When should we say,	
Let me see your hands up, baby	
Hii ni remix sawa,	this is a great remix
kwa mamanzi ni sawa	fit for all the beautiful girls.

And in one of the verses the song dwells on this desire to impress the ladies, on a reading of self and place that is dominated by the pursuit of leisure. Both success and leisure are conceived of in terms of nights of endless cavorting with the ladies:

Okay I'm called Googs	
and I come from Inner Core	[a section within Githurai]
I mean, and that's where	
na flash MCs ndani choo	I flash all the MCs in the toilet [beat the MCs at the rapping game]
Get it, get it, get it right, yoo, I'm on	
That's why the fly [sophisticated] *ladies*	
Wako [are] *busy on the floor*	

It becomes apparent therefore that in this urban environment success is in part defined and measured through the conquest of women. Seemingly the African urban landscape is still given to the commodification of women in ways that suggest conservative views of gender roles.

Of Local Mona Lisas

This persistent reading of place through a sexual grammar finds even greater resonance in "Mona Lisa" by Deux Vultures. The track appeared on the same *Ogopa 1* (2002) album that features "*Wasee Githurai.*" Whereas "4 in 1" and "*Wasee Githurai*" (re)imagine Nairobi's Eastlands, "Mona Lisa" poeticizes the Central Business District, the very heart of the city of Nairobi. Singing in praise of a beautiful city girl, Deux Vultures locate her on the prestigious Mama Ngina Street. In colonial Kenya this street was known as Queens Way. At independence the street was renamed after the first lady of Independent Kenya, Mama Ngina Kenyatta.

Naamka kumekucha	I wake up, dawn has come
Napita Mama Ngina	I pass Mama Ngina [Street]
Nasikia "eh kokoriko"	I hear [sound of a cock crowing]
(Chukua)	Take [sound of a coin being dropped]

Baada ya muda naona	After a while I see
Dame wa kisure	A smart/confident lady
Expensive kind of looking	
Utathani ametua	You'd imagine she flew [in from abroad]
Wacha nikwambie	Let me tell you
Dame alikuwa amevaa	The lady was wearing
A black stretcher	
A blue silky top	
and a pair of black sketchers	
an African queen,	
a rare kind of species none of you has ever seen	

Clearly the protagonist's choice of walking rather than driving on this street creates the opportunity for him to observe the things that happen along it at close range. Notice the juxtapositioning of Mama Ngina Street as a reputed site of privilege, with the sound of a cock crowing at dawn and then the metallic sound of a coin being dropped into a waiting receptacle. The Central Business District, and particularly Mama Ngina Street, carries all the prestige of the originally planned "green city." However, in the song "Mona Lisa" we hear sounds that suggest Mama Ngina Street has gradually been domesticated and absorbed into local urban practices. The age-old signal of daybreak—a cock crow—indicates the diffusion of urban agriculture. The jingle of coins hitting their target points to the unmistakable presence of Nairobi's street beggars into whose strategically placed bowls merciful pedestrians toss their offerings.

In colonial times the city center was a carefully planned part of the town, a showcase of Western modernity and the headquarters of consumer products. In "Mona Lisa," Mama Ngina Street's character has changed. Signs of incongruity abound, for it is along this same street that houses beggars that we encounter the expensively clad Mona Lisa. Looking like one fresh from a shopping trip abroad, she represents all that is modern and material on Mama Ngina Street, which boasts a number of top-class clothing outlets, some of them international chains. The description of Mona Lisa as an "African queen" is meant to localize her beauty. It challenges the idea that her adornments—"a black stretcher, a blue silky top and a pair of black Sketchers"—stand as the epitome of the latest in Western fashion. There is an apparent struggle here over the question of what constitutes African identity. The emphasis on African queen amounts to a cultural posturing that tries to deny the growing dominance of Western fashion and aesthetics within the local environment.

Mama Ngina Street defines both Mona Lisa and the protagonist who lusts after her. All the material trappings of modernity that are sold on Mama Ngina Street are imposed on this "rare kind of species" who is then turned into an object of male desire and fulfillment. And there are clear discourses of power and control that go with walking Mama Ngina Street. To reiterate, both the street and the African Mona Lisa represent the tensions between Western capital and the encroaching local initiative. Indeed, one can describe them both as walking sites of the perpetual contention between tradition and modernity. One can also see them as examples of the ways in which local agency continually absorbs modernity's agents creating a *bricolage* flow of influences and practices. Still, there is no denying that the ugly side of capitalism is briefly dramatized in the oblique reference to the beggar on the street. It is apparent in the dismissive aside, "*chukua*" (take), that accompanies the hastily tossed coins. This is an echo of the ways in which postcolonial nations have paid only lip-service to the growing masses of their have-nots. Second, one notes the articulation of control in the way the protagonist boasts of his hold over Mona Lisa: "*wazee kila siku wana uliza, dawa ngani nilifanya mpaka aka chiba*" (men are asking what magic potion I spun so that she could succumb to me). But even then, the protagonist repeatedly reveals Mona Lisa's very own seductive power: "*cheki Mona Lisa anaviyo tingisa, mimi nina baki nime jazzika*" (look at the way Mona Lisa swings, it leaves me utterly entranced).

In outlining this politics of control one can further argue that Mona Lisa too is the object of another form of control—that which is imposed on her by the dictates of fashion which prescribe to her what is vogue and what is outdated. Walking Mama Ngina Street, this street of liberation, modernity, and confinement gives Mona Lisa a nearly magical charm, so that much as she is herself commodified by its spaces, she in turn is bestowed by the very space with a capacity to enchant and control others. Again, by naming her Mona Lisa, after Leonardo da Vinci's portrait of beauty, Deux Vultures subvert a Western aesthetic icon, adapting it for local exigencies. They want to (re)present the idea of contemporary "African beauty" and they use a reference point that would be readily familiar to students of European history. They are perhaps alluding to the idea that local women are aesthetically equal to the classics upheld in Western art. And though the space being inhabited is a local one it retains the aura of its colonial design and demands the continued replication of aesthetic standards from another locale. Thus the artists momentarily switch to a smattering of French as a sign of their cosmopolitanism: "*Ca ve vous parlez Francais?*" In the persuasive attempts to lure Mona Lisa, the protagonist proceeds to invite her to other exciting locales around the city and beyond: "*Niku peleke Casablanca, Mombasa, Roasters, Salsa*" (Let me take you to Casablanca, Mombasa, Roasters, Salsa [dancing]).[29] Ultimately this song intimates that walking the Central Business District of Nairobi is an experience that continually thrusts one into the grip of Western modernity and its things of glamor.

CONCLUSION

Contemporary Kenyan popular music has opened up the frontiers of place through its rejection of the city as a totalizing experience, and its embrace of the newer zones in Nairobi (Nyairo 2005b; Nyairo and Ogude 2003; 2005). The spatial discourses in virtually all these songs are also engagements with class differentiation. Artists such as Ndarlin P openly sneer at middle-class aspirations and in turn celebrate ghetto existence. In giving lyrical resonance to popular idioms of class differentiation, such as *mababie*, these artists help to affirm the formation of social classes in Nairobi. Like the tunes of old that Atieno Odhiambo (2002: 264) reads in "*Kula Raha*: Gendered Discourses and the Contours of Leisure in Nairobi, 1946–63," contemporary Kenyan songs similarly persist in capturing "class differentiation within the African urban social formation" in Nairobi. The new songs emphasize the city as a place of heterogeneity, a place of ethnic and cultural variety in which people are sometimes identified and even pigeonholed on account of the way they speak/sound. The cosmopolitan potential of these sounds is evidenced in the rap songs' easy association of sounds and meanings from ethnic languages and accents as they are mapped onto the English language and also onto sociocultural nuances from Europe and America.

In large measure, these songs focus on life in Nairobi's marginal spaces. They sketch into local cultural imagination and memory the new spaces, those where native ingenuity has dictated new ways of occupying urban space, which has transformed notions of town planning by injecting the agency and enterprise of those living there. Through songs like "4 in 1" and "*Wasee Githurai*," one captures the spatial and the social geography of these areas, and gains a better understanding of the people who inhabit these spaces, and of the pleasures and dreams that daily lubricate their existence. The visual and aural images that these songs generate signal an urban essence that continually points to the social production of space in ways that are very different from the ideal(ized) city that was conceived in colonial Kenya. These songs demonstrate the informalization of urban practice. It is an informality that domesticates the urban environment, making it less alien and hostile for the residents. We see that urban space demands creative ingenuity, so that within it new norms and habits of existence are adopted. African modernity is clearly about constant newness even though this newness often stems from the powerful pull toward localized processes, such as the ethnic cuisine that is described in "4 in 1." The mimicking voice in this song mirrors not simply the class anger and envy of those in the slums observing the comforts of the upper classes, it actually parallels Nairobi's own mimickry of global concepts of town planning and urban design. It is as if to say that Nairobi only pretends to be a modern enclave whereas in fact its character is derived more from the ethnic ingenuity that has collapsed all plans of a green city and made illegal densification and informal settlements the order of the city's development.

In virtually all the song-texts I have analyzed here, the depiction of the city is never linear or uniform; it is fraught with tensions and contradictions that signal the serious limitations of the very spaces under discussion. These are songs about hunger and desire, about the inhibitions and restrictions surrounding daily existence in the city. As such, these texts never really succeed in subverting official discourses on slums and informal settlements, though we do see the artists attempts to generate new terms for reading marginal(ized) society. Like American hip-hop of the late 1980s, which moved away from "the spatial abstractions framed by the notion of 'the ghetto' to the more localized and specific discursive construct of 'the hood' " (Forman 2000: 68), Ndarlin P shuns the official term "slum." Not even the more politically correct expression "informal settlement" is found to be acceptable. In their place, the artists use "ghetto," seeing it as a more credible term to capture this existence. Perhaps ghetto is seen as a more favorable label because of its association with African American existence, which in the local Kenyan contexts is a desirable lifestyle often read as signifying positive difference and cultural agency (Behrend 2002). Alternative discourses of Nairobi's spaces also come from the way the songs show the cultural economy of informal settlements and reconfigured city estates as one that is governed by ingenious native enterprise and accompanied by romance and leisure in refreshing new ways. But even then there is a tendency to somehow undermine these alternatives in the underlying subscription to the idea that these are irredeemable urban spaces of want and violence that constitute an emergent Kenyan ghetto culture.

From these songs we also learn that space is a central element in the formation of character. As the young artists in "*Wasee Githurai*" rap personably about themselves, we realize that it is that location, that very site of marginality, impending violence with momentary distractions of partying, that have shaped these young men. They project Githurai as the cornerstone of their livelihood and identity. Indeed one could say that the characters that people all these songs are strongly defined by their structural environments. The dominant architectural modes reflect much of what de Certeau terms "surreptitious creativity," and it is precisely this moral logic that we see reflected in the characters. In other words, one can put up a case for the relationship between the spectacle of spatial "disarray" and the preponderance of violence and insecurity in Nairobi. The decay of the "Green City in the Sun" is shown to transcend mere physical deterioration. It has affected the whole system of order. In the same way that city estates long lost their original design and pattern, so too has the logic of disorder crept into the lives of city residents who have metamorphosed dramatically to embrace an inverted morality whose main guide is the ceaseless hunt for money.

Additionally, the spatial legacies of these contemporary songs problematize the praxes of "tradition" and "modernity" in entirely new ways, opening us up to the realization that cultural boundaries are continually open to (re)negotiation. Indeed, contact with place is shown to alter practice, demand changes, and accommodate innovation. Thus even where the notion of "home" is not articulated by direct naming, there is nonetheless an overt statement of place as originary, as root rather than route. The protagonists in "4 in 1," and "*Wasee Githurai*," may desire upward mobility and more privileged living spaces, but they certainly do not consider themselves to be passing through Mukuru, or Githurai, en route from some rural enclave that has a first claim over them culturally. To reiterate Alessandro Triulzi's (1996: 81) argument,

> Today's urban Africans are no longer "strangers in the city" as they were called in colonial literature: frightened peasants in an environment not their own, that was not *for* them who were passing through. Now most of them are born in the city or have adapted to it and redefined their own role in the urban context, elaborating new ways of survival, new forms of communication and connection.

Colonial policy and attitudes had colluded with ethnic cultural practice to enforce the idea that the city was only a place of temporary abode and that ancestral location was the proper formulation of home. The evidence from contemporary Kenyan popular music indicates that economic circumstances and emergent cultural alternatives have challenged the validity of this mindset.

NOTES

An earlier version of this article is contained in my unpublished PhD thesis, " 'Reading the Referents': (Inter)textuality in Contemporary Kenyan Popular Music," University of the Witwatersrand (2005).

1. Tricia Rose's (1994) study of African American hip-hop underlines the discursive senses in which this music represents the (neighbor)hood and the ghetto. She details names of groups and songs, lyrics, CD sleeves, music videos, and fashion styles as key constituents of the ways in which hip-hop symbolically (re)defines and (re)creates these spaces that embodied the neglect and discrimination of African Americans, turning them into significant makers of self and of contemporary African American culture. See also Kelly Askew's (2002) demonstration of how Taraab music grew as a popular form of expression and overran official state policy to become one of the defining hallmarks of Tanzania's Swahili identity.
2. Deux Vultures, the duo behind "Mona Lisa" (Moustafa Daudi and Thomas Gonzanga), are originally from Tanzania. I have included their work in this study first because they reside and record in Nairobi and second, because of the specific ways in which their work engages with the social geography of this city. The song appeared mid-2002 on a pirated CD entitled *Best of Kenyan Artists* whose design imitates that of Audio Vault Studios' Ivory Island Record label and the album sleeve even carries the Ivory Island logo.
3. "Green City in the Sun" is the motto of the City of Nairobi since colonial times.
4. Roger Kurtz (1998: 77) explains that the development of "Nairobi offered a perfect opportunity for colonial authorities to experiment with urban planning. Nairobi's design was the result of two predominant and not necessarily conflicting imperatives. On the one hand to create a model of the Garden City, a concept that was becoming important in British urban planning at the end of the nineteenth century; and on the other hand to create an essentially European city in the African setting based on the South African model."
5. This policy of ethnic zoning reached its peak at the onset of Mau Mau. "All Kikuyu were prohibited from entering the Eastleigh district of the city . . . . Bahati and Kariokor were made exclusively Kikuyu estates, and those Kikuyu settled in the better neighbourhood housing at Ziwani and Kaloleni were forced to move out in October 1953" (Anderson 2005: 193).
6. Kareng'ata is the name that the (mostly white) residents of Karen and the neighboring Lang'ata adopted in the 1990s as they waged their legal battles against the Nairobi City Council over poor provision of services and their right to withhold land rates.
7. Gikuyu for train, it refers to a specific dance routine. See Maina Mutonya (2005) for a discussion of *Mugiithi* performance and Gikuyu ethnic identity.
8. In " 'Reading the Referents': (Inter)textuality in Contemporary Kenyan Popular Music," I address the factors behind both the decline of the 1970s and 1980s, and also those that account for the resurgence period since the mid-1990s.
9. Personal interview, together with James Ogude, Nairobi, May 6, 2003.
10. *Ndarlin P* is a bastardized version of Anthony Alex Wainaina's sobriquet, "Darling of the People." Rendered in a Kamba accent, it promotes Wainaina's image as a master of local comic hip-hop.
11. Sheng is an urban bricolage language that combines words and structures from Swahili, English, and a variety of Kenyan ethnic languages (Githiora 2002; Nyairo and Ogude 2003).
12. The local name for private commuter vehicles. *Tatu* is Swahili for three. The name *matatu* was coined to reflect the 30 cents—3 ten-cent coins—fare that these private

vehicles charged on intercity routes in 1950s Nairobi, and which was comparatively far lower than the charges on the Municipal run bus service (Graebner 1992).

13. In this and many other instances, we see a parodying of the discourses of representation and turf wars that have typified the popularity contests between African American rappers from the East Side (Bronx, New York) tipped against their opponents from the West Side (Compton, California). See Murray Forman (2000: 81).
14. Over the last 20 years, Kenya's informal sector has come to be known by the colloquial Swahili reference for difficult working conditions *jua kali*—"scorching sun." Kenneth King (1996: 44–51) makes a detailed study of the "jua-kalification of Nairobi" and makes particular note of the way residential areas in Eastlands double up as commercial outlets. A 1972 ILO report of Kenyan employment described its informal sector as the source of livelihood for a large percentage of the urban population and categorized taxi drivers as belonging to this group of low-wage small-scale occupation. The Traffic Amendment Act (2003) was a first in government attempts to regulate public transport.
15. In March 1983, President Moi dissolved the Nairobi City Council, suspended the mayor of Nairobi, and in place of the elected council, appointed a City Commission whose mandate was to run council affairs. This Commission's performance was ofttimes compromised by shady deals and manipulation by the Executive.
16. Marc Howard Ross's (1973) study of Nairobi's Mathare Valley residents—*The Political Integration of Urban Squatters*—provides a concrete study of the possibilities and levels of social and political organization in informal urban settlements. But, and largely on account of a lack of political will and intervention, even where it exists, the ability of squatters to generate a sense of community in Nairobi's Eastlands has not led to a positive physical change in their spatial habitation or to the provision of infrastructure and social services.
17. I have reproduced the lyrics as they appear on the album without the proper Gĩkũyũ orthography.
18. The word "Buru Buru" is a corruption of the Maasai word "Emburbul," which loosely means a marshy place. However, it is the area to the far east of the estate—where Doonholm and Tena estate now stand—that previously formed swampy ground. The area where Buru Buru Estate was built was vast grassland plain.
19. Prior to 1950, Africans were expected to provide their own housing in designated "Native Locations." Furedi further argues that this colonial "color bar" that governed residential areas in the city was "partly legalized by more than 100 ordinances and was partly social." Kurtz (1998: 78) reports: "The early planning commissions—the Williams Report of 1907, the Simpson Report of 1913, and the Feetham Report of 1926—recommended explicitly racial segregation as the basis for city planning."
20. Along Jogoo Road lie Makadara, Ofafa Kunguni, Maringo, Kaloleni, Muthurwa amongst other high-density low-income estates. Along Juja Road is the expansive Mathare slum and the vast Eastleigh division, which has gradually descended into a highly populous low-income area. Komarock estate is on Kangundo Road.
21. Though *mababie* seems to connote the popular Barbie dolls, the term, as Chege Githiora (2002: 178) notes, is more likely derived from the biblical reference to the Babylonians.
22. Puff Daddy is a famous American hip-hop producer and artist; he changed his name to P. Diddy and is now simply known as Diddy.
23. In verse two, Ndarlin P, the master rapper, is introduced as coming from Sinai, another slum bordering the Industrial Area. But he goes on to brag that he is "a gee from the Westside Nailovi," which is clearly meant as a mocking taunt to imitate the territorial rivalries between American hip-hop artists (Forman 2000).

24. Aside from the obvious physical aggression that is nurtured in spaces of want and spatial congestion, colonial authorities in Kenya had established social halls with all manner of sports and recreational facilities for the residents. Amongst these were the boxing and training halls at Pumwani, Kaloleni, "Dallas" Muthurwa, Jericho, and Kariakor. Steve Waruingi, Kenya's first international medallist (Bronze, 1970 Commonwealth Games), Steve Muchoki (Gold medallist 1974 King's Cup in Bangkok), and Robert Wangila Napunyi, the first and only Kenyan Olympic Gold medallist (Seoul, 1988), all grew into their careers from these Eastlands boxing halls.
25. There are many contemporary songs such as Kalamashaka's "*Tafsiri Hii*" (1998), K-South's "Nairobbery" (1999), and Eric Wainaina's "*Usiku wa Manane*" (2001) that detail to an even greater extent than "*Wasee Githurai*" Nairobi's hideous underbelly and its capacity for rapid, ruthless violence and widespread insecurity at the hands of daring criminals and wayward security agents alike. Owing to the need for brevity however, I am compelled to leave these songs out of the present analysis of representations of the city in this chapter.
26. Zimmerman neighbors Githurai to the West.
27. *Ninanoki* is a Sheng expression meaning "I lose control."
28. "Leo ni Leo" by E-Sir is another example of the socioeconomically differentiated sense of leisure in Nairobi's up-market locations.
29. Casablanca and Roasters are popular clubs in Nairobi, and Mombasa, which is on the Kenyan coast, is the hub of the country's recreation and tourism.

BIBLIOGRAPHY

Anderson, David. 2005. *Histories of the Hanged: The Dirty War in Kenya and the End of Empire*. London: Norton.

Agnew, John, John Mercer, and David Sopher (eds.). 1984. *The City in Cultural Context*. Boston: Allen & Unwin.

Askew, Kelly. 2002. *Performing the Nation: Swahili Music and Cultural Politics in Tanzania*. Chicago: Universiy of Chicago Press.

Bachelard, Gaston. 1964. *The Poetics of Space*. Trans. Maria Jolas. New York: Orion Press.

Behrend, Heike. 2002. " 'I am Like a Movie Star in My Street': Photographic Self-Creation in Postcolonial Kenya," in Richard Werbner and Terence Ranger (eds.). *Postcolonial Subjectivities in Africa*. London: Zed Books, pp. 44–62.

Clifford, James. 1992. "Traveling Cultures," in L. Grossberg, C. Nelson, and P. Treichler (eds.). *Cultural Studies*. London and New York: Routledge, pp. 96–116.

Connell, John and Chris Gibson. 2003. *Sound Tracks: Popular Music, Identity and Place*. London: Routledge.

de Certeau, Michel. 1993. "Walking in the City," in Simon During (ed.). *The Cultural Studies Reader*. London: Routledge, pp. 151–160.

de Certeau, Michel, Luce Giard, and Pierre Mayol. 1998. *The Practice of Everyday Life*, Vol. 2. Minneapolis: University of Minnesota Press.

Fabian, Johannes. 1998. *Moments of Freedom: Anthropology and Popular Culture*. Charlottesville and London: University Press of Virginia.

Feld, Steven. 1996. "Waterfalls of Song: An Acoustemology of Place Resounding in Bosavi, Papua New Guinea," in Steven Feld and Keith H. Basso (eds.). *Senses of Place*. Santa Fe: School of American Research Press, pp. 91–135.

Finnegan, Ruth. 1989. *The Hidden Musicians: Music-Making in an English Town*. Cambridge: Cambridge University Press.

Forman, Murray. 2000. " 'Represent': Race, Space and Place in Rap Music," *Popular Music* 19 (1): 65–90.

Foucault, Michel. 1980. *Power/Knowledge: Selected Interviews and Other Writings, 1972–1977.* New York: Harvester Wheatsheaf.

Furedi, Frank. 1973. "The African Crowd in Nairobi: Popular Movements and Elite Politics," *Journal of African History* 16 (2): 275–290.

Gikandi, Simon. 2000. " 'Reading the Referent': Postcolonialism and the Writing of Modernity," in Shusheila Nasta (ed.). *Reading the New Literatures in a Postcolonial Era.* London: Cambridge, pp. 87–104.

Githiora, Chege. 2002. "Sheng: Peer Language, Swahili dialect or emerging Creole?" *Journal of African Cultural Studies* 15 (2):159–181.

Graham, Ronnie. 1989. *Stern's Guide to Contemporary African Music.* London: Pluto Press.

Graebner, Werner. 1992. *Sokomoko: Popular Culture in East Africa.* Amsterdam/ Atlanta: Rodopi.

Hanks, W. F. 1989. "Text and Textuality," *Annual Review of Anthropology* (18): 95–127.

King, Kenneth. 1996. *Jua Kali Kenya: Change and Development in an Informal Economy 1970–95.* London: James Currey.

Kristeva, Julia. 1980. *Desire in Language: A Semiotic Approach to Literature and Art.* New York: Columbia University Press.

Kurtz, J. Roger. 1998 *Urban Obsessions, Urban Fears: The Postcolonial Kenyan Novel.* Trenton, NJ: Africa World Press.

Mutonya, Maina. 2005. "*Mugiithi* Performance: Popular Music, Stereotypes and Ethnic Identity," *Africa Insight* 35 (2): 53–60.

Nyairo, Joyce. 2005a. " 'Reading the Referents': (Inter)textuality in Contemporary Kenyan Popular Music." Unpublished Ph.D. dissertation. University of the Witwatersrand.

Nyairo, Joyce. 2005b. "*Zilizopendwa: Kayamba Afrika's* Use of Cover Versions, Remix and Sampling in the (Re)Membering Of Kenya," *African Studies* 64 (1): 29–54.

Nyairo, Joyce and James Ogude. 2003. "Popular Music and Negotiation of Contemporary Kenyan Identity," *Social Identities* 9 (3): 383–400.

Nyairo, Joyce and James Ogude. 2005. "Popular Music, Popular Politics: '*Unbwogable*' & The Idioms of Freedom In Contemporary Kenyan Popular Music," *African Affairs* 104 (415): 225–249.

Ochieng, Crispino C. 2001. "Planned Housing in *Komarock* Nairobi, Changes Due to Ten Years of Illegal Densification" <www.ucl.ac.uk/dpu–projects.pdf>.

Odhiambo, Atieno. 2002. "*Kula Raha*: Gendered Discourses and the Contours of Leisure in Nairobi, 1946–1963," *Azania: Journal of the British Institute in Eastern Africa, The Urban Experience in East Africa* 36–37: 254–264.

Olson, M. 1998. " 'Everybody Loves Our Town': Scenes, Spatiality, Migrancy," in T. Swiss, J. Sloop, and A. Herman (eds.). *Mapping the Beat.* Oxford: Blackwell, pp. 269–289.

Robins, Steven. 2000. "City Sites," in Sarha Nuttal and Ceryl-Ann Michael (eds.). *Senses of Culture.* Cape Town: Oxford University Press

Rose, Tricia. 1994. *Black Noise: Rap Music and Black Culture in Contemporary America.* Hanover and London: Wesleyan University Press.

Ross, Marc Howard. 1973. *The Political Integration of Urban Squatters.* Evanston, IL: Northwestern Press.

Said, Edward. 1995. *Orientalism: Western Conceptions of the Orient.* London: Penguin.

Samper, David. 2004. " 'Africa Is Still Our Mama': Kenyan Rappers, Youth Identity, and the Revitalization of Traditional Values," *African Identities* 2 (1): 37–51.

Soja, Edward. 1989. *Postmodern Geographies: The Reassertion of Space in Critical Social Theory.* London: Verso.

Stapleton, Chris and Chris May. 1989. *Africa All-Stars: The Pop Music of a Continent.* London: Palladin.

Triulzi, Alessandro. 1996. "African Cities, Historical Memory and Street Buzz," in Iain Chambers and Linda Curti (eds.). *The Post-Colonial Question: Common Skies, Divided Horizons.* London: Routledge, pp. 78–92.

Wallis, Roger and Krister Malm. 1984. *Big Sounds from Small Peoples: The Music Industry in Small Countries.* New York: Pendragon Press.

Discography

Deux Vultures, "Mona Lisa," *Ogopa 1: Kenyan Club Classics*, Ogopa DJs, 2002

Gidi Gidi Maji Maji, "*Unbwogable*," Blu Zebra Records (Tedd Josiah), 2002

Googs and Vinnie Banton, "*Wasee Githurai,*" *Ogopa 1: Kenyan Club Classics*, Ogopa DJs, 2002

Nameless, *"Ninanoki,"* *Ogopa 1: Kenyan Club Classics*, Ogopa DJs, 2002 and *On Fire* Ogopa DJs (2003)

Ndarlin P, "4 in 1," *Kenyan, The Second Chapter*, Audio Vault Studios (Tedd Josiah), Ivory Island Records, 1999

Photographic Essay 1

Johannesburg Fortified

Martin J. Murray (Text) and
Juanita Malan (Photography)

Johannesburg in Verse

Thesis One

Johannesburg is an accidental city. No gold, no city. The gold is gone, and the big mining operations have moved on. The city remains. The end of *Apartheid* did not erase, obliterate, or suppress the spatial legacies of white minority rule.

Thesis Two

Johannesburg is a sprawling megalopolis at war with itself. The accumulation of wealth for the few is matched by the accumulation of misery for the many. The powerful, privileged, and propertied have retreated into the City of Spectacle: the Sandton City Mall, Sandton Square, Melrose Arch, Montecasino, Dainfern, and so forth. For the desperate urban poor huddled in makeshift shacks, sleeping in Joubert Park, and squatting in abandoned buildings, Egoli is the nightmare city where the hopes and dreams of a better life are overshadowed by hopelessness and despair.

Thesis Three

Johannesburg is an angular city, consisting of tall sleek buildings, encircled by high-speed freeways, bisected by arterial roadways, partitioned into fortified enclaves, protected by armies of private security police. Neighbors do not even know each other. Most of the time, they do not even want to get to know each other.

Thesis Four

Johannesburg is just about the only major city in the world without the sea, a mountain, or a river. Without the topographical beauty of Cape Town, middle-class residents of Jozy feel deprived. Whereas the Cape Town shoreline rivals the coast south of San Francisco, the old mine dumps south of the central city are just piles of yellow-colored dirt.

So what to do? With little else to brag about, city builders in Johannesburg have always sought after the biggest and the tallest buildings. The Hillbrow Tower is the highest structure in Johannesburg. Ponte City is the tallest apartment building on the African continent. At 223 meters in height, the Carlton Centre is the tallest building on the African continent. The observation deck at the top is cool place, unless you are scared of heights. A private company called Business Against Crime (renamed Cueincident) has commandeered the entire fifth floor, where it has constructed the most sophisticated Closed Circuit Television (CCTV) operation anywhere in the world outside of London. Dozens of operatives scan hundreds of monitors twenty-four hours a day, seven days a week. When I toured the facilities, I did not see any operatives shift their gaze from the six screens mounted in front of them. The war on crime never stops. No one will win.

Thesis Five

After dark, motorists do not stop for red lights. On some streets during the day, it is not a good idea to stop or even slow down. The police do not seem to mind.

Thesis Six

With an official population figure of over 350,000 residents, Alexandra township is a densely packed, overcrowded urban slum located across the N1 freeway from Sandton, the richest square mile on the African continent. The Jukskei River regularly floods, causing a great deal of hardship for the "poorest of the poor" who built shacks along its banks. When a cholera outbreak took place in 2001, leaving a number of poor black people dead, white residents in nearby middle-class suburbs went into a panic, draining their swimming pools, running up the price of bottled water, and making their maids submit to medical examinations.

Thesis Seven

If you want the real fake, go to Montecasino Shopping Mall and gambling casino. If you want the fake fake, go to Moyos Restaurant at Melrose Arch where *faux*-Moroccan waitresses will help you wash your hands "the African way." If you want kitsch, go to the downmarket theme park called Gold Reef City. You can drop 200 feet into a fake gold mine for a fake gold mining experience. Real gold mines are two and half miles deep. If you want a heavy dose of realism, go to the *Apartheid* Museum connected to Gold Reef City casino. If you want to have fun, go to FNB Stadium on the way to Soweto, and watch the Orlando Pirates beat the Mamelodi Sundowns. Be careful on the way out.

Thesis Eight

At night, the streetscape of the central city is an eerie place. Some parts—those where the big banks and tall skyscrapers are located—are bathed in the indirect light of security cameras. A few scattered fast-food outlets are illuminated. Huge stretches of the streetscape are cloaked in shadows. Black people walking on the sidewalks blend into the darkness.

Thesis Nine

The older middle-class suburbs are scattered in a wide arc around the central city, radiating from the northwest (Melville, Emmerentia) to the Far North, and from northeast (Sandton, Hyde Park, Sandhurst) to the southeast (Kensington). Whereas middle-class suburban residents ride in cars, the poor walk. For one, the pace is quick—very quick. For the other, the pace is slow—very slow. Sidewalks are not a priority in affluent neighborhoods. Suburbanites drive from one locked and secured private compound to another, taking care to check the streets for suspicious looking characters before entering or exiting cocooned enclaves. In the meantime, the legions of urban toilers—maids, cooks, child-minders, gardeners, itinerant builders, car washers, security guards, and those able-bodied young men looking for old jobs—walk along the suburban streets, taking care not to get too close to fenced-in yards lest they be attacked by vicious guard dogs.

Thesis Ten

Entrepreneurs and petty traders have come from China, settling on the eastern edge of the central city. Cyrildene has become the new Chinatown, filled with restaurants, Chinese lettering on buildings, and cheap imported goods. Meanwhile, the minuscule pocket of the original Chinese residents has fallen into disrepair. In 1902, Alfred Lord Milner authorized the importation of around 60,000 Chinese laborers to help jump-start the flagging gold mining industry after the end of the South African War. In 1906, when they were no longer needed, Chinese laborers were expelled en masse. A few avoided the dragnet, and settled at the western end of town, near Marshalltown. Many Chinese who died were buried in graves marked with Chinese characters at the old Crown Mines site. Fast-forward to the present: not much remains to signal the presence of the original Chinese community, except perhaps the Chon Hing Restaurant. Located in Alexander Street, Ferreirastown, around the corner from Swallows Inn and opposite John Vorster Square (the notorious police station), the Chon Hing is a cramped place offering inexpensive food in an abandoned and rundown part of downtown at the southwestern corner. The new Chinese barely know about the old Chinese.

Sutured City

Catwalks, skyways, and underground passageways provide modes of movement whereby the office workers can negotiate the cityscape without venturing into the dangerous streets. The creation of City Improvement Districts has enabled large-scale property owners to colonize the downtown streetscape. The ABSA "family of buildings" in the east, the majestic BankCity precinct in the west, the sprawling Standard Bank complex along Simmons Street are exemplary expressions of public–private partnerships that have partitioned the cityscape into fortified enclaves.

Photo P1.1 Sutured city

RETREAT INTO FORTIFIED LUXURY

The Greater Johannesburg metropolitan region has experienced extensive horizontal growth. Virtually all the new residential housing construction along the outer edge of the metropolis has been built behind high walls with well-guarded entry-and-exit points. Enclave housing typologies range from affordable townhouse cluster developments to exclusive gated residential communities built around artificial lakefronts, eighteen-hole golf courses, and imported parklands. Individual housing units in upscale gated residential communities are outfitted with the latest security technologies, including infrared cameras, CCTV, panic rooms, motion detectors, internal security gates, and high-voltage fencing.

Gated residential communities have sprouted like wild mushrooms on the exurban fringe. Construction protocols dictate that the corporate builders erect the elaborate front gates and high walls before they start to work on the McMansions. In contrast to Walter Benjamin who explored urban modernity by excavating its ruins, it is also instructive to anticipate where Johannesburg might be going by gazing at the City yet to Come, the new urban landscape in embryo. Photograph P1.2 captures the birth of the Future City.

SUBURBAN SECESSION

Affluent residents of older suburban neighborhoods have unilaterally erected street barricades and security fences in order to keep out unwanted Others. City

Photo P1.2 Retreat into fortified luxury

Photo P1.3 Suburban secession

officials have declared these *revanchist* actions to be illegal. Armed with lawyers, motivated by fear of crime, and energized by the rhetoric of property rights, affluent suburbanites have mounted a war of position, fending off those who would force them to dismantle their barricades.

Photo P1.4 Street hawkers

STREET HAWKERS

Curbside traders have proliferated all over the downtown streetscape of Johannesburg. The steady expansion of City Improvement Districts has effectively partitioned the central city into a seriated agglutination of fortified enclaves where itinerant hawkers are not welcome. Municipal authorities have called for strict enforcement of city bylaws to clear the sidewalks and to force street traders into officially sanctioned informal marketplaces. Profit margins are very low. These itinerant hawkers play a cat-and-mouse game with the police, who regularly harass and threaten them. Xenophobia has found a vulnerable target. Youthful gangs sometimes attack immigrant traders, stealing their goods and driving them into ethnic enclaves. Social exclusion is a banal practice interwoven into the routines of everyday life in the city.

CITY IN RUINS

Old buildings acquire the patina of history: their tired facades often retain clues (hidden in fading lettering and decaying architecture) of a once elegant past. The derelict, boarded up Chelsea Hotel in Catherine Street (at the border between Hillbrow and Berea) symbolizes the end of an era and the start of another. In the 1960s and 1970s, the Chelsea was a preferred hang-out for the bohemian, white middle class who had grown weary of the sterility of the monochromatic northern suburbs. Music, beer, and dancing. As a former patron told me, the terrace of the Chelsea was the best place to sit for a cold beer delivered by smartly dressed black waiters in dark suits with a nice view down Pretoria Street in the sunset. Starting in the 1980s, the Chelsea went into

Photo P1.5 City in ruins

decline, as Hillbrow mutated from a white, middle-class mecca of high-rise apartment buildings, nightclubs, and upscale shops, into an urban slum filled with transient work-seekers, impoverished immigrants, youthful runaways, criminal gangs, and the desperately poor who had nowhere else to go. By the late 1990s, the Chelsea had become a notorious brothel, the end of the line for underaged girls. City officials closed the place down, and surrounded the premises with concertina wire to prevent homeless squatters from moving in. That tactic has not always worked.

4

Douala: Inventing Life in an African Necropolis

Basile Ndjio

Introduction

Many contemporary African urban agglomerations manifest themselves as inverted forms of the good city (Hall 2002; Lynch 1981) or the city of tomorrow, like the one Le Corbusier (1971) dreamt of in the early twentieth century, when modernist utopianism was the order of the day. Moreover, the chaotic, informal, and dreadful character of most postcolonial African cities sets them aside from the imagined city as a humanistic place (Boyer 1983; Ferguson 1999; Holston 1989), or as the embodiment of the ideal of community (Bender 2002; Donald 1999; Young 1986). This dystopian vision of a contemporary African city is informed by the observation that, as a result of the disintegration of many sub-Saharan African states because of sustained economic decline, their urban landscapes have been transformed into what I call a *necropolis*. By necropolis, I refer to a thespian city where insecurity, violence, and terror have become the daily experience of the vast majority of city dwellers, whose lives are permanently subjugated to the power of hazard and uncertainty, and above all to the tyranny of death. In order words, the necropolis is a place where the very fact of living is abridged to the elementary art of learning how not to be turned into a *mort-vivant* (living-dead). Besides being the city of tragedy, horror, and anxiety, the necropolis is also characterized by the stunning infrastructure of decay and the architecture of decline (Courade 2000; Donald 1999; Konings 2004; Mbembe 2003; Seraphin 2000), which constitute the "physical life of crisis," as Filip de Boeck (2004: 3) observes about Kinshasa, another necropolis.

I have not chosen this concept of *necropolis* in order to update the old nihilistic literature of the early twentieth century that represented the city as a space of alienation and estrangement, a site of marginalization and exclusion of the working classes, a concentration of poverty and misery, or the breeding ground for disease and corruption.[1] Nor is it my intention to endorse the reactionary anti-urbanist ideology of the 1990s, to which Neil Smith (1996) has provided a sound critique. I instead use this concept of the necropolis to describe the new configuration of the postcolonial African city in times of economic recession and structural adjustment that have prompted not only the "privatization" of many African municipalities, but also their "criminalization" and "informalization" (Bayart et al. 1999; Bremner 2000; Chabal and Daloz 1999; Roitman 2005).

The aim of this chapter is to analyze the effect of the necropolis on its dwellers' behavior, and the various individual or collective strategies to invent a new form of life in this concrete jungle. As I discuss in the following pages, one of the ruses that enables the necropolitan dweller to cheat death or to escape tragedy consists of imagining the city as a *hedonopolis* or a *cité de la joie*, as the popular imagination calls it in Cameroon—that is, a space of pleasure and desire. I focus my analysis on the city of Douala, which is the largest urban agglomeration in Cameroon. This fluvial port city of nearly three million inhabitants (Konings 2004; Séraphin 2000; Warnier 1993) is of interest to the study of the contemporary African metropolis because it is an emblematic figure of what I call a necropolis. Indeed, very few African urban agglomerations exemplify the necropolis more than Douala—the city of crime and death, the spectacular infrastructure of lack and incompleteness, the aesthetics of ugliness, and the security-obsessed paranoia that affects the city dwellers' life. In this city, routinized violence and terror have created an intimacy between life and death, the living and the dead. A familiarity, not to say a complicity, that ends up turning what is generally experienced as tragic (death) into a comedy or hilarity.

Welcome to the *Ghettopolis*

Like many so-called Third World urban agglomerations in general, and African cities in particular, Douala is manifested above all as a *ghettopolis*. This expression refers not only to the city of destitution and misery, or to the spatial concentration of millions of destitute urban dwellers in squatters and fringe settlements, and other disenfranchised areas (Appadurai 1990; Bridge and Watson 2002; Caldeira 2000; Davis 1992), it also accounts for what Gleeson (1999) calls a "disabling city" whose physical infrastructure is falling or has crumbled. This condition of imperfection and defect often gives the urban infrastructure the character of a simulacrum, as de Boeck (2004) suggested for Kinshasa.

In reaction to the official propaganda about the *grandes réalisations* (great achievements) of President Paul Biya (in power since 1982), in May 2004 the Cameroonian independent newspaper *Mutations* published a special issue on the cities of Cameroon. Most of the contributors were sociologists, town planners, architects, and geographers. They observed that the present neglected state of many Cameroonian cities made people feel nostalgic about the former Ahidjo regime (1960–1982), and even about the colonial period when cities were at least kept clean, as one of the authors of the articles put it. For instance, in his editorial, the newspaper's editor-in-chief ironically commented that one of the greatest achievements of Biya's regime was the extraordinary transformation of most urban agglomerations of the country, most notably Douala, from the *belle ville* (beautiful city) to the *cité-poubelles* (dumping city), and to the *ville cruelle* (cruel city). In support of this point of view, the journal issued a series of pictures that dramatized to excess not only the ecology of degradation and pollution, but also the violent, murderous, and inhuman aspects of this metropolis, which formerly embodied the modernity expectations in this country. Some photos represented abandoned buildings and dilapidated roads. Others showed streets, junctions, crossroads, intersections, and other public spaces turned into rubbish dumps.

In contrast to what Achille Mbembe (2004: 373–405) has written about Johannesburg, Douala saturates its public, social, and cultural spaces not with flows of money and new technologies, commodity, and superfluity, but rather with deficiency and scarcity. This paucity makes the city look impotent and incomplete (see also Bremner 2000; Mbembe and Nuttall 2000; and Simone 2004). If Benjamin's bourgeois *flâneur* had lived in this African necropolis, he would not have enjoyed walking down the streets because the few available sidewalks have been turned into free markets by street vendors, or are constantly congested by drivers who are trying to get around the potholes that generally riddle the roads. Benjamin's famous character would also have been in danger, since at night there are no streetlights to prevent the walker from falling into one of the countless open sewers that deface the public space (Benjamin 1973). Like the local bourgeoisie who secludes itself in fortress-like enclaves, he would have contracted the pathology of agoraphobia and claustrophobia, because of the fear of contact with one of these three million *sauveteurs* (itinerant traders) and *débrouillards* (those who fend for themselves) who make their living by walking the city streets all day long, like a "commuter bus" (Moyer 2002: 185). Against his wishes, he would have become a stay-at-home, because his sensitive nose would not have withstood the nauseating odors that come from open sewers and polluted rivers. Nor would he have withstood seeing pavements being littered with shells, carcasses, and decomposing bodies, which people often step over with total indifference. Like many of the city dwellers, he would have been confronted with regular shortages of domestic gas, and power and water cuts that compel many dwellers to drink water from polluted wells, or to light up with kerosene lamps or candles. He would have experienced, too, the lack of sanitary facilities that forces residents of the destitute neighborhoods to live in "an ecology of faecal odors, piles, and channels, where cooking water, washing water, and shit-bearing water are not carefully segregated, adds material health risks to the symbolic risks incurred by shitting in public view," as Appadurai (2002: 39) observed about Mumbai.

Had the *flâneur* decided to go on a tour of the city, he would have been obliged to use the popular *bendskin* (motorbike-taxi), because it is the only mode of transport well adapted to the poor state of the city roads (Ngabmen 2002). In his wandering, he would not have found any public transportation, garden, amusement park, or educational or sport center. Nor would he have seen any museum or library that could have helped him improve his knowledge about this postcolonial city. But he would have discovered concentric zones of poverty and misery in the immense inner suburb of New Bell, the poorest and the most overpopulated neighborhood in Cameroon, where nearly one million disenfranchised urban dwellers live not only in insecure conditions, but also in a state of emergency. Downtown, he would have found streetlights and traffic lights in every junction, crossroad, and roundabout. But had he looked at them very closely, he would have noticed that most of these public facilities have lost their lamps or cables, and that they only exist as the relic of the glorious past when Cameroon was still a promising developing country, and not yet a highly indebted poor country. In the business and administrative districts, his gaze would have registered numerous wrecked buildings and impressive unfinished public constructions that have fallen into neglect because the state no longer has the financial means to achieve its delusions of grandeur and dreams of modernity. If he had entered one of these towers (which cut a fine figure when one looks at them from the outside), he would have felt stifled because the air-conditioning had stopped functioning a long time ago. Moreover, he would have been compelled to run up the stairs because the lift does not work. To his disappointment, he would have found that the telephone was not connected, and that he could not use the toilets because the taps and the flush did not function any more.

In all respects, the above comments evidence that the African *ghettopolis* is not a place for the *flânerie* and promenade for there is nothing to admire or contemplate here, because the *ghettopolitan* walker parades in a city where the general infrastructure bears the historical consciousness of decline and ruin. Moreover, in his stroll, he is likely to encounter a ferocious population that participates at different levels in an economy of violence and destruction, which has led to the transformation of this city into a necropolis (Trani 2000).

Live and Let Die in the Necropolis

On March 25, 2005, the chief of police of Kribi, a seaside town about 100 kilometers away from Douala, shot a young fisherman before the very eyes of his wife and two children. This murder caused the newspaper *Le Messager* to publish an article that was entitled: "*La République des Morts-Vivants*" (the republic of the living dead). Author Noé Ndjebet Massoussi wrote:

> What has happened in Kribi is something that many Cameroonians experience every day. Assassinations have become the citizens' cup of tea in Cameroon, which is now considered a highly indebted poor country, after almost a half-century of independence. Even strangers are not saved. From the north to the south, the east to the west, populations live in permanent dread and anxiety. Insecurity is growing and it is faceless. The situation is all the more serious as criminals are those who are responsible for the protection of citizens. You'd think you were in the Far West. As a result, the National Triangle (another designation of Cameroon) resembles a big cemetery of 475,000 square kilometers where more than 17 million living-dead are parked. For nobody knows which day or hour, much less in which circumstances, he will pass on. Every Cameroonian risks death all the time, alone or in a group, in office or at home, in public spaces or quiet places. Cameroon is nothing but a republic of the living-dead where every citizen waits all the time to be killed like a dog.[2] (My translation)

If Douala, like most cities in the country, looks like a necropolis, it is not only because the everyday life of most its dwellers is dominated by ever-present forms of risk and threat, which make life very precarious, or because violence and terror have taken here a routinized form (see Foucault 1977; Mbembe and Roitman 1995). Above all, Douala owes its necropolitan character to the fact that living in this necropolis where death has become part of everyday life implies subjugating one's life to its sovereign authority. For example, necropolitan subjects die from treatable diseases because they lack 1000 CFA francs ($1.80) to buy a pack of quinine to protect against malaria, or because poverty and misery have compelled many of them to drink water from the swamps where people often relieve themselves, or to eat unhygienic foods in the *tourne-dos* (a popular eating house), which are often set up beside rubbish dumps or open sewers. They perish in numerous car accidents because they are forced to take *cargos* (very old buses) whose brakes are not working, or which young car cleaners-turned-drivers drive without mercy. People are killed also because they have no money or valuables to offer to the *braqueurs* (armed robbers) who have taken over much of the city. Some of them are put to death because they have had an argument with a member of the forces of law and order who have taken on themselves the right to decide who might live or die, or to dispense what the Cameroonian journalist Melvin Akam has called the "justice of Kalachnikov."[3] That is an absolute justice, which offers the defendant or offender only the right to be riddled with bullets. Still others encounter death as a result of torture in police stations and other detention camps because they are unfortunate enough to be arrested during a police raid, or because they are suspected of being thieves.

Let us take one example to substantiate these broad statements. On January 23, 2001, members of the dreadful *Commandement Opérationnel*, a special armed forces unit that was created in February 2000 to fight organized crime in Douala, arrested nine young men (aged between 17 and 23) from Bépanda, a popular neighborhood in the city. The arrestees allegedly stole an empty gas bottle from a young lady whose lover was a gendarme who was connected to this special unit. For about a week, the unfortunate young men endured all kinds of brutality in the detention camp where they were kept in custody. Finally, their executioners took them to a place named Logbadjeck (at the outskirts of the city), where they executed them together with 56 other young men who were arrested the same week. This massacre only extended the list of victims of this death squad, which, according to several human right organizations, killed nearly 12,000 Cameroonians between February 2000 and March 2001.[4]

But the singularity of this postcolonial necropolis is that victims of the state machinery of death and destruction, whether it is called *Commandement Opérationnel*, *Opération Vautour*, or *Opération Scorpion Noir*, often enthusiastically join their perpetuators in the necropolization of Cameroonian society. Indeed, since the mid-1990s, the generalization of what is known today in Cameroon as *justice populaire* (popular justice) has become the embodiment of this process of transforming Cameroon into a huge cemetery, a culture of death that seems to be the only thing that brings together the rulers and the populace. For example, one is beaten or stoned to death, crucified, burnt alive, or hanged by an excited mob, and sometimes by almost the entire population of a neighborhood, because one has stolen an object, no matter whether this item is a can, a cell phone, a bunch of bananas, a cloth, or a chicken. It may happen as well that you are a victim of the collective paranoia, simply because someone has found you prowling the neighborhood at night, and has shouted, "stop, thief!" In recent years, most neighborhoods in Douala, as in many cities in the country, have set up what it is popularly known as *groupes d' auto-défence* (self-defense groups), members of which seem to have reduced their actions to the capture and execution of thieves or suspected thieves. In many respects, the most efficient self-defense group is "the one which never allows thieves to escape from the neighborhood alive," as one of the leaders of a self-defense group in Douala once declared in *Cameroon Tribune*, a pro-governmental newspaper.[5]

For instance, most recently, one local newspaper reported a story about two young men (aged 20 and 23), whose mortified bodies were abandoned in a rubbish dump that was in the vicinity of the Quartier Madagascar, a popular neighborhood in Douala. According to the reporter, the local population lynched the unfortunate young men because they had attempted to break into a shop. They were unfortunate enough to be caught by the shopowner who alerted his neighbors. After a laborious manhunt that mobilized almost the entire neighborhood, the delinquents were finally captured and then attached to a stake where they were submitted to all kinds of brutality, which finally led to their demise. The reporter explained:

> One of the criminals is laid on his side, his hands tied behind his back, his body scorched like an ill-roasted *michoui* (spit-roast lamb). The other one is laid down 20 meters away from his unfortunate companion. His head, like the rest of his body, has been completely disfigured by the blows he had received. Gasoline cans, bludgeons, bars of iron, sticks, stones, pieces of board, which had served to kill them, are still at the scene.[6] (My translation)

Some of the perpetrators whom the reporter interviewed, legitimated their act by quoting the fact that people were fed up with the general insecurity that prevailed in Douala.

This "*vindicte populaire*" (popular condemnation), as the newsman put it, recalls a macabre scene that CRTV, the state-controlled television, broadcast on November 27, 2002. Residents of Elig-Edzoa, a popular neighborhood in Yaounde (the capital of Cameroon), beat to death three young men who allegedly stole two goats, and then attached their corpses to the stolen animals. For about five minutes, viewers could watch the locals kicking or spitting on these mutilated bodies invaded by flies. It was emotive to hear these men and women explaining to the journalists how they had tortured and humiliated their victims before putting them to death. Some of them even prided themselves on having participated in what they described as the *mise à mort des voleurs* (killing of the thieves). One middle-aged man who pretended to be a member of the neighborhood self-defense group told the reporters:

> This action [he meant the killing of the three young men] is a dissuasive measure against thieves. We want to make them understand that, death is the only thing that awaits those who steal in our quarter. Nine criminals have already been killed here. And we will keep killing them, as long as thieves make life hard for us.[7]

This last decade, the necropolization of the Cameroonian society has also taken the form of an exuberant propagation of innovative witchcraft-related practices, which often imply ritual killings, zombie conjuring, child abuse, satanic practices, and clandestine theft and sale of the organs of young people for magical purposes. For example, in April 2003, the entire Quartier Aréoport, a densely populated neighborhood on the outskirts of Douala, was plunged into mourning after the discovery of the mutilated bodies of nine children (the victims were aged between six months and six years old) in the trunk of a car parked in front of a concession. Most of the victims, who were females, had their head, eyes, or genital organs amputated. The police investigation revealed that the car's owner and his wife killed the adolescents in order to sell their body parts to a mystical organization with which they were reportedly connected.[8] Though this murder was infamous, it was far from being an unprecedented or baffling crime in a city where it has become almost banal to see dismembered bodies or parts of bodies on the streets, or to find human embryos or newborn babies near a rubbish dump.

The general practice of euthanasia in most medical institutions of the country is another remarkable expression of the necropolization process. Euthanasia refers here not to the practice of putting an end to the suffering of patients who are condemned to death, or to the medical killing of those who are in the terminal phase of their illness. In the necropolis context, this expression accounts for the routinized practice of abandoning patients to their fate, of exposing their lives to death, or of increasing the risk of death for them, either because they have no connection with the staff or because they cannot bribe the doctors or nurses. Cameroonian prisons, detentions camps and police stations, notorious for their inhuman conditions, are not the only places where what Mbembe (2003: 11–40) has translated as "necropolitics" is put into practice. Local hospitals too manifest themselves as a *place de la mort* (space of death), in opposition to a general perception of medical institutions as a *place de la vie* (space of life). Symptomatic in this respect are the public hospitals, which have become for the most part a *mouroir*, as the local population derisively calls them. By *mouroir*, they mean not a twilight house or a place where the moribund spend the last moment of their lives, but rather a location where one enters alive and walks out only as a dead person. This expression also accounts for a place where there is no longer a distinction between the space of death and the space of life, or between the expectation of birth and the expectation of death, for the very act of delivery often leads to death.

In most public hospitals for instance, people die through neglect because the nurse who was supposed to be watching over a patient was instead busy watching a football match or gossiping with a colleague. It happens as well that one dies while delivering, because the medical staff is incompetent, or rather because the maternity hospital lacks everything. This is what happened to a 35-year-old lady who died recently while delivering in a district hospital in Douala because she was given an inappropriate medicine. Instead of stimulating labor as expected by the practitioners, the drug induced anomalous bleeding, which caused her to fall into a coma. She finally passed away while she was being transported to a private hospital whose intensive care unit was still operational.[9] The victim was one more name in the long list of women who die every year in the maternity hospitals in this country. For example, in a special issue the newspaper *Mutations* published in

February 2005 on maternal mortality in Cameroon, it was revealed that delivering in public hospitals carried a high risk, for more than 80 out of every 1,000 expectant mothers die there every year. In some public medical institutions, especially in the so-called regional hospitals and medical district centers, the rate of maternal mortality is nearly twice the national average. According to the same newspaper, many women, and even those from lower social classes, prefer to pay high fees in private hospitals where they are well treated, rather than going to public hospitals where they run a risk of "dying on the delivery table."[10]

Living in the necropolis entails making death one's intimate. Symptomatic of the intimacy that has been created between the living and the dead is the transformation of many cemeteries and communal graves into playgrounds, farms, or living spaces for many destitute urban families. The foreign visitor who happens to stroll around Douala will be impressed not only by the number of gravestones in front of people's houses but also by the number of families who live in the burial grounds, which have become the only places where the poor can afford to buy land in the city. Since 1995, local authorities have been struggling to keep squatters out of the cemeteries. For example, in reaction to the invasion of cemeteries and communal graves by destitute families, in November 2003 the municipal authorities of the Douala District II undertook a clean-up campaign that led to the destitution of hovels and dumps that were set up in these burial grounds.

As I discuss in the following pages, in Africa necropolises where people are familiar with misfortune, death has ceased to be considered an imaginary or an invisible ghost that hides behind the shadow of existence. It is no longer a mysterious hand that deprives us of the delights of life. Moreover, its omnipresence has led here to its banalization and theatricalization.

Banalization and Theatricalization of Tragedy

Besides being a place where life is no longer regarded as sacred, the necropolis is also a space where death and tragedy have become banal or have taken on a theatrical expression. For instance, in early February of this year, a gang of armed robbers murdered a prosperous Chinese businessman who was based in Douala and seriously wounded his wife. In reaction to this aggression, members of the Chinese community who lived in this city attempted to organize a peaceful demonstration in the streets of Douala. The subdivision officer of the Douala District I banned this march and threatened to arrest the demonstrators because they were "making a big fuss about a single death," as he put it. He even refused to receive the bereaved family who came to complain about the growing insecurity in the city, for "the death of a man in a city where hundreds of people are killed every day was not an exceptional event that was worth dwelling on."[11] But we will let ourselves be misled by this example, if we think that in the necropolis, the banalization of death is only the work of the state power that has turned from protector to predator. It is a behavior that is shared as well by the commoners, whose attitude toward the dead bears witness to their active participation in the process of desacralization of death.

One of the most ignoble forms of banalization of tragedy and death in this city is less the reluctance to assist someone whose life is in danger than the habit of denying the dead the right to be buried decently. People dehumanize dead bodies by associating them with a carcass or waste that can be dumped into a dustbin, or can be abandoned either in the streets at the mercy of vultures and other stray dogs, or in dilapidated and overloaded mortuaries. For example, as recently as November 2004, the newspaper *Le Messager* published a list of 175 corpses that were abandoned by families in the mortuary of the Laquintinie Hospital in a single month. As the identity of the deceased evidenced, most of them were either suspected *braqueurs* (robbers) who were executed by the security forces during their operations or *gardés à vue* (offenders) who died during bruising interrogations in the police stations and other detention camps. But some of the unfortunates were inmates of the disreputable New Bell prison, which is often compared to a "death camp" (see *Mutations* June 18, 2004). In an interview he granted to the same journal, the director of the aforementioned hospital revealed that every month, more than 225 abandoned corpses were buried in the communal grave of Bois des Singes, so as to "decongest the hospital mortuary which could no longer cope with the increasing number of bodies."[12]

But it happens that instead of burying these corpses people use them to supply the prosperous traffic of bodies that has become widespread in the country, and in which undertakers play a decisive role. For instance, in early June 2004, a scandal about the disappearance of corpses in some mortuaries in Douala and Yaoundé hit the headlines of several local newspapers. According to one of the journals that reported the story, families who went to collect the remains of their deceased relative in the mortuary were offered another corpse because someone who passed himself off as one of the deceased's close parents had already carried away their "corpse." One middle-aged man whose cousin's body disappeared in the morgue of the Yaounde Central Hospital explained:

> That afternoon, I and other members of the family went to the morgue of the Yaoundé Central Hospital to wash the corpse of my cousin who had died two days earlier. But to our surprise his remains were no longer there. The corpse that the undertakers persistently presented to us was not our cousin's. It was of a male much older than him, and who probably had died three or four weeks earlier. Moreover, the deceased had a shaven head, whereas our cousin had long hair. One of the undertakers earnestly suggested that we accept this body, because, according to him, a body was a body, no matter whether it was of an old or young man, a fresh or frozen body. It was only after some "Big Men" of our family threatened them with legal action that the undertakers revealed the address of the man to whom they sold our cousin's corpse. After several hours of search, we were lucky enough to find the man in a bar in Yaoundé. He turned out to be an intermediary. The information he provided us with helped us to intercept our cousin's corpse, which was headed for Mbalmayo.[13] (My translation)

One can find a striking similarity between this routinized traffic of bodies that allow unpaid state agents to earn some money, and the commodification of the corpses of victims of the Sam-Effoulam catastrophe in Yaounde by the local population. On February 14, 1997, some residents of this popular neighborhood in Yaounde derailed a tanker that transported the petrol destined to the *Société Camerounaise de Dépots Pétroliers*, a parastatal company. As usual, this "accident" offered the locals who crowded on the accident spot the opportunity to collect the petrol that escaped from the tanks, which would be resold later to car users. But, the merrymaking turned into a tragedy when, in his eagerness to make the most of this unexpected godsend, one of the looters was so imprudent as to throw a cigarette end on the ground. This caused a huge explosion that killed more than 200 people and wounded several hundred others. Word had it that all the victims were autochthons from that neighborhood, because the *allochthon* residents had allegedly been expelled already from the accident scene by the former, on the grounds that the accident occurred on their soil (Geschiere and Nyamnjoh 2000: 423–452). But, when the government decided to offer bereaved families 200,000 CFA francs (nearly U.S. $400) for each corpse, Cameroonians from different ethnic groups and neighboring towns ostentatiously mourned for people with whom they had no connections, just because they could get their share of the state money. At the Yaounde military base where the corpses were displayed, it was pathetic to see all these men and women jostling, squabbling, or exchanging blows for a cadaver that would enable them to earn 200,000 CFA francs. Some cunning people found it less laborious to collect abandoned bodies from municipal mortuaries, and then went and traded them with corrupt state agents. To facilitate their transactions, some of them even took care to burn their "cadavers," so as to make them look like burn victims of the Sam-Effoulam catastrophe. A man even prided himself on having *recupérer* (collected) five corpses that brought him one million CFA francs (U.S.$2,000). One can understand why the newspaper *Le Messager* (February 21, 1997) talked of "*Les cadavers qui font le bonheur des autres*" (the cadavers that make other people's fortune).

Another aspect of the banalization of death in this necropolis is the common practice of desecrating cemeteries and gravestones, a practice that is revelatory above all of the little respect that many necropolitans pay to the dead. In the article "*De L'Histoire sous le Cimetière*" that focuses on the cemeteries in Douala, Djimeli (2005: 3–4), reveals that most of the burial grounds in the downtown have been turned into a "place of defecation," because of the lack of public toilets. Moreover, a number of sepulchers and mausoleums have been deprived of their epitaphs and wreaths. This is the case in the Catholic cemetery of Bonadiboung, which was erected in the late nineteenth century by the first European missionaries who arrived in Cameroon. This cemetery, which is located at the heart of the city, is one of the most plundered graveyards in Douala, for it is essentially made up of highly decorated or extravagant graves of Europeans and wealthy Douala natives (the autochthonous populations of Douala) who pay a high price to be buried in this prestigious cemetery. For example, during the show *SOS Solidarité*, which the state-controlled television (CRTV) broadcast in May 1996, it was revealed how some criminal groups made use of mad people squatting in this cemetery for their trafficking in human remains. A lunatic man who was interviewed during this program explained to the reporters how he and his cronies were given 1,000 CFA francs (U.S.$2.00) or a pack of cigarettes in order to burst open the coffins or to dig up corpses. He even disclosed the names of some local politicians and administrative authorities who were allegedly implicated in this trade. Following these embarrassing revelations, the government ordered the suspension of the program. Moreover, disciplinary actions were taken against the reporters for *manquement à l'éthique professionnelle* (violation of professional ethics) and *faute grave* (gross misconduct), as the then minister of communication called it.

From Necropolis to Hedonopolis

Despite the pervasiveness of death and tragedy, despite its pathological and chaotic character, the African necropolis is far from corresponding to Dear and Wolch's *Landscapes of Despair* (1987). In their "practice of everyday life" (de Certeau 1984), the necropolitan subjects endeavor to dramatize a culture of life and insouciance that deprives death of what Morin (1976) upholds as its essence: its tragic, scandalous, and traumatic character (see also Jankélévitch 1977). Moreover, this last decade has witnessed the necropolitan dwellers' project to transform the city of death that they live in into a city of life, and also to create a place of pleasure and enjoyment that can function as a panacea for their social and economic distress, or at least can drive them into realms of fantasy and hallucination. I call this fantastic world *hedonopolis.*

Hedonopolis is the expression I use to describe what is popularly known in Cameroon as the *cité de la joie.* Contrary to the city of desperation where people succumb to despair and fatality, or submit their lives to the authoritarian power of death, the city of enjoyment, as the popular imaginary in Cameroon represents it, is a place where death itself has been mortalized or zombified, for the necropolitan subjects no longer experience it as a tragic and distressing event. I do not mean that people are no longer afflicted by the death of their relatives, or that they have ceased to mourn their parents or friends who have passed away. What I want to emphasize is that, in the hedonopolis, mourners are turned into revelers, for tragedy and catastrophe are generally associated here with the aesthetics of pleasure and enjoyment. Paradoxically, tragedy is often the only event that livens up gloomy poor neighborhoods, or exhilarates destitute urbanites who live an empty existence. As a matter of fact, death is what brings people together, makes bars and brothels thrive, or enables undertakers, photographers, musicians, prostitutes, pickpockets, and hawkers to earn some money. You often hear the locals referring to the demise of their neighbors as the *mouvement dans le quartier* (animation in the neighborhood), which offers them the opportunity to *se gâter avec la bière et les femmes* (to "spoil" oneself with drinks and women). When there is no mishap in a neighborhood, it seems as if all its residents have died, because there will be no lavish celebration, no noisy music to play, no women to court or men to seduce, no malicious gossip to exchange, no rumor to spread, no quarrel or brawl to engage in, no money to earn, and so on.

It is in this respect that one can understand why here burials, which are supposed to be sorrowful and distressed moments, have been turned into festivities that generally end with drunken orgies. Moreover, many people attend funerals less out of compassion for the bereaved family, more as an occasion to sell their goods, feast, or engage in an orgiastic carnival. Indeed, during the funerals, especially the lavish ones that generally attract a huge crowd of revelers, it is common to see men and women of different ages getting drunk, being jubilant, fighting over a piece of chicken, or relieving themselves in public. It is not unusual as well to see young female dancers dropping down their skirts, prostrating in insensibility, ostentatiously exhibiting their nipples, or offering their denuded backsides to their male partners. In their excitement, you will often hear some frenzied revelers saying that the "*deuil est bon*" (funerals are good), or regretting that there were not deaths everyday in their neighborhood. The singer Kon Mbogol, in his critical song (*Likalo: Message*), points out the seamy behavior of many Cameroonians:

> Funerals are no longer what they used to be in the past.
> Please tell me, why funerals have become today the occasion of festivity among
> The Bassa, Ewondo, Duala, Bamileke and Hausa!
> You have to see what happens at the day of the funeral.
> When a wealthy man dies,
> People attend the burial in large numbers,
> Not to mourn the deceased.
> For some, it is an opportunity to eat beef and mutton, drink whisky and Champagne,
> And for others, it is an occasion to seduce the widower and share the heritage.

The hedonopolis is also a place where any disaster or misfortune that affects the neighborhood, the city, the region, or the country is seen above all as an opportunity to earn money. More explicitly, when a catastrophe occurs somewhere in the city or region, people will pass themselves off as disaster victims at the expense of real victims, just to get aid from the state or international organizations, even if they live far afield from the disaster area. Few will hesitate to strip the dead of their assets, because they consider that they no longer need to wear expensive clothes or jewels. For example, on December 3, 1995, a civilian airliner, a Boeing 737 that belonged to the Cameroon airlines company, crashed into the swamp area of Youpwe near the Douala international airport, killing more than 50 out of 78 passengers and members of the crew. On hearing that there was an air crash, the local population ran up to the scene, not only to rescue the victims but also to strip them of their possessions. One of the survivors I met by chance in 2002 in the departure lounge of the Charles de Gaulle international airport (Paris) revealed the "Cameroonian mentality" to me during our discussion:

> The three young men who came to rescue me dispossessed me of my belongings. While two of them were carrying me to their canoe, the third one was rummaging through my pockets. I saw him unfastening my jewels and my watch. But I could not resist him, not only because my strength was failing me, but also because I ran the risk of being abandoned to my fate in this infested area. Before losing consciousness, I even saw them and other guys robbing the dead, since most of the passengers were businessmen and high-profile bureaucrats. I had never seen people sinking as low as these young men did. I think that we are losing moral values in our country.

Topographically, the city of enjoyment and ecstasy is the concentration of popular drinking houses, bars, night clubs, brothels, prostitution hotels, hostels, cabarets, close houses, and clandestine video parlors where teenagers are allowed to watch pornographic movies, drink alcohol, or smoke cigarettes. Most of these spaces for pleasure and frenzy are located in popular and disadvantaged neighborhoods that are notorious for being *hot spots.* Here, lower social categories and impoverished middle classes find through drink, sex, and torrid popular music the means to escape from distress, sorrow, and anxiety (Ndjio 2005). This is the case of New Bell, the most populous neighborhood in Douala, where nearly one million men and women "live to the rhythm of libido," as the newspaper *Le Messager* (October 25, 2004: 4) once wrote.

New Bell in particular, and Douala at large, is a place where people invent life or cheat death by investing their bodies in what de Boeck (1998) aptly calls the "economy of ejaculation," of which bars and houses of pleasure have become the iconic figure. The economy of ejaculation refers here not only to the conspicuous consumption of beer and sex, but also to the general practice of debauchery, lechery, and infidelity, which is one of the most remarkable aspects of this hedonistic culture that makes this city resemble the biblical Sodom and Gomorrah. In this archipelago of profligacy and immorality, venality has taken the form of corruption of minors, normalization of pedophilia, banalization of adultery, popularization of prostitution, and so on and so forth. Douala, like many other urban agglomerations of the country, is a place where keeping several young mistresses who are often younger than one's granddaughter, or appearing in public with one's immature *meilleure petite* (young favorite lover) or toy-boy have become appropriate if not routine forms of behavior. Symptomatic in this respect is the incredible number of students or schoolboys and girls that one encounters in houses of pleasure together with their old lovers (*Le Messager*, March 25, 2004).

Douala is also a location where partners regularly catch each other *in flagrante delicto*, commiting adultery in a brothel or hostel. This behavior has led the locals to consider infidelity as a sign of sexual vitality and potency, or to steer clear of condoms, because they allegedly "kill pleasure," as one young lady earnestly declared in the newspaper *Le Messager* (March 17, 2004: 5). Some are even doubtful about the reality of AIDS (SIDA in French), which they often translate as "*Syndrome Inventé pour Décourager les Amoureux*" (invented syndrome to discourage lovers).

In the hedonopolis, even the popular culture is affected by this Epicurean culture. For example, much of the popular music such as *Bikutsi*, Soukous, *Coupé-Décalé*, *Makossa, Mdombolo*, and *Bend-skin*, which are often dubbed "pornographic music" (*Le Messager* June 14, 2002), exalts above all sensuality, voluptuousness, and eroticism. It is a kind of music that drives its dancers to a primal state or arouses a wild emotion from those who dance it, for this musical genre equates the act of dancing with that of copulating. Its lyric itself is a panegyric discourse not only about permissiveness and intemperance, but also about nymphomania and frivolity.

CONCLUSION

This study has suggested that the chaotic and murderous character of contemporary African metropolis offers a dystopian vision of the city, which challenges the utopian representation of the city that is still dominant in

Western academia. The necropolis, as I have called it, is not only the city of death and terror; it is also the landscape of disability and breakdown, in which most of its dwellers live in a state of emergency, which leaves no time to *flânerie* and reverie. As the chapter has revealed, the iconic figure of the necropolitan identity in public is not Benjamin's dandy *flâneur* of the nineteenth century who lived on the boulevards, and made the streets and cafés of Paris his drawing room, but rather the resourceful *sauveteur* who strives through legal and illegal means to make a living on the street. Like the ragpicker and other wretched of the earth so well depicted in Zola's *L'Assommoir* (1970), he represents the other modernity or the dark side of globalization (Castells 1989; Sassen 1998; 2000). Whether he/she is a hawker, sorcerer, hooker, robber, profaner, or trickster, the *sauveteur* is above all someone who, in his/her everyday practice, endeavors, by means of resourcefulness, ruse, trickery, mischievousness, or violence, not only to transform his/her living conditions, but also to invent a new form of life. This individual or collective mode of life creation goes along with what Michel de Certeau (1984: 25) calls "the process of appropriation of the topographical system," and above all the imagination of the city as the hedonopolis.

In conclusion, contrary to what the readers might think, this essay is less a narration on the sovereign power of death on people's lives than on the transformation of tragedy into comedy and farce. It is a chronicle of the individual or collective effort to fantasize a space of freedom that enables the necropolitan subject to enfranchise himself or herself of the tyranny of death and tragedy.

Notes

This research was made possible thanks to the grant from WROTO (Netherlands Foundation for the Advancement of Topical Research). I owe an intellectual debt to my colleagues from the Amsterdam School for Social Science Research, especially to Peter Geschiere, Eileen Moyer, Joost Beuwing, and Francio Guadeloupe.

1. For a critical analysis of this approach see Bridge and Watson, 2002; Vidler, 1992.
2. In *Le Mesager online*, March 28, 2005: 3. See also *Mutations online*, March 29, 2005.
3. Cf. his article: "*Le Pouvoir de tuer*" (the power to kill) in *Le Messager online*, November 12, 2003: 2
4. Cf. *Le Mesager*, March 19, 2001; May 10, 2001: 2; *La Nouvelle Expression*, March 16, 2001.
5. See *Cameroon Tribune*, February 24, 2005: 3.
6. See *Le Messager online*, March 24, 2005.
7. *Cameroon Tribune*, November 28, 2002: 4. See also *Mutations*, November 28, 2002.
8. Cf. *Le Messager*, April 14, 2003; *La Nouvelle Expression*, April 21, 2003: 9.
9. See *Mutations online*, March 24, 2005: 5.
10. See *Mutations online*, February 23, 2003: 3–5.
11. See *Le Messager online*, February 16, 2005.
12. See *Le Messager* November 14, 2004: 3.
13. *Mutations*, June 18, 2004: 4. On the traffic of bodies in mortuaries, see also *Le Messager*, June 1, 2004.

REFERENCES

Appadurai, Arjun. 1990. "Disjuncture and Difference in the Global Cultural Economy," *Public Culture* 2 (2): 1–24.

Appadurai, Arjun. 2002. "Deep Democracy: Urban Governmentality and the Horizon of Politics," *Public Culture* 14 (1): 21–47.

Bayart Jean-François, Stephen Ellis, and Béatrice Hibou. 1999. *Criminalization of the State in Africa*. Oxford: James Currey.

Bender, Thomas. 2002. *The Unfinished City: New York and the Metropolitan Idea*. New York: New Press.

Benjamin, Walter. 1973. *Charles Beaudelaire: A Lyric Poet in the Era of High Capitalism*. London: New Left Books.

Boyer, M. Christine. 1983. *Dreaming the Rational City*. Cambridge, MA: MIT Press.

Bremner, Lindsay. 2000. "Reinventing the Johannesburg Inner City," *Cities* 17 (3): 185–193.

Bridge, Gary and Sophie Watson. 2002. *The Blackwell City Reader*. Oxford: Blackwell.

Caldeira, Teresa. 2000. *City of Walls: Crime, Segregation, and Citizenship in São Paulo* Berkeley: University of California Press.

Castells, Manuel. 1989. *The Informational City*. Oxford: Blackwell.

Chabal, Patrick and Jean-Pascal Dalloz. 1999. *Africa Works: Disorder as Political Instrument*. Oxford and Bloomington: James Currey/Indiana University Press.

Courade, Georges (ed.). 2000. *Le Désarroi Camerounais: L' Epreuve de L'Economiemonde*. Paris: Karthala.

Davis, Mike. 1992. *The City of Quartz: Excavating the Future in Los Angeles*. London: Verso.

de Boeck, Filip. 2004. "The Possibilities of the (Im)possible: Kinshasa and Its Heterotopia." Paper presented during the conference on "Exploring the Wealth of the African Neighborhood: the Sustainability and Creativity of Urban Life." Africa Studies Center, Leiden, Netherlands, September 16–17.

de Certeau, Michel. 1984. *The Practice of the Everyday Life*. Berkeley: University of California Press.

Dear, Michael and Jennifer Wolch. 1987. *Landscapes of Despair: From Deinstitutionalization to Homelessness*. Cambridge, MA: Polity.

Djimeli, Antoine. 2005. "L' Histoire sous le cimetière," *Le Messager*, February 23: 3–4.

Donald, James. 1999. *Imagining the Modern City*. Minneapolis: University of Minnesota Press.

Geschiere Peter and Francis Njamnjoh. 2000. "Capitalism and Autochthony: The Seesaw of Mobility and Belonging," *Public Culture* 12 (2): 423–452.

Ferguson, James. 1999. *Expectations of Modernity: Myths and Meanings of Urban Life on the Zambian Copperbelt*. Berkeley: University of California Press.

Foucault, Michel. 1977. *Discipline and Punish: The Birth of the Prison*. New York: Pantheon.

Foucault, Michel. 1986. "Of Other spaces," trans. J. Miskowiec, *Diacritics* 16: 22–27.

Gleeson, Brendan. 1999. *Geographies of Disability*. London: Routledge.

Hall, Peter. 2002. *Cities of Tomorrow*. [Third Edition] Oxford: Blackwell.

Holston, James. 1989. *The Modernist City: An Anthropological Critique of Brasilia*. Chicago: University of Chicago Press.

Jankélévitch, Vladimir. 1977. *La Mort*. Paris: Flammarion.

Konings, Piet. 2004. "Bendskin Drivers in Douala's New Bell Neighborhood." Paper presented during the conference on "Exploring the Wealth of the African Neighborhood: The Sustainability and Creativity of Urban Life." Africa Studies Center, Leiden, Netherlands, September 16–17.

Le Corbusier. 1971. *The City of Tomorrow and Its Planning*, 3rd edition. London: Architectural Press.

Lynch, Kevin. 1981. *The Theory of Good City Form*. Cambridge, MA: MIT Press.

Mbembe, Achille. 2003. "Necropolitics," *Public Culture* 15 (1): 11–40.

Mbembe, Achille. 2004. "The Aesthetics of Superfluity," *Public Culture* 16 (3): 373–405.

Mbembe, Achille and Janet Roitman. 1995. "Figures of the Subject in Times of Crisis," *Public Culture* 7 (2).

Mbembe, A. and Sarah Nuttall. 2004. "Writing the World from an African Metropolis," *Public Culture* 16 (3): 347–372.

Morin, Edgar. 1976. *L' Homme et la Mort*. Paris: Edition du Seuil.

Moyer, Eileen. 2002. "In the Shadow of the Sheraton: Imagining Localities in the Global Spaces in Dar es Salaam, Tanzania." Unpublished Ph.D. dissertation. University of Amsterdam.

Ndjio, Basile. 2005. "Carrefour de la Joie: Popular Deconstruction of the Postcolonial Public Sphere," *Africa* 75(3): 265–294.

Ngabmen, Henri. 2002. "Libéralisation de l'exploitation des transports collectives urbains a Douala: Mise en oeuvre d'une nouvelle approche." Unpublished paper, Yaoundé, Institut des Transport et des Stratégies de Développement.

Roitman, Janet. 2005. *Fiscal Disobedience: Anthropology of Economic Regulation in Central Africa*. Princeton and Oxford: Princeton University Press.

Sassen, Saskia. 1998. *Globalization and Its Discontents*. New York: The New Press.

Sassen, Saskia. 2000. *The Global City: New York, London and Tokyo*. Princeton: Princeton University Press.

Séraphin, Giles. 2000. *Vivre à Douala: L'Imaginaire et l'Action dans une Ville Africaine en Crise*. Paris: Karthala.

Simone, AbdouMaliq. 2001. "On the Worlding of African Cities," *African Studies Review* 44 (2): 15–43.

Simone, AbdouMaliq. 2004. "People as Infrastructure: Intersecting Fragments in Johannesburg," *Public Culture* 16 (3): 407–429.

Smith, Neil. 1996. "After Tomkins Square Park: Deqentrification and the Revanchistcity," in A. King (ed.), *Re-presenting the City*. London: Macmillan, pp. 93–107.

Trani, Jean-François. 2000. "Les Jeunes et le travail à Douala: La galère de la deuxième generation après l'indépendance," in Courade (ed.). *Le Désarroi Camerounais. L' Epreuve de l"économie-monde*, Paris: Karthala, pp. 153–176.

Vidler, Anthony. 1992. *The Architecture of Uncanny*. Cambridge, MA: MIT Press.

Warnier, Jean-Pierre. 1993. *L'Esprit d'Entreprise au Cameroun*. Paris: Karthala.

Young, Iris Marion. 1986. "The Ideal of Community and the Politics of Difference," *Social Theory and Practice* 12 (1): 1–26.

Zola, Emile. 1970. *L'Assommoir*. Trans. Leonard Tanscock. Harmondsworth: Penguin.

II

Political Economy, Work, and Livelihood

The rapid growth of cities in Africa has gone hand-in-hand with confrontations over the use of urban space. As the urban wealthy have increasingly retreated behind walls and barriers, the urban poor have inventively converted places of the city to uses that were never intended. In the face of an acute shortage of decent and affordable housing, homeless squatters have invaded abandoned buildings, converting them into makeshift accommodation, and newcomers flocking to the cities and towns have constructed self-built housing on the urban fringes, or wherever they can find unused and open space. Curbside traders have commandeered sidewalks, street corners, and public parks, transforming downtown areas into vast open-air marketplaces. Residents who live in authorized housing have often subdivided their units, crowding desperate rent-paying tenants into tiny spaces. For the most part, this transformation of urban space has taken place in defiance of existing legal regulations and the efforts of municipal authorities to enforce them. Municipal authorities have responded in various ways to this informalization of urban life, ranging from an insouciant, hands-off *laissez-faire* approach to co-optation or outright suppression.

Struggles over access to and use of urban space occur not only between urban residents and city officials entrusted with the enforcement of law and order. The construction of places in the city is a complex, and layered, process, where their use is never fixed or permanent. It is often the case that rival groups making alternative claims to the same localities come into conflict with one another, sometimes leading to uneasy accommodation and other times to bitter confrontations.

The introduction of "free-market" policies to replace what once were centrally planned economies in many countries in Africa has not only opened up new opportunities for local entrepreneurs to tap into the emerging global marketplace, but also led to massive layoffs of wage-paid employees in the formal economy as state enterprises have downsized, off-loaded, and privatized their assets. In Africa, trade liberalization, privatization, and free-market policies have not led to a rise in private entrepreneurial investments with a commensurate increase in wage-paid employment.

The essays in part 2 illustrate how urban residents engage in various kinds of informal appropriation of space, of land acquisition, and land use. Municipal authorities respond to what they regard as the inappropriate use of space in ways that reflect not only their perception of how the urban landscape should be ordered and administered, but also their limited capacity to do so. We seek to shed light on how new urban spatial arrangements, interpersonal networks, and embryonic forms of self-organization are emerging from the failures of municipalities to deliver adequate services and to provide sufficient opportunities for socioeconomic advancement. In chaotic cities where the urban poor cannot count on the municipal authorities for assistance, the need to improvise, to go it alone, has provided fertile ground for the emergence of new types of relations and exchanges, strategies of survival and subsistence, and modes of solidarity and resistance. It is in the polymorphous and seemingly chaotic logic of the evolving postcolonial megacities of Africa that we may discover the emerging signs of new urban identities in formation.

The historical conjuncture of neoliberal reforms, the implementation of Structural Adjustment Programs (SAP), and collapsing urban economies has resulted in the loss of city jobs, the downsizing and outsourcing of municipal services, and the cutbacks of subsidies for housing and basic urban infrastructure. Because these population increases have not been matched by opportunities for wage-paid employment, expectant work-seekers in the cities and towns have been forced to find other means to generate income. Unregulated, unlicensed income-generating activities exhibit considerable differentiation, ranging from licit barter and trade to illicit smuggling, drug-dealing, and commercial sex (Nordstrom 2004). Some informal economic activities provide the semblance of a social safety net, whereas others serve as the launching pad for capital accumulation.

Assessing the overall socioeconomic impact of the informal economic activities requires an understanding of the type and level of activities, the resources mobilized to support their operation, and the nature of the social relations that structure them (Hansen and Vaa 2004: 81). The operational principles governing informal economic activities vary greatly, ranging from small-scale microenterprise activities operating on a shoestring, to large-scale mercantile-commercial operations involving well-entrenched trading diasporas with far-flung networks of dealers, middlemen, and brokers, where goods, money, and sometimes people are passed along transnational commodity chains.

To the extent that urban residents are no longer able to ensure the satisfaction of their basic needs through normal channels and in predictable ways, they have come to rely on *provisionality* and innovation. Without the certitude of regular work and a permanent place of habitation to call home, urban residents are cut loose from structured responsibilities and long-term commitments to locality. As a consequence, they are able to move more freely and at a moment's notice to forge tactical alliances cobbled together out of mutual need, and to experiment with multiple identities that may perhaps mask their true intentions.

Besides the broad range of improvised and provisional exchanges, the mobilization of economic resources in poor communities largely depends upon the confluence of familial, entrepreneurial, religious, and ethnic networks and collaborations. As a result, individual choices often conform to both strict rational economic calculation and the norms of reciprocity, mutual aid, and "sharing the wealth." Under these circumstances, it is not unusual to find microenterprises that limp along, remaining inefficient in accordance with a strict capitalist logic because of an unwillingness to shed casual workers who have no other source of income (Simone 2004).

The identities of African urban residents are elastic and fungible, hybrid and socially constructed. As people on the move, immigrants and political refugees have proven themselves particularly adept at negotiating this fluid and ephemeral terrain to their advantage. Depending upon the circumstances, African migrants who move from city to city typically fashion new identities and affinities. These do not replace older ones, but merely substitute for these as the circumstances warrant. Kinship, common language, and religious affiliations might be operative at home, but in countries other than their own, migrants might seek wider connections rooted in shared regional origins, or nationality.

In her study of the dynamics of the informal economy in Nairobi, Elizabeth Campbell shows how refugees, particularly those coming from Somalia, live a kind of dual existence. On the one hand, they play a key role in organizing informal economic activities from the strong point in Eastleigh. On the other hand, local Kenyans regard them with a great deal of suspicion, accusing them of exacerbating the problems of joblessness in the city, and heaping scorn on them as exploiters. The vast majority of refugees in Nairobi are there illegally. While they face widespread institutionalized discrimination, they have nonetheless managed to construct complex networks that link together their countries of origin, their countries of asylum, and the countries of resettlement. These transnational linkages have enabled many urban refugees in Nairobi to become successful entrepreneurs and prominent businessmen, particularly in the informal marketplace. Contrary to official claims and local xeonophobic belief that they absorb local resources, these urban refugees—especially those from the Horn of Africa, Central Africa, and other parts of East Africa, operate within largely self-sufficient communities. The slum neighborhood of Eastleigh has become the heart of the immigrant and refugee communities in Nairobi. Immigrant entrepreneurs have reconstructed the built environment, transforming what was once an abysmal slum area into a thriving center for informal trade. In demonstrating how globalization from below actually works in practice, Campbell looks at how urban refugees, particularly Somali immigrants, have forged a viable socioeconomic beachhead for themselves in Nairobi while at the same time negotiating an intensely hostile environment. With access to new information technologies, global telecommunications, and electronic money transfers, Somali entrepreneurs in Eastleigh have successfully established worldwide business networks and commercial connections that have bypassed large-scale banking enterprises, tax collectors, and the regulations of formal trade.

As urban agglomerations that emerged on the margins of modernity, cities in Africa bear the spatial imprint of metropolitan colonialism. As a general rule, the built environment of African cities consists of fragments cobbled together over a long period of time in the vain hope of creating some semblance of order and coherence. As cities in Africa have become more integrated with the global economy, they have experienced diverse kinds of "enclave development" that has broken the urban landscape into distinct fragments. In the headlong rush to promote tourism or to foster development, city builders have imported readymade spaces—such as shopping malls with their distinctive stylized building typologies, gated residential communities with their *faux*-European motifs, and enclosed official complexes. As a general rule, these are unceremoniously injected in the local urban landscape with little regard for existing vernacular architecture, the built environment, and the aesthetics of scale (Gandy 2005).

Cities are networked and connected in ways that move beyond the flows of people, ideas, and commodities. With the end of *apartheid* and the transition to parliamentary democracy, large-scale corporate enterprises with their headquarters in South Africa have begun to invest in other parts of the African continent. While the huge mining companies, construction firms, and defense industries have received a great deal of attention, large-scale commercial enterprises have been largely ignored. The construction of retail shopping centers with their financial origins in South Africa have proliferated in cities and towns across the African continent. In her study of Shoprite, one of the leading retail grocery chains in South Africa, Darlene Miller shows how the importation of modular types of business enterprise (bringing together South African–made commodities, architectural designs, and labor–management relations) has dramatically disrupted local urban economies in cities like Maputo.

Like dozens of other port cities that line the coastal areas of Africa, Luanda is an old city that can trace its origins back literally hundreds of years. The contemporary physical layout of the city bears the spatial imprint of colonial city planners who fashioned a streetscape to accommodate far different patterns and rhythms of urban life. Whereas cities in African may be "off the map" in terms of their connections with the dominant urban agglomerations at the apex of the world economy, the emergence of new identities and subjectivities amongst urban youth in particular reflect a deep emersion in—and attraction for—globalized consumer preferences.

In describing how suffocating traffic congestion is literally "killing" Luanda, Anne Pitcher (along with Aubrey Graham) uses the fixation that residents have with cars as a point of departure to explore both unanticipated use of the streetscape of the city and also the rise of consumer culture in a country emerging from decades of civil war and flush with the monetary proceeds of oil wealth. In their view, cars in Luanda have become objects of commodity fetishism. In a situation similar to what Rem Koolhaas (2002) describes for Lagos, the agonizingly slow pace of vehicular traffic in Luanda results in an unplanned and yet a new functional use for urban space. In a stunning and ironic reversal of the conventional understanding of fixed marketplaces and mobile consumers, traffic jams effectively establish a monetary exchange mechanism by creating a systematic interface between street vendors—who circumambulate the highways clogged with stalled vehicles—and their "captive cargo" of potential consumers (Koolhaas 2002). Pitcher (with Graham) argues that the proliferation of late-model cars that have transformed the streets of Luanda into a nightmare of traffic congestion reflect the rise of a globally conscious, middle-class consumer culture linked to iconic symbols of social status. They also show how alternative vantage points of city users—particularly impatient car drivers, nimble-footed pedestrians who must maintain constant vigilance against the reckless driving habits of car owners, and itinerant street vendors—shape their experience of urban living, and give different views to what it means to live in the city.

As a mode of engagement with city life, photography offers a visual display that words can only describe. In her photographic exhibition of Luanda, Aubrey Graham explores the cult of the automobile and the cottage industry of car washers, car guards, and repair activities that it has spawned. Just as Baudelaire's celebrated, site-seeing *flaneur* represented the quintessential middle-class resident of great pedestrian-friendly European cities of the nineteenth century, the impatient automobile driver gives substance and meaning to distended, overcrowded megalopolises like twenty-first century Luanda.

Miriam Grant's essay is based on her latest research project within her larger longitudinal study of the human geographies of Bulawayo, Zimbabwe, over several decades. In this case, Grant's focus is on the implications of the precipitous free-fall of the Zimbabwean economy for the youth of Bulawayo. Drawing on interviews with youth that she has followed through four successive surveys, Grant provides a very lively picture of the lifeworlds of young job-seekers in the city in a time of the AIDS pandemic, increasing state repression, and economic catastrophe. In articulating the strategies young women and men engage in to survive, she is questioning the ultimate utility of the currently trendy fixation in development studies with social capital as a curative dynamic. She extends the discussion of youth strategies into the vital and poorly understood analysis of mentoring, assessing the ways that mentoring differs distinctly by gender.

In cities in Africa, the collapse of state enterprises and the shrinking opportunities for regular work in wage-paying employment has dramatically transformed the terrain of social reproduction and survival. Under circumstances where increasing numbers of extended family members have come to depend on the salaries of single wage-earners, socioeconomic survival entails a great deal of individual initiative. As the burden of socioeconomic survival has shifted away from conventional social collectivities (such as trade unions, business associations, and other solidaristic organizations) toward individuals and households, greater value is placed on the autonomy of operations than on fostering social interdependency and promoting social collaboration. Without strong institutional supports for social solidarity and cooperation, individuals and households are compelled by economic necessary to step out on their own, to "go their own way." In this way, urban residents are less rooted in place, and more dependent upon networks that connect disparate places.

As Grant's essay shows, there is a growing body of scholarly literature that focuses on the role of women in the informal economy (Tripp 1992; 1997). In their investigation of the informal economy in Kinshasa, Guillaume Iyenda and David Simon argue that opportunities in the informal economy have enabled women to gain access to economic power and social mobility, and thereby narrow the conventional gap in gender inequality. In a stunning reversal in the conventional patterns of retail commerce, the decline in popularity of downtown Kinshasa stores has paralleled the growing importance of street-vending. Increasing numbers of women informal traders purchase commodities from wholesalers (who are predominantly businessmen of Pakistani or Lebanese origins) in geographically dispersed sites throughout the city. With the virtual collapse of the formal banking system, ordinary people—but especially informal traders—have turned to informal financial arrangements that are based on trust and self-interest.

Part 2, then, brings us to the nitty-gritty details of economic existence for urban Africans. For citizens of cities in Africa, the sociologies and geographies of working, or of conjuring a livelihood, are dominated by the confrontation with an economic context that combines perpetual local crises with a global political economy increasingly detrimental to those livelihoods. Fluidity and flexibility in the conjuring, from Nairobi to Luanda to Maputo to Bulawayo to Kinshasa, do create economic possibilities, but within systems that seem to quickly crush them out and force new strategies into existence.

References

Gandy, M. 2005. "Learning from Lagos," *New Left Review* [NS] 33: 37–53.

Hansen, K. and M. Vaa. 2004. "Economy, Work and Livelihoods," in K. Hansen and M. Vaa (eds.). *Reconsidering Informality: Perspectives from Urban Africa*. Uppsala, Sweden: Nordiska Afrikainstitutet, pp. 81–83.

Koolhaas, R. 2002. "Fragments of a Lecture on Lagos," in O. Enwezor et al. (eds.). *Under Siege: Four African Cities. Freetown, Johannesburg, Kinshasa, Lagos, Documenta 11, Platform 4*. Ostiledern-Ruit, Germany: Hatje Cantz, pp. 173–184.

Nordstrom, C. 2004. *Shadows of War: Violence, Power, and International Profiteering in the Twenty-First Century*. Berkeley and Los Angeles: University of California Press.

Tripp, A. M. 1992. "Local Organizations, Participation and the State in Urban Tanzania," in G. Hyden and M. Bratton (eds.). *Governance and Politics in Africa*. Boulder, Colorado: Lynne Riener, pp. 221–241.

Tripp, A. M. 1997. *Changing the Rules: The Politics of Liberalization and the Urban Informal Economy in Tanzania*. Berkeley and Los Angeles: University of California Press.

5

Economic Globalization from Below: Transnational Refugee Trade Networks in Nairobi

Elizabeth H. Campbell

Introduction

Refugees in Nairobi are simultaneously accepted, needed, and depended on as key actors in the local economy and rejected as illegal foreigners, accused of compounding problems of joblessness and poverty in the city. Although the vast majority of Nairobi's refugees live illegally in the city and face widespread institutionalized discrimination, they have managed nonetheless to forge multistranded social and economic relations that link together their countries of origin, countries of asylum, and countries of resettlement (Horst 2003; 2004). These transnational networks have helped many urban refugees become successful entrepreneurs and prominent businessmen, particularly in the informal marketplace. Contrary to the official state position and the xenophobic local belief that refugees are a drain on limited national resources, urban refugees, stemming from throughout the Horn, Central, and East Africa, are largely self-sufficient. Firmly entrenched in Eastleigh, the heart of the African immigrant community in Nairobi, these transnational migrants have cultivated an ability to operate successfully within a socially hostile and economically depressive environment.

Most research on refugees in Kenya however focuses on refugee camp situations (Crisp 2000; 2003; de Montclos and Kagwanja 2000; Horst 2001; 2003; 2004; Hyndman 2000; Mwangi 2005). Until recently, urban refugees in general have been largely ignored (Al Sharmani 2003; Grabska 2005; Jacobsen 2001; 2003; 2005; Kibreab 1996; Landau 2003; Landau and Jacobsen 2004; Maxwell and El-Hilaly 2004; van Hear 2003a, b). When they are mentioned, they are usually depicted only as victims of discrimination and targets of police abuse and not empowered social actors (Human Rights Watch 2002; Verdirame 1999; Verdirame and Harrel-Bond 2005). Moreover, much refugee literature fails to engage with the field of migration studies, which has long argued that other immigrant communities, like refugees, are engaged in a series of transnational social and economic networks (Horst 2001; 2003; 2004). This chapter thus addresses the gap in the literature on urban refugees and challenges the more common approach of highlighting only the vulnerability and lack of legal standing of urban refugees by revealing them as successful entrepreneurs and traders. It also draws on immigration and migration literature to better understand urban refugee livelihood.

The chapter contextualizes urban refugees locally, within the specific history and development of Nairobi, and globally, within the framework of economic globalization and transnational migration flows. Economic globalization is used here to mean "an emerging vision of the world and its resources as a globally organized and managed free trade/free enterprise economy pursued by a largely unaccountable political and economic elite" (McMichael 2000: 354). This vision is dominated by transnational corporations (TNCs), whose size, influence, resources, and global reach have turned them into the world's most powerful social actors (Cavanagh 1996; Derber 1998; Korten 2001). The immediate effect of globalization, characterized by neoliberal economic policies, privatization, and state deregulation, has been a widening gap between rich and poor (Kim et al. 2000; McMichael 2000; Portes 1997). Transnationalism is used here to mean the processes by which refugees create and sustain multi-stranded social relations that link together their countries of origin, countries of asylum, and countries of resettlement (Basch et al. 1994; Horst 2003).

The frameworks of economic globalization and transnationalism are central to the discussion concerning urban refugee economic survival. Indeed, the possibilities, limitations, and realities of urban refugee livelihoods and trade networks are integrally bound to the structure of the global political economy and the strengthening of transnational relations within it (MacGaffey and Bazenguissa-Ganga 2000). For example, neoliberal economic reforms in Kenya, aimed at jump-starting economic growth and providing jobs for the poor, have resulted in the rapid growth and expansion of the informal economy, in which refugee businesses are deeply embedded (Little 2003; McMichael 2000; Portes 1995; Portes et al. 1989; Tripp 1990). The growth of the informal economy, a defining feature of economic globalization, is directly linked to the increased power and profits of global corporations that have systematically disrupted local and regional economies (Jhabvala et al. 2003; McMichael 2000; Portes et al. 1989). The economic activities that sustain urban refugee communities, like TNCs, capitalize on differentials of advantage created by state boundaries (MacGaffey and Bazenguissa-Ganga 2000; Portes 1995; 1997). The main difference is that these communities operate at the grassroots level and usually outside the so-called formal marketplace.

Most research on refugees, however, is not contextualized within this larger framework. Crisp (2003a) argues that the field of refugee studies has in fact been "notoriously ahistorical," where researchers are preoccupied with the latest emergency and the responses to it. Even in protracted refugee situations like Kenya, the studies often begin with the initial mass influxes and rarely analyze previous refugee flows or important historical, social, economic, and political conditions in the countries of asylum. The lack of historical and even theoretical coherence in the field can also be partially explained by the nature of international aid itself. That is, resources directed toward conflicts are reactive and often short term. This ahistorical approach is nonetheless shortsighted, especially in formerly colonized countries like Kenya, which inherited a colonial legal system and an established colonial practice toward refugees and foreigners, much of which is evident in today's policies toward urban refugees.

Nairobi: The Birth of a Transnational City

The colonial policies of social and spatial segregation used by the British against the indigenous African population are virtually identical to the policies used today by ruling African elites against refugees and other black immigrants in Nairobi. At the onset, the social policies employed by the British ensured that Nairobi was an exclusive city, belonging to some groups and not to others. This idea and social practice has remained a salient feature in the historical development of the city, contributing to the continual discrimination against refugees and immigrants living in Nairobi. For ruling elites and citizens alike, black foreigners have come to replace indigenous black Kenyans as "the source of all the city's ills," including rising levels of violent crime and unemployment (Andambi 2003; Awori 2004; Musau 2003; Rutinwa 1999; UNHCR BO Nairobi 2003; 2004b).[1] The constraints of the pre-independence days still form an important basis for explaining the underlying dimensions of social space in Nairobi today.

Nairobi has always been a transnational city, linking Europe, Africa, and Asia socially, culturally, and economically. Extensive trade networks reaching throughout these continents and the rest of the world have deepened throughout the decades. Somalis in particular built upon these trade networks established long before colonization, which deepened during the building of the Uganda Railway, and which intensified after the collapse of the Somali state and with the subsequent influx of rather wealthy Somali refugee businessmen into Nairobi. At the same time, Nairobi was spatially designed to separate the three main communities into distinct neighborhoods and areas of the city. A variety of colonial laws and policies reinforced the spatial segregation and ensured that the majority of public services were disproportionately allocated to the wealthy European neighborhoods. In addition, its origins were predicated upon economic exploitation of black Africans, who, for the better half of the twentieth century, were only legally allowed in Nairobi as temporary workers to serve the interests and functions of the white city (Barber 1967; Barnett and Njama 1966; Collier and Lal 1986; Davidson 1968; Mariotti and Magubane 1973; Tiwari 1972).

Prior to British colonial rule in the nineteenth century, Nairobi did not exist as an urban center. It was only when the Uganda Railway reached Nairobi in 1899 that the area began to develop (Hake 1977; Hill 1957, Hirst 1994; Huxley 1969; Robertson 1997; Uganda Railway ca.1908; van Zwanenberg 1975). When Nairobi was formally designated as the capital of the colony in 1907, the British further accelerated their development efforts, turning the area into a rapidly emerging commercial center. The city, however, was built on a swamp, which led to several sanitation and other health concerns and prompted authorities to appeal to London to remove the entire town to more solid ground (White et al. 1948). Winston Churchill (1908: 19) himself responded and wrote: "It is now too late to change, and thus lack of foresight and of a comprehensive view leaves its permanent imprint upon the countenance of a new country." In light of the undesirable situation, the colonial authorities again appealed to London and requested to formally segregate the city, as in South Africa, between the colonial administrators and the railway workers (Robertson 1997). Their request was again rejected. Instead, the British moved away from the railway headquarters, where the heaviest concentration of laborers and traders resided in overcrowded barracks, and into the neighboring hills. From the onset, then, Nairobi was thus segregated, between the "sticky morass of the subordinate railway quarters" and the "palatial residences of the Railway officers" (Grey 1903: 21)—"a perfect Apartheid city without trying" (Lonsdale 2002: 220).

In order to enforce racial segregation, pass laws for Africans began in 1901.[2] At the time there were no locations in Nairobi where Africans were allowed to live independently of their employment (Barnett and Njama 1966; Collier and Lal 1986; Macharia 1992). By 1906 there were seven, albeit small, separate sections developing in the city: (1) the railway center; (2) the Indian bazaar; (3) the European business and administration center; (4) the railway quarters; (5) the Dhobi or (washermen) quarter; (6) the European residential suburbs and coffee estates; and (7) the military barracks outside of town (White et al. 1948: 14). The basic outlines of Nairobi's commercial and administrative core were laid down within a few weeks of the establishment of the town in a pattern that has endured to the present day. In addition to the bazaars, both established and casual traders from the coast as well as other people attracted by the project—or displaced from it— contributed to the growing number of Indians, Arabs, Somalis, Swahilis, and other Africans already associated in some way with the railway. These people were viewed by the colonial authorities with great disdain and seen mostly as unnecessary surplus labor that was a threat to the health and well being of the city (Hake 1977; Lee-Smith 1988; White et al. 1948).

The settlers continued to appropriate huge areas of Kikuyu and Masai land, and the local Africans were given tribal designations and specific locations or reserves in which to live (Barnett and Njama 1966; Kanogo 1987; Mariotti and Magubane 1973). The designated native reserves were deliberately overcrowded, as British settler Lord Delamere made sure in his 1912 appeal to the Labor Commission where he argued that the areas should be small enough to discourage a self-supporting level of production and encourage a shift to wage labor to service the growing white city (Barnett and Njama 1966). This, coupled with policies of taxation, consequently, as expected, prompted an outflow from the reserves into Nairobi (Burton 2002; Mariotti and Magubane 1973).

Ultimately, half of Kenya's arable land was appropriated by the British; thus, as more families and communities faced displacement through new labor regimes, large-scale cash-crop farming, and the general deepening of capitalist relations, there was indeed rapid rural to urban migration (Aaronovitch 1947; Barnett and Njama 1966; Burton 2002; Collier and Lal 1986; Curtis 1995; van Zwanenberg 1975). No longer able to ignore the growing presence of Africans in the city, coupled with a severe and readily apparent housing crisis, in 1919 the colonial government created designated "native areas" in town. Still, the Nairobi City Council continued to forbid any African to reside permanently in the city. The colonial government continued to treat Africans as short-term wage earners and temporary residents, since their "real" homes were somewhere in the rural areas (Aaronovitch 1947; Macharia 1992; Mariotti and Magubane 1973). Consequently, the segregated "native areas," located to the east of the railway and downstream from the industrial discharge, were designed on the cheapest possible basis. In addition, the 1922 Vagrancy Ordinance, which allowed the police to pick up anyone who appeared to be loitering and unemployed and return him to his rural home, continued to also further entrench the illegality of the black African presence in Nairobi.

After more than three decades, in 1928 the colonial government formally acknowledged for the first time the urban African presence through the establishment of the Municipal Native Affairs Officer for Nairobi (Robertson 1997).[3] Nonetheless, between 1932 and 1947, the City Council spent only one to two percent of its revenue on services for Africans (van Zwanenberg 1975). The vast majority of the revenue went toward roads, water, public lighting, and sanitary services in the vast, sparsely populated, white suburban areas. The attitude of municipal authorities toward African housing was well expressed in 1930:

> It seems only right that it should be understood that the town is a non-native area in which there is no place for the redundant native, who neither works nor serves his or her people. The exclusion of these redundant natives is in the interests of natives and non-natives alike . . . (van Zwanenberg 1975: 268)

By 1940 the pattern of residential racial segregation in colonial Nairobi was firmly entrenched. Low-density European housing was located away from the swampy areas on the highest ground to the west and north of the central business area in forested areas and on large plots. These areas consisted of, among others, Karen, Muthaiga, and Westlands. The majority of Nairobi's Asian population lived in residentially zoned areas across the Nairobi River from the bazaar and commercial zone, Ngara and Eastleigh. The wealthiest moved into Parklands, more spacious plots just to the north. African housing was concentrated in Nairobi's Eastlands, Pumwani, Shauri Moyo, and Karikor, east of the railway yards, with the industrial zone to the south and the Mathare River to the north. At independence in 1963 it was estimated that 50 percent of Nairobi's total population (70 percent of the African population) lived in Eastlands, which at that time accounted for only 10 percent of the total housing area (Etherton 1971: 3). The African population in Nairobi always outnumbered the white settler population, hovering between 60–70 percent until independence, at which point it increased to approximately 80 percent (Robertson 1997).

The postindependence era has been characterized by a persistence of deepening structural inequality. Newly elected African elites traded laws, policies, and practices based on racial segregation for those based on class segregation. Although the three Nairobis—European, Asian, and African—became more racially mixed, the city was resegregated along class lines (Robertson 1997; Tiwari 1972). These characteristics of a city increasingly divided economically remain salient today. Kenya is among the top five countries in Africa with the worst income-distribution rate, and among the top ten most unequal in the world. In addition, recent reports indicate that people are poorer today than they were in 1990, with growing inequality particularly between 1994 and 1999.[4]

The late 1980s and 1990s marked the period during which structural adjustment programs were firmly entrenched, debt repayments mushroomed and were strictly enforced, public firms were privatized, and the country was forced to liberalize trade (Aseto and Okelo 1997; Freund 1998; Prah and Teka 2003).[5] With the deepening of economic globalization and the decline of postindependent national development, Nairobi's economy has stagnated and declined (Freund 1998; Frobel et al. 2000; Himbara 1994; Kim et al. 2000; Leys 1974; McMichael 2000). The levels of absolute poverty have continued to increase from 48 percent in 1990 to 56 percent in 2002 (Mwangi 2005). Many Kenyans, however, have sought to understand these massive structural reforms in part by blaming refugees and other black immigrants, whose mass influx into Nairobi in the early 1990s coincided with the implementation of these changes. Indeed, the huge numbers of refugees who sought asylum in Kenya from the wars in Sudan, Somalia, and the Great Lakes brought forth a lot of animosity and xenophobic feelings toward refugees in general but urban refugees in particular (Juma 1995; Kagwanja 1998; Khalambe 2004; Kimbewe 2003; Kroner 2002; Meru Njuri Ncheke Elders 2003; Murunga 2004; Musyemi 2004).

Many public officials have been quick to blame foreigners and refugees in particular for growing levels of economic and physical insecurity. In 2002, over 1,000 "illegal immigrants" were arrested as part of a countrywide crackdown on crime. Later in the same year, police arrested over 800 foreigners in "aliens-infested Eastleigh Estate."[6] Vice president and minister for Home Affairs, Moody Awori, (2004: 8) recently remarked: "The government is concerned with this group of asylum seekers [urban refugees], as they are likely to be engaged in activities that are contrary to their stay in this country."

Kenyans also increasingly view urban refugees as economic threats, taking over jobs and markets that rightly belong to them. "The plight of Kenyan workers will further be compromised by the introduction of this [refugee] Bill as it allows refugees to enter the local job market" (Khalambe 2004). "Plans to table a refugees Bill is ill-advised. The Bill will allow refugees to obtain citizenship and give them rights like other Kenyans. They will be able to compete with the locals for jobs and businesses. This will create unnecessary competition and disadvantage Kenyans, ultimately pushing them into poverty" (Kimbewe 2003). Urban refugees "could be the missing link in the ever soaring crime rate in Nairobi. But now Kenya has to deal with a different type of refugee altogether—the economic refugee."[7] Finally, in his study on the matatu sector, Kagwanja (1998) wrote that the locals are increasingly hostile toward refugees, who are squeezing the Kenyans out of the matatu sector. These widely held views, if nothing else, reveal the economic success of most refugees in the city, debunking the myth that refugees are an economic burden. At the same time, these comments also make it quite clear that refugees are not welcome in the city.

High levels of economic insecurity in Nairobi have indeed led the victims of structural economic changes to blame foreigners for their plight—a common and well-documented response to large-scale global economic restructuring that leaves huge groups of people unemployed and impoverished. The rise of the service economy and the informal market, in which refugees are concentrated, do indeed threaten the formal economy in which many Kenyans are employed. This is not however because of the influx of refugees but rather due to the consequences of economic globalization that has squeezed out well-paying, long-term formal jobs in favor of short-term, temporary, low-paid work. Such work can be found in the growing number of "sweat shops" in Nairobi's Athi River export processing zone or along the busy commercial streets of Eastleigh. Without legal access to the formal market, it follows that most urban refugees are employed in the informal sector. As the people and institutions responsible for these structural economic changes do not mill the streets of Eastleigh, it is easier to blame the refugees—"the foreign invaders"—who live there. It is worth noting that when it comes to blaming others for job loss in Kenya, other "foreign" populations such as Europeans and North Americans are never targeted by the same xenophobic attitudes.

As policies central to the economic globalization project continue to impoverish the African continent, refugees face rising levels of xenophobia by host populations, who view them as economic migrants and "job stealers." The problems of Nairobi have always been blamed on a "forbidden" or "illegal group" perceived to be disrupting what would otherwise be a prosperous city. The British colonial government has a well-documented history of pointing fingers at the "illegal" black Kenyans who "plagued" the city, bringing with them disease, crime, and everything undesirable. Today, independent Kenyans have kept this history alive by showing the same attitudes toward refugees—the new "illegal" foreigners in the city. It is thus not surprising that the encampment policy, vagrancy laws, lack of work permits, and other policies directed toward urban refugees are not only modeled after but also applied in the same spirit as colonial laws and policies historically directed toward urban Africans.

Though black Africans today control the Nairobi City Council, they define inclusion and exclusion and what is "rightly theirs" in relation to foreign black Africans, especially refugees, and not other groups such as Europeans or Asians, who are seen as assets to the economic growth and well being of the city. At the same time, however, Nairobi's refugees have become such an integral part of the urban fabric that their forced removal would be disruptive to the local economy. In the same way the British settlers both needed African labor in Nairobi and objected to their presence in the city, many refugees today live under similar circumstances. This idea that a group of people is simultaneously needed for economic purposes and rejected socially has a long history in Nairobi; one that developed long before the mass influx of refugees.

Refugees and African Immigrants in Eastleigh

Kenya has been a leading refugee hosting state throughout the twentieth century. By 1988 there were approximately 12,000 refugees in Kenya: the majority were Ugandan and lived in Nairobi (UNHCR BO Nairobi 2004a). These refugees enjoyed full status rights (outlined in the 1951 UN Refugee Convention), including the right to reside in urban centers and move freely throughout the country, the right to obtain a work permit and access educational opportunities, and the right to apply for legal local integration (UNHCR BO Nairobi 2003). The political crises, impacted greatly by the end of the Cold War, in the Sudan, Somalia, and Ethiopia in 1991–1992 and later Burundi, Rwanda, and the Democratic Republic of Congo led to a large-scale influx of refugees into Kenya. The numbers jumped from roughly 12,000 to 120,000 in 1991 to over 400,000 in 1992 and eventually stabilized around 220,000 by the end of the decade (UNHCR BO Nairobi 2004a). These numbers overwhelmed the government's refugee protection capacity, resulting in its collapse and the eventual withdrawal of Kenyan authorities from all refugee affairs. The state mostly viewed the new asylum seekers as threats to national security and economic burdens, marking a shift in refugee protection in Kenya (Juma 1995). Today the vast majority of refugees are not allowed to leave or reside outside of the isolated camps, they are no longer granted work permits, and have been denied opportunities to legally integrate in Kenya (UNHCR BO Nairobi 2003). Though the majority of Kenya's refugees now reside in these camps, several thousand live illegally and largely undocumented in Eastleigh, one of the most densely populated, low-income areas of Nairobi.

Lacking in all public services, including proper drainage and sewage systems, dusty roads overcrowded by a mixture of street vendors and *matatus* (minibuses)—the city's main form of public transportation—dominate Eastleigh's landscape. Of the two main roads running through Eastleigh, one, Second Avenue, has been permanently closed for several years. Huge craters, potholes, and pools of standing water make the road un-navigable. Water supplies are inefficient and many must make illegal connections to the city's pipes. Garbage collection, though recently improved, was once nonexistent. In 2001, an inspection carried out revealed that Eastleigh had the biggest mounds of garbage, some 5,000 tons.[8] Commercial development is rapid and unregulated. If the sparsely populated, well-planned, regularly serviced suburb of Muthaiga, nestled near the Karura Forest and whose residents manage the formal economy, represents the epitome of European (and now also wealthy black) Nairobi, the residential community of Eastleigh represents the opposite. Once a thriving Asian community, Eastleigh today is dominated by African refugees, especially Somalis, hence the name "Little Mogadishu," and also Ethiopians, Congolese, Burundians, Rwandans, Ugandans, and Eritreans, employed largely in the informal economy. Black Kenyans now comprise a small minority of the population.

Eastleigh, located just a few kilometers from Nairobi's Central Business District at the center of the general Eastlands area in which African residences were first authorized by the former colonial government, was established by British investors between 1910 and 1914 (Hake 1977).[9] Before the development was completed, the investors disposed of their unfinished interests to an Indian businessman. Before long the area was dominated by a largely Asian residential community, which also established small shops and other businesses in the area. After independence, the Asians were the first to feel the effects of the "Africanization of Nairobi," and they quickly fled from Eastlands to wealthier, more isolated communities (Tiwari 1972). The Asian exodus from Eastleigh began in 1955, and by 1970 it was largely occupied by Africans, with predominantly Kikuyu landlords. The area was also repopulated by a large number of Somalis, who numbered among those who were in the initial trade caravans from the coast and were present from the onset of the building of the railway in Nairobi (Tiwari 1969). Their presence thus served as a "pull factor" for many Somali refugees who came to Nairobi in the early 1990s to both escape the violence in their country and partake in and benefit from the growing businesses and developing trade networks. As the Asian landlords sold their property largely to Kikuyus in the 1950s, Kikuyus are today quickly selling their properties to Somalis, who now hold a majority of properties in Eastleigh and also comprise the majority of tenants.[10]

As Nairobi's city center and spacious suburbs once drew Europeans, South Africans, Asians, and others from around the world to participate in the benefits of the growing formal economy, today Eastleigh draws large-scale and small-scale traders alike to participate in the largely informal economy. As Iddi Musyemi, a Kenyan and life-long resident of Eastleigh remarked: "Today Eastleigh is the global capital of Nairobi. On any given day, aside from the permanent refugees living here, you can find Tanzanian, Ugandan, and other traders here pedaling their wares and purchasing materials to sell in their countries."[11] In 2001, 55 people were arrested in Eastleigh and charged with illegally entering the city and working without permits. Among them were Palestinians, Bangladeshis, Nigerians, Tanzanians, and people from the Central African Republic, nationalities largely not represented in the refugee populations in Kenya.[12]

Eastleigh's growing importance in the informal economy should not be ignored. Thirty years ago, one-third of Nairobi's population was living in unauthorized housing and had probably created by that time something over 50,000 jobs, which did not appear in any official statistics (Hake 1977). At the time, this "self-help city" was building more houses, creating more jobs, absorbing more people and growing faster than the "modern city" (Hake 1977). This trend continues today. The vast majority of large-scale and smaller-scale businesses and traders operate without the necessary permits and outside the watchful eye of the City Council.[13] Eastleigh is now the epicenter of the booming informal economy, marked by multistory shopping malls. With the best prices in town, Kenyan consumers and merchants are increasingly dependent upon the cheap goods and services provided largely by urban refugees. "Eastleigh is neither formal nor informal, but rather a location where unsanctioned trade is increasingly out in the open . . . In some respects, it symbolizes a graphic form of resistance to an economic and political system that excludes it" (Little 2003: 166). As much as it may have been excluded, it is now part and parcel of the urban fabric of Nairobi. No matter the outcomes of the current peace processes being negotiated, with multi-million shilling investments and prosperous businesses, refugees in Eastleigh are there to stay.

REFUGEE BUSINESSES AND LIVELIHOODS: THE CASE OF THE SOMALIS

Throughout the 1990s Eastleigh was transformed from a residential community to the commercial center of Eastlands, and increasingly much of Nairobi.[14] Based on a land transfer policy known as "willing buyer, willing seller," and with little to no governmental oversight, like in the colonial era, largely Somali businessmen in Eastleigh bought up residential blocs and turned them into multi-million shilling retail malls and commercial enterprises of various sizes. The rapid shift from a predominantly residential area to a commercial one has reduced the number of rentable rooms for an increasing population, thereby pushing many long-term inhabitants, especially Kenyans, out of Eastleigh into neighboring slums or estates and raising the rents for those who can afford to remain. Hence, Eastleigh businesses have brought tremendous competition to the marketplace, which has had a negative effect on many of the Asian businesses in particular. The Asian community has hitherto controlled most of the retail business in Kenya, yet the owners of these businesses can now be seen purchasing their wholesale merchandise from Somalis. One such owner of a city center hardware store stated: "Most Asians don't like to admit it, but the Somalis are really cutting into our businesses. They are willing to live and work in Eastlands, areas where most Asians won't even visit."[15]

The cornerstone of this development, the famous "Garissa Lodge," serves today as a symbol of refugee businesses in Eastleigh. Many Somalis resided in this former guest house before its transformation into a modern retail shopping mall, officially renamed Little Dubai but popularly referred to as "Garissa." From a small-scale "black market" trading in hotel rooms, today Garissa houses 58 stalls in which everything from designer clothing to electronics is sold at some of the cheapest prices in all of Nairobi. According to Mahmoud Noor, a Somali trader, "real business at Garissa Lodge took root after [trade] liberalization, especially when used clothes were allowed."[16] Trade liberalization in Kenya coincided with the influx of Somali refugees, offering them an edge in already established yet more covert business transactions. With their businesses deeply entrenched in the informal economy, they benefited from trade liberalization because they were able to more easily move goods across the borders and sell them openly. Much of the literature on globalization points to the strong relationship between trade liberalization and the growth of the informal economy and/or black market, or as it is referred to in Kenya, *jua kali* (under the sun) workers (Jhabvala et al. 2003; Kagwanja 1998; Kim et al. 2000; Macharia 1992; McMichael 2000; Portes 1997). Informalization involves two related processes: the casualization of labor via corporate restructuring and the generation of new forms of individual and collective livelihood strategies (McMichael 2000). In 1999 there was over 1.2 million micro and small enterprises in Kenya involving some 3.7 million people. This number jumped to 4.2 million the following year (Mitullah and Wachira 2003). Though seen by large multilateral agencies such as the International Monetary Fund (IMF) and World Bank as a form of subversion or as a reservoir of labor in need of development (Schneider and Enste 2002), it is really nothing more than a survival technique when no other job opportunities or source of income in the formal economy exists. This is especially the case for refugees who often have no legal authority in the marketplace. Many entrepreneurs in the informal economy, however, have experienced great success, turning their *jua kali* businesses into contemporary shopping malls. In light of this, it is thus important to measure the success, failures, and limitations of urban refugee businesses and livelihoods within the framework of economic globalization and the increasing informalization of the economy in particular.[17]

Due to its low prices, Garissa Lodge, and many others like it, now draw Kenyans from throughout Eastlands and from all over Nairobi. As individual consumers increasingly turn toward Eastleigh to purchase a wide variety of items at cheaper costs, so do commercial businesses. From hardware stores to fruits and vegetable stands, the merchandise is increasingly purchased wholesale from refugees in Eastleigh. At ten electronics stores on two main thoroughfares in Nairobi, Tom Mboya Street and Moi Avenue, each business owner stated that the vast majority of the merchandise being sold, including radios, televisions, VCRs, DVD players, cameras, and stereos, was purchased from Somali dealers who had cheaply imported it from Dubai in particular. Unlike most of the unregulated businesses in Eastleigh, those in the city center are more strongly regulated and are required to pay rent and taxes and obtain the necessary permits from the City Council. When asked if they thought that businesses in Eastleigh were cutting into their overall profit margin, some of the owners responded that luckily many Kenyans fear going to Eastleigh and only shop in the city center. Others, including Mr. Mwangi Mbugua and Mr. Sarindar Singh, said that Eastleigh businesses are strong competitors and that one day they suspect Eastleigh will really be the main commercial center of Nairobi.[18]

Impressive multistory shopping complexes such as Garissa and Amal Shopping Plaza were both built in areas in which multi-family housing units previously existed.[19] Though legally zoned a residential area, Somalis, often by bribing officials, have been successful in turning these buildings into commercial enterprises. In one year between September 2003 and August 2004, eight different residential structures, in which thousands of people lived, were converted into commercial businesses in Eastleigh proper. Aside from these larger commercial structures, it is also common for Somali businessmen to convert the lower portion of a residential bloc into a coffee house, such as the recently opened Karmel Restaurant on Second Avenue and 9th Street. Others include Tasneem and Ramada Hotel, the most popular restaurant in Eastleigh specializing in Somali cuisine. From rather dilapidated residential buildings, Somalis have transformed Eastleigh's structures into well-built and freshly painted buildings. In fact, there is much more new construction taking place in Eastleigh than in any part of the city center, where buildings continue to deteriorate and go without the necessary services and maintenance.

Aside from large-scale shopping malls, Somalis also own a large number of guest houses or lodges. Many camp refugees without family or friends in Eastleigh stay in these hotels when visiting Nairobi. Somalis also own several bus lines with routes between Nairobi and the refugee camps as well as throughout Kenya and East Africa. They also own significant numbers of *matatus*, the main form of public transportation for refugees and Kenyans alike. *Matatus* began as an illegal, informal mode of transportation in Nairobi, and were only officially permitted in the 1970s (Lee-Smith 1988). The growing influence and importance of the informal sector since the late 1980s forced many to rely on cultural networks to cushion against state retrenchment and the social effects of structural adjustment programs (Kagwanja 1998). Somalis, with particularly strong familial and kinship ties between their countries of origin, country of asylum, and the Western diaspora, were in strong positions to capitalize on these networks and mobilize needed funds to purchase and operate *matatus*. Moreover, of the Somali refugees who settled in Eastleigh in the 1990s, many were successful businessmen and brought with them entrepreneurial experience and capital. The liberalization of trade, intended by policymakers to strengthen the formal economy, has actually created new opportunities for Somali refugees living and working in Nairobi. With less government regulation in general, Somalis have capitalized on the freer flow of goods and services to build their businesses and strengthen their networks. One of the ways in which they have financed these endeavors is through the growth of their informal banking system or *hawilaad*.

Formalizing and Financing Informal Trade

Most refugee traders and business owners in Eastleigh are required to bribe officials in order to avoid arrest and detention for illegal presence in Nairobi or for failure to have a work permit or operating license. In many cases, refugees also pay bribes in order to obtain the necessary licenses and permits. In 2003 a local government minister temporarily suspended licenses of all textile shop owners in Garissa Lodge for paying lesser fees than required for the permits. The minister went on to say, "There must be a conspiracy between City Council workers and these traders owning wholesale shops to deny the council of revenue because the traders are being charged like people operating kiosks."[20] In a more recent example, just down from the Eastleigh traffic circle toward Section III on the right-hand side, one of the newest planned Somali shopping malls, *Al-Haqq Plaza*, is now under construction. Previously a residential estate, friends of the investors indicated that "an arrangement" was made between authorities in the City Council and the businessmen.[21] Since many large-scale investors have such enormous up-front capital, in a country in which open corruption is part and parcel of daily life, it is rather easy for them to pursue their commercial plans.

Indeed, according to Transparency International, Kenya (TIK), Kenya is among the top five most-corrupt countries in the world (Njeru 2004). Nearly three-quarters of all respondents in a recent crime victim's survey reported that their business had been involved in bribery in the past year, with almost everyone claiming that an ethos of corruption and bribery prevailed throughout the commercial sector (Stavrou 2002). Over three-quarters of the business people said that is was necessary to bribe public sector officials if they needed something to be done. Three-fifths of the respondents felt that such bribery was the norm, and they saw it as part of their business practice, almost as an additional tax that had to be paid to ensure the desired service. Almost all respondents felt that bribery had assumed alarming levels of acceptability among Nairobi residents. TIK has noted, however, that low income or unemployed people—and to which refugees should be added due to their illegal status in Nairobi—are significantly more vulnerable to corruption than wealthier people. Unemployed and poor people experience bribery in more than two-third of their encounters with municipal authorities (stavrou 2002).

Corruption in Kenya and especially in Nairobi has a significant impact on refugee businesses. For wealthy entrepreneurs, the system often works to their advantage, enabling them to purchase desired properties and turn them into commercial enterprises, despite zoning laws or other restrictions. For less wealthy and poor refugees (the majority), bribery—or extortion—is a source of abuse and harassment in which hard earned wages often disappear into the hands of eager police, leaving the person with no money and hence nothing with which to buy necessary daily staples. In light of this widespread corruption, it is virtually impossible to distinguish between the formal (official) and informal (unofficial) economy. For instance, powerful businessmen "buy" the needed authorization from officials (who are presumably regulating the formal economy) to sanction the building of large retail complexes in the informal economy—yet which have all of the traits of belonging to the formal economy in terms of size, numbers of employees, and profit. In this example, there is a strong relationship between official regulatory agencies sanctioning large-scale, informal businesses, which should be but are not subjected to the same tax laws as similar businesses in the city center. In Nairobi, the division between formal and informal spheres is not easy to distinguish, since illegal practices regularly occur in the formal sector, and the informal sector is dominated by well-organized and highly sophisticated economic networks (Hibou 1999).

The government of Kenya has long been involved in the 'unofficial' export of goods and services. The most recent and most devastating such example was the infamous "Goldenberg Scandal," in which a complex web of politicians and businessmen managed to defraud the government of billions of shillings through creating fictitious exports to attract foreign currency (Maiko 2003; Mutua 2000).[22] As politicians and wealthy businessmen looted the government coffers, one example was highlighted by the Kenya Revenue Authority (KRA). In 2001 the KRA intercepted and impounded 17 trucks that were sneaking contraband goods worth millions of shillings into the city, destined, the authorities said, for Eastleigh's markets, especially Garissa. The goods, valued at 1.6 million Ksh., were imported through Dubai via Eldoret International Airport, where they were then transported by road to Nairobi to various traders. The traders were caught in this particular instance evading taxes and duties (ironically, probably by the same people who initially accepted the bribe to avoid them), and the incident reveals how most business in Eastleigh is conducted. As one cargo inspector noted, all of the clothes on sale in Eastleigh come through one container freight service in Mombasa, where there is only one customs officer and one Kenyan Bureau of Standards authority. There is thus little preventing one from giving bribes to the officer to undervalue the goods. By 2003, corruption at Eldoret Airport was so endemic that all cargo flights were cancelled. Somali traders or freight companies owned by Somali networks in Eastleigh and coming mostly from the port of Dubai imported the majority of the goods targeted for cancellation (Githongo 2003).[23]

The mobile phone revolution, engulfing much of Nairobi in the late 1990s, coupled with the rise of computerized informational networking, has contributed significantly to the growing effectiveness of informal trade (Castells 2000; MacGaffey and Bazenguissa-Ganga 2000). The recent introduction of mobile phone networks in the refugee camps in mid-2004 has greatly impacted trade networks between the camps and Nairobi as well. Using these technologies, Somali companies based loosely around family and clan networks receive goods from Kenyan *jua kali* importers in Dubai and other countries, ship them to Kenya on behalf of the importers and clear the goods for collection in Nairobi. The receiving office is usually an individual on a mobile phone operating somewhere in Dubai. Goods destined for export to East Africa are collected from one's point of purchase and are simply marked with the shipper's name and address, consignment weight, and destination. The total transit charges are limited to a dollar value per kilo of the consignment's weight irrespective of the nature of the cargo. The importer need not even be present in Dubai to make the actual purchases, as the Eastleigh office can orchestrate the whole process (Githongo 2003). These networks, like TNC activities, are grounded precisely on the differentials of advantage created by state boundaries. Refugee traders use the same logic as global corporations, except they manoeuver informally at the grassroots level (Portes 1997).

Facilitating this trade is an informal banking system, known as *hawala* or *hawilaad* (meaning "transfer" in Arabic), which enables the transfer of cash in any denomination and in almost all currencies throughout the world and at a much cheaper rate than the formal competitor, Western Union (Little 2003). To send or receive cash from Eastleigh to Dubai, Cairo, London, Johannesburg, Sydney, Minneapolis, or San Diego, Somalis and others deposit the equivalent value in a local currency at a given location. Hawilaad transactions are guaranteed and usually completed within one hour. Credit, by transferring funds through the use of promissory notes, is mediated through these informal money houses, often a one-room shack, and middlemen who are essential to the overall operation. *Al Barakaat*, once among the largest *hawilaads* handling some $140 million in annual transfers, had branches throughout the world, including Eastleigh. Its largest source of remittances was from Somalis living in the United States. This bank was forced to close its operations after September 11, when top U.S. officials argued it was laundering money to terrorists and al-Qaeda in particular (Crawley 2001). The bank and its investors suffered huge losses, but individual Somalis were easily able to use alternative *hawilaads*. Despite the collapse of the state in Somalia, telecommunications and money-wiring services are booming industries that continue to facilitate trade networks and bring more capital into Eastleigh (UNDP 1998). Little (2003: 164) has written:

> . . . the Somali system is inherently expansionist . . . As a livelihood system, it effectively adapts to uncertain circumstances, incorporates occupied populations, and mobilizes social relations over vast territories. No matter where one is in Somalia or outside among the diaspora, the extensive kinship system creates potential alliances, an attribute that nicely complements mobile pastoralism. The same logic of extension and alliance also accommodates geographically dispersed trading networks as they seek new markets and partners.

Eastleigh's growing influence cannot be underestimated. Eastleigh is an openly informal marketplace, neither hidden from nor embraced by authorities.

Regardless, it is a central part of Nairobi's economy. Aside from offering all of the goods and services imagined at the cheapest price in all of Nairobi, thereby attracting both individual consumers and purchasers from a variety of businesses, the Somalis have also created low-wage, unskilled work for many Kenyans in Eastleigh. This work includes cleaning, employment as casual workers unloading boxes of goods, washing, shoeshine, or basic repairs. Most interviewed agreed that though the jobs were not very glamorous, the Somalis tended to pay more than Kenyans, roughly 150–250 Ksh. ($2–3.30) a day compared to 80–100 Ksh. ($1.06–1.30) typically earned from Kenyans when engaging in the same work.[24]

Other types of work done mostly by Kenyans and generated from Somali businesses included the collection of discarded cardboard boxes. Once retrieved from the different shopkeepers, the cardboard was resold to the recycling center for roughly 5 Ksh (6 cents) per kilogram. Kenyans working in this business were able to make between 100 and 250 Ksh. (U.S.$1.30–3.30) daily. More lucrative jobs included working on Somali-owned *matatus* as a tout or a money counter or collector. Some Kenyans are even offered jobs as construction workers. Others have profited from mechanical repairs of Somali-owned vehicles. With the general infusion of capital in the area, Kenyan residents of Eastlands increasingly turn toward Eastleigh to eke out a meager living. For many, chances to earn a day's wage are higher in Eastleigh—the informal economy—than in the city center, where formal businesses already have a regularly employed staff. As Godfrey Icharia said, "It's easier to find a Somali willing to pay you a couple hundred shillings to do some work for him than it is to beg from the Asian businessmen in town. Anyway, you save on transport costs by not travelling into town."[25] For the majority of refugees and Kenyans, the so-called informal economy today in Eastleigh provides more hopeful possibilities of survival than the formal one.

Small-Scale Somali Businesses and Traders in Eastleigh

In addition to large-scale businesses in the wholesale, retail, housing, and transportation industries owned by a few wealthy male refugees, there is also a wide variety of smaller-scale trade networks and businesses, in which the majority of refugees work, including large numbers of women. Where the wealthy, largely Somali, refugees are able to profit from a corrupt City Council, less wealthy and poor refugees suffer from constant harassment and abuse. The class differentiation among and between refugee communities is important to highlight, as the level of wealth often determines the level of protection and security a refugee is able to buy in Nairobi. In fact, the Eastleigh Business Community (EBC) was largely set up to curb excessive police abuses and to regularize the relationship between the two entities.[26]

Most Somali refugees living in Eastleigh are indeed economically poor. Some survive by working for other wealthier Somalis. Others, including many women, are able to open their own road-side stands selling fabrics, textiles, undergarments, scarves, shoes, perfume, dishware, music tapes and CDs, fruits and vegetables, electronics, coffee, and tea. Many engage in the rather lucrative business of selling *miraa*, a mild narcotic that grows in abundance in the Mt. Kenya region of the country. A day's supply for a single person goes for between 300 and 500 Ksh.; sellers can make about 20 Ksh. in profit from one sale. Women especially do washing and other household chores for wealthier Somalis often in exchange for rent and/or food. There are many Somali-owned telephone calling centers and Internet cafes. Some are taxi drivers, shuttling customers up and down the busy commercial thoroughfare and throughout the city.

There is also a widespread trade in cattle. Seventy percent of the cattle sold at Garissa, a small town on the Kenyan–Somali border, are destined for Nairobi; 16 percent of all cattle consumed in Nairobi come from Somalia (Little 2003). Many engaged in cattle trade in Nairobi also engage in retail, butcheries, grain trade, and skins and hides trade. Nassir Ali is one such example. He works in the cattle trade transporting the animals from Garissa to Nairobi. During the dry season when the movement of animals is slow, he runs a small retail shop selling the latest imported ladies fashions, including dresses, scarves, long skirts, and blouses. His shop, located in the "Little Dubai" Shopping Plaza in Eastleigh's main shopping district, does good business. "I make enough money for my wife and four children, and I also help support the families of my two brothers."[27] Ali went on to explain that when he is moving cattle, he is also moving his merchandise to and from Nairobi.

Goods imported without taxation or duty into Somalia are easily brought to Kenya and sold at the cheapest possible prices in Eastleigh, undercutting many Kenyan competitors who do not have access to these networks. This small-scale border trade is a key component of refugee livelihoods in Eastleigh. In 2001 the Kenyan authorities, citing concerns with gun smuggling and contraband goods, closed the Somali–Kenyan border. The effects were devastating. An estimated 500,000 *miraa* farmers suffered massive losses, as they were unable to sell their product in Somalia.[28]

As largely nomadic pastoralists, many Somalis have successfully adopted migration strategies necessary for the survival of livestock toward retail and other trade (Horst 2003; Hyndman 2000; Little 2003). Divided between Somalia, Kenya, and Ethiopia, ethnic Somalis build upon these social relations in neighboring countries to establish successful regional trade networks today, selling everything from shoes to perfume. An increasingly large Somali diaspora, stretching from Australia to Canada and in almost every country in-between, including Iceland and Greenland, has in the last fifteen years certainly widened the scope and size of these networks, bringing ever more capital to Eastleigh in particular. Independent from international aid and without protection or assistance from the Kenyan government, urban refugees have successfully carved out spaces in which to live and work in Nairobi. Kenyans living in Eastleigh increasingly turn toward these refugees for jobs and work opportunities, highlighting the significance of refugee entrepreneurs and business owners in the city.

Impact of Refugee Livelihoods and Businesses in Nairobi

Before the onset of economic globalization in the 1970s, most Africans ridiculed those wishing to be traders, as the real opportunities were believed to be in public service (MacGaffey and Bazenguissa-Ganga 2000). Since then, as the purchasing power and job security of civil servants has been gradually eroded, traders are largely considered to be the people with the wealth (MacGaffey and Bazenguissa-Ganga 2000). As neoliberal economic reforms have spread throughout Kenya and the African continent, the size of the government and the scope of its activities has indeed declined (Aseto and Okelo 1997; McMichael 2000). At the same time, similar employment opportunities have not emerged in the formal private sector, leaving larger and larger numbers of people outside of the newly restructured economic framework. These people have thus turned to the informal economy for economic survival. Likewise, urban refugees, who have no legal right to work or live in the city, are also immersed in the informal economy. These refugees have capitalized on and strengthened existing trade networks as well as forged new ones in light of state retrenchment and deregulation of many industries. As largely nomadic pastoralists, Somalis in particular have successfully adopted migration strategies necessary for the survival of livestock toward retail and other trade (Horst 2003; Little 2003).

Today, most of Nairobi's refugees are highly mobile individuals engaging in networks that extend through time, space, and various cultures to circulate commodities between countries (Horst 2003; MacGaffey and Bazenguissa-Ganga 2000). As such, refugees, like other migrants and traders, now have vested economic interests in Eastleigh. War may have brought many refugees to Eastleigh in the first place, but peace negotiations alone will not necessarily take them back home. Throughout years and even decades of protracted political crises, urban refugees in Nairobi have found ways to tap into trade networks and build businesses in the informal economy. The operators of these networks will not simply uproot their investments to return to countries where such opportunities may not exist. Still, official state pronouncements and local popular opinion regards urban refugees with great disdain, repeatedly calling for their complete removal from the city. Refugees are constantly used as scapegoats for the city's high levels of poverty and unemployment, despite their well-known entrepreneurial successes.

Similar to the way in which indigenous Kenyans were simultaneously needed and rejected by the colonial city council in Nairobi, refugees and other African migrants now fill this ambiguous position. Urban refugee trade networks are central to the livelihood of many people living in Nairobi, yet the refugees themselves face high levels of xenophobia and discrimination. Despite the discrimination, urban refugees, like indigenous Africans under the colonial regime, are fully integrated into the fabric of the city. No matter the desires of the locals or the authorities, removing all of the refugees from Nairobi is unlikely. Since the growth of the informal economy is a defining feature of globalization, it is likely that it will only continue to grow and expand in the coming decades, further entrenching refugee businesses in Nairobi. Legal local integration of these successful entrepreneurs is thus a viable solution to their situation of protracted exile.

NOTES

The bulk of the research, funded by the Fulbright International Institute for Education, was conducted in Nairobi between September 2003 and August 2004. The research was based at the United Nations High Commissioner for Refugees Branch Office Nairobi (UNHCR BO Nairobi). In addition to conducting interviews with and examining internal documentation of UNHCR and government agencies, ethnographic work was carried out in the refugee-dominated area of Eastleigh. This chapter stems in part from over 150 structured, unstructured, formal, and informal interviews of refugees from the Somali, Ethiopian, Ugandan, Congolese, Rwandan, Burundian, and Sudanese communities. Moreover, semi-structured surveys were used to gather pertinent data on pricing and trade networks.

1. See also "Tighten Control at Borders," *The Nation*, December 20, 2003; "Report Calls for Control of Immigrants," *The Nation*, June 10, 2004; and "Illegal Immigrants Blamed over Insecurity," *East African Standard*, February 3, 2003.
2. Pass laws required that all black Kenyans be in possession of passes that stated whether the holders were legally entitled to work in the city, whether or not they had completed their contractual obligations, and whether they could leave the city.
3. Though the colonial government also discriminated against the Asian population, compared to black Africans, Asians enjoyed more political power and economic opportunities, not least their ability to reside legally in Nairobi.
4. See "Poverty on the Rise," *East African Standard*, June 25, 2004; and "Our Unequal Kenya," *The Nation*, October 27, 2004.
5. Some of the companies that privatized include Kenya Airways (1996), Port Authority and Railways (2001–2002), Telecommunications (Telcom) (2000), Kenya Power and Lighting Company (2002–2003), Kenya Tea Development Authority (1991), Kenya Oil Refinery (2002–2003), East Africa Portland Cement Company (2002–2003), and various water distribution systems (1998–2000).
6. Not a single recognized refugee has been found guilty of any terrorist act in Kenya. See "840 Foreigners Arrested in Nairobi," *East African Standard*, May 31, 2002; "Over 1,000 'Illegal' Immigrants netted in Police Swoop," *The Nation*, February 8, 2002; and "Kenya Warned against Crackdown on Ethiopian, Somali Refugees," *BBC News*, June 10, 2002 <http://news.bbc.co.uk>.
7. See "Our Own Illegal Trafficking Syndicate," *East African Standard*, November 2, 2001.
8. See "Council Cracks Down on Illegal Water Connections," *East African Standard*, August 15, 2003; and "City hall to Clear Garbage," *The Nation*, June 21, 2001.
9. Today the area of Eastlands consists of the estates and blocs of Biafra, Buru Buru, California, Dandora, Donholm, Eastleigh, Embakassi, Gikomba, Githurai, Huruma, Jericho, Kahawa, Kariobangi, Kariokor, Kasarani, Kayole, Komarock, Majengo, Mathare, Mlango Kubwa, Mukuru, Pangani, Pumwani, Shauri Moyo, Starehe, Umoja, Zimmerman, and Ziwani.
10. Attempts to gain official documentation from the Nairobi City Council to support this claim proved impossible. The claim is thus supported by a door-to-door survey of Eastleigh's main business street, in which it was found that 45 of 50 businesses and 41 of 50 residential buildings, constituting a mere sample, were owned by ethnic Somalis, both Kenyan and Somali nationals, some of whom were officially registered refugees.
11. Interview with Iddi Musyeni, Kenyan Eastleigh resident, November 4, 2004.
12. See "Illegal Immigrants in Court as Crackdown Intensifies," *The Nation*, October 17, 2001.
13. In the above-mentioned survey of 50 businesses, it was also found that not a single business paid formal rates or taxes to the city government. Most of these businesses did however pay bribes regularly to police of City Council officials.
14. See "A Tale of a City without a Plan," *The Nation*, January 10, 2002.

15. Interview with Narayan Mehta, Asian businessman, Nairobi City Center, June 30, 2004.
16. Mr. Mahmoud Noor cited in Mung'ou (2000).
17. Interview with Calum Mclean, UNDP-Somalia Official Nairobi, October 30, 2003; Interview with Tula Muhamud, Kenyan Somali businessman from coastal areas, May 8, 2004; and Interview with Sudhir Vidyarthi, hardware shopowner, Nairobi, March 16, 2004.
18. Interview with Mwangi Mbugua, Eastleigh businessman, October 12, 2004; and Interview with Sarindar Singh, Eastleigh businessman, October 13, 2004.
19. See "A Tale of a City without a Plan," *The Nation*, January 10, 2002.
20. See "Minister Suspends Licenses for Textile Shops," *The Nation*, October 23, 2003.
21. Interview with Ali Moalin, Somali businessman in Eastleigh, April 3, 2004.
22. See also "Kenya Looting Goes to Court," *Africa Analysis*, March 7, 2003; and "The Goldenberg Scandal: Powerful Forces behind Kenya's Most Devastating Economic Fraud," *The Nation*, February 28, 2003.
23. See "KRA Seizes 17 Trucks in TRax Evasion Scandal," *East African Standard*, December 15, 2001; and "Scandals and Intrigues at Kenya Ports Authority," *The Nation*, November 26, 2003.
24. Interview with Mohammed Abdu Ali, Somali businessman, originally from coastal areas now resident of Eastleigh, April 4, 2004.
25. Interview with Godfrey Icharia, Kenyan resident of Eastleigh, June 3, 2004.
26. See "Eastleigh—Kenya's Somali Capital," *East African Standard*, November 4, 2002.
27. Interview with Nasir Ali, Somali businessman in Eastleigh, August 10, 2004.
28. See "Gunrunning is Out of Control, Admits State," *The Nation*, February 14, 2001; and "Ban on Trade Raises Questions," *The Nation*, July 31, 2001.

BIBLIOGRAPHY

Aaronovitch, S. and K. Aaronovitch. 1947. *Crisis in Kenya*. London: Lawrence & Wishart.

Al-Sharmani, Mulki. 2003. "Livelihood and Identity Constructions of Somali Refugees in Cairo." American University Cairo, Forced Migration and Refugee Studies Working Paper Series No. 2 (July) <www.auegypt.edu/fmrs>.

Andambi, Arthur. 2003. "Kenya's Refugee Policy." Lecture given at the Moi University Center for Refugee Studies Regional Conference on Curriculum Development. Eldoret, Kenya, November 16–19.

Aseto, Oyugi and Jasper Okelo. 1997. *Privatization in Kenya*. Nairobi: Basic Books.

Awori, Moody A. A. Honorable. 2004. "Remarks by the Vice President and Minister for Home Affairs Hon. A. A. Moody Awori, EBS MP during the Official Opening of the Joint Strategic Planning Workshop for the 2005 Kenya Refugee Programme Held at the Hotel Intercontinental, Nairobi. 16–17th February 2004—9:00 a.m." pp. 1–20.

Barber, William J. 1967. "Urbanization and Economic Growth: The Cases of Two White Settler Territories," in Horace Miner (ed.). *The City in Modern Africa*. New York: Frederick A. Praeger, pp. 91–126.

Barnett, Donald and Karari Njama. 1966. *Mau Mau from Within: An Analysis of Kenya's Peasant Revolt*. New York: Monthly Review Press.

Basch, Linda, Nina Glick Schiller, and Cristina Szanton Blanc. 1994. *Nations Unbound: Transnational Projects, Postcolonial Predicaments and Deterritorialized Nation-States*. Amsteldijk, Netherlands: Gordon and Breach.

Burton, Andrew (ed.). 2002. *The Urban Experience in Eastern Africa c. 1750–2000*. Nairobi: British Institute in Eastern Africa.

Castells, Manuel. 2000. *The Rise of the Network Society*, 2nd edition, Vol. I. Oxford: Blackwell.

Cavanagh, John. 1996. "Global Economic Apartheid." *Alternative Radio*. Takoma Park, MD <www.alternativeradio.org> September 19.

Churchill, Winston. 1908. "My African Journey," quoted in L. W. Thorton White et al. *Nairobi: Master Plan for a Colonial Capital*. London: His Majesty's Stationary Office.

Collier, Paul and Deepak Lal. 1986. *Labor and Poverty in Kenya 1900–1980*. Oxford: Clarendon Press.

Crawley, Mike. 2001. "Somali Banking under Scrutiny," *Christian Science Monitor*, November 28.

Crisp, Jeff. 2000. "Africa's Refugees: Patterns, Problems and Policy Challenges." UNHCR Evaluation and Policy Analysis Unit, New Issues in Refugee Research Working Paper No. 28 <www. unhcr.ch>.

Crisp, Jeff. 2003a. "Closing Keynote Address." In Joanne van Selm et al. (eds.). *The Refugee Convention at Fifty: A View from Forced Migration Studies*. Oxford: Lexington Books, pp. 219–229.

Crisp, Jeff. 2003b. "No Solutions in Sight: The Problem of Protracted Refugee Situations in Africa." UNHCR Evaluation and Policy Analysis Unit, New Issues in Refugee Research Working Paper No. 75 <www. unhcr.ch>.

Curtis, John. 1995. *Opportunity and Obligation in Nairobi: Social Networks and Differentiation in the Political Economy of Kenya*. Munster, Hamburg: Lit Verlag.

Davidson, Basil. 1968. *Africa in History*. New York: Macmillian.

de Montclos, Marc-Antoine Perouse and Peter Mwangi Kagwanja. 2000. "Refugee Camps or Cities? The Socio-Economic Dynamics of the Dadaab and Kakuma Camps in Northern Kenya," *Journal of Refugee Studies* 13 (2): 205–222.

Derber, Charles. 1998. *Corporation Nation: How Corporation Are Overtaking Our Lives and What We Can Do about It*. New York: St. Martin's Press.

Etherton, David. 1971. *Mathare Valley: A Case study of Uncontrolled Settlement in Nairobi*. Nairobi: Housing Research and Development Unit, University of Nairobi.

Freund, Bill. 1998. *The Making of Contemporary Africa: The Development of African Society since 1800*. Boulder, CO: Lynne Rienner.

Frobel, Folker, Jurgen Heinrichs, and Otto Kreye. 2000. "The New International Division of Labor in the World Economy," in Timmons Roberts and Amy Hite (eds.). *From Modernization to Globalization: Perspectives on Development and Social Change*. Oxford: Blackwell, pp. 257–273.

Githongo, Gitau P. 2003. "Those Magnificent Somalis in Their Flying Informal Networks." *The East African Standard*, July 28.

Grabska, Katarzyna. 2005. "Living on the Margins: The Analysis of the Livelihood Strategies of Sudanese Refugees with Closed Files in Egypt." American University Cairo, Forced Migration and Refugee Studies Working Paper Series No. 6 (June) <www.auegypt.edu/fmrs>.

Grey, Olive. 1903. *Picturesque British East Africa*. London.

Hake, Andrew. 1977. *African Metropolis: Nairobi's Self-Help City*. London: Sussex University Press.

Hibou, Beatrice. 1999. "The 'Social Capital' of the State as an Agent of Deception or the Ruses of Economic Intelligence," in Jean-Francois Bayart, Stephen Ellis, and Beatrice Hibou (eds.). *The Criminalization of the State in Africa*. Oxford: James Curry, pp. 69–113.

Hill, Mervyn F. 1957. *Permanent Way: The Story of the Kenya and Uganda Railway*. Nairobi: East African Railways and Harbours.

Himbara, David. 1994. *Kenyan Capitalists, the State and Development.* Boulder and London: Lynne Rienner.

Hirst, Terry. 1994. *The Struggle for Nairobi: A Documentary Comic Book.* Nairobi: Mazingira Institute.

Horst, Cindy. 2001. "Vital Links in Social Security: Somali Refugees in the Dadaab Camps, Kenya." UNHCR Evaluation and Policy Analysis Unit, New Issues in Refugee Research Working Paper No. 38 <www. unhcr.ch>.

Horst, Cindy. 2003. "Transnational Nomads: How Somalis Cope with Refugee Life in the Dadaab Camps of Kenya." Ph.D. dissertation. Research Institute for Global and Development Studies, University of Amsterdam, Amsterdam, The Netherlands.

Horst, Cindy. 2004. "Money and Mobility: Transnational Livelihood Strategies of the Somali Diaspora." Global Migration Perspectives No. 9. Geneva: Global Commission on International Migration, October <www. gcim.org>.

Human Rights Watch. 2002. *Hidden in Plain View: Refugees Living Without Protection in Nairobi and Kampala.* New York: Human Rights Watch.

Huxley, Elspeth. 1969. *Settlers of Kenya.* Nairobi: Highway Press; London: Longmans, Green and Co.

Hyndman, Jennifer. 2000. *Managing Displacement: Refugees and the Politics of Humanitarianism.* London and Minneapolis: University of Minnesota.

Jacobsen, Karen. 2001. "The Forgotten Solution: Local Integration for Refugees in Developing Countries." UNHCR Evaluation and Policy Analysis Unit, New Issues in Refugee Research Working Paper No. 45 <www. unhcr.ch>.

Jacobsen, Karen. 2003. "Local Integration: The Forgotten Solution," *Migration Information Source* <www.migrationinformation.org>.

Jacobsen, Karen. 2005. *The Economic Life of Refugees.* Bloomfield, CT: Kumarian.

Jhabvala, Renana, Ratna Sudarshan, and Jeemol Unni. 2003. *Informal Economy Centerstage: New Structures of Employment.* New Delhi/Thousand Oaks, CA: Sage.

Juma, Monica Kathina. 1995. "Kenya: NGO Coordination during the Somali Refugee Crisis, 1990–93," in Jon Bennett (ed.). *Meeting Needs: NGO Coordination in Practice.* London: Earthscan, pp. 89–117.

Kagwanja, Peter Mwangi. 1998. "Investing in Asylum: Ethiopian Forced Migrants and the Matatu Industry in Nairobi," *Les cahiers de l'IFRA* 1 (March/April): 51–69.

Kanogo, Tabitha M. J. 1987. "Kikuyu Women and the Politics of Protest: Mau Mau," in Sharon MacDonald, Pat Holden, and Shirley Ardener (eds.). *Images of Women in Peace and War: Cross-Cultural and Historical Perspectives.* Houndmills, Basingstoke, Hampshire: Macmillan Education in association with the Oxford University Women's Studies Committee, pp. 78–99.

Khalambe, Tenu. 2004. "A Plan to Enact Refugee Law Likely to Affect Locals," *The Nation*, November 3.

Kibreab, Gaim. 1996. "Eritrean and Ethiopian Refugees in Khartoum: What the Eye Refuses to See," *African Studies Review* 39 (3): 131–178.

Kim, Jim Yong, Joyce Millen, Alec Irwin, and John Gershman (eds.). 2000. *Dying for Growth: Global Inequality and the Health of the Poor.* Monroe, ME: Common Courage Press.

Kimbewe, Wycliffe. 2003. "Shelve Refugee Law, It is Likely to Affect Many," *The Nation*, December 17.

Korten, David. 2001. *When Corporations Rule the World.* Bloomfield, CT: Kumarian Press.

Kroner, Gudrun Katharina. 2002. "Social and Political Impact on Somali Refugees in the Diaspora," in Susanne Binder and Jelena Tosic (eds.). *Refugee Studies and Politics:*

Human Dimensions and Research Perspectives. Vienna: WUV Universitätsverlag, pp. 139–170.

Landau, Loren B. 2003. "Forced Migrants in the New Johannesburg." Forced Migration Working Paper Series No. 8 <http:/// migration.wits.ac.za>.

Landau, Loren and Karen Jacobsen. 2004. "Refugees in the New Johannesburg," *Forced Migration Review* 19 (January): 44–46.

Lee-Smith, Diana. 1988. "Urban Management in Nairobi: A Case Study of the Matatu Mode of Public Transport," in Richard Stren and Rodney White (eds.). *African Cities in Crisis: Managing Rapid Urban Growth.* Boulder, San Francisco, and London: Westview, pp. 276–304.

Leys, Colin. 1974. *Underdevelopment in Kenya: The Political Economy of Neo-Colonialism 1964–1971.* Berkeley: University of California Press.

Little, Peter. 2003. *Somalia: Economy without State.* Oxford: James Curry.

Lonsdale, John. 2002. "Town Life in Colonial Kenya," in Andrew Burton (ed.). *The Urban Experience in Eastern Africa c. 1750–2000.* Nairobi: British Institute in Eastern Africa, pp. 207–222.

MacGaffey, Janet and Remy Bazenguissa-Ganga. 2000. *Congo–Paris: Transnational Traders on the Margins of the Law.* Bloomington: Indiana University.

Macharia, Kinuthia. 1992. "Slum Clearance and the Informal Economy in Nairobi," *The Journal of Modern African Studies* 30 (2): 221–236.

Maiko, Deremo. 2003. "Heads to Roll Over Goldenberg Scandal." News From Africa, April <www.newsfromafrica.org>.

Mariotti, Amelia and Bernard Magubane. 1973. "Urban Ethnology in Africa: Some Theoretical Issues." in William Arens (ed.). *A Century of Change in Eastern Africa.* The Hague and Paris: Mouton, pp. 249–273.

Maxwell, Laura and Aya El-Hilaly. 2004. "Separated Children in Cairo: A Rights-Based Analysis." American University Cairo, Forced Migration and Refugee Studies Working Paper Series No. 5, September <www.auegypt.edu/fmrs>.

McMichael, Philip. 2000. *Development and Social Change: A Global Perspective.* Thousand Oaks, CA: Pine Forge Press.

Meru Njuri Ncheke Elders. 2003. "The Position of Meru Njuri Ncheke Elders on the Somali Question." Submitted to UNHCR BO Nairobi, December 8.

Mitullah, Winnie V. and Isabella Njeri Wachira. 2003. "Informal Labor in the Construction Industry in Kenya: A Case Study of Nairobi." Geneva: International Labor Organization <www.ilo.org>.

Mung'ou, Titus. 2000. "Mystery Deepens as Traders Are Burnt Out," *The Nation*, December 19.

Murunga, Godwin. 2004. "Refugees at Home? Coping with Somalia Conflict in Nairobi, Kenya." Council for the Development of Social Science Research in Africa <www. codesria.org>.

Musau, Jelvas. 2003. "Major Issues in Refugee Protection: Speaking Notes for the East African Workshop for Curriculum Development in Forced Migration Organized By the Center for Refugee Studies, Moi University." Eldoret, Kenya, November 16–19.

Mutua, Makau. 2000. "A Scandal that Could Topple Kenya's Shaky Democracy," *Boston Globe*, June 17.

Mwangi, Annabel. 2005. "Refugees and the State in Kenya: The Politics of Identity, Rights and Displacement." Ph.D. dissertation. University of Oxford.

Njeru, Mugo. 2004. "Graft: Kenya Still among the Worst," *The Nation*, December 10.

Portes, Alejandro (ed.). 1995. *Economic Sociology of Immigration: Essays on Networks, Ethnicity and Entrepreneurship.* New York: Russell Sage.

Portes, Alejandro. 1997. "Globalization from Below: The Rise of Transnational Communities." UK Economic and Social Research Council Transnational Communities Programme Working Paper Series, WPTC-98–01 <www.transcomm.ox.ac.uk>.

Portes, Alejandro, Manuel Castells, and Lauren Benton (eds.). 1989. *Informal Economy: Studies in Advanced and Less Developed Countries.* Baltimore: Johns Hopkins University.

Prah, Kwesi Kwaa and Tegegne Teka (eds.). 2003. *Chasing Futures: Africa in the 21st Century—Problems and Prospects.* Capetown: The Center for Advanced Studies of African Society and Addis Ababa: Organization for Social Science Research in Eastern and Southern Africa.

Robertson, Claire C. 1997. *Trouble Showed the Way: Women, Men, and Trade in the Nairobi Area, 1890–1990.* Bloomington and Indianapolis, IN: Indiana University Press.

Rutinwa, Bonaventure. 1999. "The End of Asylum? The Changing Nature of Refugee Policies in Africa." UNHCR Evaluation and Policy Analysis Unit, New Issues in Refugee Research Working Paper No. 5 <www. unhcr.ch>.

Schneider, Friedrich with Dominik Enste. 2002. *Hiding in the Shadows: The Growth of the Underground Economy, Economic Issues 30.* Washington, DC: International Monetary Fund.

Stavrou, Aki. 2002. *Crime in Nairobi: Results of a City-Wide Victim Survey.* Nairobi: UN HABITAT.

Tiwari, R. C. 1969. "An Analysis of the Social Agglomerations among Asians in Nairobi," *Scottish Geographical Magazine* 85 (2):141–149.

Tiwari, R. 1972. "Some Aspects on the Social Geography of Nairobi, Kenya," *African Urban Notes* 7 (1) (Winter): 36–61.

Tripp, Aili Mari. 1990. "The Informal Economy and the State in Tanzania." In M. Estellie Smith (ed.). *Perspectives on the Informal Economy: Monographs in Economic Anthropology,* No.8. Lanham, MD: University Press of America, pp. 49–69.

Uganda Railway. Ca. 1908. *The Uganda Railway: British East Africa, from Mombasa to Lake Victoria Nyanza, and by Steamer Round the Great Lake.* London: Waterlow and Sons.

UN Development Program (UNDP). 1998. *Human Development Report: Somalia.* Nairobi: UNDP.

UNHCR Branch Office Nairobi. 2003. *Annual Protection Report.* Internal document.

UNHCR Branch Office Nairobi. 2004a. "UNHCR in Kenya." Internal document.

UNHCR Branch Office Nairobi. 2004b. "Meeting Minutes GOK and UNHCR Workshop Concerning Refugee Bill." Hilton Hotel, Nairobi, July 6–7.

Van Hear, Nicholas. 2003a. "From Durable Solutions to Transnational Relations: Home and Exile among Refugee Diaspora." UNHCR Evaluation and Policy Analysis Unit, New Issues in Refugee Research Working Paper No. 83 <www. unhcr.ch>.

Van Hear, Nicholas. 2003b. "Refugee Diasporas, Remittances, Development and Conflict." Migration Information Source, June 1 <www. migrationinformation. org>.

van Zwanenberg, Roger M. A. 1975. *Colonial Capitalism and Labor in Kenya, 1919–1939.* Nairobi: East African Literature Bureau.

Verdirame, Guglielmo. 1999. "Human Rights and Refugees: The Case of Kenya," *Journal of Refugee Studies* 12 (1): 54–77.

Verdirame, Guglielmo and Barbara Harrell-Bond. 2005. *Rights in Exile: Janus-Faced Humanitarianism.* Oxford and New York: Berghahn Books.

White, L. W. Thornton, L. Silberman, and P. R. Anderson. 1948. *Nairobi: Master Plan for a Colonial Capital.* London: His Majesty's Stationary Office.

6

Changing African Cityscapes: Regional Claims of African Labor at South African–Owned Shopping Malls

Darlene Miller

Introduction

> The rights of those who labor to exercise some level of individual and collective control over labor processes (over what is produced as well as over how it shall be produced) is crucial to any conception of democracy and freedom. Long-standing concerns over the conditions of labor and the right of redress in the event of unreasonable burdens or sufferings (such as those that result in shortened life expectancy) need to be reinforced on a more global scale . . . It also highlights respect for the dignity of labor and of the laborer within the global system of production, exchange and consumption.
>
> (Harvey 2000: 249)

On August 27, 1997, Shoprite supermarket opened its doors in Maputo, the capital city of Mozambique. In most cities of the United States, the opening of a food store would elicit only minor attention, perhaps a side-column in the local news. In Mozambique, Shoprite's arrival was an event. The store was swamped with people who had been crushing its designer-tiled entrances to gain access to the store when it opened. Much fanfare, hype, and local town gossip had preceded this event. On the day itself, celebrities were in attendance and a public rally was held at the Center. The two major newspapers in the country ran frontpage coverage of Shoprite's opening. Months after the event, debates continued to rage in the newspapers and amongst Maputans about the benefits and disadvantages to Maputo and Mozambique of this new South African arrival.

Shopping in southern Africa had a racial geography since the growth of the mining towns and the brutal separation of black people from land ownership in the 1900s. When beautiful malls were built in South Africa in the 1960s, they were built close to white suburbs and in the central business districts where Africans could only visit with special pass books. As a young girl growing up in a "colored" area in Lansdowne, Cape Town, we bought groceries at a Shoprite supermarket "on the other side of the tracks." This store was the second store opened by Shoprite's founder, Mr. Barney Rogut, in 1967. Its first store was opened in 1966 in Wynberg, Cape Town, an area bordering a middle-class "colored" suburb and wealthier white suburbs. The little Shoprite supermarket on the "white side" of Lansdowne (marked off by the bridge over the railway tracks) that I walked to on bare feet is now part of the largest retail chain in Africa. Shoprite's "Cape to Cairo" expansion is part of a new phase of retail accumulation in the 1990s, made possible by 37 years of racialized retailing and the exploitation of black labor in South Africa. This essay foregrounds the workers of southern Africa whose labor power is often hidden from view when the story of wealth and power accumulation in South and southern Africa is told (Meyer 2002).

The end of apartheid rule in South Africa in 1994 opened up a new regional moment and a new regional space, where the "definition of the possible" for the southern African region changed and South Africa was reintegrated into the region (Simon 2001: 377–405). South Africa's transition conferred a new respectability on the region's policies and projects, catapulting South Africa from pariah to regional liberator. Democracy, however, has had many unintended outcomes. At the same time as the incumbent President Thabo Mbeki declared his *African Renaissance* in the early 1990s, many southern African countries deepened economic liberalization and privatization and released state enterprises for sale to mainly private, foreign investors (BusinessMap SA 2000; 2001; Nkiwane 1999; Soderbaum 2002: appendix, table 8). Liberated by South Africa's democratization from the limits of racialized capitalism, restless South African retail capitalists were now free to explore new possibilities for accumulation in the rest of Africa (Adedeji 1996; Ahwireng-Obeng and McGowan 1998a, b).

This essay argues that the new investment activities of South African retailers in Africa shape regional geographic imaginaries. About four times more is exported from South Africa to other parts of Africa than is imported. South African investment has increased from R9 bn. to R30 bn. between 1997 and 2002. South African investment in SADC between 1994 and 2003 was 25 percent of total FDI flows into the region (Daniel et al. 2003; Miller 2005; UNCTAD World Report 2005). Regional perceptions of South African economic strength are reinforced by the African retail expansion of South African multinationals, of which the Shoprite-owned shopping malls are a major part. The changing environment of consumption in host countries and the character of the new retail investment, specifically shopping malls, provide the context for changing regional imaginaries. The high levels of visibility of the retail sector bring with it a new set of expectations in host countries about democratic South Africa's regional role. If expectations of regional development for host countries are frustrated in some ways, a renewed charge of South African regional exploitation in the post-apartheid era will open up the possibility of enhanced tensions between South Africa and its African neighbors (Kenny 2001). Regional debates have questioned South Africa's regional hegemony and charged that South Africa is the principal beneficiary of post-Apartheid regional integration (Bond et al. 2001; Miller 2001; Naidu 2004: 205; Clarke et al. 1999).

Workers complained bitterly in strikes at Shoprite in Zambia that the company had benefited from its African expansion to the detriment of the workers in the host countries. Claims of an "African Renaissance" will become unsustainable in the face of growing regional dissatisfaction.

New political fault-lines are cohering around these growing expectations of the benefits that South African economic expansion should have for local communities and host countries. This essay first discusses the concept of "geographical imaginaries," drawing on an earlier article. The section that follows provides a brief overview of retailing in southern Africa. The post-Apartheid regional moment and the expansion of South African multinationals have opened up new sites of contradiction between African workers, on the one hand, and South African capital, on the other, as well as new loci of conflict between African citizens (and local farmers) and South African multinational corporations. These points of tension are modest but significant new "spaces of hope" in African cities threatened by stagnation and unemployment, with possibilities for new regional resistances. The essay concludes with a report on a controversy over dumping at the *Centro Commercial* in Mozambique, and a strike by Shoprite workers at Manda Hill shopping mall in Zambia as cases of new regional resistance (Miller 2005).

"Malling" Africa—Changing Geographic Imaginaries and Regional Claim-Making

Though "Afropessimism" dominates contemporary accounts of African societies (Arrighi 2002; Ferguson 1999; Saul 1993; Saul and Leys 1999), these analyses overlook or underestimate the impact that new South African investment is having on southern Africa and the continent more generally. Stagnation and decline are the overarching metaphors of Afropessimists for a continent redlined by "globalization" and devastated by the AIDs epidemic. Whereas other less-developed regions of the world have enjoyed significant growth spurts, sub-Saharan Africa's share of world GNP has fallen dramatically (Arrighi 2002). Conflict and genocide have sown devastation and warlordism in the midst of this material deprivation. Yet, in the midst of this ailing social environment, a new development has emerged. A new regional moment is shaping the workplace experiences of African workers and leading to new, boundary-drawing strategies for African workers (Miller 2005; Morris 1993). Southern Africa is dominated by South Africa, the region's economic subhegemonic power. Uneven capital flows concentrate money and power in particular geographical places to the detriment of others, leading to unequal levels of development between and within regions and nations and the underdevelopment of "developing" nations (Arrighi and Saul 1973: 145; Harvey 1989: 176; Southern African Regional Poverty Network (SARPN) Pretoria 2004; Weeks and Mosley 1998). Whereas natural geographical conditions explain the initial contours of uneven development, social forces intervene in the more complex processes of differentiation and equalization that occur under capitalism (Smith 1984: 99–103). Sometimes referred to as "enclave economies" or economic islands, capital accumulation develops the most profitable sectors of the economy to the detriment of other sectors, creating uneven capital flows (Butts and Thomas 1986; Seidman and Makgetla 1980). South Africa has been the chief beneficiary within the southern African region of uneven regional development, comprising $130 bn. of the ten main countries $160 bn. in 1998 output. In 2001, South Africa's total exports ($3.7 bn.) were five times that of its imports ($856 mn.) in Africa. Relations of economic dependency have thus continued into the post-Apartheid phase.

Workers at Shoprite in post-Apartheid Southern Africa are implicated in a politics of scale where rights and claims may be asserted at local, metropolitan, regional, national, and global levels. I employ the concept of "claim-making" to delineate these spatialized contestations and competing regionalisms. Claim-making as a concept delineates these spatialized contestations and competing regionalisms. "Scalar" translations—pragmatically shifting reference points between one geographical level and another—shape the ways in which local resistance achieves national, regional, or global purchase. How do the reference points of workers—constructed through race, gender, class—assume a geographical dimension?

Perrot (1986) elaborates on the formation of working-class dispositions through a concrete historical analysis of the French working class in the nineteenth and twentieth centuries. The concept of dispositions, he contends, shows how workers see themselves as part of a greater whole. He points to the referential moment in working-class dispositions, arguing that workers construct their images of themselves in relation to some other. Perrot analyzes the French working class and asks a relevant question: "How did he (the worker) conceive of this whole over time and space?"

> This working class defined itself by its enemies, its limits, its consciousness of a shared "fate" and a shared exploitation, its vision of the future. All of this, often voiced by militants who were both mediators and spokesmen, was crystallized in words and images, a language that became an instance of reality, a reference that in turn structured the imagination. (Perrot 1986: 94)

To shift from the national level to cross-national and regional imaginaries, the historical work of Cooper (1996) and Silver (2003) is evocative. Cooper's study of "the labor question" in French and British Africa shows how the geographical idea of "empire" was inserted into African working-class imaginaries in the first half of the twentieth century, thus providing useful cross-cultural insights. African trade unionists used European labor standards as a reference point for their own claims. Workers appropriated specific geographical and hegemonic representations of empire into their claim-making. The absence of any reference to regional levels of claim-making in Cooper's account may suggest that the regional level was not relevant to workers' claim-making processes during the colonial period.

If the phase of empire suggested European metropolitan conditions as the universal frame of reference for African workers, how does southern Africa insert itself into workers' regional imaginaries? The regional moment in working-class dispositions begs a deeper understanding of how the region is produced and how the politics of boundary-making should proceed. "Making" boundaries points to the geographical envisioning—or "imaginary"—on the part of workers. Historically, race, gender, ethnicity, and nationality were employed in various ways by workers and labor movements to exclude some sections of the global working class from this associational community. North–South divisions and tensions between workers in northern, highly developed countries and workers in less developed regions of the south are an example of the geographical contours of such boundary-making processes. Pragmatic solidarity strategies between workers of the north and south can be inspired by these differences in the geographies of labor. Making these exclusionary boundaries is often a defensive strategy actively employed by workers themselves, as Arrighi (1990: 93–94; Arrighi et al. 2003) points out with reference to the early days of the neoliberal counterrevolution:

> Whenever faced with the predisposition of capital to treat labor as an undifferentiated mass with no individuality other than a differential capability to augment the value of capital, proletarians have rebelled. Almost invariably they have seized upon or created anew whatever combination of distinctive traits (age, sex, colour, and assorted geographic specificities) they could use to impose on capital some kind of special treatment. As a consequence, patriarchalism, racism and national chauvinism have been integral to the making of the world labor movement. . . . and live on in one form or another in most proletarian ideologies and organizations.

Thus, divisions within the working class are not made only by "class enemies," but are actively constructed from within. Silver (2003) identifies three forms of boundary-drawing strategies: labor market segmentation, bounding citizenship, and exclusionary, nonclass identities (e.g., race, ethnicity, gender). Adapting Perrot's question, we may then ask, "How did she (the worker) conceive of this whole over regional time and space?" How do workers' notions of inclusion and exclusion take on a geographical character? If working-class dispositions and the establishment of collective identities require a common set of values and goals, how do these common objectives become articulated at a particular geographical scale?

Shoprite workers at the shopping malls in Lusaka privilege the regional over the local or national scales in their geographic reference points. Shopping mall workers are included in the "space of consumption" through their position as company employees. Their claims, however, are directed at the regional company and its head office in South Africa and to a lesser extent at their national governments, rather than at their local managers. Though national and other levels retain importance for workers, regional claim- making has become an important spatial strategy for retail workers at these shopping malls. The Shoprite workplace is an important agent of a new regional imagination amongst these retail workers. Workers claim inclusion into the regional company on an equal basis with South African workers, privileging ties to South Africa that go through the company. The South African reference point in workers' claims is interpreted here as a geographic imaginary expressed as regional claims.

In the war-torn landscape of Mozambique and the economic reversals in Zambia, the shopping mall becomes the symbolic container of a renewed stab at modernity (Goss 1993; Jackson 1996; Marks and Bezzoli 2001; Morris 1993). During the period of nationalized industry in Mozambique and Zambia, local Indian traders and the government owned shops and wholesale stores. These stores experienced constant commodity shortages. Lack of infrastructure development in the cities and poor service provision also contributed to economic decline and stagnant urban centers, where peeling building facades were a graphic index of urban decline. The decline of national economic growth and commodity prices for key mineral exports led to demoralization and failed expectations in the nationalist projects of Zambia and Mozambique. In the uneven African cityscape, these bright, modern outlets are part of a new urban development—in contrast to the old central business districts, which are decaying (Marks and Bezzoli 2001). When South African investors build new shopping centers in these impoverished African cities, the contrast between these new malls and the old city environment produced an apparent urban "dualism," where modernity and urban underdevelopment stood side by side.

Struck by the image in Lusaka of women in traditional wraps and head cloths carrying water in clay pots, against the background of a gleaming office block, Ferguson, however, challenges these "dualist habits of thought" that contrast urban and rural. Rejecting the binaries of "traditional" and "modern" when confronted by the extreme unevenness of Zambian urban development, he argues that such mixtures are in the nature of development in less-developed contexts (Ferguson 1999: 85). Ferguson's observations support Trotsky's notion of the "leap-frog" character of development in less-developed societies:

> The laws of history have nothing in common with a pedantic schematism.
>
> Unevenness, the most general law of the historic process, reveals itself most sharply and complexly in the destiny of the backward countries. Under the whip of external necessity their backward culture is compelled to make leaps. From the universal law of unevenness thus derives another law of combined development—by which we mean a drawing together of the different stages of the journey, a combining of separate steps, an amalgam of archaic with more contemporary forms. (Trotsky 1977: 27)

Ferguson's (and Trotsky's) cautions notwithstanding, the insertion of the most modern technologies into declining African landscapes produces a cultural rupture that penetrates ever-widening social layers and has dramatic social consequences. Such truncated commodification of society such as shopping malls changes everyday life in a far-reaching way, particularly in the sphere of consumption. The diversified consumption that the shopping mall allows serves different local markets.

The impact of expanded commodity distribution on social relations in African countries is observed by earlier writers. Almost two decades ago, Phimister highlighted the development of new needs in Africa with the advance of commodity relations and the corresponding withdrawal of labor from agriculture. Observing these changing urban environments and the creation of "new needs" between 1890 and the 1950s, Arrighi and Saul highlight the transformative nature of internal consumption patterns: "In analyzing the process whereby the sale of labor-time became a necessity for the African population of Rhodesia, attention must be focused upon . . . the transformation of 'discretionary cash requirements' into 'necessary' requirements" (Arrighi and Saul 1973: 199).

The dominance of money in social relations expands as cash is required to participate in the new realms of social exchange. Local consumption patterns shift as more local consumers are drawn into the new shopping mall consumption. The shopping mall becomes the conduit for drawing larger numbers of African citizens into the money economy and circuits of capital accumulation. New consumer needs and lifestyles emerge as old, traditional social relations are disrupted to make way for global, consumer lifestyles. The presence of these shopping mall outlets dramatically alters urban imaginaries and the landscapes of consumption, even for those who are unable to participate in these new "cultures of consumption."

UNEVEN REGIONAL DEVELOPMENT AND SHOPRITE'S RETAIL EXPANSION IN THE 1990S

Uneven regional development continues in the geographies of the new shopping malls. As local economies declined in Africa during the subsequent phases of nationalization and structural adjustment, African cities registered these declines dramatically. The geography of malls in Zambia and Mozambique follows the models of American cities, sidestepping the clutter of the old CBDs and opening up shopping malls in undeveloped land within driving distance of these old CBDs. The stark contrast of these glitzy malls with dilapidated urban environments testifies to the uneven and combined nature of capitalist development, where less-developed countries often taken a dramatic and truncated step into advanced urban technologies. Successive phases of retail development in South Africa have agglomerated resources, infrastructure, technical know-how, and capital for reinvestment within powerful corporate entities. The post-apartheid opening that is currently being captured by South African retail multinationals has been facilitated by strong phases of national retail accumulation in South Africa, on the one hand, and weak phases of national retail accumulation in Mozambique and Zambia, on the other (Ariyo and Afeikhena 1999: 201–213; Kolala 2000; Pitcher 2003: 28–32).

As one of the largest retail multinationals in South Africa, Shoprite made R70 mn./$10 mn. available for reinvestment in Africa in 1999.[1] With an overtraded local market, it leveraged its powerful conglomerate toward an African expansion. Other retail multinationals faced with a similarly crowded local market have employed expansion strategies in other global regions such as Europe and Australia. General Equity unit trusts at seven percent make up the third biggest slice in South African retail behind banks, financial services, and mining resources, the same sectors expanding in Africa. The Shoprite group's historical experience in Africa since the 1960s through their clothing chain, Pep Stores, and their supermarkets in the black-run "homelands" (nominally independent states) of South Africa gave them some organizational advantages. This experience with black consumer markets, their surplus capital, and bold organizational leadership in the company's upper echelons positioned them to best penetrate a consumer market perceived as "high risk" and with low consumer savings. Their absorption of other retailers such as OK Bazaars added to this sense of "African know-how."[2]

The retail sector in South Africa has been in a long-term low for a number of years. Competition is tough and South African retailers have used strategies of consolidation, new kinds of retail stores, and expansion into other parts of Africa to cope with these challenges. Managers describe the domestic market as "sluggish and capricious" and marketing directors say they have never seen such "deep lows and high peaks" of consumer spending. Financial analysts argue, however, that the 85 percent rise in the Retail Index since its September 1998 low, suggests a continued recovery in the retail sector. Over the past few years, competition has narrowed to three large players, Shoprite, Pick 'n Pay, and Spar (Tiger Foods) as consolidation of the retail industry has occurred. As Shoprite lost market share in South Africa to large competitors such as Pick 'n Pay and Spar's flexible, new "action stores," Shoprite, along with other South African retailers such as Game, Steers, Debonairs, Engen, ProFurn, the J D Group, and Wimpy have used expansion into other African countries as a response to heightened competition. Shoprite has taken its excess cash and headed for the African countries north of South African borders, extending as far as Egypt in North Africa.[3]

A pattern in this new retail investment is the opening up of new shopping malls with a supermarket (Shoprite) as an anchor store. These shopping malls make a dramatic change to the local consumption and urban environments. The South African multinational retailer, Shoprite, has spearheaded this kind of development in fifteen (one in four) African countries. Shoprite forms a joint consortium with a local minority shareholder. The consortium owns the new shopping mall. Other companies, primarily South African, rent retail space in these stores, from which a significant proportion of Shoprite's profits derive. A characteristic cluster of stores is Hi-Fi Corporation (belonging to the ProFurn group), Truworths, First National Bank, Game Discount stores, Edgars, and fast food stores such as Debonairs and Steers. There has also been an increase in local spending and domestic credit that has increased local demand for goods. Inflow of grants and development finance has contributed to increased liquidity in some countries (Brümmerhoff 1998). The rapid increase in money supply in a number of countries could be related to major credit extension to the private sector and credit granted to government structures. This is particularly applicable to Zambia and Zimbabwe where, according to statistics compiled for the Committee of Central Bank Governors, total domestic credit extension showed sharp increases during 1997.

Internal consumptive markets are also heterogeneous. Despite high levels of general poverty, internal elites have significant savings and consumptive capacity, sometimes generated by earnings in foreign currency (dollars, rands). Local expatriates, government elites, and middle-class professionals are significant customers for the new supermarkets. Some of these markets have local peculiarities. For example, company management reported that Angolan diplomats and international community workers cross the border for olive oils, bakery items, and other specialist items at the rural supermarket in Solwezi province, a market that Shoprite management in Zambia have learnt to cater to in this branch.[4] Trade unionists also argued that there was pent-up demand that had no outlet as long as the retail and services sectors were run as poorly stocked, state-owned enterprises. People had money, they report, but had to go to South Africa to buy commodities that they now find inside Zambia at South African companies.[5] Tourism is a new area of demand that affects the shifting patterns of consumption in many African countries. The prevalence of tourism in recent economic activity demonstrates the nature of Africa's economic growth sites. Foreign and South African tourists are propelling a highly skewed economic development that caters to the consumptive activities of leisure classes whereas local development is neglected. Middle-class consumers in Mozambique may shop at the same South African store in the capital, Maputo, or in the Johannesburg border town of Nelspruit (Soderbaum and Taylon 2003). Working-class consumers have made use of Shoprite's promotional activities to buy basic consumer items such as fish oil, eggs, washing powder, rice, bread and milk (although these promotions appear to be less now as the company is more established and tax breaks for the company's first five years in both countries are over).

Demand for goods from Shoprite's supermarkets also comes from the informal sector. Informal traders in Mozambique and Zambia source some of their basic items from Shoprite. In Zambia, one store in Lusaka has been converted into a primarily wholesale store to cater for small shop owners from rural areas. In rural areas where Shoprite has outlets, informal traders buy from Shoprite and resell to local consumers, sometimes just outside of the company's premises.[6] New patterns of consumption and distribution thus develop as the Shoprite supermarkets and shopping centers extend from the city into rural towns (Larmer 2005).

While deindustrialization could be seen as a threat to Shoprite's growth in African countries, the withdrawal of large companies from a local environment can stimulate Shoprite's growth as competition intensifies and Shoprite is able to eliminate smaller, local competitors. In the Copperbelt, Anglo-American's pull-out in 2001 led to smaller businesses going under and the capture of local market share for Shoprite that had previously belonged to these competitors.[7] Though distribution to the informal sector may be better served by the expansion of wholesale stores, Shoprite is wedded to its shopping mall style of development. The company aims for a uniform brand image in its supermarkets and the shopping mall creates an appropriate consumer environment for the Shoprite brand. There is a fear from managers that if their style of operation differs from its South African style of operation in less-developed African locales, it will be subject to charges of racism.[8]

The African retail expansion is a step toward South Africa's global expansion. The expanded African market is absorbing surplus capital in South Africa and commodity surpluses from South Africa, potentially expanding the manufacture of goods inside South Africa. South African retailers benefit from regional economies of scale as they expand their distribution to regional consumer markets. In contrast to Afropessimist accounts of Africa's marginalization, the expansion of South African companies produces dynamic economic and social relations that change the geographic imaginaries of workers at these foreign, South African firms, as the case studies that follow demonstrate.

Centro Commercial in Maputo, Mozambique

> Shoprite is a filthy-rich multinational, (with) billions of US dollars in property. Shoprite has had the chance to grow with Apartheid. Mozambican traders have had to fight war and the competition of the informal sector . . . Many people were very happy when Shoprite opened. People went there in their droves. I was the only one objecting . . . What kind of regionalization is this?[9]

The Shoprite store is situated on the edge of the Maputo CBD. It is located in an L-shaped, single-storey mall of shops, many of them South African–owned (Truworths, Pep stores). To access the store by car, one often has to cross large "dongas" (huge holes in the road), with construction work-teams competing with cars. Once in the enclosed and guarded parking area of the mall, neat cobbled stones cover the parking area. The mall's entrance is made of beautiful modern paving, and the welcoming entrance to Shoprite is the wide, brightly lit doorway characteristic of many First-World supermarkets. Once inside, fresh dairy products, rows of fresh fruit, signs denoting "specials" on promotion and aisle demarcations, rows (about 8) of neatly attired black women cashiers, black male floor managers in corporate-style shirts and dark pants race around with clipboards monitoring the shop-floor. Cashiers speak English if requested: in short, everything you would expect if you walked into a well-run American supermarket. Given the generalized context of straw shacks, ailing infrastructure, "shibalo" labor relations between Portuguese expatriates and subservient, multitasked locals, entering Shoprite is like crossing a boundary in space and time, a truly breath-snatching experience. Like southern Africa, the contours of uneven development are starkly visible at this local scale as well. The First World shopping experience belies the Third World urban degradation beyond the paved parking lot of the *Centro Commercial* (Commercial Center). Flanked by a diversity of housing, the Center is sandwiched between beautiful houses and middle-range apartments on its east—what Mozambicans have called "cement city." To its north and west there is a sprawling, high-density township abuzz with people, informal markets, and stalls selling secondhand clothing. Old and dilapidated formal structures of stone or brick township housing are hemmed in by informal cane housing in the fronts and backs and the roads are sandy and potholed.

Modeled on the U.S. shopping mall, the Shoprite Center—*Centro Commercial*—takes up about 12,500 square kilometers for the shops and 12,500 hectares for the car park of downtown municipal property. The Center entailed an initial capital outlay of R5.4 mn. (less than US$1 mn.). To a statistical observer, this event carries little meaning. To local Maputans, however, this store has changed the nature of their lives as consumers dramatically. No longer limited to shopping in open, "mosquito-infested markets" as one resident described them, shopping at Shoprite marks a new consumer era for Maputans. This includes those with very little money who make regular use of the promotional sales at the store. For many Mozambicans, Shoprite's investment is "um bom investamente," a good investment. There are new jobs where there were no jobs. Shoprite has built new infrastructure and imported new consumption patterns. Consumers have access to a range of commodities that they had limited access to in the recent past—fruit juices, processed meats, different kinds of cleaning detergents, and so on. Maputans who aspire to modern "cultures of consumption" may find new commodities and services in cell-phone shops, CD stores, banks, and clothing shops that are increasingly accessible through television and other visual media.[10] Internal opinion is divided, however.[11] Local traders think that the special privileges given to Shoprite by the state and the local municipality give Shoprite an unfair advantage (as the opening quote by the *Metical* editor suggested). One issue where growing regional tensions are evident is the periodic controversy around "dumping" from South Africa. About two years ago a huge public furor erupted in Maputo. The agent of consumer modernization in Mozambique, Shoprite, was caught dumping expired foodstuffs on the shelves of its ritzy new store in the *Centro Commercial*. The reaction to this discovery was loud and contentious. Maputan consumers asked whether South Africans thought they could be sold rotten wares. Was this to be the *African Renaissance*, South Africa using the region as its backyard for dumping, they asked in public commentaries? The local reaction suspiciously wondered whether Shoprite was selling perishable goods that could not be sold in South Africa to Maputan consumers.

When interviewed, Shoprite management tried to explain that the expired dates were not intentional but a consequence of Shoprite's regional distribution mechanisms. Retail companies characteristically buy discounted goods wholesale that have short expiry dates. This system, they argue, worked well for South African stores. Mozambique obtains its stock from the warehouse in Gauteng, South Africa. New problems were encountered with the cross-border regional distribution system. Border problems sometimes caused distribution delays. Also, as a store that targets working-class consumers, turnover was not always as quick in Maputo as in South African stores, hence the unanticipated expiry of goods.

Some Maputans disputed Shoprite's explanations. They are accustomed to buying groceries and other durable goods from Nelspruit, the South African–Mozambican cross-border town that Maputans call "Thank-you, Maputo" (because of the Mozambican subsidy to the town's phenomenal economic expansion in the last decade). Some consumers went back to shopping at the same Shoprite in Nelspruit, a porous site on the Mozambican–South African border. More forgiving consumers or those with less choice said they needed to "give Shoprite a chance." Black Mozambican trainee managers at Shoprite-Maputo, caught in the middle of local loyalties and company loyalties, argued that this was the kind of regional development that was to be expected.

> Turnover in South Africa is difficult. They finish their stock in Maputo. Of course they do things to suit them. They are the big ones so what they want, happens. It's a story. It happened before. It won't change. Dumping in Africa has always been happening. It's happening now in a modern way. (Interview, Mozambican Trainee Manager, Mozambique, September 1999)

Most black Mozambican managers identify with the company's reliance on South African supplies, arguing that controversies over dumping obscure the extent to which consumer standards have been improved by Shoprite's retailing presence. This controversy over dumping has also been an issue in Zambia in the past, pointing to regional concerns over the impact of South Africa's expansion on local supply chains and the competitive advantages of large, foreign multinationals over local villagers, traders, and businessmen. In a similar contestation over the regional benefits of Shoprite's expansion, workers at the new South African–owned shopping malls occupy a contradictory location in relation to the privilege of employment in countries with unemployment levels ranging between thirty and fifty percent, and the problems they encounter at these companies.

Malls and the Supermarket as a Workspace: Comparing Manda Hill (Lusaka, Zambia) and Centro Commercial (Maputo, Mozambique)

While Ferguson's workers attest to "ethnography of decline,"[12] being part of a shopping mall locates Shoprite workers in the heart of urban capitalism. South African stores have placed these retail workers within a realm of expectation offering modernity after Zambia's failed copper dreams. Hence the company's claim that Shoprite is providing "world-class merchandising."[13] Working in this "space of consumption" puts the employee in the midst of this promise of modernity. Retail workers share this space, even when they are excluded as consumers. The grandeur of their work environment is not lost on the Shoprite staff.

> We have seen different kinds of food displays and sometimes on our plates, if we manage to buy them.[14]
>
> I see Shoprite as a powerful company . . . even the way their buildings are, the way they display their merchandise.[15]

Manda Hill Complex in the capital city of Lusaka is a centerpiece of Shoprite's Zambian investment, with a cost of U.S.$20 mn. for the shopping center. Employees and managers were drawn from the state shops when the company first started out in Zambia. The center takes up 22,260 square meters, of which Shoprite occupies 4,608 square meters.[16] The complex is 20 percent owned by Zambia Venture Capital and 80 percent Commonwealth Africa Investment, the name under which Shoprite trades in Zambia. There are about 56 tenants at the store. Shoprite and Game (general merchandising retail multinational)—both South African owned—are the two anchor tenants. Shoprite-Manda Hill (in Lusaka) is by far the largest of the firm's 18 Zambian supermarkets.[17] It is not only Manda Hill's larger physical size that makes it Shoprite's Zambian flagship, but also because Manda Hill has been the only shopping mall of its kind to date. The Shoprite supermarkets represent a new phase in South Africa's relations with the region. The new Shoprite *Centro Commercial* heralded a new era in retailing for many ordinary Mozambicans who in the past were excluded from the hotels and stores developed for the tourists and foreign aid communities. Shoprite-Manda Hill has had a similarly dramatic effect on urban lifestyles and consumer choices in Lusaka, Zambia. This confers an enhanced status on workers outside of their workplaces, a status that does not correspond to their conditions within the workplace.

Workers are aware of their relatively privileged position, not least because they were specially selected from around the country to make up the staff at this store. They are also aware of the improved retail ambience of Shoprite-Manda Hill. In all 11 stores that I visited, workers followed the uniform dress code of the company, projecting a pristine image that corresponded to the upmarket environs of the mall. Interviewed workers often cited the Shoprite uniform as one reason why Zambians initially assumed that Shoprite staff were part of a labor elite. The suggestive, imaginary reach of the mall brings the expanded global consumptive universe within the reach of the retail worker. Any perceived or real deprivation due to wage levels is thrown into sharp relief when working in such commodity havens, a contrast that creates the equivalent of Hirschman's (1981) "tunnel effect," whereby increased hopes for social mobility are frustrated by social inequality.

Both Zambian and Mozambican workers enjoy an enhanced status as workers at a powerful, South African multinational company with branches all over Africa. In these poor environments, their smart uniforms and appearance set them apart from poorer nationals. Unlike workers from the older mining and manufacturing sectors, these retail workers work in a modern shopping mall environment that is cleaner and smarter. Despite this "foreign enclave" status, almost 90 percent of workers in both cities responded that there was nothing about work at Shoprite that they loved and had to be coaxed to find something positive to say about their work environment. Once they were coaxed, they were able to find positive elements in their work, but their embittered feelings made their initial response to this question a highly negative one. Workers in Zambia and Mozambique find their work conditions degrading because of low wages, long hours, and multi-tasking. These conditions are offset for more skilled workers (clerks and controllers) who feel that they have benefited from multi-skilling. The ravages of unemployment are also avoided through work at Shoprite. Even if their work conditions are unsatisfactory, it is better than the insecurity of life without a job.

Both sets of workers felt that the extent of South African control over the shop floor undermined the autonomy and efficiency of local management for whom they had little respect, with only one or two exceptions. All workers looked to South Africa as the standard-bearer of the region based on its higher levels of industrialization and their knowledge of better conditions for workers. Workers similarly ignored the internal heterogeneity of South African retail workers, creating an idealized notion of retail work in South Africa based on some inaccurate assumptions. Though they are correct about the better conditions for workers in South Africa, the declining conditions and growing insecurities of South African workers were something they were largely unaware of.

The Shoprite company magazine and transport workers in the regional firm emerged as important sources of information for workers in both countries. The newspaper is distributed regularly on the shop floor from head office and workers circulate amongst themselves the copies that they receive and what they have read. Images of festivities attached to particular social occasions such as weddings, engagements, and birthdays had a profound impact on workers in countries where these crucial social occasions are becoming an unattainable luxury. High levels of local poverty and unemployment and illness and death due to AIDS and other causes stretches workers' wages across extended family and friendship networks, causing stress and high levels of responsibility for these relatively younger workers. Porous regional borders also allow information about South Africa to circulate amongst southern Africans. Workers were unaware of the *African Renaissance*.[18] For workers, Shoprite's geographic expansion in Africa is a far more immediate example of a *Renaissance* than the grander political aims of an *African Renaissance*. Enhanced regional expectations were linked to the perceived profitability and success of this large, South African multinational.

Regional claims were strongly evident based on the idea that all workers in a company should get not equal pay but the same pay for the same work. The right to profit-making and economic expansion was acknowledged by workers, but the decent treatment of workers was a corresponding outcome that they expected from this economic success. Workers attributed uneven standards between themselves and South African workers to the effect of regional discrimination by South Africa against poorer countries that South Africa could take advantage of. Notions of regional geometries of power were thus prevalent amongst workers.

Despite the overwhelming similarities in the responses of workers in both countries to the same set of questions, there are significant differences in the conditions of work between workers at Shoprite-Maputo and workers at Shoprite-Manda Hill. An approximate regional geometry of standards suggests that Zambian Shoprite workers have the worst conditions when compared with South African and Mozambican Shoprite workers. This could be one factor in the strike that took place in Zambia in June 2003. Conditions of Shoprite workers in Zambia appear to be the worst amongst the three countries. Zambian permanent workers were doing the most overtime and unpaid overtime work for the least wages per month when compared with Mozambique and South Africa.

Exploitation of Shoprite workers through the use of casual labor appears to be the pattern in Mozambique. Shoprite-Maputo workers are also paid well below averages for formal sector workers in the national labor market. Casual workers in South Africa are paid around 1.7 times more than their Zambian counterparts. Casual workers in Mozambique, although they earn more per month, earn less in real terms as they are working a full week of 49.7 hours. The category of casual worker ("eventuals") is being used in violation of the Mozambican Labor Law through the repeated renewal of these contracts.

Casual workers in South Africa and Zambia work between 19 and 24 hours per week, so there is a relationship between their low wage rates and their under-employment. South African permanents are earning almost twice as much as permanent workers in Mozambique who also earn more than their Zambian counterparts. The cost of casual labor is cheaper in Mozambique but only constitutes a minority of the workforce, unlike in Zambia. This is possibly because these casuals are full-time equivalents, whereas in Zambia two casual workers make up one full-time equivalent. Mozambican workers earn less than other formal sector workers in their national labor market. Zambian permanent workers earn more than the $59 minimum legislated wage for shop-workers in the grade of cashier. However, this does not indicate what the actual average minimum wage is in the retail and services sectors. (The wage rates are for workers in the rate of shelf-packers. Clerks earn higher incomes than those cited here.)

Though most workers in Zambia were unionized and had a Recognition Agreement with the company, workers in Mozambique had been unable to get the majority of votes needed for a Recognition Agreement. The company was thus able to restrict wage increases and abuse labor legislation restricting the renewal of contracts for casuals. Uneven union representation did not, however, protect the Zambian workers from becoming the most exploited amongst Shoprite workers in the three countries (Adler 1997; Adler and Buhlungu 1997).

There was a suggestion from Shoprite-Maputo workers that, though the status of workers has been elevated in South Africa after democratic transition, their status has been downgraded in Mozambique. Although Zambian workers articulated a consistent lack of faith in the nation-state and a realization that they were on their own, Mozambican workers at Shoprite still seemed to suffer from feelings of betrayal and abandonment by the country as a whole and by the government. These differences could play an important role in the morale of workers and their capacity to strike, with the realism of Zambian workers aiding their resistance whereas the frustrated hopes and demoralization of Mozambican workers disable their capacity for collective action.

There was a greater ambivalence amongst Mozambican workers about the positive impact of foreign investment for the country. They were almost unanimous that the foreign investors were a good idea, unlike their more critical Zambian counterparts who observed that South Africa benefits more than Zambia in the economic relationship with South African companies. Although both Zambian and Mozambican workers articulated the same regional claims for inclusion into the company, a more critical regionalist disposition was emerging amongst the Zambian workers. As their expectations of South African foreign investors were declining, they demonstrated a willingness to voice a counterhegemonic disposition to the regional freedom for foreign investors. For the Shoprite-Zambian workers, the interests of workers and the interests of the country had to correspond. They could not accept that their interests as workers were not the same as that of the country; hence their argument that the failure to treat workers as human beings necessarily meant the companies were not good for Zambia. The Mozambican workers, on the other hand, felt that they had to suppress their separate, sectional interests for the sake of the country. As workers, their problems were subordinate to the larger problems of the country's economic growth. The supermarkets appeared to benefit the country in a variety of ways, including that they embodied development for Mozambique. Their exploitation was one unfortunate outcome of a process that was essentially good for their country. Mozambican workers did not cite racist attitudes amongst South African "Boers" as a reason for regional discrimination. This is perhaps because their contact with white management is mostly with Portuguese expatriates.[19]

Unlike the Zambian workers, workers in Mozambique did not comment on the shopping mall ambience of their workplace or the wider choices available to consumers. They recognized that Shoprite and South African companies were creating much-needed employment and that Shoprite was a large multinational company. They seemed to be less impressed with the "cosmopolitan" space of the shopping mall and more aware of their uniforms and appearance in the community and the false impressions their neat uniforms created.

In Zambia, new foreign investors brought renewed "expectations of modernity", and the failure of foreign investors to live up to these expectations has provoked militant criticism in the public sphere and even within the ranks of government.[20] Failures of previous "expectations of modernity" such as that in the 1960s and 1970s have perhaps endowed Zambians with a greater realism and empathy for the plight of workers who bear the brunt of failed economic initiatives. For Mozambique, this is their first round of "expectations of modernity," given a past of civil war and limited capitalist development. There are still illusions that capitalist modernity will lift the country out of its devastated national state, and the increasing growth rate in Mozambique and rapid urban development underway reinforce these illusions.

Public discourse about foreign investors has shifted more rapidly in Zambia. The disastrous effects of wholesale privatization are already economically visible. The deputy minister of labor attacked the role of private investors, saying they had raided the Zambian economy and that, in effect, the Zambian government had paved the way for this "accumulation by dispossession" (Harvey 2003).[21] Mozambican public discourse still points to the necessities of neoliberal privatization and they are still very uncritical about the intervention of new foreign investors.

Within their workplaces, interviews with workers showed a high level of dissatisfaction. Workers made comparisons with South Africa workers and regional claims were emerging. Different conditions and different national realities, however, create different capacities for resistance and the assertion of regional demands. National differences in the responses of workers seem to suggest defeatism amongst the Mozambican workforce. Whereas workers have the same regional claims, their regional dispositions and expectations vary. In Zambia, regional claims were cohering into regional demands (as the strike discussed below shows), whereas in Mozambique regional claims were leading to feelings of disempowerment and alienation. The regional claims of workers can therefore have different regional outcomes, depending on a range of contingent and historical factors.[22]

The Mozambican workers that I interviewed in Shoprite suggested that their national counterparts were still infused with the "expectations of modernity" that new foreign investment could bring, comprehensible perhaps against a backdrop of civil war, urban breakdown, and restricted capitalist development. The suggestion is that there are still perceptions that capitalist modernity and South African investment will lift the country out of its devastated national state. The increasing growth rate in Mozambique and the rapid urban development underway reinforce these perceptions. Mozambican public discourse still points to the necessities of neoliberal privatization and they are still very uncritical about the intervention of new foreign investors. As can be seen from the case studies, there are high levels of comparability in the regional perceptions of workers at Shoprite in Mozambique and Zambia in relation to their workplaces. For these workers, the "definition of the possible" had indeed taken on a new regional dimension.

"Spaces of Hope" and the Strike at Manda Hill

When workers began a three-day work stoppage at the eighteen Zambian stores of Shoprite, on June 21, 2003, this was surely no extraordinary event. But African labor has traveled a convoluted path. This strike marks a turning point in labor relations for Zambian workers. Cowed by chronic unemployment, a discredited ex-president who was elected into government office after being the trade union federation's president, a ravaged economy, and aggressive, "no-holds-barred" privatization, risking dismissal would appear foolhardy for any "rational economic actor." Yet these workers put their livelihoods, and the livelihoods of the extended families they support, on the line. This was, indeed, a remarkable dispute. This strike marked a turning point in labor relations for Zambian workers and was one of the first strikes in the foreign stores of Shoprite, now Africa's largest retailer.

The strike attracted a lot of public attention. Newspapers headlined reports of the strike, Zambian TV headlined the strike action for two days, interviewing workers on TV, radios ran updates about the strike, and human rights groups also commented on the strike. "After the down-tools we were receiving a lot of comments from the people—the public—saying that the worker is not being cared for. Letters were being written."[23] The first demand was around wages, the primary issue in the strike. Workers said they are unable to support themselves on their current wages. Casual workers felt particularly aggrieved at their income. Permanent workers also spoke out about the bad conditions of casual workers. The second concern was that the increase should be a large increase—*demands began at 300 percent of existing wages*—as they believed only a significant increase would begin to solve their problems. Significantly, they had learnt from their attendance at a South African trade union meeting in South Africa that they were the lowest paid in the region, and were very disgruntled about this. They also wanted the Zambian Human Resources manager removed. Their understanding was that an HR manager should act as a mediator between management and the workers, and therefore also represent their interests. Not only was he not playing the mediating role, he was also a Zambian. As a Zambian, he should be able to identify with the problems of Zambian workers.

Workers expressed strong feelings of bitterness over the company's perceived lack of empathy with the challenges that confront them. From the interviews I conducted with some of the workers who had gone on strike, they argued that the exchange between management and workers has been unequal. The investment has been successful and expansion has been possible for the company. Workers at the company, however, experience financial difficulties. According to these workers, Zambians have allowed South Africans a period of unfettered access to their national economy. South Africans appear to be abusing Zambia's invitation, in their view. The multinational encounter, therefore, is an unequal one.

Regional trade union collaboration between South Africa and other southern African countries emerged as one impetus behind the retail sector strike. In October 2002, South African Commercial and Catering Workers Union (SACCAWU), the South African retail sector trade union affiliated to Congress of South African Trade Unions (COSATU), organized a national shop stewards' council in Port Elizabeth. This three-day meeting included the attendance and presentations by company head office management on the first day. Represented at this meeting for the first time were trade union and worker delegates from six other southern African countries (Lesotho, Swaziland, Zimbabwe, Zambia, Malawi, and Namibia). At this meeting, SACCAWU's Research Unit made a presentation on shoprite's African expansion. Perhaps more importantly, the southern African delegation actively and informally exchanged information during their time together at this meeting. When the Zambian delegate returned to Lusaka, he was armed with a comparative analysis of wages at Shoprite in the region. From this comparison, Zambian workers saw that the company pays them the least in the region. They corroborated this information with their own gathered while training new Shoprite employees from newly opening stores in other African countries. This information was an important consideration for workers when they decided to embark on strike action in June 2003. Workers and the Deputy Minister of Labor believe that the company should not have been given "carte-blanche" when they came into South Africa.[24]

> It's maybe because of the way they came in. They were given a lot of respect. They were given the freedom to do anything . . . even if there's a problem they are able to stand; no one will convince them or chase them back to where they came from. So they've got freedom.[25]

Though workers at Shoprite tend to look to South African companies for an improvement in their lives, their perceived exclusion and the denial of their regional claims is producing contradictions that have made them turn against the company. As a result of the lack of national expectations, workers have pragmatically set their sights on the regional company. National demands have given way to regional claims. These regional claims are aimed at the company rather than the political institutions of the region such as the Southern African Development Community (SADC). The regional company is the place where their demands for fair working conditions should be met. Discriminatory treatment of South African workers and their regional counterparts was a source of tension in the past; in the present context, new regional expectations will make such discrimination untenable.

CONCLUSION

Regional developments in post-Apartheid southern Africa have spawned two important phenomena. The first is the growth of South African investment in the region (and the continent more broadly). The second is the self-representation by these South African investors as agents of an *African Renaissance*. These significant structural and ideological developments have created a new context for workplaces in southern Africa. The foreign branches of South African retail companies have given a high visibility to South Africa in the region. Expanding against the backdrop of a declared *African Renaissance*, the style of expansion and the workplace practices of these companies open up a new set of capital–labor dynamics and contradictions.

Despite the significant differences in the national histories of Mozambique and Zambia, workers at these workplaces articulated the same claims for regional inclusion in the firm. Whereas worker claims may be directed at a colonizing power such as Britain or France, at the nation-state in favor of national social compacts, or at the local level toward an individual company, the current geographic pragmatism of workers at Shoprite turns their focus to the regional company and its South African base as a reference point.

Both Zambian and Mozambican groups saw their futures in individualistic terms. Their goals were houses, cars, good jobs with good salaries, decent education for their children. Their political sensibilities (reformist) emphasized the individual attainment of these objectives. Through their work they would have to secure advancement for themselves and their families. There was no sense that the government would help one attain these objectives in any way. In this sense, the political sensibilities of these workers are post-nationalist and market oriented. Unlike South African workers who still look to the government for employment programs and national redistribution initiatives, workers in Zambia and Mozambique have put aside any claims on the nation-state for redistribution. Unlike the period of national liberation when workers were characterized as "rent-seeking elites," workers in these countries now express a strong realism about fending for themselves. Any charges of "cultures of dependency" would not stand up to scrutiny in relation to these workers. They have decided they are on their own as a political class. There is no evidence of any illusions about the nation-state. In this sense they have moved beyond the South African experience where many workers still retain some faith in the government they have installed in power. They have seen through the failures of the national liberation (NIEO) experiment and now articulate a market-based demand. Company citizenship is where they locate their entitlement, and it is in the company that all workers in the same grades should be equal.

There was no awareness of the way that casualization has undermined the conditions of both permanent and temporary workers in South Africa. This is partly attributable to the impressionistic way in which knowledge of South African work conditions has been gathered. The nuances of conditions in the South African labor market are not a concern to workers for whom the injustice of being paid amongst the least in the Shoprite region is their central concern. The new regional imaginaries that emerge out of the regional firm and the new shopping malls open up new possibilities and contradictions. Growing regional contradictions are embodied in the multinational dispute between the multinational South African retail company, Shoprite, and its foreign workplaces. The strike at Shoprite in Zambia (and in 2004 in Malawi) points to some of the potential outcomes of these new contradictions. Bi-national disputes have regional consequences and influence how the local public reacts to disputes and controversy between host country nationals and South African companies. If the relations between South African companies, on the one hand, and host country workers or consumers, on the other hand, are fractious, this will undermine South Africa's proclaimed leadership role in post-Apartheid southern Africa.

Charges of "Yankees of Africa" and South African "sub-imperialism" point to an unanticipated faultline of political struggle in southern Africa—a new tension between democratic South Africa and the countries and working classes who were to benefit from this political unity at the regional level. A new imprint has been left on the continent: one that potentially reproduces the global relations of Empire at the regional level. Uneven regional development and heightened regional expectations are already producing Hirschmann's "tunnel effect" (Hirschmann 1981) amongst retail workers at Shoprite, whereby increased hopes for social mobility are frustrated by social inequality. If South Africa is perceived by other southern African countries as the primary beneficiary of post-Apartheid regional economic development, with deepened regional inequality as the outcome of South Africa's democratic expansion, new regional resistance becomes both possible and likely. New cases of local resistance point to new regional claims in the demands of local communities, where South Africa becomes the reference point for new regional demands.

NOTES

A shorter version of this article appeared in *Africa Development* 31 (1) (2006): 27–47.

1. Shoprite Company reports, 1999–2005 <www.shoprite.co.za>.
2. Interview with G. Fritz, General Manager of Zambia Shoprite, November 2000; *Financial Mail* July 11, 1997; Macmillan 2005; Makoka 2005; Meyer 2002: 24–43; Portes 2003; Weatherspoon and Reardon 2003.
3. <www.shoprite.co.za>.
4. Interview with General Manager, Zambia, August 2003.
5. Interviews with NUCIW officials, Lusaka region, August 2002.
6. This is a tension-ridden collaboration as an incident in Solwezi showed when one of these traders came into the store and loudly shouted slogans protesting against Shoprite. This incident was partly provoked because the shop was regulating the amount of its supplies to the traders.
7. Telephone Interview with Zambian Regional Manager, April 2002.
8. Interview, G. Fritz with General Manager of Zambia Shoprite, November 2000.
9. Interview with Carlos Cardoso, Metical Editor, August 1999. Cardoso was assassinated in November 2000. His assassination was linked to his investigation of the privatization of Mozambique's largest national bank, Commercial Bank of Mozambique (BCM).
10. Interviews with Jose Cabaco, Investment Advisor; Carlos Cardoso, Editor, Metical; Shoprite workers, local residents; Shoprite Mozambican managers; September 1999. The Editor of Metical, a local faxed newspaper, estimated that the land cost $2.20 per square meter. Land in the downtown area normally costs $100 per square meter. The cheapest land in that area is $30 per square meter.
11. As the opening quote by the Metical editor suggested.
12. Ferguson (1999: 12) comments on the overwhelming sense of "decline and despair" he found while doing his research on the Copperbelt in Zambia.

13. <www.shoprite.co.za>.
14. Interview with male permanent worker, August 2000.
15. Interview with male permanent shelf-packer, August 2002.
16. Email communication with Center Manager, Kangwa Mukuka, October 5, 2002.
17. The three other medium-sized outlets are in Lusaka and in the Copperbelt towns of Ndola and Kitwe. The remaining 14 stores employ fewer than a hundred workers each.
18. Yet when informed by the researcher, they generally thought it was a good idea.
19. A limitation in the research is that the focus on relations with South Africa failed to sufficiently explore the peculiarities of the Portuguese–Mozambican relationship.
20. Interview with Deputy Minister of Labor, August 2003.
21. Interview with Deputy Minister of Labor, Lusaka, Zambia, August 2003.
22. The stores were opened within a year of each other, so neither store is significantly older than the other—*Manda Hill* in 1996 and *Centro Commercial* in 1997.
23. Interview with NUCIW Negotiation Team Leader and Deputy General Secretary for Finance, Kitwe, August 2003.
24. Interview with Deputy Minister of Labor, August 2003.
25. Interview with Focus Group, Shoprite-Manda Hill worker (September 2003).

Bibliography

Adedeji, Adedeji (ed.). 1996. *South Africa & Africa. Within or Apart?* Cape Town: SADRI Books; London and New Jersey: Zed Books; Ijebu-Ode: ACDESS.

Adler, Glenn. 1997. "Zambia's Second Subordination, Re-Colonisation through Neo-Liberalism," *South African Labour Bulletin* 21 (3): 51–54.

Adler, Glenn and Sakhela Buhlungu. 1997. "Labor and Liberalisation in Zambia," *South African Labour Bulletin* 21 (3): 48–50.

Ahwireng-Obeng, Fred and Patrick McGowan. 1998a. "Partner or Hegemon? South Africa in Africa. Part One," *Journal of Contemporary African Studies* 16 (1): 165–195.

Ahwireng-Obeng, Fred and Patrick McGowan. 1998b. "Partner or Hegemon? South Africa in Africa. Part Two," *Journal of Contemporary African Studies* 16 (2): 5–38.

Ariyo, Ademola and Jerome Afeikhena. 1999. "Privatization in Africa: An Appraisal," *World Development* 27 (1): 201–213.

Arrighi, Giovanni. 1990. "The Developmentalist Illusion: A Reconceptualization of the Semiperiphery," in William Martin (ed.). *Semiperipheral States in the World-Economy.* New York: Greenwood Press, pp. 11–42.

Arrighi, Giovanni. 2002. "The African Crisis: World Systemic and Regional Aspects," *New Left Review*. [NS] 15 (May–June): 5–36.

Arrighi, Giovanni and J. S. Saul. 1973. *Essays on the Political Economy of Africa.* New York and London: Monthly Review Press.

Arrighi, Giovanni, Beverly Silver, and Ben Brewer. 2003. "Industrial Convergence and the Persistence of the North–South Divide." *Studies in Comparative International Development* 38 (1): 3–31.

Bond, Patrick, Darlene Miller, and Greg Ruiters. 2001. "The Production, Reproduction and Politics of the Southern African Working Class: Economic Crisis and Regional Class Struggle," in *The Global Working Class at the Millenium.* London: Merlin Press; New York: Monthly Review Press, pp. 119–142.

Brümmerhoff, W. 1998. "Report on Meeting of Central Governors," Southern African Development Community, October.

BusinessMap SA. 2000. *SADC Investor Survey. Complex Terrain.* BusinessMap SA Report, Johannesburg, South Africa.

BusinessMap SA. 2001. *Regional Investor Survey 2001.* BusinessMap SA Report, Johannesburg, South Africa.

Butts, Kent H. and Paul R. Thomas. 1986. *The Geopolitics of Southern Africa. South Africa as Regional Superpower.* Boulder and London: Westview Press.

Clarke, Marlea, T. Feys, and E. Kalula. 1999. "Labor Standards and Regional Integration in Southern Africa: Prospects for Harmonization," Development and Labor Monographs. No 2. Institute of Development and Labor Law.

Cooper, Frederick. 1996. *Decolonization and African Society. The Labor Question in French and British Africa.* Cambridge, New York, Melbourne: Cambridge University Press.

Crush, Jonathan. 1994. "Post-Colonialism, De-Colonization, and Geography," in Anne Godlewska and Neil Smith (eds.). *Geography and Empire.* Oxford, UK and Cambridge, USA: Blackwell, pp. 333–349.

Daniel, John, Adam Habib, and Roger Southall. 2003. *State of the Nation.* Cape Town: HSRC Press.

Fashoyin, T. and S. Matanmi. 1996. "Democracy, Labor and Development: Transformation Industrial Relations in Africa," *Industrial Relations Journal* 27 (1): 38–49.

Ferguson, James. 1999. *Expectations of Modernity. Myths and Meanings of Urban Life on the Zambian Copperbelt.* Berkeley, Los Angeles, London: University of California Press.

Fisher, Fozia. 1978. "Class Consciousness among Colonized Workers in South Africa," in Lawrence Schlemmer and Edward Webster (eds.). *Change, Reform and Economic Growth in South Africa.* Johannesburg: Ravan Press, pp. 197–223.

Goss, Jon. 1993. "The 'Magic of the Mall': An Analysis of Form, Function, and Meaning in the Contemporary Retail Built Environment," *Annals of the Association of American Geographers* 83 (1) (March): 18–47.

Harvey, David. 1989. *Limits to Capital.* New York, Oxford: Blackwell.

Harvey, David. 2000. *Spaces of Hope.* Berkeley and Los Angeles: University of California Press.

Harvey, David. 2001. *Spaces of Capital. Towards a Critical Geography.* New York: Routledge.

Harvey, David. 2003. *The New Imperialism.* Oxford: Oxford University Press.

Hirschman, Albert. 1981. *Essays in Trespassing.* Cambridge: Cambridge University Press.

Jackson, Kenneth. 1996. "All the World's a Mall: Reflections on the Social and Economic Consequences of the American Shopping Center," *American Historical Review* 101 (4): 1111–1121.

Keet, Dot. 1999. "Globalisation and Regionalisation: Contradictory Tendencies, Counteractive Tactics, or Strategic Possibilities?" *FGD Occasional Paper* No 18, April.

Kenny, Bridget. 2001. " 'We Are Nursing These Jobs': The Impact of Labor Market Flexibility on South African Retail Sector Workers," in Neil Newman, John Pape, and Helga Jansen (eds.). *Is There an Alternative?* Cape Town: ILRIG, pp. 90–107.

Kolala, Faith. 2000. "South African Retail Firms in Zambia." Workshop on SADC Industrial Development, Development Policy Research Unit, Namibia, September 29–30.

Larmer, Miles. 2005. " 'For How Long Are We Going to Sacrifice?': Reaction and Resistance to Neo-Liberalism in Zambia," *Review of African Political Economy,* 32 (103): 29–45.

Macmillan, Hugh. 2005. *An African Trading Empire. The Story of Susman Brothers & Wolfsohn, 1901–2005.* London, New York: I.B. Taurus.

Makoka, Donald. 2005. "The Emergence of Supermarkets in Malawi: Implications for Agrifood Markets and the Small Farmer," in Tsutomu Takane (ed.). *Agricultural and Rural Development in Malawi: Macro and Micro Perspectives*. Chiba, Japan: Institute of Developing Economies, pp. 121–139.

Marks, Tafael and Marco Bezzoli. 2001. "Palaces of Desire: Century City, Cape Town and the Ambiguities of Development," *Urban Forum* 12 (1): 27–48.

Meyer, Juanita. 2002. "The Profit Zone: Shoprite, Pick 'n Pay, Spar & Woolworths: An Analysis of the Profit Strategies of Four South African Food Retailers," M.B.A. Dissertation. University of Stellenbosch.

Miller, Darlene. 2001. "Contesting Regionalism in Post-Apartheid Southern Africa," in Neil Newman, John Pape, and Helga Jansen (eds.). *Is There an Alternative? South African Workers Confronting Globalisation*. Cape Town: ILRIG, pp. 162–178.

Miller, Darlene. 2005. "New Regional Imaginaries in Post-Apartheid Southern Africa—Retail Workers at a Shopping Mall in Zambia," *Journal of Southern African Studies* 31 (1): 97–125.

Morris, Meaghan. 1993. "Things to Do with Shopping Centers," in Simon During (ed.). *The Cultural Studies Reader*. London, New York: Routledge, pp. 391–409.

Naidu, Sanusha. 2004. "South Africa and Africa: Mixed Messages," in E. Sidiropoulos (ed.). *Apartheid Past, Renaissance Future*. Johannesburg: South African Institute of International Affairs, pp. 205–220.

Nkiwane, Thandeka. 1999. "Contested Regionalism: Southern and Central Africa in the Post-Apartheid Era," *African Journal of Political Science* 4 (2): 126–142.

Perrot, Michelle. 1986. "On the Formation of the French Working Class," in I. Katznelson and A. R. Zolberg (eds.). *Working-Class Formation. Nineteenth-Century Patterns in Western Europe and the United States*. New Jersey, Oxford: Princeton University Press, pp. 71–110.

Pitcher, M. Anne. 2003. *Transforming Mozambique: The Politics of Privatization, 1975–2000*. Cambridge and New York: Cambridge University Press.

Portes, Alejandro. 2003. Rapporteur comments prepared for Conference on African Migration in Comparative Perspective, Johannesburg, South Africa, June 4–7.

Saul, John. 1993. *Recolonization and Resistance in Southern Africa in the 1990s*. New Jersey: Africa World Press.

Saul, J. and C. Leys. 1999. "Sub-Saharan Africa in Global Capitalism," *Monthly Review* 51 (3): 13–30.

Seidman, Ann and Neva Seidman Makgetla. 1980. *Outposts of Monopoly Capitalism. Southern Africa in the Changing Global Economy*. United Kingdom: Zed Press; Connecticut: Lawrence Hill & Company.

Silver, Beverly. 2003. *Forces of Labor. Workers' Movements and Globalization since 1870*. Cambridge: Cambridge University Press.

Simon, David. 2001. "Trading Spaces: Imagining and Positioning the 'New' South Africa within the Regional and Global Economies," *International Affairs* 77 (2): 377–405.

Soderbaum, Fredrik. 2002. *The Political Economy of Regionalism in Southern Africa*. Sweden: Department of Peace and Development Research, Goteborg University.

Soderbaum, Fredrik and Ian Taylor. 2003. *Regionalism and Uneven Development in Southern Africa. The Case of the Maputo Development Corridor*. Burlington: Aldershort.

South African High Commission. 2005. *Report on the Financial Sector, Lusaka, Zambia*. Pretoria: Southern African Regional Poverty Network (SARPN).

Smith, Neil. 1984. *Uneven Development: Nature, Capital, and the Production of Space*. New York, NY: Blackwell.

Swyngedouw, Erik. 2000. "Authoritarian Governance, Power, and the Politics of Rescaling," *Environment and Planning D: Society and Space* 18 (1): 63–76.

Trotsky, Leon. 1977. *The History of the Russian Revolution.* London: Pluto Press.

UNCTAD World Report 2005.

Weatherspoon, Dave and Thomas Reardon. 2003. "The Rise of Supermarkets in Africa: Implications for Agrifood Systems and the Rural Poor," *Development Policy Review* 21 (3): 333–355.

Weeks, John and Paul Mosley. 1998. "Structural Adjustment and Tradeables: A Comparative Study of Zambia and Zimbabwe," in Len Petersson (ed.). *Post-Apartheid Southern Africa. Economic Challenges and Policies for the Future.* London and New York: Routledge, pp. 171–200.

7

Cars Are Killing Luanda: Cronyism, Consumerism, and Other Assaults on Angola's Postwar, Capital City

M. Anne Pitcher with Aubrey Graham

If the bicycle embodied the contradictory effects of twentieth-century colonialism in Africa, then surely the car serves a similar purpose with regard to the postcolonial moment on the continent today. The automobile's association with cosmopolitanism and modernity, urban living and elite values is evident in the expression of individual desires and in the tropes of mass advertising. Yet, its dependence on oil links it undeniably with the resource curse that has cruelly plagued so many African countries. The many potholed roads on which it travels in Angola, in Congo, or in Uganda underscore the failures of developmentalism and modernism, and expose the sabotage and neglect occasioned by intractable conflicts from western to southern Africa.

Furthermore, the car's real and imagined impact on mobility gives it a use value and an iconic status that few other machines can match. From Cape Town to Fez, the "automobility" of the continent's inhabitants has exploded over the last 50 years enabling them to increase circuits of both informal and formal trade, and to enhance political links with far-flung parts of their countries.[1] It facilitates the exploration of other cultures and religions beyond one's borders and enables cooperation with neighboring countries on joint projects such as game parks or the prevention of malaria. At the same time, the proliferation of cars is both the cause and the consequence of the growth of criminal networks. As means of transport, cars, or more accurately, SUVs, buses, pick-up trucks, and heavy transport vehicles make possible the expansion of illicit trade from drugs to diamonds within and without Africa. As commodities, these vehicles are part and parcel of that trade—in fact, carjacking is one of the most lucrative crimes in southern Africa. Beyond its uses and abuses, the car symbolizes wealth, conveys status, and defines the elite. Coveted by many and possessed by few, the luxury car confers an almost magical power on its owner.

Yet, particular cultural and socioeconomic contexts clearly influence the modalities, meanings, and status of cars and trucks in Africa. In this essay, we intend to explore these issues within the urban milieu of Angola's capital city, Luanda. Angola is a resource rich country where a nearly 30-year conflict for control over revenues from oil and diamonds brought unimaginable misery and, ironically, inconceivable wealth. In Luanda's postwar landscape, pent up demand, and a surfeit of cash produced by oil and the war business have translated into a desire for cars of every conceivable make and model from late model Hummers to beat-up, secondhand Toyota Corollas.

Few places are more spatially ill suited to cars, SUVs, and trucks than Luanda. Founded in the sixteenth century, its built environment reflects the aesthetic conventions, social mores, and organizational requisites that defined earlier periods in the city's history. Superimposed on this historical imprint are the architectural, administrative, and environmental effects of major political and economic events of the last two centuries such as colonialism, the discovery of oil, the achievement of independence, civil war, and lastly, the growth of consumerism. Today, the city struggles to accommodate, feed, water, and move an estimated three and a half million people in a space built for much smaller numbers and previously served by narrow footpaths or cobbled streets.

The profusion of cars, minivans, trucks, and motorcycles in Luanda reflects the changes that have beset the city over the years, but also it shapes the city in dramatic and particular ways. Here, we examine three dynamics of cars (and related motorized vehicles) in the capital: as a means of transport, as commodities, and as status symbols. How has the dramatic growth of cars in the last decade impacted the city and its inhabitants? How does the exchange of new and used cars both reflect and shape social relations? What do cars mean to ordinary Angolans and how do they influence the experience of the city? How do they mark status and indicate wealth? Although we treat each dynamic separately for analytical purposes, all three of them overlap and intertwine. They illustrate that motorized vehicles have had contradictory effects on urban culture and the built environment of Luanda. They blight the landscape and pollute the air. They also connect the city to the countryside, and link the capital to the rest of Angola. Their purchase and sale crisscross the boundaries between the formal and informal sectors, licit and illicit transactions. They reflect the country's enormous mineral wealth and define class differences in the city.

Although there has been an explosion of writing on cities in Africa in recent years, there has been little attempt to theorize the relationship between the car and the city. This lacuna parallels that in the more general theoretical literature (see Carrabine and Longhurst 2002; Sheller and Urry 2000). Moreover, in spite of a number of works that have documented the growth of licit and illicit trade, the expansion of the informal sector, the increasing diaspora of transnational traders, and extensive global commodity chains, few works have highlighted the sale and purchase of cars as central components of the vast legal and extralegal trading networks that interlace the continent or arrive at and depart from its ports. Furthermore, a number of scholars have reflected on the growth of consumer culture and the changing orientation of status markers in urban areas, yet few have privileged the car in their analyses nor shown how they are visible manifestations of simmering class conflict.

This essay seeks to address these issues by juxtaposing the immobility of the urban landscape with the mobility of motorized transport. It argues that cars alter the way that cities are experienced. Like other cities whose origins predate the invention of motorized transport, parts of Luanda reflect the aesthetic conventions of earlier periods when the urban elite was expected to see and be seen—to stroll through the city as spectators and to learn from it. Although conventions no doubt varied across time and space, and from one urban designer to another; as Boyer claims, eighteenth- and nineteenth-century planners represented cities as works of art. "Historical monuments and civic spaces as didactic artifacts were treated with curatorial reverence" (Boyer 1998: 33–34).

Cars subvert the intention behind this earlier convention because they reconfigure, and in this case, thwart the position of the *flaneur*. They are "inimical to the sociality of the urban" to cite Mendieta (2005: 196). In the contemporary period, cars force a renegotiation of physical space and a rethinking of the economic advantages of a fixed business location. In cities like Luanda, they enable the growth of informal trade because traffic jams and the lack of parking aid the *ambulante*—the mobile trader. These social and environmental challenges reveal that patterns of mobility and immobility are just as critical as the built environment to an understanding of urbanism in Africa.

Second, our study of cars as commodities forces us to recognize the blurred boundaries between licit and illicit trade, the formal and informal, business and politics, and the public and private. Car ownership has not exploded in spite of the war in Angola, but because of it. SUV purchases have not increased in spite of the resource curse, but because of it. Lastly, growing and unequal patterns of consumerism in Luanda, of which luxury cars and four-wheel drives form a central part, cannot be attributed to the formal adoption of neoliberal policies. Rather, they are owed to the stealth privatization and lucrative deals initiated by, and for the benefit of, the political and economically powerful within and beyond Angola. The study of car sale and purchase, use and maintenance, in Luanda offers specific insights into the performance of shadow and concrete power relations and the uses of patronage in a postwar, oil-rich African country confronting the transcontinental expansion of consumer culture. Further, the car's iconic status calls attention to the multiple expressions of identity and stratification in African cities. Not only the sheer number of cars, but also the symbolic and financial value accorded to particular makes and models in Luanda reflect intertwining international and national influences on urban tastes and choices. Particular cars symbolize the importance of their owners and act as telling markers of social status in the city. They compete against, as well as reinforce, earlier sources and symbols of social hierarchy.

POWER AND THE CITY

The present Angolan economy is directly linked to the global demand for gas-powered vehicles. After Nigeria, Angola is the second largest producer of oil in Africa. Oil accounts for 96 percent of its recorded export revenue; signature bonuses, corporate taxes, and the extralegal trade in oil reinforce its importance in the Angolan economy (Hodges 2004: 141–164; Nordstrom 2005: 148).[2]

Most of the oil is produced via joint ventures between the state and private multinational oil companies. Following Angola's independence in 1975, the ruling MPLA (Popular Movement for the Liberation of Angola) party espoused Marxism–Leninism and established a command economy. Most major industries, including Angola's largest export earner, the oil sector, had, and continue to have, extensive state involvement and oversight. In the oil sector, however, private investors have always played an important role and have colluded with the government to produce the intricate, hidden networks and patterns that characterize the sector. They enjoy privileged access to the highest levels of government. The state-owned oil company, Sonangol, engages in joint ventures with approximately 30 private British, American, and French oil companies in order to research and develop its extensive oil reserves. These private companies bear the cost of exploration and development in exchange for a percentage of the profit (de Fátima 1997: 19–22; Global Witness, 1999: 5).

Oil exports presently bring in an estimated $7–8 billion dollars a year in revenue but they have brought troubles too. From independence until 2002, the MPLA government was embroiled in a long-standing civil conflict against the Union for the Total Independence of Angola (UNITA) that was financed and prolonged by resources—notably oil in the case of the government and diamonds in the case of UNITA. Cold war politics also exacerbated and sustained the war, which until the 1990s took place mostly in the central and southern provinces and along the border with the Democratic Republic of the Congo (formerly Zaire). The war cost the lives of thousands, drove many more thousands to provincial towns and to the capital of Luanda, debilitated infrastructure, and devastated agricultural production and manufacturing (see Cilliers and Dietrich 2001; Gleijeses 2003; Hodges 2004). Oil production was unaffected by the war because it is largely located offshore. Moreover, Angola's role as oil supplier stifled the growth of investment in diverse sectors of the economy. Known as the Dutch disease, the dominance of a precious commodity such as oil can drive up the exchange rate and inhibit investment in other sectors of the economy such as agriculture and non-oil related industry (Kyle 2002). Conversely, a strong currency cheapens the cost of imports and feeds an appetite for consumer goods.

The global demand for oil helped to produce these common and alarming characteristics of a resource-based economy. But as a major participant in the production of oil, the Angolan government was also responsible for the outcome.[3] Early on, the adoption of a command economy was reinforced by centralization due to the war, enabling the ruling party to extend and strengthen state intervention in almost every aspect of the economy. Sonangol controlled most upward and downward linkages in the oil sector, crowding out the entry of independent private firms (Hodges 2004: 147–150). Further the state nationalized former colonial companies in everything from sugar to cotton. In manufacturing, there were state companies for beverages and tires; in services—a state company for insurance, for the print and broadcast media, and for the import/export trade.

Despite its early allegiance to Marxism–Leninism and the creation of a command economy that was supposed to benefit workers and peasants, the government used the income from oil and other productive enterprises not only to finance the war but also to construct a highly authoritarian state. To accomplish this, the government employed the oil revenue to create a kind of pacted autocracy, concentrating wealth in the hands of a few, powerful families, who either occupy or have direct connections to the highest offices of the state. The links include the president of the Republic as well as those advisors who directly answer to him known as the *homens do futungo* or "men of the futungo"—which is the name of the president's private residence outside of Luanda (Aguilar 2001: 7). They also extend to high-ranking officers in the Angolan military, Sonangol, and the heads of ministries. In addition, they move beyond Angola to include international investors (see Le Billon 2001; Messiant 2001). Our best guesstimate is that approximately 3,000 individuals constitute the core of this state apparatus, but there are layers and layers of beneficiaries who use their access to the state to receive lucrative deals, accept bribes, or rent seek from state-owned enterprises. Their loyalty is maintained through favors, but also it is shored up by the widespread use of discretionary power, even deadly force.

The focal point for the expression of political power, the conclusion of business deals, and the exhibition of status is the city of Luanda. Like a magnet, it draws the wealthy and the poor, the demobilized, the dislocated, the hawkers, criminals, and opportunists. But the myriad legacies of the city's 400-year-old history frame transit patterns, public spaces, and social interaction in the city. From its initial settlement above the horseshoe-shaped bay of Luanda on the Atlantic coast in the northern part of Angola, the city has spread east, north, and south. Its topography reflects the limitations imposed by its location on the coast and the aesthetic conventions that governed an earlier period. Streets in the *baixa* or the "lower" area near the coast, which is one of the historic parts of the city and its central business district, are narrow, almost intimate. As they mimic the contours of the bay and curve sinuously around the coast, they intersect other streets at odd angles. They bow before important landmarks like a monument or church, stopping to form a graceful square or a small circle. They bend around hills or avoid them all together, coping with the terrain in a manner consistent with the demands and the technology available in the seventeenth and eighteenth centuries not the twenty-first century.

Layered on top of these earlier developments are the social preferences, economic needs, and political changes that arose from the seventeenth to the twentieth centuries. Production and trade, of course, expanded greatly over hundreds of years, initially to cater to the voracious demands of slave traders, and then to meet the needs of the colonial power, Portugal, and its subjects. Consistent with these changes, the urban population and subsequently the boundaries of the city grew. By the 1950s, Luanda had 300,000 inhabitants; nearly two decades later it had 800,000 residents. The infrastructure required to cater to their need for water, electricity, sanitation, roads, and transport also expanded but did not keep pace with demand. As a result, neighborhoods such as Rangel, Bairro Popular, and Cuca lacked paved roads, streetlights, and sidewalks that existed in older residential and commercial parts of the city (*Angolense* 2002; João, 2004).

After independence, Luanda visually and spatially began to reflect the priorities of the Marxist–Leninist government. After coming to power, the MPLA nationalized much of the housing that formerly belonged to Portuguese settlers, renting it out at low cost to supporters of the regime. Although the city only sporadically experienced actual fighting between 1977 and 2002, the lengthy war introduced a steady stream of emigrants and displaced persons fleeing the violence in the rest of the country. It diverted resources that might have gone to city planning, rehabilitation, and road repair; it introduced shortages of basic consumer goods; and demanded sacrifices that most of the population had to bear. Equally, the war also distracted the government so that zoning regulations were neither passed nor enforced (Jenkins et al. 2002). By 2004, the city had approximately three and a half million people (*Angolense* 2002).

Musseques (literally sandy places) or urban shantytowns housing emigrants and displaced persons mushroomed in order to accommodate this gargantuan demographic shift. In the older parts of the central city, makeshift dwellings squeezed in alongside a sixteenth-century fortress; underneath twentieth-century, high-rise apartment buildings; on the sides of hills; beside bridges; and even in underground sewers. Over time, small, informal businesses sprang up to cater to, or to create, increased demand for goods and services. By 2005, shops selling auto parts operated out of former schools and a multitude of activities had sprung forth from homes. Single-family dwellings became warehouses for secondhand clothes, small appliances, and foodstuffs sold on the streets and in open-air markets by Malians, Senegalese, and more recently, the Chinese. Beauty salons, bars, and discotheques invaded residential areas, undeterred by government threats that "their days [were] numbered" and that they would be relocated elsewhere because they did not conform to commercial zoning policy (Gomes 2005). These changes and the continued failure of the government to provide for the welfare of its urban residents produced an urban zone distinguished by overcrowding, burnt out streetlights, rotting garbage, and overfilled sewers.

Urban growth also extended beyond the historic zone to encompass previously open land in and around the city—the peri-urban areas. These areas witnessed exponential increases in the 1990s yet without most of the accompanying infrastructure necessary for urban living such as sewerage, sanitation, water, roads, hospitals, and schools. Rather than provide these services, the government ordered forced evictions in numerous locations from Boavista, a very old shantytown in northern Luanda to Soba Kapassa, a planned community in the south. In Boavista, the government claimed that landslides during the rainy season were a serious hazard warranting forced removal. However, an added reason for the removals may have been that the *musseques* were spoiling the view from the new hillside home of the president's mother and they were located on prime commercial real estate. To carry out the evictions, the government used the one institution that is not lacking in the peri-urban areas, the *fiscais* (translated as fiscal agents or inspectors but colloquially referred to as *fiscais ninjas* due to their brutal tactics) to raze the homes of 4,000 people in 2001 (Amnesty International 2003; Pearce 2001).

Similar incidents of violent, arbitrary acts by these inspectors and the police have occurred with little warning elsewhere in the peri-urban areas (Neto 2003: 15). Several times, the government has followed through on threats to end the operation of informal businesses in open-air markets and on the sides of streets, which reportedly provide work for 60–70 percent of the population (IRINnews.org 2004). Looked at more broadly, the Angolan government's approach to displaced people and informal vendors forms part of a familiar pattern of forced removals practiced by many African governments across the continent. In neighboring Zimbabwe, for example, President Mugabe recently authorized the removal of approximately 300,000 people on the outskirts of Harare, again employing the convenient trope of unsafe conditions and poor sanitation.

In stark contrast to the deterioration caused by population growth, commercial expansion, and government neglect were the effects of the government's steady cultivation of the elite. Fed by the proceeds from oil, those who constituted the top echelons of political and economic power adopted consumption patterns that were equivalent to those of the upper middle class in the United States. Some of them lived in gated communities that resembled those in Florida, they wore clothes purchased at smart boutiques in Paris and Milan, and they drove luxury sedans and four-wheel drive vehicles. Unlike the vast majority of the city's income earners who toiled in squalid surroundings, some worked in strikingly beautiful government buildings painted various shades of a stunning mauve color. Dating back to the seventeenth century, these carefully preserved architectural gems are sprinkled throughout the *baixa* near the waterfront, or they cluster in the *Cidade Alta* (literally high city), a section of Luanda perched on a hill overlooking the bay. *Cidade Alta* contains some of Luanda's oldest churches, the presidential palace, and other government offices.

By the twenty-first century then, Luanda reflected all of the contradictions, conflicts, mistakes, and choices of the preceding years. After Tokyo, it was the second most expensive city in the world (Messiant 2001: 294). Well-appointed, furnished apartments costing as much as $15,000 a month to rent stood next to buildings that should have been condemned. Raw sewage ran alongside brand new Volvo SUVs and Toyota Prados. Hawkers lined congested streets and sidewalks, selling everything from sunglasses to the kitchen sink, and government soldiers-turned-private security personnel closely guarded the freshly painted buildings occupied by the ruling elite.

Slow Cars, Dangerous City

Among the conflict and wealth, poverty and luxury, overcrowding and neglect are cars. Cars are the most visible manifestation of Angola's oil wealth and the consumption patterns it produces. They facilitate convergence of the diverse inhabitants of the city and yet visually they represent the palpable disparities between them. They are highly prized not only as commodities but also as status symbols. There are three dynamics of the car in the city and each one of them affects the built environment and reflects the social milieu of Luanda in different ways: the car as means of transport, the car as commodity, and the car as status symbol.

The first dynamic is the most obvious one: the car as a means of mobility. The growth of cars, SUVs, and trucks has transformed the use of public space in Luanda, reorganized conceptions of the city, and changed relations between the city and the countryside. As more and more people come to Luanda, the use of motorized transport of all kinds has increased. Someone arriving in Luanda by air from abroad or from the countryside by car or bus is not only struck by the eighteenth-century architecture and the city's crescent shape along the sea, but also by the enormous number of cars on the streets, in driveways, on the sidewalks, and in parking lots. One Angolan emigrant who returned to Luanda in the mid-1990s described the experience as culture shock, he could not believe how the city had changed with the increase in population and the number of cars.

As Sheller and Urry (2000: 739) have observed, cars bring both flexibility and coercion. They represent freedom but they can also be inhibiting. In Luanda, cars enable their occupants to negotiate the city in new and different ways and ironically thwart that very process due to their abundance. Half of all cars in the country are in Luanda, and, half of the country's traffic accidents occur there too. Most of the growth in motor vehicles has occurred since the early 1990s with noticeable spikes in car purchases occurring after 1992 and 2002. The dates are significant for they coincide with important political changes in Angola and with the rising price of oil over the last 15 years. In 1992, Angola held its first democratic elections after a peace accord between the ruling MPLA government and the armed opposition UNITA concluded nearly two decades of war. The peace accord and preparation for elections drew the politically powerful from both sides and from other political parties into the capital city. Although the opposition rejected the outcome of the elections and the fighting began afresh, the process allowed Luandans to imagine the possibility of peace. This imagining, along with increased revenue in the 1990s owing to the exploitation of new oil fields offshore, and the continued flow of illicit goods such as "blood diamonds," fueled an increase in consumption, including cars. When the war drew to a close in 2002, car purchases jumped again. Linked to the pathologies of resource curses and constant warfare, the car ironically also promised freedom and peace.

Whereas before 2002, the constraints of the war prevented regular movement to and from the suburbs and the countryside, the end of the war has triggered a transportation revolution. Those who can afford it are moving to new middle-class housing developments outside of Luanda and relying on personal transport to commute to the city for work. Others are reconnecting with the countryside and in doing so, they are facilitating the rebirth of trade. Equally important, movement from the city to the countryside is enabling Luandans to come to terms with the impact of the war on their relatives, and on the country itself. In an interesting way, travel by car may be building nationalism just as widespread use of the Portuguese language mitigates ethnic differences across the country according to Hodges (2004: 25). Luandans who rarely or never left the city during the war to travel to the interior, now spend weekends getting to know other parts of the country. They see the ravages of gunfire and the effects of prolonged shelling on the built environment of towns. They witness the mined fields, the abandoned factories, and burnt out vehicles. They confront the desolation and ruin of provincial capitals, smaller towns, and rural areas.

But if Luandans are finally getting the chance to know their country from behind the wheel of their cars, then they are getting to know it very slowly.

Because as liberating as the car is, it is also inhibiting. Everywhere outside of Luanda there are potholes. Where the war raged, the "bush has eaten the roads"—to borrow a line used to describe the aftermath of the war in neighboring Congo (*The Economist* 2005: 22)—so connecting with the hinterland by car, SUV, or bus can take hours. One resident of Luanda decided after the war ended that she would get to know the rest of the country by taking weekend trips to the countryside. The only difficulty is that even to drive 100 kilometers can take a long time. Moreover, degraded infrastructure and faulty workmanship have hindered emergency support and supplies to neighboring provinces. To get to Uige, for example, where an outbreak of the deadly Marburg virus recently occurred, took approximately nine hours by SUV. Even though it is only located 300 kilometers from Luanda, the degenerated road impeded a timely arrival.

Within the city, transit slows to a snail's pace owing to the traffic congestion. From 7 a.m. to 7 p.m. on weekdays, the historic center of Luanda is jam-packed because that is where the services and the formal sector jobs are. Few cars can move easily in a city built in the sixteenth century with roads that initially accommodated horse drawn carts in single lanes. How to get somewhere, in or out of the city, what roads to take, and when to leave, now seem to be all consuming tasks that recent efforts by city authorities to improve the traffic flow have done little to assuage (Dambi 2004: 30–33). What Dominique Malaquais describes for Cameroon also seems apropos for Angola. She states: "Transit, the distances between places, the experiences and the time getting there and back, the itineraries followed in doing so, routes often improvised or un-anticipated, commonly take precedence over places where one stops, where the body stands still" (Malaquais 2004).

In fact, the congestion is so bad and the commute time so long that it is affecting the family life and sociability of middle-class Luandans, as it has in other parts of the world where living in the "exurbs" has become the norm (Lyman 2005: 41). Following the customs of the Portuguese colonial period, it is typical for the middle class to return home for a meal in the middle of day. But it is now so time consuming to return home for those who live even the smallest distance from work that many are opting out of the family meal in the middle of the day. Thus some of the customs that came with Portuguese colonialism may be altered just because they are inconvenient.

If population explosion and unemployment have fuelled the growth of informal trade, traffic jams have influenced the spaces in which the trade takes place. Trapped in their cars, drivers and their occupants become the objective of the many *ambulantes* or mobile traders who traverse the city. Traffic jams throw into question the value of a physical location for conducting business. With so many people confined to their vehicles, it makes sense to move trade into the street, to shift business from the formality of a building to the informality and individuality of the driver and the trader. On a scale greater than that in Lusaka or Maputo, the trader comes to the driver in Luanda and he/she comes with items as small as a bic pen or as large as a microwave. This reorientation of business away from a fixed space makes contextual nonsense of the idea envisioned by twentieth-century urban planners in other parts of the globe of the "city as spectacle," as a place where pedestrians stroll along, window shopping at their leisure in spaces that have aesthetically ransacked previous architectural styles and conventions to visually seduce the contemporary consumer to part with her money (Boyer 1998). Neither a reimagined, reinvented Arcades project nor a "cathedral of consumption"—a mall (see Ritzer 2005)—currently exist here, although they live in the imaginations of many and it is just a matter of time before they arrive.

For the carless, the challenges of mobility in Luanda are even worse. Those without vehicles are resigned to the "public" transport system or to private Toyota Hiace taxivans called *azuis e brancos* (blues and whites) due to their lively blue and white striped colors.[4] With regard to the former, the government reformed the public transport system in 2001. In addition to improving the fleet of the state company responsible for public transport, it awarded concessions to three private companies to provide transport services in and around Luanda. Although government subsidized fares make this an inexpensive option, many passengers prefer private taxis because their routes are more numerous and they allow passengers to bring bags and shopping on board (Rodrigues 2002: 14).

Of the latter, about 1,400 private taxis are legally registered to operate in Luanda and its environs, but many more are believed to be operating illegally. To stay in business, the nonregistered pay bribes to the police who frequently rely on street kids as the intermediaries for the cash payment (*Folha 8* 2005b: 19). Hence the other name for the blues and whites is *candongueiros*, which is a figurative expression meaning "illegals." Although blues and whites offer advantages over public transport, trips can still be uncomfortable, inconvenient, and expensive. Ideally, a taxivan can carry about ten people comfortably, but during peak hours each one is crammed with twenty or more passengers. Moreover, for those who live far from the city center, trips may last for hours because passengers must take three or four blues and whites to get to their destination. Additionally, unlike before independence, there are few designated stops for blues and whites in the congested capital. They stop anywhere and everywhere to let passengers on and off, including the middle of the street (Chambassuco 2005). Further, *candongueiros* can be expensive. To travel from *Roque Santeiro*, a huge market located a few miles outside of the city, into the *baixa* where many services are, can cost 50 *kwanzas* or about 60 cents. The cost increases as the distance lengthens.

By choice or necessity, the remaining carless are pedestrians who now confront formidable obstacles as they try to negotiate a city that in a different context and a different era would be a *flaneur*'s dream. Small roads and the near absence of parking garages means that drivers disrespect existing laws on parking and privatize the sidewalks, forcing pedestrians into the street where alas they must battle even more cars. The risk to pedestrians from poor driving and excess speed (relatively speaking) has become so great that more pedestrians than occupants of cars die in traffic accidents (*Folha 8* 2005a: 18). Not surprisingly, one young man we talked to said even if the distance were very short, he would rather drive than walk. Such an attitude seems common among car drivers in Luanda. As in the United States, SUVs and the like are a defense against the urban, they are personal fortifications chosen to ward off the threat of the city (Campanella 1997: 32). Cocooned in their cars, drivers and their passengers can avoid dealing with the social and ethical consequences of poverty and war including abandoned and orphaned street children, maimed civilians and soldiers, and the economically active men and women of the "informal sector." Inside their 4 by 4s, occupants can seal themselves off from Luanda's pickpockets, petty criminals, scam artists, and organized gangs in a manner that pedestrians cannot. No wonder drivers now use their cars even to go a mere 200 meters and any pedestrian who can afford it finds another means of navigating the battleground that defines Luanda's city "space" (dos Santos 2005).

THE BUSINESS OF CARS

The automobility brought by motorized vehicles may not meet the expectations of most drivers and passengers, but Luandans of all ages and classes still consider cars a highly valued commodity and there are enough dealerships in the city to prove it. With names such as Unicar, Autoworld, Facar, Servauto, and Auto Kumba, the car business in Luanda is booming. To understand who is buying, who sells, and why cars mean so much, requires an understanding of the configurations of Angola's economy; the system of rewards in the country and the centrality of the car in this system; the use and availability of credit; and Luanda's housing market. Primarily, in Angola's resource-rich, postwar environment, the government, including the military, is using its access to oil wealth to win friends and isolate enemies, and to create and maintain a network of obligations and dependencies that will translate into votes, loyalty, or silence. Audis, Toyota Prados, and BMWs are the glue that joins together the intricate parts of this system of favors. Thus, government ministries and prominent people connected to government are amongst the major purchasers of cars.

Moreover, beyond the use of cars as the key item in the government's bag of favors, offering cars to supporters is a palliative measure, designed to avoid the adoption of public solutions to collective problems by disarming opponents one by one. A long time observer of the Angolan government described it like this: "If there is a lack of light, the elite resolves the problem by buying a generator. If there are potholes in the road, it buys 4 by 4s" (Nelson Pestana, interview). So rather than solve the problems of lack of electricity, or numerous potholes, or poor public transportation through policies that benefit the general welfare, the government adopts private solutions that pacify potential critics but worsen the public problem.

Examples abound of the purposes to which political influence in the car sector is put. It is alleged that a prominent general linked to Angolan intelligence distributed dozens of Toyota Prados, "the Jeep of the moment," to powerful supporters of the regime (Neto 2005). It is rumored also that the government purchased a fleet of Audi A6s for every member of parliament, including the opposition. Top government officials routinely receive expensive cars as part of the perks of their position. For example, the Ministry of Finance reportedly purchased 250 vehicles for the personal use of its top personnel. In addition, seeking to supplement their paltry salaries, the government grants generous lines of credit to state officials to purchase personal vehicles. Further, the government has bought trucks from the Chinese to give to approximately 1,500 Angolans who lost their vehicles during the war. Such a gesture invited speculation that the government trying to buy votes prior to the elections, which supposed to take place in 2006 (*Agora* 2005: 9). Perhaps, but it illustrates also how central the gift of cars is to addressing certain postwar grievances.

Of course, the government is not the only source of the demand for cars. There is a coterie of oil and diamond companies, embassies, banks, insurance agents, and national and transnational nongovernmental organizations that purchase cars for their employees. In addition, although bank loans are difficult to secure in order to start a business, many banks offer credit for car purchase as long as the person applying for credit has a job. Thus, middle-class Angolans who do not qualify for cars under any of the above categories may be able to purchase them with a bank loan. Since the government-set exchange rate for the *kwanza* is overvalued, they benefit from a favorable exchange rate on the price of imported cars. Moreover, although the supply of gasoline is erratic owing to the lack of an in-country refinery, its cost is low. A liter of gasoline in Angola is about one-third that in Europe.[5]

Lastly, for those who must travel from the new gated communities in the suburbs as well as those who cannot afford to move to a nicer home, cars have become a highly valued commodity. To understand how cars intersect with the housing issue, one must recognize the public and private dimensions of the housing problem in Luanda. With regard to government owned housing, the costs and priorities of war diverted financial resources vital to upgrading and expanding the housing stock. Although government-set rents are low, the houses and apartments are in poor condition and badly in need of repair (see Jenkins et al. 2002: 145–147). Tenants are unwilling to make repairs either because of the high cost or because they feel insecure about their tenancy.

To remedy the situation, the government has adopted a private solution. Since the early 1990s, it has selectively sold some of the stock at rock bottom prices to current occupants and to the well connected (Hodges 2004: 137). Further, it has turned a blind eye to the private real estate and rental "market" that is operating in certain parts of the city. With regard to the real estate market, a one-bedroom apartment in the *baixa* can sell for $80,000 (*Jornal de Angola* 2005:16). Since sale prices bear little relation to the mean income in the country, however, this market is only for the rich. The average yearly salary of an unskilled public worker in Angola is between U.S.$1,500 and $2,000 per year and that of a skilled worker is between U.S.$7,000 and $12,000 per year (Camara de Comércio e Indústria Portugal-Angola 2003/2004: 44). Such incomes make the purchase of a home from anyone other than the government nearly prohibitive for most.

In addition, for those who can arrange alternative accommodation, there is another private solution—the rental "market." Renting out one's apartment or house provides an opportunity to earn the money to purchase it later and to supplement one's income. Owing to the severe housing shortage and the wealth brought by oil and diamonds, war, and/or patronage, the cost of rents in the high end of the "private sector" has skyrocketed. Renting one floor of offices in a high-rise office complex can cost $120,000 a month whereas a nice apartment, suitable for a visiting dignitary or an ambassador but not a luxury apartment by any means, can cost $15,000 a month. As long as the rental and real estate market remain restricted, they offer another form of patronage to those lucky enough to take advantage, but again they are not public solutions.

Since real estate and rental markets are so distorted, most residents in or near the historic city center are reluctant to move from their rent controlled homes and apartments. Forced to stay put, that small fraction of the population with disposable income have chosen instead to put their money into cars. There are approximately 46 dealerships in Luanda selling every make and model of car and truck including Hummers, Cadillacs, Volvos, Chevies, and Prados. According to estimates, there are 7,000 cars imported into Angola every month and ten percent of them are new. Several dealers we spoke with also confirmed that business was good. With respect to used cars, the Malians and the Congolese run huge used-car lots located just outside the historic city; further, there is a vast network of buyers and sellers bringing cars illegally into Angola every day.

Examining the car trade also offers the observer much insight into how formal and informal, licit and illicit business is conducted in the capital and who controls it. Regarding the formal sector, one reason there are so many dealerships is that the overhead is so low. Showrooms are rented. Most dealers do not keep a stock of cars in their showrooms so they have no inventory. Rather, they take orders and then import the cars from abroad. Moreover, the mark up is around 30 percent so it is a lucrative business even if only one car is sold a month. Sample prices are given in table 7.1.

Prices of used cars run the gamut from tens of thousands of dollars to several hundred dollars. In a daily newspaper, a 1993 Jeep Cherokee was offered at $7,500 and this was the least expensive vehicle for sale that day. The most expensive was a Volvo truck advertised for $35,000 (*Jornal de Angola* 2005: 16). Cheaper cars can be found for an average of around $3,000 in the second-hand car markets. Although we were unable to document the extent to which these used cars were actually stolen cars, both anecdotal evidence and rumor suggested that some of the more common used-car makes and models were

Table 7.1 Costs of selected car makes and models in Angola versus the United States (in U.S. dollars)

Make and Model	Angola Total (including Taxes, Shipping)	United States Base Price
Mazda 6	31,074	19,000
Mazda Single Cab Pickup 4×4	24,045	15,000
Volvo S40	45,500	30,000
Volvo S60	59,800	36,000
Volvo S80	65,000	42,400
Volvo XC90	89,650	51,000
H2 Hummer	100,000	52,000
Volkswagen Touareg (4×4)	80–109,000	44,000

Source: Angola vehicles: dealership visits in Luanda, and selected magazine and newspaper articles; U.S. vehicles: dealership Internet sites.

stolen cars driven across the many borders that Angola shares with its neighbors. Left-hand drive vehicles were said to come from Congo whereas right-hand drive cars were smuggled into the country from Zambia and South Africa. Presumably, the trade also goes in the other direction.

But who is selling these cars? With names like Mitsubishi, Toyota, Volkswagen, and Chrysler their foreign provenance is easily discernible. It is their domestic journey that is more obscure. As one might expect in a country where most power resides in the office of the presidency, the lucrative end of the car trade is infiltrated by those in, and with, connections to political power. So not only do those in positions of authority buy cars for their own use and for their networks of patronage, but also they are deeply entangled in the car trade as importers, traders, insurers, and dealers. It is highly structured and strenuously controlled and layers and layers of it are hidden and unrecorded. What is visible gives a glimpse of the extent to which political and economic power in the country is interlaced, interwoven, and thoroughly intertwined with transnational power flows and commodity chains. A former functionary in the National Bank of Angola, for example, now has interests in the Zuid/Mazda car-truck dealership (Santana 2003). The owner of a trucking company that made money transporting internally displaced persons during the war was on the central committee of the MPLA. Two corporate heavyweights in the economy, Sonangol and the African Investment Bank (BAI) jointly own a BMW dealership. Not surprisingly, these two companies were the biggest purchasers of a top of the line, late model BMW on display at the 2004 Annual car show in Luanda (*Angolense* 2004: 2).[6] In turn, both parties are shareholders in an insurance company that provides all types of insurance, including automobile coverage (Diário da República 2003).

Car sales form part of an intricate web of horizontal and vertical linkages connected to car repair and car washing that blur the boundary between the formal and the informal sector. Though still conforming to certain patterns, exit and entry to these enterprises become easier as the return becomes less lucrative. In the formal sector, passenger and merchandise transport in 2002 accounted for approximately nine percent of the commercial activity carried out by a sample of 306 traders in the suburbs of Luanda who were interviewed by a weekly journal. Car sales and car accessories accounted for another two percent of the activity of this sample of the formal service sector (*Angolense/Consulteste* 2002: IV).

Alongside the formal sector, informal car-related activities have mushroomed. There is a huge trade in stolen car parts, and markets that deal exclusively in car accessories and parts are scattered throughout the suburbs. Even in the same location as a legally registered car repair business, street vendors sell exhaust pipes, mufflers, steering wheels, car seats, spare tires, and, in the summer, windshield wipers. Just within sight of a legalized competitor, they carefully stack up their tires or mufflers, or advertise their panel beating skills, waiting for a customer looking for a deal (Rodrigues 2005: 14).

Numerous, too, are the many car washers in and around the city, who reported when we asked them that the price of washes can vary between 100 and 500 *kwanzas*. To receive 500 *kwanzas* (about $6) per car is a good fee but business is erratic and unpredictable. Car washers might average two cars per day or none at all. Grown men and teenage boys work Monday to Saturday on a range of cars. Some rarely wash the same cars two days in a row whereas others seem tied to a set of cars connected to employees at certain businesses. The latter group washes the same cars everyday, even getting to know the car owners. Some of the teenagers earn money for school through car washing, others spend their money on expensive shoes. The hunger for expensive shoes even by car washers brings us to a final and related issue we wish to discuss briefly in this chapter, the use and acquisition of status symbols in post-war Luanda. For status conscious Luandans of all ages and income levels, cars are the objects of their greatest idolatry.

"Cardolatry" and Class Difference in Luanda

The language used to describe the articulation of power in postwar Angola is full of words such as "secrecy," "mystery," "shadows," "invisibility" (see Nordstrom 2004). Deals are said to have been concluded "in secret." Trade in guns, or cars, or drugs are said to take place in the "shadow economy." The men surrounding the president are said to be "mysterious." The exact number of the wealthiest of the elite is "unknown." Bank accounts are "hidden"; the origins of an individual's wealth, "buried." But a clean, steel grey Toyota Prado driven by a man whose $1,000 suit complements the color of the car establishes a visual limit to the secrecy of shadow networks in politics and finance.[7] The deal may be hidden but it produces blatant, visible results. And it is the embodiment of these two seemingly disparate, but intertwined and interconnected expressions of power—secrecy on the one hand, conspicuous consumption on the other—that makes cars the subjects of admiration as well as scorn by Luandans.

One Angolan journalist describes this phenomenon as "cardolatry" (viaturolatria), a term he borrowed from the Mozambican writer Mia Couto, who is now observing a similar development in his own country. Of its expression in Angola, Aguiar dos Santos writes:

> . . . beginning with government elites, we are succumbing to the fetish of the top of the line car, to the vanity of possessing various status symbols in the garage, to out-of-control sons of ministers smashing up official cars on the weekends, or to the anarchy of seeing cars with Angolan Armed Forces license plates being driven by young people or civilian women. (dos Santos 2005: 3)

It is hard to say when the "cardolatry" began, but Aguiar dos Santos suggests that it began right after independence, "contaminating" those in the state apparatus and then working its way along to the families of those in power and then the newly rich from the provinces. Whenever it started, the national, mostly male (it is quite clearly gendered) obsession with cars has accelerated since the end of the war. As Ross (1995) writes with regard to France after World War I, some Angolans seem to be experimenting with changes in taste and culture, and indulging in the frivolity that follows a formal peace. They are exercising personal choices in a space and place where broader rights and democratic freedoms have been circumscribed by the use of discretionary political power and the constraints of war. Lacking the power to decide the fate of their country, at least they can choose the color and make of their cars.

Ackbar Abbas's reflections on Hong Kong offer an interesting parallel to Angola. Abbas writes that "Historical imagination, the citizens' belief that they might have a hand in shaping their own history, gets replaced by speculation on the property or stock markets, or by an obsession with fashion or consumerism" (Abbas 2002: 5). In Angola, the adornment of cars with images of Che Guevara, the quintessential heroic revolutionary, rather drives home the point that even for those with disposable income, the choices are confined to commodities—not political leaders with integrity.

Car lovers are aided in their selection by the global explosion of consumer culture and the media through which it operates—the Internet, advertisements, magazine articles, and mail order catalogs (see Storper, 2001). Although "cathedrals of consumption" such as megamalls, casino complexes, and theme parks are in their infancy in Angola, most of the Angolan elite has experienced them in Cape Town or Houston; Lisbon, Paris, or Rio de Janeiro. Closer to home, "chapels of consumption" in the form of spotlessly clean showrooms containing a small number of cars in pristine condition whet the consumer appetite in Luanda. Here, professionally dressed salespersons patiently explain the technical and aesthetic features of a particular make and model. Since stock is limited and test driving unthinkable, what reality lacks, the virtual can provide. Billboards and magazine advertisements link cars to "love at first sight," or to "adventure and comfort in the same space." Internet adverts, blogs, and websites provide endless virtual spectacle: entertainment and information about every make and model of cars is easily available with a few clicks.

Even those who cannot afford a car experience its thrill vicariously through games, dreams, and the Internet. It seems ingrained in the masculine culture of the city. One driver we talked with told us that as young kids, boys will play a game at school called "Burro" that is similar to "hangman." One player will think of a make of car and the other boys will have to guess what it is he is thinking of. Even if a player loses, continuous iterations of the game familiarize the players with all the makes of cars. As boys get older, they turn to magazines and the Internet to expand their knowledge. At several Internet cafes across the city, we watched as male customers rotated between pornography and luxury car sites seeking vicariously to satisfy their lust. Boys, too youthful to drive, spend 100 *kwanzas* or a little over a dollar per half an hour at an Internet cafe to ogle the flashy pictures of the newest model Ferraris and Land Rovers. Other school-aged adolescents, when asked about cars, responded that they wanted Jaguars, Lincolns, Jeep Grand Cherokees, and Porches.

Many people we talked with about cars agreed with the musings of Leno, an Angolan fence-painter, who stated emphatically: "If you have money, you *must* buy a car" (emphasis original); nearly everyone we spoke with easily rattled off what car they would buy *if* they had money. But not everyone does have money so cars have become a class marker and a statement about identity. Part of the reason for this concentration on the car has to do with the existing social geography of Luanda. As stated above, housing shortages, the degradations of buildings in the peri-urban areas and the historic center, insecurity of tenure, and high rents have trapped inhabitants in inadequate housing situations. Because the built environment has failed them, people prefer to put their money in mobile form.

As O'Dougherty observes in her discussion of the car in Brazil, "cars offer ready opportunities for nonverbal, unambiguous public display of wealth" (O'Dougherty 2002: 45). Like Brazilians, with whom they appreciate being compared, some wealthy Angolans view the car as the ultimate status symbol. What is so striking about this in the Angolan case is that the wealth is obtained so secretly and yet displayed so publicly. A handy rule of thumb was that the higher one was in government, then the better the car. Government officials were said to drive "the car of the year" or rather brand new cars. One respondent noted that even if they did not like the way a car drove, members of the elite would buy a car just because it was prestigious: "Like now the Hummer is better than the Toyota Prado, so Prado owners are buying Hummers," one respondent acknowledged. The irony is alarming: refurbished armored transport vehicles used by the American military now roam the streets of postwar Luanda shielding their occupants from the aftershocks of a war in which Western powers were implicated.

Respondents acknowledge that some people used luxury cars as a way to "trick" others into thinking they had more money than they did and to keep up with the upper class. One journalist who has attempted to delineate the various socioeconomic classes in Luanda refers to this second group as the "class of those who have little and appear to have much. They talk big but they throw out only trifles" (Cardoso 2005: 21). Their masquerade acts to camouflage their real social standing.

For those wealthy enough to afford a luxury car, the automotive display of plumage is extravagant. While their vehicles serve the express purpose of effective transportation between two points, there exist a plethora of fashion-over-function vehicles, such as the popular, upmarket SUVs (Hummers, Toyota Prados, Mercedes, and Land Rovers) and small sports cars, (BMW Z3s, Shelby Cobra Coupes, Mercedes S-class) These luxury, late model automobiles often sell for between U.S.$50,000 and $120,000. Owning one of these flashy cars goes beyond the need for simple transportation; owners are making a statement, and a very expensive one at that. The logic of their purchase rests on the understanding that a car signifies more than a functional piece of technology: it denotes economic superiority and security, it is a statement about class and about identity.

These new, expensive, shiny automobiles turn pedestrian and hawkers' heads as they roll slowly through the incessant stop and go congestion of the city. The cars provoke talk. They are part of an ostentatious expression of real or presumed economic security. Real or a well-constructed veil, the impressive nature of the auto-commodity derives respect and admiration as a status symbol. The importance lies not in the way the cars drive or their ability to maneuver obstacles,[8] but rather in the way that one looks sitting behind the wheel and in the fact of possession. As Gilroy observes with regard to car worship by African Americans during the late twentieth century, "Motor vehicles were the public ciphers of celebrity" (Gilroy 2001: 94), or in the Angolan case, of power.

So intertwined is this power with the car in Luanda's social relations that daily discourse links position with the make and model of a car. Miller's study of

Trinidadian automotive culture argues that this means of referencing people by their automotive choice, and therefore, economic capability, demonstrates the car's acceptance by society. Miller notes, "The identification of persons by their associated cars is not the exception but the norm of daily social discourse" (Miller 2001: 19). Such a norm is replicated in Angola. Street kids gossip that a woman driving a cherry red BMW Z3 is the lover of someone powerful. Or a security guard describes a banker by his choice of cars. The guard waves his arm toward the adjacent bank and says, "The man with the silver H2 Hummer works there." In doing so, the street kids and the guard acknowledge the status attached to such expensive luxury vehicles.

Some status conscious Luandans have even taken the car culture and symbolic, social identity to a new extreme by dressing like their cars. For example, one woman we spoke with said that her neighbor runs a bakery and has at least five cars. "On Monday," she sighs, "it's the Jeep, Tuesday, the Corolla, Wednesday, a Land Cruiser, Thursday a Mercedes . . . And the worst part," she rolls her eyes, "is that he matches his cars to what he drives. Blue, yellow, red, he has an outfit that works well with each car." However bizarre, this is by no means an isolated observation. Several respondents noted that the elite and the pretenders to the elite make every effort to look as flashy as possible in their cars, matching their clothing to the car, donning sunglasses, crisp shirts, pressed pants, shined shoes, and ensuring that the car is washed in their drive every morning.

Ranking drivers according to their cars, however, belies another sentiment that coexists with cardolatry—a sense of deprivation. For the fact of the matter is that not everyone can afford a car—not those living beside the fort, in the drains, and on the slopes of Boavista; not the thousands who take the blues and whites; not students or beggars; maimed, young soldiers or car washers. And one wonders, in this postwar urban environment, whether the dreams of car ownership are enough to assuage the nightmare of forced removals, to lessen the anger at the lack of jobs, to obliterate the disgust with the corruption and the secret deals, and to compensate for the absolute lack of goods.

The presence of clean, new cars surrounded by garbage, by shoeless young boys in ragged pants, exposes the stark economic disparities in Angola. It is a country where the majority has little or nothing with which to purchase a healthy meal or even a glass of water. It ranks as one of the poorest in the world. Infant mortality is alarmingly high. Malaria is rampant and other diseases like the recent Marburg virus decimate the population until the outbreaks are belatedly brought under control by a combined effort of transnational and national health organizations. Expensive cars are visual manifestations of the concentration of wealth in the hands of a few, the business of war, nontransparent deals, or, at the very least, of gross insensitivity. One day, those who sit within them may be asked to account for their actions.

Conclusion

Luanda is a historic city ravaged by nearly 30 years of civil and transnational conflict. Displaced women cook meager rations on charcoal fires in makeshift dwellings. Former soldiers barely out of their teens hang around on street corners looking for something to do. Children make homes in abandoned cars and disused cargo containers. Grown men wash themselves in manholes and hawk small appliances on the side of the road. Yet, ironically, the "business of war"—the illicit trade of diamonds, drugs, and arms; the struggle for oil reserves that are the second largest in Africa, the reliance on patronage by a ruling party eager to keep its friends close and its enemies closer has put money in the pockets of a few. Their wealth has produced a pattern of consumption and a culture awash in portable commodities from cell phones to clothes, and from computers to cars.

Of these, the car occupies a highly complex position in the cityscape. In Africa where distances are great and mobility is the *sine qua non* of economic survival, the availability of a car opens up limitless possibilities for engaging in commerce. But our reference in the title to cars killing Luanda operates at a number of levels. It is meant to suggest that the demand for gasoline for our cars in the West helped to finance an incessant war that destroyed lives and landscapes. It is a reference to the traffic jams and pollution caused by an explosion of cars in the context of a built environment that had its origins in the premotorized era. It is an allusion to the stranglehold that powerful elites have on productive enterprise and the means of consumption in the economy. And lastly, it is a reference to the clean, top of the line car as a symbol of the widening cultural and economic abyss between the wealthy and the poor. Ironically, this blatantly visible manifestation of the secret and shadowy uses of power may act as a catalyst for real social change in the coming years.

NOTES

We would like to thank the American Political Science Association small grants committee and the Colgate University Research Council for funding fieldwork in Luanda in July 2003 and May–June 2005, respectively. We appreciate the support and the interest in this project shown by the many Angolans that we met and we are grateful for the help of the *Arquivo Histórico Nacional* (National Historical Archives) of Angola for locating relevant sources. We thank also Marissa Moorman; participants in the "Urbicide" conference at the University of Durham, England; and the editors of this book for their comments on an earlier version of this chapter.

1. The term "automobility" is from Sheller and Urry (2000: 738–739).
2. Carolyn Nordstrom (2004; 2005) has called attention to the operation of the unrecorded, informal, and illicit sector in conflict/postconflict Angola and elsewhere. We say more about this in the context of cars below.
3. On the role of governments in creating and reproducing the "paradox of plenty," see Karl (1997).
4. Unlike Lusaka where personal vehicles may become informal taxis if a driver sees a pedestrian walking along the side of the road, this phenomenon was less apparent in Luanda, though we were told anecdotally that it occurs. Individual arrangements could also be made with friends or the owners of restaurants to hire a driver, but it was quite expensive. In contrast to the year before, repeated efforts to reach by phone the one official taxi service, Macon taxis, were unsuccessful nor were any Macon taxis seen on the streets during our fieldwork in May–June 2005.
5. A refinery is under construction. I thank Marissa Moorman for this point.

6. Each BMW was reported by *Angolense* to cost $262,000 or, rather, double the price of BMW's 7 Series luxury car in the United States. Excluding taxes and the cost of shipping, the mark up appears to be extremely high.
7. A Toyota Prado is similar to a Toyota Land Cruiser in the United States; the base price in the United States is $56,000.
8. Cameroonian Taxis, which dominate the streets in the capital city of Yaoundé, exist for reasons beyond the look they create. Drivers take pride in painting slogans on their bumpers, "Don't be Jealous" or "God will Save" but their cars are homogeneous, yellow Toyota Corollas or a like yellow car. Their drivers praise them for their maneuverability or their low gas mileage, as they negotiate traffic and potholes, but the status of driving a taxi in Yaoundé does not compare to that of commanding a luxury vehicle in Luanda.

Bibliography

Abbas, Ackbar. 2002. *Hong Kong: Culture and the Politics of Disappearance.* Minneapolis: University of Minnesota.

Agora. 2005. "Avante camaradas," May 21: 9.

Aguilar, Renato. 2001. "Angola's Incomplete Transition." United Nations University/WIDER Discussion paper, 2001/47 (August).

Amnesty International. 2003. "Angola—Mass Forced Evictions in Luanda—a Call for a Human Rights-Based Housing Policy." Working Paper, AI Index: 12/007/03 (November).

Angolense. 2002. "Luanda: 426 anos de história," 167 (January 26–February 2): 14–15.

Angolense. 2004. "Os novos BMW e o fim do pudor," 296 (September 18–25): 2.

Angolense/Consulteste. 2002. "Sondagem: Como os comerciantes angolanos vêem os seus homólogos estrangeiros," 168 (February 2–9): I–XII.

Boyer, M. Christine. 1998. *The City of Collective Memory: Its Historical Imagery and Architectural Entertainments.* Cambridge: MIT Press.

Camara de Comércio e Indústria Portugal-Angola. 2003/2004. Anuário de Angola. Lisboa.

Campanella, Thomas J. 1997. "Mythologies of the Sport-Utility Vehicle," *Harvard Design Magazine* (Fall): 29–32.

Cardoso, José. 2005. "A divisão de classes 'à maneira angolana,' " *Semanário Angolense* 3 (116) (June 11–18): 21.

Carrabine, Eamonn and Brian Longhurst. 2002. "Consuming the Car: Anticipation, Use and Meaning in Contemporary Youth Culture," *The Sociological Review* 50(2) (May): 181–196.

Chambassuco, Martins. 2005. "Taxistas exigem paragens sinalizadas," *Folha 8*, May 28: 18.

Cilliers, Jakkie and Christian Dietrich (eds.). 2001. *Angola's War Economy: The Role of Oil and Diamonds.* Pretoria: Institute for Security Studies.

Dambi, Luís. 2004. "Luanda muda de cara," *Angola Figuras e Negócios* 5 (45) (September): 30–33.

de Fátima, Velasco. 1997. "Sebastião de Sousa e Santos, Presidente do Conselho de Administração da SONANGOL-Holding," *Angola Ilustrada* 5 (June–August): 19–23.

Diário da República. 2003. "AAA-Serviços do Risco, Lda," Serie III, January 31.

dos Santos, Aguiar. 2005. "A 'viaturolatria,' " *Agora* 426 May 28: 3.

Economist, The. 2005. "Africa's Unmended Heart," June 11.

Folha 8. 2005a. "Motorista assassina pequeno de 12 anos," May 14: 18.

Folha 8. 2005b. "Motáxi está a bater na Guimbi," May 14: 19.
Gilroy, Paul. 2001. "Driving while Black," in Daniel Miller (ed.). *Car Cultures*. Oxford and New York: Berg, pp. 81–104.
Gleijeses, Piero. 2003. *Conflicting Missions: Havana, Washington, and Africa, 1959–1976*. Chapel Hill: University of North Carolina Press.
Global Witness. 1999. *A Crude Awakening: The Role of the Oil and Banking Industries in Angola's Civil War and the Plunder of State Assets*. London: Global Witness.
Gomes, Júlio. 2005. "Estranhas metamorfoses das casas comerciais." *Agora*, May 14: 22–23.
Hodges, Tony. 2004. *Angola: Anatomy of an Oil State*, 2nd edition. Bloomington: Indiana University Press.
IRINnews.org. 2004. "Closure of Markets Undermine Informal Economy," April 6 <http://www.irinnews.org/report>.
Jenkins, Paul, Paul Robson, and Allan Cain. 2002. "City Profile: Luanda," *Cities* 19 (2): 139–150.
João, Emanuel. 2004. "Problemas de Luanda não se resolvem com paliativos." *Angolense* 291 (August 14–21), 12–13.
Jornal de Angola. 2005. "Classificados," June 11: 16.
Karl, Terry Lynn. 1997. *The Paradox of Plenty: Oil Booms and Petro-States*. Berkeley: University of California.
Kyle, Steven. 2002. "The Political Economy of Long Run Growth in Angola—Everyone Wants Oil and Diamonds but They Can Make Life Difficult." Working Paper No, 2002–07 (April), Cornell University.
Le Billon, Philippe. 2001. "Angola's Political Economy of War: The Role of Oil and Diamonds, 1975–2000," *African Affairs* 100: 55–80.
Lyman, Rick. 2005. "In Exurbs, Life Framed by Hours Spent in the Car: Time for Family and Community Eroding," *New York Times*, December 18: 41.
Malaquais, Dominique. 2004. "Douala/Johannesburg/New York: Cityscapes Imagined." Dark Roast Occasional Paper Series, Isandla Institute, No. 20, Cape Town, South Africa.
Mendieta, Eduardo. 2005. "The Axle of Evil: SUVing through the Slums of Globalizing Neoliberalism," *City* 9 (2) (July): 195–204.
Messiant, C. 2001. "The Eduardo dos Santos Foundation: Or, How Angola's Regime is Taking Over Civil Society," *African Affairs* 100 (April): 287–309.
Miller, Daniel. 2001. "Driven Societies," in Daniel Miller (ed.). *Car Cultures*. Oxford and New York: Berg, pp. 1–33.
Neto, Gilberto. 2005. "Governo de auto-golos," *Angolense* 321(March 19–26): 6.
Neto, Salas. 2003. "Demolições demitiram Alves." *Semanario Angolense* 1 (3) (March 22–29): 15.
Nordstrom, Carolyn. 2004. *Shadows of War: Violence, Power, and International Profiteering in the Twenty-First Century*. Berkeley: University of California Press.
Nordstrom, Carolyn. 2005. "Extrastate Globalization of the Illicit," in Catherine Besteman and Hugh Gusterson (eds.). *Why America's Top Pundits Are Wrong: Anthropologists Talk Back*. Berkeley: University of California Press, pp. 138–153.
O'Dougherty, Maureen. 2002. *Consumption Intensified: The Politics of Middle-Class Daily Life in Brazil*. Durham: Duke University Press.
Pearce, Justin. 2001. "Luanda's Evicted Neighborhood," *BBC News*, July 30.
Pestana, Nelson. 2005. Interview with Angolan academic and journalist, Luanda, June 1.
Ritzer, George. 2005. *Enchanting a Disenchanted World: Revolutionizing the Means of Consumption*, 2nd edition. Thousand Oaks: Pine Forge Press.

Rodrigues, Agostinho. 2002. "Um sistema que se regenera sem solucionar os seus problemas," *Angolense* 166 (January 19–26): 14–15.

Rodrigues, Agostinho. 2005. "Sucatas têm os dias contados," *Angolense* 325 (April 16–23): 14.

Ross, Kristin. 1995. *Fast Cars, Clean Bodies: Decolonization and the Reordering of French Culture.* Cambridge: MIT Press.

Santana, Mário. 2003. "O privado é que está a dar," *Semanario Angolense* 1 (3) (March 22–29): 2–3.

Sheller, Mimi and John Urry. 2000. "The City and the Car," *International Journal of Urban and Regional Research* 24 (4) (December): 737–757.

Storper, M. 2001. "Lived Effects of the Contemporary Economy: Globalization, Inequality, and Consumer Society," in J. and J. Comaroff (eds.). *Millenial Capitalism and the Culture of Neoliberalism.* Durham, NC: Duke University Press, pp. 88–124.

Photographic Essay 2

Luanda, Angola

Aubrey Graham (Photography) and
M. Anne Pitcher (Text)

Photograph P2.1

A common scene all over urban Africa—two women carry T-shirts on their heads while they walk along the Marginal in Luanda. As the background suggests, the city's architecture reflects the aesthetic conventions of the eighteenth and nineteenth centuries with the modernist visions of late colonialism and early independence.

Photo P2.1 A mosaic of aesthetic conventions

Photo P2.2 Urban comfort meets social exclusion

PHOTOGRAPH P2.2

Urban comfort and convenience meets social exclusion. A right-hand drive Mitsubishi Pajero darts past old, rusted sea containers used by displaced people for housing. Pedestrians must navigate the same potholed streets—at considerable risk to their lives.

PHOTOGRAPH P2.3

Wild Conqueror tires compete for space with beer cans and loose trash. In a city where services fail to meet the needs of 3.5 million people, garbage collection poses a daunting problem.

PHOTOGRAPH P2.4

A car washer hand dries the car he has just washed. Car washers make from 100 to 500 kwanzas per car depending on the neighborhood, but business is erratic. Car washers around the city are numerous so days may go by without having a car to wash.

PHOTOGRAPH P2.5

In Luanda, shoe care is as important as car care and there are many shoeshiners located around the city. Here, a young shoeshine boy sets up shop just in sight of some car washers. Shoeless himself, he waits for the right pair of shoes to come along.

Photo P2.3 Life in the trash lane

Photo P2.4 The business of car washing

Photo P2.5 From car care to shoe care

Photograph P2.6

Events in Angola's history, from colonialism to the war, make the present difficult for young people in the city. To survive, many must creatively combine trade on the street, shoeshining, car washing, and other informal activities. Given the grim past, many would rather dream about the future. What these young men want is a car to go with the car seats.

Photo P2.6 Imagined mobility

8

Human Capital, Embedded Resources, and Employment for Youth in Bulawayo, Zimbabwe

Miriam Grant

Introduction

Zimbabwe's economic crisis has been more than a decade in the making. The nation's debt level precipitated imposition of the World Bank/IMF sponsored Economic Structural Adjustment Program (ESAP) in 1991–1992. This led to massive retrenchments in the formal sector, imposition of user fees for health and education services, and sudden and frequent increases in the costs of basic foodstuffs and services. By 1995, the UNDP found that 45 percent of all households nationally had incomes below the food poverty line and 42 percent of urban households were poor (Raftopoulos et al. 1998).

Following this initial period, Zimbabwe has been in a spiral of "nearly uninterrupted economic chaos" since 1998 (Bond and Manyanya 2003). The statistics from this state of escalating decline are stunning in both national scope as well as impact on barely subsisting individual households. Annual inflation rates exceed 622 percent, and an estimated 75 percent of Zimbabwe's employable population is unemployed. Those who are employed face curtailed factory hours, which often equate to a three-day work week. Eighty-one percent of the population is below the Poverty Datum Line, 47 percent of Zimbabwe's population is critically undernourished and it was estimated that in 2004, 7.5 million out of a total population of 12 million needed food assistance due to poor crop production (Bloch 2004). Over the past couple of years, economic and political instability have further exacerbated retrenchments and food and basic commodity shortages, which means that the vast majority of households cannot meet minimal basic needs. At the intra-household level this means that children, youth, and the elderly—particularly females—tend to be the most socially and economically vulnerable (Grant 2003). One significant outcome of this economic chaos is Zimbabwe's inability to create enough jobs for the hundreds of thousands of new young entrants to the job market annually (Raftopolous et al. 1998).

Another significant outcome is the large number of children who are forced to drop out of school (Mvududu and McFadden 2001) and who have diminished chances of ever returning to school (Grant 2003). The economic crisis as well as deepening poverty due to the impact of HIV/AIDS has meant that many households have been forced to choose between buying food and paying school fees. Girls and orphans are often the first to be denied schooling (Mwanza 1999). By 1999, only 70 percent of children were completing primary education (Nkala 2004).

The AIDS pandemic has hit Zimbabwe hard, during a time when the government has drastically cut back spending on the health sector and user fees have increased. By the end of 2001, UNAIDS estimated that 2.3 million Zimbabweans were living with HIV/AIDS and of these, two million were adults aged 15–49, with an adult prevalence rate at 33.7 percent (up from an estimated 25.06 percent at the end of 1990). Zimbabwe's adult HIV prevalence rate is the third highest in the world after Botswana (38.8 percent) and Swaziland (34.5 percent) (UNICEF 2002). Life expectancy is expected to decrease to 35 years or lower by 2010. In Bulawayo, the country's second largest city (population close to one million) and the site of this research study, by the year 2000, the overall death rate of 13.7 (per 1,000 population) had more than doubled in a decade, and HIV-related diseases were the leading cause of death in all age groups from 1 to 64 years.

The high rate of AIDS mortality, increased number of orphans, declining economic conditions, and high levels of unemployment have combined to increase the dependency ratio in Zimbabwe to an estimated 98 people per 1 gainfully employed person. Not surprising, the informal sector, driven by the high rate of unemployment, is now the largest employer in Zimbabwe (Nkala 2004). However, within the informal sector there is a wide range of economic return, and many activities such as small-scale vegetable selling and hairdressing bring in meager sums.

In the midst of severe economic, political, and social crises, youth in Zimbabwe are attempting to establish themselves as independent economic and social actors. In this context, the geographies of household survival and social identity are in constant flux as households change and reconfigure to ensure survival. As Simone (2001) indicates, contestation and negotiation for scarce resources, position, and power have emerged as integral elements of everyday life. The first research question of this chapter is what are the economic pathways of these youth and what is the importance of human and social capital in these pathways? The second research question is how fundamental is the role of mentoring in the social and economic development of youth and is there a difference between mentoring of males and females? Social capital is determined as an investment in social relations with expected returns in the marketplace, which can be economic, political, labor, or community. In this context, social capital is viewed as an asset due to actors' connections and access to resources in the network or group of which they are a part (Lin 2001: 19–20). Ensher (1998; in Bennetts 2003) views mentoring in terms of social exchange theory where individuals will form, maintain, or terminate relationships with others with respect to how they perceive the benefit and costs of such relationships.

This research is based on a longitudinal study of male and female youth from 1998 to 2004 in three high-density suburbs in Bulawayo. The larger study examines educational background, economic and household circumstances and vulnerability, support networks, and the dreams and aspirations of youth and how this fits with later circumstances. The methodology includes a household dyad approach with interviews of youth and their household heads or guardians, who were asked about the concerns they had for youth under their care. The original sample size was 60 youth (31 males and 29 females) plus 60 household heads. This essay is based on a smaller subset of the original study, and includes 12 males and 11 females who were interviewed in 1998, 1999, 2001, and 2004. Although follow-up until 2001 produced a larger sample size (see Grant 2003), 2004 follow-up reflects attrition of many youth moving away to seek employment or to marry. In addition, the 2004 interviews asked much more explicit detail about the role of mentors in the lives of youth. Although this is a small sample, the longitudinal nature of the study allows us to unpack processes at work, including relationships with mentors, and constraints and opportunities as youth attempt to establish themselves as social and economic actors under increasingly constrained circumstances.

Official definitions of where childhood ends and adulthood begins differ between and within individual countries. Glaser (2000: 3) asserts that youth should be understood as a phase of socialization rather than as a fixed category. For the purposes of this chapter, and in keeping with other research on the topic, "youth" begins at 15 years of age when teenagers begin to move toward adulthood, and includes those up to the age of 29 in 1998. However, it is recognized that there are sociological differences within this category, for example, between a 24-year-old youth who is married and has her or his own household and a 28-year-old youth who may be single and still living at home with his or her parents.

HUMAN CAPITAL DEVELOPMENT

In its first decade after Independence in 1980, Zimbabwe invested heavily in education. Schools were built and staffed all over the country, and especially to service burgeoning cities. As a result, this generation of youth should in fact be much better educated than their parents, many of whom have migrated to town from the rural areas and who would have had their own education limited under the racial restrictions of the white minority Smith regime (1965–1979). Many youth should have completed their O-level examinations at the end of high school, and may have had the opportunity to engage in available training courses before entering the work force. One would predict that the higher the level of education, the greater the probability of employment.

Almost three-quarters of our youth wrote their O-level exams at the end of high school (with varying degrees of success), 9 percent had some secondary and 17 percent had finished elementary school. All of the youth who had dropped out of school who did not reach O levels cited lack of school fees to continue. Of male school dropouts, one was from a poor male-headed household whose father and brother later died from HIV/AIDS, and two were from low-income households headed by their grandmothers. Of female school dropouts, one was from an economically desperate household where the father later died, another was from a female-headed household, and another was a niece who came into the city from the rural areas to stay with her aunt and uncle; both her father and uncle later died. Loss of productive male household heads and nuclear family members would severely curtail money available for school fees. These households not only lost income from working members, but also would have used savings and any available resources to pay for both medicine and funerals.

Parents and guardians are facing increasingly difficult economic situations just as youth need more economic resources such as school fees, fees for courses, and to launch themselves successfully. Many parents have been retrenched and are still looking for work in the city whereas others have retreated to the rural areas but are unable to send in enough money for escalating school fees. There is also widespread belief that the formal education system is outdated and, many would contend, largely irrelevant, and thus many school leavers lack the skills, resources, and guidance needed to enter either the formal or informal economy (Grant 2003: 417). To help counter this situation, various courses are available from a wide range of sources including some Bulawayo City Council Youth Centers as well as many private "colleges" and entrepreneurs. Youth Center courses range from cutting and design, cooking, welding, and carpentry and vary from short term to durations of two or three years, including apprenticeship training. However, many of these courses have been curtailed due to City Council budget restrictions. Some youth were able to secure household or extended family resources for several courses, which would indicate that families were able to free money to invest in youth so that they would hopefully secure decent employment and help to support other family members. Thus, these youth were using their social capital to increase their human capital. All youth who benefited from courses had reached O levels, which would indicate that families at that time had the resources to pay for school fees. Slightly more than a third of the youth took courses at some stage and of these, five took one course, two took two courses and one took three courses. The second prediction is that those who took courses would have a higher probability of being employed, but of course, courses need to correspond with job fit, especially within this very restrictive economic environment.

Accumulating human capital is strong in this group of youth. Almost three-quarters reached their secondary school O-level exams, and 35 percent were able to take further training courses. This level of human capital development should provide youth with enough credentials and leverage to capture employment opportunities in either the formal or informal sectors. In the next section, we explore the economic pathways of these youth to examine the influence of both human and social capital on their present employment status.

Economic Pathways of Youth

In an attempt to categorize monthly earnings, I have designated low wage or low self-employment as any monthly income below 500,000 Zimbabwean dollars (hereafter Z$) and high wage or high self-employment as a monthly salary at or above Z$500,000 (U.S.$1 = Z$6,000 on the black market). Though this is an arbitrary division, given the highly volatile economic climate and the small sample size, it's helpful to separate highly vulnerable households from those which are less vulnerable, and recognize that there is a major range, with some individuals earning more than Z$1 million per month. However, this arbitrary cut off line serves to emphasize the vulnerability of many youth and their respective households.

A high percentage (48 percent) of youth is unemployed at present and this is heavily influenced by the 73 percent of females who are unemployed. None of the female youth had been able to secure low-paying wage employment, whereas this was the most important category for male youth. Two-thirds of male youth were employed in low wage/self-employed activities but no one from this group had access to high-wage jobs. Only two females were in the high self-employed category and no one had access to a high-wage position. These figures underscore the difficult economic climate and the scarcity of well-paying activities. What we would like to do now is to unpack this data retrospectively and examine economic pathways for each gender, from 1998 to 2004 inclusive and stated ambition in 1998. Table 8.1 presents education level, courses, and involvement of relatives in support roles for female youth. The phases roughly correspond with the initial interviews (1998) plus years of follow-up interviews (1999, 2001, 2004).

Table 8.1 allows us to view the economic journeys of these young women. Of the three who progressed from unemployed to employed, one was working in South Africa and one was a commercial sex worker who had done some prostitution prior to our 1998 interview. Three others went from being employed in 1998 (two low S/E and one high wage) to being unemployed in 2004. Slightly more than half (55 percent) of this small group were able to secure temporary employment at some stage during the seven-year period and almost all individuals secured this work through relatives.

Youth #8 has been consistently unemployed, with the exception of a three-month high-wage temporary job that Mom helped her attain. Although Youth #19 had a low self-employed job selling vegetables—which Mom taught her to do—for three of the four phases, she is now unemployed also. Youth #23 also went from low self-employment to a temporary low in-kind job with relatives (who paid with food and other commodities) to unemployment. Youth #52 is still engaged in low self-employment (selling freezits), which a cousin helped her fund. Youths #58 and #59 also engaged in temporary jobs secured by relatives. Despite starting with a high-wage one-year contract job, and taking a computer course funded by family members, Youth #27 is presently unemployed. Two female youth have left for South Africa—one is living with a relative there and is engaged in high self-employment and the other youth in looking for work. Relatives play an important role for these youth in securing temporary work for them or in funding and teaching them how to run a microenterprise. Thus, social capital in the form of embedded resources from family members appears to play a more important role than human capital in employment status and access, even though many jobs are temporary and

Table 8.1 Employment phases and courses of female youth

Youth #	Age	Education	Phase 1	Phase 2	Phase 3	Phase 4	Ambition
8	20	Gr. 7	Unemployed	Unemployed	3 month temp. job—high Wage (Mom)	Unemployed	Nurse
19	35	O levels	Low S/E (Mom taught)	Low S/E	Low S/E	Unemployed	Dressmaking
23	25	O levels	Low S/E		Low in kind labor (for relative)	Unemployed	Marketing
27	27	O levels	High wage (1-year contract)	Unemployed	Computer course (family)	Unemployed	Teacher/Nurse
45	24	O levels	Unemployed	Store till course (Uncle)	Unemployed	Computer course (Canadiancontact); unemployed	Caterer
50	26	Gr. 7	Unemployed (previous CSW)	Unemployed		High S/E (CSW)	Sell goods From Botswana
51	26	Gr. 10	Unemployed	Low wage (temp.)	Low S/E	Unemployed (looking in RSA)	Sell goods from Botswana
52	28	O levels	Unemployed			Low S/E (cousin helped)	Secretary/ Nurse
57	23	O levels	Store till course (Mom); unemployed	Unemployed	Unemployed	High S/E in RSA	Hotel Caterer
58	27	O levels	Unemployed		Short temp. (relatives); unemployed	Unemployed	Dressmaking/ Typing
59	24	O levels	Unemployed	Red Cross course (Dad)	Unemployed	6 month temp. low wage (Uncle); unemployed	Tourism

almost two-thirds of this group is unemployed. Sadly, not one respondent has been able to reach her ambition (as stated in 1998). Ambitions stated would be within the reach of this highly educated group only if they had been able to take the necessary training and could access necessary equipment, such as sewing machines. Perhaps Youths #50 and #51, with lower education levels, were the most practical in their stated ambition to be able to buy goods in Botswana for resale in Zimbabwe, but even this requires seed funding.

Four female youth have had training courses. Two have taken courses in operating a store till, one a Red Cross assistant course, and two have taken computer courses. All of these courses were funded by family members but three of the four youth who took courses are unemployed. This emphasizes the disjuncture between types of courses being offered and employment opportunities in either sector. It may also indicate lack of knowledge about what types of jobs are available and level and type of training that would be needed to be eligible for these jobs.

To better understand why so many female youth are unemployed and why many went from being economically active to economically inactive, we need to further unpack the context of their lives. How do household configuration, employment status, and dependency ratios impact on employment? How do parental status and economic activities of partners influence female youth? In addition, mentors are a key source of social capital and we need to know what types of mentoring are being offered, geographic proximity of mentors, and how this impacts on youth. Table 8.2 shows household, parental, and mentor details.

If we go back to Youth #8, we discover that there are three different household members working—all at high wage. Even though this youth did a high-wage temporary job, there would be no pressure on her to find work since the household is in excellent shape, especially compared with many others. Since the youth has experience with high wage, she would be less inclined to try low wage S/E or formal employment. At 20 years of age, and with three high wage earners in the household, she is probably waiting for marriage and may remain unemployed until she finds a husband.

Youth #19 is divorced, and living with her boyfriend and their child. The two children from her previous marriage live with her parents in the rural areas. She sold vegetables at a stand in her yard until her present boyfriend joined her, and since he is earning high wages, they have likely both decided that she should stay at home and look after their child. Youth #23 is in an extended family household since both parents divorced and remarried and Mom has gone to the rural areas. With three high-wage earners in the household, this youth may be just waiting to marry her boyfriend, who has migrated to the United Kingdom in search of work. Households for Youths #27 and #59 both have very high dependency ratios (6:0). Youth #27 heads a household comprising two siblings and three extended family orphans who are all youth. Although Mom and Dad are based in the rural areas, they are engaged in high-earning activities and, along with one of their sons, send remittances to help keep the household going. Youth #59, despite doing a Red Cross course and a low-wage temporary job, is presently unemployed. However, she has gone through a divorce and now is living back home with her parents and siblings. Dad is retired, her

Table 8.2 Households and mentors for female youth

Youth #	Youth Economic Status	Household Typology	# Modes of Livelihood	High Earnings?	Dependency Ratio Dep.: Indep.	Mentor 1	Where?	Mentor Economic Status	Youth: # Kids/ marital status
8	U	Female HH	3	Y	3:3	Mom	Home	High wage	0/single
19	U	Male HH	1	Y	2:1	Boyfriend	Home	High wage	3/divorced
23	U	Male Ext. HH	3	Y	2:3	Uncle	Home	High wage	0/single
27	U	Female youth HH	3 (remit)	Y	6:0	Mom	Rural	High S/E	1/single
45	U	Male HH	2	Y	7:2	Mom	Home	U	0/single
50	High S/E	Female HH	1	Y	5:1	Mom	Home	U	1/single
52	Low S/E	Male HH	2	Y	2:2	Husband	Home	High S/E	2/married
58	U	Male HH	1	Y	3:1	Husband	Home	High S/E	2/married
59	U	Male HH	1	N	6:0	Mom	Home	U	1/divorced

Notes: The two female youth who went to South Africa are excluded from this table.
Remit, remittances; U, unemployed; Ext., extended family. Modes of livelihood are the total number of sources of income, including lodgers. If two household members work at the same source of income, such as selling vegetables, this is listed as one mode of livelihood. If remittances are made to the household on a monthly basis, each is counted as a separate mode. Dependency ratio is the number of dependents (including children and unemployed household members) to independents, or those who are earning income.

siblings are unemployed, and the only source of income is a lodger in an already crowded household.

Although Youth #45 took a store-till operation course (funded by an uncle) and a computer course (funded by a Canadian family) she remains unemployed. This household survives on one low self-employed source and one high wage, which combine to support seven other people, five of whom are of working age. After securing family funds and external funds for her courses, it's unlikely that anyone else in the extended family is willing to invest more funds either for a course or to establish a microenterprise. Given the high number of dependents, this household would be quite vulnerable.

Youth #50 is the only female youth, who has remained in Bulawayo, in the high self-employed category. However, the household situation has been very difficult. In 1998, Dad was still in the household but at 66 was unemployed. Mom used to support the family as a domestic servant, but she was sick in 1998 so a son was sending them remittances. Youth #50 had tried some commercial sex work prior to the interview, but had stopped since she had a young baby. Three years later, Mom was still sick and unable to work, there were two youth and two children in the household, Dad was very ill and staying in the rural areas, and they were in arrears for water and electricity. A nephew who was in the army had been helping them, but had since died.

> We have no words to describe the way we are living. The children are not educated so there is no work for them. We have gone three days without food. An older sister has gone to a relative for help. (HH #50)

By 2004, this youth had returned to being a commercial sex worker, and likely felt she had no choice in order to survive for today and put food on the table and pay the bills. Youths #52 and #58 are married with two children. Both husbands engage in high self-employment so their wives are more than likely expected to fulfill traditional female roles, although Youth #52 sells "freezits" to supplement the household income. Youth #52 also reports that she sometimes helps her husband sell vegetables and they argue about what he has done with the money he earns. Although she names her husband as her mentor, it was her cousin who loaned her money to establish her own microenterprise.

There is strong evidence that sex role attitudes prevail with respect to role and duties of female youth. Female youth who lived in households that are less vulnerable appear to be helping with household and childcare duties and waiting to get married without engaging in economic activity in the meantime. This is reinforced by evidence that households which could free resources to help youth establish microenterprises have chosen not to do so, including the husband for Youth #52. In addition, low-wage jobs for female youth are absent from the group, with the exception of short intervals of temporary jobs secured by family members. Ambitions stated in table 8.1 also reflect traditional female jobs and careers such as nursing, teaching, and secretarial work although some hoped for careers in hotel catering and tourism.

Traditional female roles of beer brewing and commercial sex work exist in all Zimbabwean cities, and from our data we know that the female youth (#50) from one of the most vulnerable households has chosen to engage in commercial sex work to support five dependents. Female Youths #45 and #59 are in precarious situations in highly vulnerable households and may not be able to access any embedded resources in the form of seed money from extended family to start microenterprises. Four female youth have children, and three of these youth and their children stay at home with their parents. This supports Schlyter's (1999) findings in George compound, Lusaka, that single daughters and their children tend to live at home with their parents. Youth #19 has sent two children from a previous marriage back to the rural areas to live with her parents, and has had a child with her present boyfriend in the hopes that they will marry. Traditional roles of marriage, childbearing, and household work are predominant with these female youth despite the fact that their education levels are higher than the previous generation.

This chapter now examines economic paths and household details for male youth and then examines the role of mentors for all youth. Table 8.3 outlines economic pathways for male youth.

For male youth, even though two-thirds were unemployed in 1998, 75 percent of this subgroup was engaged in an economic activity by 2004. Of the 75 percent who were working by 2004, 78 percent were helped by family or friends in either actually securing the wage or S/E activity or paying for training/teaching them job skills. These male youth are able to access embedded resources within the family to improve both their human capital as well as their economic circumstances. Youths #46 and #47 played soccer for low wage (which varied by game outcome) and both had temporary factory jobs in the company that sponsored the soccer team. Youth #21 is the only high earner and is a self-employed brickmaker. His uncle taught him the skills, paid for a business course, and helped to set up his small business. The only male youth who has reached his ambition is Youth #42, who has his own microenterprise for repairing radios and TVs. Despite overall high levels of education, almost all males are engaged in low-income activities. To determine circumstances, as well as the situations for Youths #13, #20, and #56, we turn to table 8.4 for household typologies and the status of mentors.

Youth #13 comes from a household where there are two sources of high earnings. Family members paid for his courses, and may be allowing the youth to wait for a technical job that would fit his qualifications. Youth #20, who is also unemployed, has both parents working (one high/one low earnings) plus the household receives decent remittances from two siblings who are working in South Africa. For now, the pressure is not on this youth to engage in even low-paying economic activities. Youth #21 is from an unusual and highly vulnerable household. This youth and his aunt are low-income earners who are supporting six dependents: three friends, two uncles, and a niece. The two uncles are widowers who lost their wives to AIDS, and the youth also lost his Mom to AIDS. This household has had tremendous expenses in the form of medication and funerals. None of the five dependents who are old enough to work are working. Youth #41 is also from an extended family household. Headed by his Mom, the household includes two unemployed siblings plus a nephew—all of whom depend on this youth's low-wage earnings. This household also has suffered major loss and hardship with AIDS deaths of Dad and a brother.

Table 8.3 Economic pathways of male youth

Youth #	Age	Education	Phase 1	Phase 2	Phase 3	Phase 4	Ambition
13	24	O levels	Welding apprenticeship course (Brother) Temp. job	Computer Course (Dad); peer education course (free)	Technical course (Dad)	Unemployed	Welder
20	24	O levels	Unemployed		Low wage and in-store training	Unemployed	Manager
21	24	O levels	Unemployed	Business course (Uncle)		High S/E	Engineer
22	26	Gr. 7	Unemployed	Low wage	Low S/E	Low wage (relative)	Make leather goods
25	25	O levels	Unemployed		High wage	Low wage (Friend)	Mechanic
29	24	O levels	Unemployed	Unemployed—looking in Harare		Low wage (Dad)	Engineer
31	24	Form 1	Unemployed	Unemployed	Unemployed	Low S/E (Mom)	Computers
41	26	Gr. 7	Low S/E (Dad)	Temp. low wage	Unemployed—looking in mine	Low wage (Brother)	Farmer
42	25	O levels	Low S/E (Friend)	Low S/E	Low S/E	Low S/E	Electronics (S/E)
46	29	O levels	Low S/E + low wage	Low S/E + low wage	Low S/E + low wage + low wage temp. (Employer)	Low S/E + low wage	Truck driver
47	32	O levels	Unemployed	Low wage + low wage (Employer)	Low wage	Low wage	Brickmaker
56	24	O levels	Unemployed	Carpentry course (Dad)	Driving course (Sister)	Unemployed	Mechanic

Table 8.4 Households and mentors for male youth

Youth #	Youth Economic Status	Household Typology	# Modes of Livelihood	High Earnings?	Dependency Ratio Dep:Indep	Mentor 1	Where?	Mentor Economic Status	Youth: # Kids/ Marital Status
13	U	Male HH	2	Y	5:2	Dad	Home	U	Single
20	U	Male HH	4 (2 remit)	Y	4:2	Dad	Home	High wage	Single
21	High S/E	Female HH	2	Y	1:2	Mom	Home	Low S/E	Single
22	Low wage	Male HH	2	N	1:2	Grandma	Home	U	Single
25	Low wage	Female HH	2	N	6:2	Aunt	Home	Low wage	Single
29	Low wage	Male HH	3	Y	1:3	Dad	Home	Low wage	Single
31	Low S/E	Female HH	2	Y	1:2	Mom	Home	High S/E	Single
41	Low wage	Female HH	1	N	4:1	Friend	Nearby	Unknown	Single
42	Low S/E	Youth male HH	2	Y	3:2	Brother	Home	High wage	2/married
46	Low S/E+ Low wage	Youth male HH	1	N	3:1	Girlfriend	Nearby	Unknown	Single
47	Low S/E	Youth male HH	1	N	6:1	Sister	Home	U	Single
56	U	Male HH	2	N	4:2	Pastor	Nearby	High wage	Single

Youth #56 has benefited from two family sponsored courses but remains unemployed. This is not a well-off household and combines one low wage with one low S/E to support four other people. The youth now wishes to take a motor mechanics course and is hoping that someone in the family will support this.

With one exception, all males are single. Other than trying to provide subsistence to household members, these males would all want to make enough money to save up for lobola (or bride price) in order to get married, especially given an average age of 25 for single males. Given present earnings and the overall economic climate, many must be very discouraged at marriage prospects anywhere in the near future.

Male youth are much more likely than female youth to be engaged in low-wage/low S/E activities. Two-thirds of the females who have remained in Bulawayo have children, half of these live with a husband or boyfriend and the other half are at home with at least one parent. Even though female youth generally have equal educational qualifications to their male counterparts, they for the most part are acting within traditional sex roles and staying at home to look after children and the household. Better education levels and more training courses do not lead to high wage or high self-employment, with the exception of one male youth. What role do mentors play in the well-being of youth? Is social capital from mentors more important to success than education and courses? Do they tend to mentor males and females differently? The next section examines these issues.

Mentoring and Social Capital

Traditionally mentoring is visualized as a one-to-one relationship between an older experienced adult and a young mentee (Flaxman et al. 1988). In their study on a typology of mentoring, Philip and Hendry (1996: 192–193) identify five mentoring styles:

(1) *Classic mentoring*, a one-to-one relationship between an adult and a young person where the older, experienced mentor provides support, advice, and challenge.
(2) *Individual-team mentoring*, where a group looks to an individual or small number of individuals for support, advice, and challenge.
(3) *Friend-to-friend mentoring*, which often gives a "safety net," especially for young people who may be distrustful of adults.
(4) *Peer group mentoring*, where an ordinary friendship group takes on a mentoring role at specific times.
(5) *Long-term relationship mentoring* with "risk taking" adults.

In their study on benefits of mentoring for engineering students, Wallace and Haines (2004) make use of Kram's (1985) framework; specific benefits of mentoring functions including career development benefits, psychosocial benefits, and role-modeling benefits. Psychosocial benefits include providing advice, support, and counseling to help build competence and confidence, whereas role modeling is defined as the chance for protégés to observe mentors being successful in their personal and professional lives (Bruce 1995 in Wallace and Haines 2004: 3–4).

For female youth who were in close contact with their mentors ($n = 8$), with one exception all mentors were at home with them. Three had sex symmetry mentoring, two with both Mom and Dad and one with a husband and a sister; two had Mom only as a mentor and three had males only: two husbands and an uncle. Only half of these eight females had been able to secure help from mentors (in either funding courses or microenterprises) but none had received any help from mentors during 2004. Almost two-thirds (63 percent) had received help from extended family members at some stage, but only two had benefited from their help in 2004. The majority of female youth have classic mentoring from one or both parents although three include either their husbands or boyfriend. Female youth generally view mentors as a source of material support and advice, as evident from some direct comments:

> My mentor [Mom] helps by buying medication, food, shelter, and school fees. In the future, she will help with a good education, a job, and a good marriage, through giving me advice on choosing the right man, a man who can take good care of me. (Youth #8)

> [Mom and Dad] are looking after my son who is in the rural areas with them. Since the father of the son is in South Africa, they pay school fees for the other members of the family. They will help in the future by giving me advice on how to earn a living by doing computer courses. They give parental guidance and support the whole family with food, clothing and rent. (Youth #27)

Where female youth have lost one or both parents, a husband or boyfriend may take over the role of mentor, often with help from one of the youth's siblings.

> My boyfriend is taking good care of us- me and the baby. He makes sure that we don't sleep on empty stomachs; he also buys clothes so he's the only person that I'm truly dependent on. We are still planning for the future to get married and buy a house. [Although not listed as a mentor] since my Mother died, my sister looks after me and is like a mother to me now. She's always giving me advice on being good to my boyfriend since she also depends on him now. (Youth #19)

Psychosocial mentoring is a major part of mentoring for female youth, and may be more important that any career development since it is generally assumed in Zimbabwean culture that female youth will soon marry and become mothers. Thus role mentoring for females is more likely to apply to their social reproductive roles than careers. One youth (#27) describes the close bond with her mother, "She's my guide and my light so I very much doubt if ever I'll ever do anything without her being around." Only one female youth (#59) implies some connection between advice and achievement, "They [mentors] should give us love and comfort. They should encourage us to do great things in life."

In contrast with female youth, slightly more than half (58 percent) of male youth were engaged in economic activities in 2004 directly as a result of help from mentors or family/friends. Only 25 percent of male youth received instrumental help from mentors, thus family and friends were more important in helping to train them or set them up in wage or self-employment activities. A higher proportion of female youth were able to secure help from their mentors, but male youth were much more successful at accessing embedded resources of family and friends to engage in economic activities. Social capital from networks is the key to success for these male youth. One quarter of male youth, including two youth household heads, were unable to access help from either mentors or family/friends and this accentuates their vulnerability.

Sex symmetry for male youth mentors includes three pairs of both parents, followed by six female-only mentors (Mom, grandmother, aunt, sister, and girlfriend) and three male-only mentors (friend, brother, and pastor). Help from mentors—and anticipated help—for male youth includes money, jobs, and concerns about *lobola*:

> They [Mom and Dad] have given me education and proper shelter. They will get me a good job and by paying lobola/bride price which I know I cannot afford. (Youth #13)
>
> [Dad] tells me that my life is what I make it and I have to work hard to make a decent living. (Youth #20)
>
> [Mom] has made me grow up to be a respectful and hard working someone on which I'm very thankful. For as long as she's alive and we're together I know I'll have a brighter future. (Youth #21)
>
> [Mom] helps by paying the rent, food and clothing. I think she will help me finish my education to get a job. (Youth #31)
>
> [My pastor] gives me money when possible and may help me get a job. (Youth #56)

Given extremely harsh social times with the AIDS pandemic, psychosocial benefits from mentors would be critical to the health and longevity of youth:

> I talk daily [with Mom and Dad]. They are very talkative on issues such as drinking and drugs. Even though I don't drink or take drugs it gets so difficult for my parents to believe me since I have friends who smoke and drink. (Youth #13)
>
> Mom tells me there should be no sex before marriage because of AIDS. (Youth #20)
>
> They are my sisters. I think they are the closest people to tell my problems. I think they are the right people to help because we don't have any living parent. (Youth #47)
>
> [My pastor] gives me prayers, preaching, advice about self respect, trustworthiness, and avoiding peers who are bad. (Youth #56)

All youth were asked whether their mentors discussed the following topics with them: boys/girls, marriage, HIV/AIDS, drinking and drugs, work and money. Female youth who had sex symmetry mentors all discussed marriage, HIV/AIDS, drinking and drugs, and money. Female-only mentors for female youth discussed all topics whereas male-only mentors concentrated on girls/boys, marriage, and HIV/AIDS and did not discuss work or money matters as much. Sex symmetry mentors for male youth all talked about HIV/AIDS, drinking and drugs, and money issues, followed in importance by work. Lone female mentors all discussed HIV/AIDS with their protégés, followed by equal emphasis on drinking and drugs, work, and money. Male-only mentors discussed all topics, however, with less emphasis on marriage.

When we compare all mentors and topics discussed for male and female youth the mentoring patterns are different. Altogether, female youth are not receiving as much mentoring as males. All mentors for male youth discussed HIV/AIDS and money, followed in importance by drinking/drugs and work, with less emphasis on girls/boys and marriage. The three most important topics for female youth include marriage, HIV/AIDS, and money, followed by girls/boys, drinking/drugs, and finally work (with just over half receiving any mentoring about work). This reinforces stereotypical gender roles with respect to young females and work, despite their high levels of human capital.

Discussion and Conclusion

Opportunity structures for youth in Zimbabwe at this time are extremely constrained. There are few formal-sector jobs and many of these are low wage. Given the hundreds of thousands of retrenchments, competition for any decent high-earning formal jobs would be intense, and those without experience would be seriously disadvantaged, although social capital in the form of connections to the right people may mean more than experience for decent-paying positions.

For youth, the accumulation of human capital does not appear to help at all. Reaching O levels at the end of high school does not have any benefits as far as qualifying one for a decent-paying job and this links with the present job structure in Zimbabwe. Some youth have abandoned any hope of securing steady employment in Zimbabwe and have made their way to South Africa (often illegally) in order to try to find jobs. Since this sample includes only two females who stopped school at Grade 7, one cannot generalize, but it would be helpful to know whether females who have their O levels are less inclined to engage in commercial sex work.

Investing in courses does not work either, since most courses do not fit available job opportunities. There would be few store-till operators needed, and even there, store owners would be inclined to train staff who had worked with them for a long time and whom they trust. The one successful male took a business course, which has helped him to run his brick molding business. Most youth who took higher skill courses such as computers, welding, and driving are unemployed and may have a very long wait before their training converts into a job opportunity in that specific field.

Social capital is essential to success in the economic pathways of youth. Male youth especially were able to call upon embedded resources from family and friends to establish themselves either in low-wage or low self-employment activities. Social capital is much more important a factor in success than human capital. The assets that male youth are able to call upon and to use make all the difference in their abilities to try to support themselves and their households.

This fits with Ncube's (1998: 18) assertion that "in the African cultural context, childhood is not perceived and conceptualized in terms of age but in terms of intergenerational obligations of support and reciprocity."

Female youth were often able to call upon some social capital, but this was not consistent across the time spectrum and usually did not convert into permanent economic activities. Social capital did give some female youth access to short-term jobs, which would temporarily help both financially and with respect to experience, but female youth were unable to call upon embedded resources to the same extent as male youth. Despite high levels of human capital for female youth, this generation of young women continues to be constrained by a social system with fairly rigid concepts of sex role for females, and this translates into expectations and opportunities for employment. Female youth who are parents but who are not connected with a partner are unlikely to engage in economic activity. This may change as children grow up, or as households become more vulnerable.

Mentoring is critically important in the social and economic development of youth. Some mentors have helped to launch male and female youth at one stage or another, and many have paid for courses. Mentors are important for job contacts, for financing for microenterprises, and for using their own social capital to link youth with extended family members who are willing to invest in youth.

Psychosocial benefits of mentoring are just as important as economic benefits, especially within a framework of severe economic and social crises. In a country where the average life expectancy may drop to 35 years or lower in five short years, counseling about relations before and after marriage and about HIV/AIDS in particular are vital. Many youth have been forced to grow up very quickly, and in some cases to become the household head while they are still teenagers, due to the loss of one or both parents. Households are reconfigured in many ways and more households—however precarious economically—must take in orphans as the pandemic wreaks havoc across the fabric of the extended family and society. Many households survive on low wages or low earnings in self-employment and both economic and social mentoring are critical as households face uncertainty and continued hardship.

Female youth seem to be falling through the cracks of mentoring. They receive less mentoring than their male counterparts and their mentoring is on more traditional topics such as relations between the sexes and marriage. Very few female youth receive mentoring about work. Since many male youth have single female mentors (usually Mom) and still receive mentoring about work, then this indicates further evidence of assigning females to traditional roles, despite their education levels. Many mentors of female youth may be just waiting for female youth to marry, and thus are not concerned with the present idleness of their protégés. Given present uncertainties in both the economy and the household, potential productivity, skills transfer, potential success, and development of independence is lost. Social mores and gender role expectations have not yet caught up with current reality.

It is straightforward and easy to make recommendations; however, the following recommendations look forward in time to what is hoped will be a renewal and a better future within Zimbabwe:

(1) A complete change is needed in the formal education system. Youth should be taught skills that will convert easily into a livelihood, whether in the formal or the informal sector. Skills training should include elementary business courses.
(2) Female youth should be allowed to train for any occupation. This will entail a long process of change to promote changes in societal gender roles.
(3) When the economy recovers, support for apprenticeship programs and a registry for unemployed youth should be established. A youth employment center could provide some accreditation of courses, advertise those courses, and provide career counseling.
(4) School curriculum should include sex education, including HIV/AIDS, and should also include career counseling.
(5) Micro-finance programs need to be established to help youth who have a clear business plan and who need to establish their own microenterprises.
(6) City Council Youth Centers should be revitalized so that training courses, recreation and peer education can continue to reach as many youth as possible. New centers will have to be built to service newer suburbs.
(7) A formal mentoring system should be developed for both male and female youth at these centers, with female youth being made a priority.

Social capital and embedded resources are absolutely critical to youth and will remain so for a long time into the future. Government, NGOs, and other organizations will need to prioritize youth once the geography of economic chaos is suspended. As Youth #19 expresses about the future, "I hope to be someone who does a lot to help myself and my family but I'm not making enough."

Note

I would like to acknowledge the generous support of the International Development Research Centre for initial research and the University of Calgary's URGC for supporting follow-up interviews. I would also like to acknowledge Dr. Valerie Haines and Mr. Dumisani Banda for their important contributions to this project.

References

Bennetts, C. 2003. Mentoring Youth: Trend and Tradition, *British Journal of Guidance and Counseling* 31 (1): 63–76.

Bloch, E. 2004. "The Private Sector and the National Budget," in *Poverty Reduction Forum Zimbabwe, Budget Series Workshop Report.* IDS, UNDP, pp. 11–13.

Bond, P. and M. Manyanya. 2003. *Zimbabwe's Plunge: Exhausted Nationalism, Neoliberalism and the Search for Social Justice.* Pietermaritzburg: University of Natal Press.

Bruce, M. 1995. "Mentoring Women Doctoral Students: What Counselor Educators and Supervisors Can Do," *Counselor Education and Supervision* 35: 139–149.

Ensher, E. 1998. "Mentoring as a Process of Social Exchange: A Theory Based Approach," in *Proceedings of Diversity in Mentoring 1998*. Western Michigan University, International Mentoring Association, Michigan.

Flaxman, E., C. Ascher, and C. Harrington. 1998. *Youth Mentoring: Programs and Practices*. New York: Columbia University, ERIC Clearinghouse on Urban Education.

Glaser, C. 2000. *Bo-Tsotsi: The Youth Gangs of Soweto, 1935–1976*. Portsmouth, NH: Heinemann.

Grant, M. 2003. "Difficult Debut: Social and Economic Identities of Urban Youth in Bulawayo, Zimbabwe," *Canadian Journal of African Studies* 37 (2 and 3): 411–439.

Kram, K. E. 1985. *Mentoring at Work: Developmental Relationships in Organizational Life*. Glenview, IL: Scott, Foresman.

Lin, N. 2001. *Social Capital: A Theory of Social Structure and Action*. Cambridge: Cambridge University Press.

Mvududu, S. and P. McFadden. 2001. *Reconceptualising the Family in a Changing Southern African Environment*. Harare: University of Zimbabwe Publication.

Mwanza, A. (ed.). 1999. *Social Policy in an Economy under Stress*. Harare: SAPES Books.

Ncube, W. 1998. *Culture, Tradition and Children's Rights in Eastern and Southern Africa*. Brookfield, VT: Ashgate.

Nkala, P. 2004. "The Social Sector and National Budget: A Focus on Social Welfare, Education, Agriculture and Informal Sector," in *Poverty Reduction Forum Zimbabwe, Budget Series Workshop Report*. IDS, UNDP, pp. 14–25.

Philip, K. and L. Hendry. 1996. "Young People and Mentoring—Towards a Typology? *Journal of Adolescence* 19: 189–201.

Raftopoulos, B., T. Hawkins, and D. Amanor-Wilks. 1998. *Human Development Report: Zimbabwe*. Harare: UNDP, Poverty Reduction Forum, Institute of Development Studies.

Schlyter, A. 1999. *Recycled Inequalities: Youth and Gender in George Compound, Zambia*. Uppsala: Nordiska Afrikainstitutet.

Simone, A-M. 2001. "On the Worlding of African Cities," *African Studies Review* 44 (2): 15–41.

UNICEF. 2002. *Hope Never Dries Up: Facing the Challenges: Situational Assessment and Analysis of Children in Zimbabwe*. Harare: UNICEF.

Wallace, J. and V. Haines. 2004. "The Benefits of Mentoring for Engineering," *Journal of Women and Minorities in Science and Engineering* 10: 1–15.

9

Gender Relations, Bread Winning, and Family Life in Kinshasa

Guillaume Iyenda and David Simon

Introduction

The World Summit on Social Development in 1995 gave momentum to the fight against poverty, and one of the most important issues in this process was the achievement of all social goals, with particular emphasis on gender equality and gender participation in development. Since then, the discourses on gender participation in the fight against poverty in the Third World have evolved further, not least with respect to the Millennium Development Goals, all of which have implicit gender aspects. However, several (achieving universal primary education, eliminating gender disparities in all levels of education, and reducing maternal mortality by two-thirds) are explicitly gendered.

These goals have great resonance for the Democratic Republic of Congo (DRC), one of the most war-ravaged and thus impoverished countries in Africa, despite its vast natural wealth. Nevertheless, the debate in the DRC on gender and development commenced well before the 1995 summit. In the early 1970s, the Congolese government launched a campaign on *Emancipation de la Femme Zaïroise*. It advocated special strategies to support women by promoting their emancipation from the household. It worked to build and raise women's consciousness and to make them more aware of their responsibilities as mothers and workers outside their households. Over many years, successive Congolese governments have enunciated discourses about the improvement of women's participation in development. However, they have deliberately ignored the implementation of their own discourses, forgetting that "planning for low-income women in the Third World must be based on their interests—in other words, their prioritized concerns" (see also Evans 1992; Moser 1993: 37; Ostergaard 1992; Rai 2002; Standing 1992).

Although successive Congolese governments have signed numerous international commitments to recognize and strengthen equality between men and women, gender inequality persists throughout the country. Women remain more vulnerable to chronic poverty because of gender inequality in the distribution of income within households and their limited access to productive inputs and properties. Indeed, the UN Economic Commission for Africa does not regard the DRC as on track to meet any of the MDGs, let alone the gender-focused ones (UNECA 2005).

Nevertheless, the country's economic bankruptcy has precipitated many changes in people's daily practices. The role of gender in urban survival strategies has received increased attention over the last decade. Some academic research has been carried out and the public has also become aware of the implications of gendered relations in urban development. The involvement of women in household livelihoods and survival strategies has increased, precipitating significant changes in gender relations. Since the economic crisis deepened, many women have become the main breadwinners for their households. This is true in many other countries too. Research in Dar-es-Salaam revealed that, "while there are indications that men are handing over more of the responsibility for supplying the needs of the household to women, evidence shows that this is because the husband's wages no longer meet the household's basic needs" (Koda and Omari 1991: 120).

Accordingly, our principal focus is the analysis of gender relations and especially the increasingly pivotal roles of women in breadwinning in many Kinshasa households. We demonstrate how the pervasive crisis has reduced gender inequality within households and how women in Kinshasa now play a crucial role in generating household incomes. "Breadwinning involves not only paid employment, but also the day-to-day obligation to earn money for the financial support of the family" (Potuchek 1997: 4). This study defines a breadwinner as someone who provides his/her family with the financial or other means of survival, regardless of the sector or nature of employment.

The transformations taking place within Congolese society have exacerbated the impoverishment of many households. However, the current crisis has weakened gender differentiation and the gender hierarchy imposed on women for generations. Particularly in Kinshasa and other larger urban areas, it has allowed women to gain economic power and ownership of assets, to become socially more mobile, and to increase their participation in income-generating activities for their households, especially within informal economic activities. Nevertheless, the complexity and sensitivity of the issues provided a formidable research challenge.[1]

THE CITY OF KINSHASA

History of the City

Before Belgian colonization in the nineteenth century, Kinshasa, a conglomerate of Teke and Humbu villages, was a centuries-old and important trading center on the Congo River (De St Moulin 1976: 463; Vansina 1973: 250–251, 259–226). However, colonization heralded a familiar story of displacement and economic marginalization through direct and indirect expropriation of businesses, livelihoods, and influence. Crucially, the Belgians pushed the indigenes away from the riverbank to build a European city called Leopoldville near the place where Henry Morton Stanley had settled in 1842. Its growth was stimulated by completion in 1911 of the railway from Matadi on the coast. In 1920, Leopoldville was connected to the village of Kinshasa by road, and three years later the Congolese capital was transferred from Boma to Leopoldville (Map 9.1).

The district of Kinshasa was created by decree on August 10, 1923. In 1941, Kinshasa became a city and in 1951 its official boundaries were extended from 46 to 75 square kilometers. In 1954, with the creation of annexed zones and their organization into districts like existing parts of the city, the urban area covered 1,977 square kilometers. A dramatic further extension in 1968 to reflect rapid *de facto* urbanization gave Kinshasa a *de jure* extent of 9,965 square kilometers (Mwanza 1997). Although the built-up area has doubled in surface area again since then, it is difficult to ascertain its true size as no such data are kept and the city is expanding daily. The Bureau d'Etudes d'Aménagement Urbain et d'Urbanisme (BEAU), the state office responsible for urbanization and urbanism, was looted in 1991 and 1993 and now opens only irregularly as it lacks funding or government support.

The majority of the city's early inhabitants were men, who constituted the main labor force. Until 1945, black workers lived near the city of Leopoldville. After World War II, new areas were built, especially in what subsequently became the current districts of Kasa-Vubu and Linguala. After 1950, the city was extended and new planned districts were built, including Bandalungwa, Kalamu, Matete, and Lemba (map 9.1).

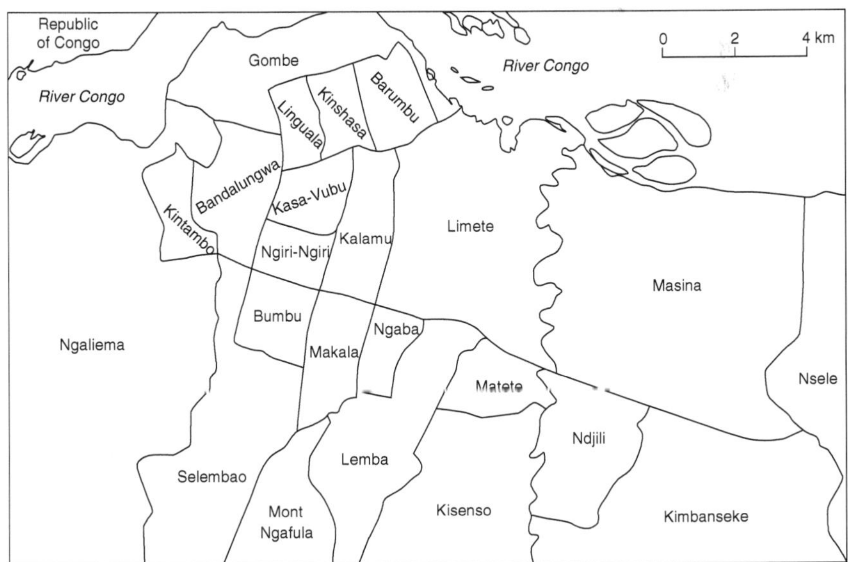

Map 9.1 Map of Kinshasa.

Source: Amended from Institut Géographique de Kinshasa, 2001.

Kinshasa's Population

Despite strict administrative control of rural–urban migration throughout the colonial period, Kinshasa's population of 30,000 in 1880 had risen to 400,000 at Independence in 1960. At Independence, the new indigenous political leaders immediately ended the controls and the city's subsequent rapid population growth (Table 9.1) has posed serious problems since the state lacks the means to satisfy people's shelter, infrastructure, and employment needs (Piermay 1997: 227).

With the level of misery that people face in Kinshasa, one might expect a net exodus to rural areas. Yet, net migration to Kinshasa and other cities continues to rise. This shows how desperate and untenable the rural situation has become. The economic destruction, closure of many companies in rural areas, the lack of basic commodities such as soap, salt, palm oil, pharmaceuticals, and clothing, and the displacement caused by the brutal and long-running civil wars in rural areas and other cities of the country explain this increase.

Under such circumstances, and given the state of the BEAU, it is clearly impossible to ascertain recent or current populations with any degree of accuracy. Ironically, these difficulties echo those for earlier eras highlighted by Fetter (1987: 85–89), who argued that census reports from the Belgian Congo (Zaire) and other African countries must be treated with extreme caution. Currently, the most populous districts in Kinshasa are Kimbanseke in the extreme east and Ngaliema in the extreme west (Map 9.1), each of which has nearly 400,000 inhabitants. The post-Independence districts of Masina (called *Chine populaire* by the residents), Kisenso, and Selembao each have nearly 300,000 inhabitants as a result of unregulated and uncontrolled expansion.

Urban Infrastructure

Electricity was introduced early in 1902 and the paving of streets commenced in 1931. The first running water was installed in the white people's city in 1923

Table 9.1 Evolution of Kinshasa's population

Period	Population	Growth Rate (%)
1924–1929	25,000–26,000	0.96
1929–1934	46,088–27,910	−10
1934–1940	27,910–49,972	10
1940–1945	49,972–101,501	15
1945–1950	No data	No data
1950–1955	201,905–365,905	13
1955–1959	365,168–402,422	2.5
1959–1967	402,422–901,520	10.6
1967–1976	No data	No data
1976–1980	1,748,000–2,400,000	8
1980–1984	2,400,000–2,664,200	2.6
1984–1991	2,664,200–3,119,869	2
1991–2000	3,119,869–6,062,000	11.4

Sources: De St Moulin October 1977; INS 1992; 1993; Piermay 1997. There are many inconsistencies among the sources.

but not until a decade later in indigenous cities, and then only in the form of public fountains. The rectangular, single-storey colonial housing constructed for Africans was often deemed culturally inappropriate since it precluded people from sitting together in the compound and spending most of the time outside the house (Nzuzi 1992).

To deal with post-Independence population growth, the Office des Cités Africaines (OCA) was replaced by the Office National des Logements (ONL) with a mission to conceive, to finance, and build housing at moderate cost for low-income people (Mwanza 1997: 42). Failing to achieve real success, the ONL was replaced in 1971 by the Caisse Nationale d'Epargne et de credit Immobilier (CNECI), but by 1981 it was bankrupt. In fact, 70–75 percent of houses in Kinshasa have been built by their owners. This explains the serious environmental, erosion, and administrative problems facing the city. Some streets are too narrow to accommodate cars; many are unnamed, and some have more than one name and/or unnumbered houses.

In the field of transport, people in Kinshasa face a nightmare. Mismanagement of public companies and the lack of political will prevented the government from investing in this sector. Today, like in many other sectors, all transport infrastructure is in an appalling state and has deteriorated steadily. The crisis is mainly due to the lack of fuel, a shortage of equipment and spare parts, inadequate maintenance of the transport network, and a lack of funds for new infrastructure projects. A state-owned public transport company no longer exists throughout the city. All public companies in cities have ceased to deliver services and are bankrupt. In 1974, for example, two major companies were operating 1,700 buses in Kinshasa and Lubumbashi. This number fell to 137 in 1977 and nowadays there are fewer than ten state-owned public buses operating in Kinshasa (World Bank 1980: 17). Urban dwellers currently use private services, which are also in very poor condition but at least still operate to some extent. In many cases, people resort to walking.

Kinshasa's industrial sector has been neglected for nearly a quarter of a century. Industry in the DRC accounted for 15.6 percent of GDP in 1994, down from 33 percent in 1980, and well below the sub-Saharan African average of 30 percent (EIU 1999–2000: 26). Virtually all manufacturing activities have also declined inexorably on account of the shortage of imported spare parts, the riots and lootings of 1991 and 1993, mismanagement, a lack of local purchasing power, and, in the case of clothing, the availability of cheap secondhand imports from Europe, which also have a certain status value (Banque Centrale du Congo 2001: 10). Therefore, the tertiary sector now dominates Kinshasa's economy, accounting for 73.9 percent of all urban activities, comprising primarily small and medium commercial (39.1 percent), administrative (23.9 percent), and other tertiary services (2.2 percent; see Mwanza 1997: 57–58). The secondary sector provides only 16.9 percent of jobs and the primary sector under 8 percent, mainly in urban agriculture and fish breeding. Nevertheless, Kinshasa's urban primacy means that it dominates the national economy, accounting for between 19 and 33 percent of all firms or establishments in each sector (INS 1993).

GENDER AND FORMAL EMPLOYMENT IN KINSHASA

Until the mid-1970s, jobs in Kinshasa were provided principally by the formal sector and were located in two main zones: Gombe (the downtown area) and Limete (the industrial area) (map 9.1). Since the formal sector has ceased to provide employment for most of the economically active population, the location of jobs has shifted from the former colonial city to the entire urban area, and the organizational basis of employment has also changed radically. People now locate their enterprises according to the ease of obtaining raw materials, supplies of goods, and reaching customers. Therefore, the easy way to trade (and to avoid paying the rent, energy charges, or tax) is outside Gombe and Limete. In Kinshasa, street traders gain access to land for their activities in different ways. Those who sell on the street do not pay for the land or the portion of street or sidewalk where they trade. They pay only a daily equivalent of between U.S.$0.50 and U.S.$1.00 to market controllers or to police officers who harass them hourly. Those traders who decide to erect stalls buy their plots from market controllers appointed by the mayor of the district.

Within formal employment in Kinshasa, patterns of gender segregation have changed. Although in some areas of the city the situation varies according to the livelihood of the head of the household (HHH), women are now equally involved in breadwinning. Since the deepening of the crisis, there has been an explosion of commitment by urban women in income-earning productive work, over and above their traditional domestic reproductive roles, in the manner described by Caroline Moser (1993: 40). In response, the Congolese government has, since the late 1980s, updated and changed family law and introduced many amendments regarding women's working conditions. The *Code de la Famille* (the Congolese Family Code) has emphasized women's rights and entitlements to resources. Currently, equality between men and women at work is guaranteed by law. Salary disparities and sexual discrimination at work have been abolished and the right of women to attain managerial positions within any organization has been reinforced.

Women working in the formal sector are concentrated in NGOs and civil society, nursing and health work, teaching, secretarial work, and administration, with small proportions in management and directorships (figure 9.1). Most nurses work in different clinics close to their homes and at Kinshasa University. Although the law has changed in their favor and the principle of equal wages for equally qualified people doing the same job has been applied, few women have yet reached managerial or directorial positions within public and private companies. Nevertheless, more women now earn the same wages as men. Although married women do not benefit from some fringe benefits such as health costs for their children, substantial improvement has occurred for literate women.

Nevertheless, formally employed women often complain about the persistence of patriarchal gender stereotypes. Many have been offered only jobs of lower status and fringe benefits. Within formal enterprises, people commonly explain gender differences in employment by means of traditional patriarchal assertions that women are less productive, physically weaker, less educated, spend fewer hours at work because of their household responsibilities, and are often absent from work (Iyenda 2002).

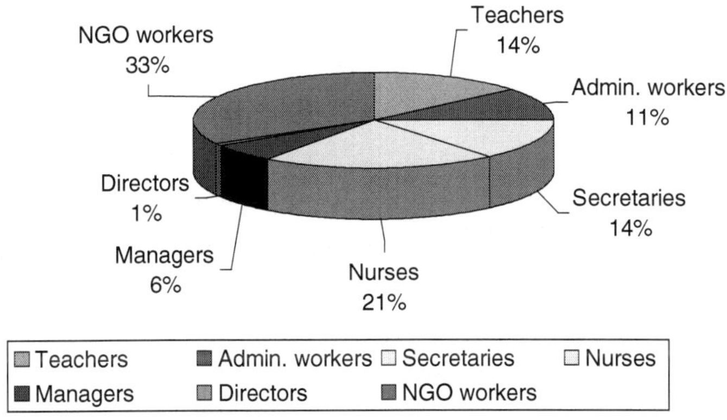

Figure 9.1 Involvement of women in formal employment in Kinshasa.
Source: Field Research in Kinshasa, May 2001.

Contrary to these accusations, women workers are actually as productive as men in the labor market and compete on equal terms. The views of the personnel and training managers in four companies we interviewed supported this finding:

> We always want to work with women and if everything depended on us, we would employ more women than men. Women are well-organized, fast workers, fast learners and serious in the execution of their tasks. Women are multi-skilled, they hate unfinished work and they always do everything with precision and attention. In our day-to-day work, we have found that with the same qualification and the same experience in the same job, women are more productive and more efficient than men. (Iyenda 2002: 343)

Another issue faced by women in formal employment in Kinshasa is sexual harassment from male counterparts or bosses, some of whom continue to see women in particular categories of jobs as "loose." Men in management positions often demand sexual favors from women, even married women, in return for job favors or cash. The lack of female representation in unions makes them more vulnerable. In Kinshasa, women are underrepresented in trade unions and, therefore, their issues are less debated, reinforcing their weaknesses in the labor market (see Elson 1991; Iyenda 2002; Molyneux and Razavi 2002; Rai 2002).

Gender and Informal Sector Activities in Kinshasa

The sharp rise in unemployment since the early 1980s, coupled with the problems experienced by women in the formal sector, both necessitated and facilitated the involvement of Congolese women in self-employment and informal economic activities. Indeed, one of the main characteristics of unemployment in the Congo is that it is not generally frictional (i.e., short term or occasional) but structural and hence of long duration. Without any financial support or form of social security, most long-term unemployed become destitute and their living conditions deteriorate further. Therefore, many women have chosen to work on their own informally and to combine their economic activities with household tasks.

Sources of Commodities

In the early 1990s, the political situation in the Congo changed dramatically and led to a deep crisis with profound effects on people's lives. Just after January 1993, unemployment rose sharply and the state descended into bankruptcy. Without secure incomes, urban dwellers' spending dropped sharply and most were able to satisfy only basic needs. Therefore, the clientele of urban supermarkets and wholesalers shrank dramatically. At the same time, the phenomenon of huge street markets called *Kuwait* arose in residential areas. All manner of looted and contraband goods and merchandise from stores, warehouses, offices, and people's houses were sold in *Kuwaits.* As the number of customers in the main downtown commercial centers diminished and street vending activities grew, wholesalers began providing street entrepreneurs with goods to meet this new situation. The use of the term *Kuwait* exemplified people's dark humor in dire situations, reflecting Saddam Hussein's then recent invasion and looting of Kuwait.

Many women working within the informal sector now obtain their goods on credit or with cash from wholesalers, who are mainly Lebanese or Pakistani. Everyday, the women queue in front of different downtown stores to receive or buy their merchandise, and the number of providers of goods to informal sector operators has been rising continually. As street enterprises fall beyond the formal tax system, more and more business people make their living by providing them with goods, thus avoiding the need to keep real business accounts. Traders from nearby counties supply many of the nonmanufactured goods for sale, and other merchandise is sourced through fraud and contraband.

Table 9.2 reveals the substantial extent and diversity of women's involvement in informal activities and self-employment, including many forms of vending and personal services but not manufacturing or repairs. Taking informal activities in the four surveyed districts as a whole, about 91 percent of women own their businesses, while 8 percent are employees and only 1 percent is in training. Among the 91 percent who are their own bosses, 44 percent work with relatives (children, especially girls, nephews, cousins, grandchildren) on a regular basis whereas 47 percent work alone. Those who work as paid employees are working as servers in bars or restaurants, as hairdressers, and in beauty salons. The apprentices are found in sewing shops.

Gender and Vending Activities

Vending refers to the sale of items such as those listed in table 9.2 as well as imported secondhand clothes and shoes. These are numerous and geographically widespread throughout the city. They are not measured because it is impossible for the government or local authorities to obtain accurate data on the activities as people move constantly, go bankrupt, and change businesses

Table 9.2 Involvement in Informal Activities by Gender in Kinshasa, 2001

Activity	Gender				Total (%)	
	Male		Female			
	No	%	No	%		
Cobblers	12	5.88	0	0	2	1.6
Shoeshiners	4	7.2	0	0	4	3.2
Street money-dealers	5	9.09	7	10	12	9.6
Barbers	2	3.6	0	0	2	1.6
Mechanics	3	5.4	0	0	3	2.4
Street artisans	2	3.6	0	0	2	1.6
Trolley owners	7	12.72	6	8.57	13	10.4
Small shop keepers	6	10.9	8	11.42	14	11.2
Tire repairers *(Quado)*	4	7.2	0	0	4	3.2
Cooked foods sellers	3	5.4	9	12.85	12	9.6
Vegetable sellers	0	0	14	20	14	11.2
Cakes and pastry sellers	4	7.2	9	12.85	13	10.4
Manufacture products sellers	13	23.6	5	7.1	18	14.4
Cereal and tubers sellers	0	0	8	11.42	8	11.4
Frozen fish, meat, and poultry	0	0	4	5.7	4	5.7

Source: Field research in Kinshasa, March–May 2001.

regularly as some grow while others vanish within days. Goods sold by women differ in type and importance. Our field research revealed that hundreds of women sit at intervals along the curb, displaying their goods on the sidewalk. In commercial streets, they sit in niches between the shops. Others use portable stalls made mainly from wood and erected daily on the streets. Well-established traders with large quantities of merchandise rent small shops or kiosks as sales points.

The busiest period is between 10 a.m. and noon. As many households currently consume only one meal per day, people prefer to do their shopping then before cooking a meal that is consumed at around 4–5 p.m. Afternoon sales peak between 5 and 8 p.m. in markets called *wenze ya bitula* (literally markets of the unsold) which stay open until late.[2] Here, people generally sell their remaining perishable goods, which they are unable to store because of a lack of freezers. Therefore, these goods are sold at half price or less.

Nowadays, a substantial number of women in Kinshasa sell goods just to survive. Most of them earn about U.S.$8.00 profit per day on a turnover of U.S.$26.00. This they use to buy food for their households and meet other needs. Family members and children of women involved in vending activities in Kinshasa recognize real changes since their mothers became involved in vending activities, not only economically but through a restored sense of vibrancy and purpose in the households.

In Kinshasa, life in many households had become impossible without the involvement of the wives, who have increasingly taken on men's roles, providing all the necessary financial and material resources. In the process, personal ties allow women to cope with the crisis in different ways. They help one another and the most vulnerable people to obtain assistance and to solve day-to-day problems. In many cases, people lend money to their neighbors, kin, and other relatives without charging interest. Their only objective is to see others becoming independent, instead of having to ask for money daily.

We met women selling fresh cassava roots and leaves on the pavement in Boulevard Lumumba in Masina and Kingasani. Many had worked on the street for ten years, changing their selling activities whenever the market became unstable and gradually finding new commodities according to demand and available opportunities. Many of these women stated that financial support for their household was the main reason and the primary motivation for them to work. Their labor was central to the life of their households, since many of their husbands' monthly incomes would barely cover the cost of a ten-kilogram basket of corn flour. Nothing now differentiates these women from men in terms of breadwinning and financial support of the household, as they always use their incomes to take care of children, pay their bills, and cover most household expenses.

Some women work an average of 112 hours per week. Most wake up at 5 a.m. and get to bed at 10 p.m. each day. Their situations are worse when they have small children. Many have no leisure time and once they are up in the morning, they do not rest until they are back in bed. As Momsen (1993: 1) argued, many women bear a double or triple burden of productive as well as domestic and reproductive work.

Furthermore, households in which relationships are transparent and more egalitarian between men and women are better off and face fewer difficulties than others. They use their resourcefulness to manage their households better and to allocate their income more effectively. They have become self-sufficient and are able to support their children. Thus women are now critical to the very survival of their households through their involvement in income-earning projects (see also Tripp 1997: 240).

Gender and Informal Financial Networks

The lack of saving opportunities for poor people and their inability to access the formal banking system have induced poor people in Kinshasa to revert to generations-old saving practices. Although during the precolonial period the practice did not involve money in its modern form, savings mechanisms were common in all Congolese communities. Nowadays, 38 percent practise the *likelemba*, 41 percent of them use the saving system called *carte*, and 2.84 percent of interviewed women work as money changers (Figure 9.2).

Rotating Credit (*Likelemba*)

In markets, bus terminals, ports, lorry terminals, and on streets, women have organized themselves within informal financial assistance organizations called *likelemba* (rotation) in Lingala. Each association operates as a small financial cooperative and comprises 5 to 15 members (sometimes up to 20). At the end of every week or fortnight, the group's cashier receives a deposit of an agreed amount of money from each member. The total is then given to one member at an agreed time and the exercise rotates to cover all members of the association

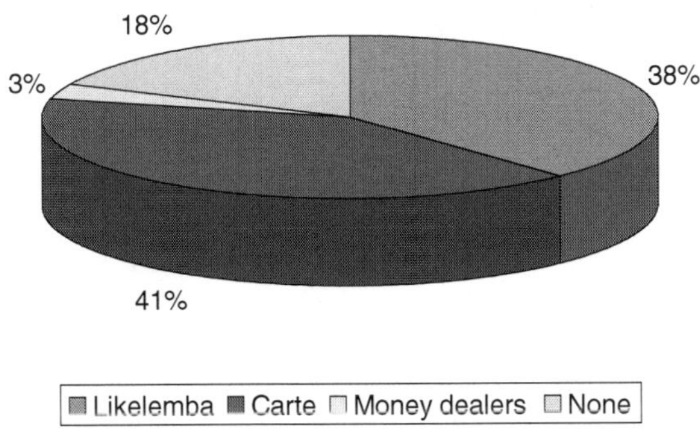

Figure 9.2 Involvement of women in informal financial networks.
Source: Field Research in Kinshasa, May 2001.

in turn. Some women belong to two or more *likelemba* and are able to earn up to U.S.$500.00 per rotation.

Many women recognized that the practice of *likelemba* allows them to purchase household appliances such as a stove, TV set, fridge, or other goods that they were unable to buy with their own income. Others used the money to expand their capital and start more profitable new businesses or to expand their existing activities. In such cases, the rotation system played the role of credit agencies. Similar findings on informal financial networks were reported in Tanzania, where these self-help strategies (called *upatu*) allowed women in poor areas of Dar-es-Salaam to solve many daily problems (Koda and Omari 1991: 117–131). Such rotating credit schemes occur widely in sub-Saharan Africa. *Likelemba* in Kinshasa is not only practised by poor women or men but also by middle-class people. Even people working in the formal sector are now deeply involved in the practice. That *likelemba* has been practised in the DRC for generations demonstrates that an indigenous institution may be more durable and effective—not least in situations of stress—than externally inspired and imposed organizations.

Shopkeeper Credit (*Carte*)

With the collapse of the formal banking system and its accessibility solely to the rich, poor people in Kinshasa have developed their own informal financial networks and systems to save their money. Forty-one percent of interviewed women in Kinshasa use a savings system called *carte* (the French word for "card"). The system works as follows: in a street or an area, some well-known and long-standing residents who run shops in which they sell different kind of goods and merchandise, help others to save money. Based on trust and honesty, neighbors and local acquaintances open savings accounts with the shopkeeper. For each customer, the shopkeeper uses a card on which is recorded all amounts credited to the account and other transactions made by the customer during each month. At the month's end, customers withdraw their cash balance as an interest-free lump sum, enabling them to purchase merchandise or to meet other financial demands.

It is mostly women who use these services, which play the same role as banks and building societies in Western(-ized) societies. By using the *carte* system, women avoid the risk of thieves, including children in their houses, their husbands' misuse of money, and other unplanned spending. These women have the responsibility of looking after the whole household and being sure that their needs are satisfied. They are at home with their children all the time and can help when a child falls ill, even at night, when their fathers often go out or are drinking in bars with mistresses. Therefore, the women have to be sure that they have something in their pockets to deal with unexpected problems. Similarly, Tripp (1997: 246) has observed that women are often perceived by both men and women as more capable of saving than men because it is primarily the women's responsibility to make sure that the needs of the household and children are met.

Money Changing

Money changing, another profitable informal business, emerged just after Independence but became legitimate after the end of the one-party state in 1990. At that time, the kleptocratic president, Mobutu Sese Seko, and his followers started to bribe politicians and ordinary people to remain in his party. Thus, hundreds of million U.S. dollars and billions of local currency were used as bribes countrywide. As most recipients did not want to keep this money in local currency, which was devaluing hourly, they changed it into foreign currencies, mainly U.S. dollars, Belgian, and French francs.

With the subsequent collapse of the formal banking system, companies, multinationals, NGOs and international organizations, ministries, even diplomats and embassies have resorted to buying foreign currency on the street. The most popular places in Kinshasa for such activities are the central market and Ngobila Beach (in Gombe), Lemba Terminus (in Lemba), Rond Point Ngaba (in Ngaba), IPN (in Ngaliema), Bandalungwa Tshibangu (in Bandalungwa), Masina Petro-Congo (in Masina), Yolo-Mundelengulu, Yolo-Kapela, Avenue Oshwe (in Kalamu), and Avenue Kanda-Kanda (in Kasa-Vubu) (see map 9.1). The biggest of all is "le Chateau," located in front of the American Embassy in Kinshasa and near the Belgian Embassy (in Gombe), where millions of dollars are traded daily. According to our informants, large amounts of counterfeit dollar banknotes belonging to Mobutu, his generals, and followers were traded there daily during the 1990s, with the knowledge of American diplomats.

Most foreign currency dealers are Congolese women. These hard currencies are sold by travelers, embassy staff, political leaders, high-ranking army officers, and other business people. Buyers come from all levels of society: students, local business people, travelers, diplomats, companies, and members of the public who need foreign currency. Profit is made in the same way as in other businesses and according to the law of supply and demand. The dealers include a profit margin in their buying and selling exchange rates; this is deducted from total cash-in-hand at the end of each day. Another source of profit is currency speculation, which depends on the level of inflation, as the Congolese currency fluctuates daily, and sometimes even hourly.

Women predominate in money-changing activities because of the trust involved (MacGaffey and Bazenguissa 2000: 107–112).[3] Unable to work alone, these women are often helped by young men to seek out customers and to lift heavy bags and cases of banknotes. Despite being illegal under Mobutu, he and his leadership clique actually encouraged and fuelled these activities, which continued under Laurent Kabila before eventually being legalized by Joseph Kabila in 2001. In contrast to other African countries, where money-changing activities often have an ethnic dimension, Congolese money dealers are ethically diverse and come from all provinces of the country. Money changing is a highly desirable informal activity in Kinshasa, being preferred by literate unemployed people to urban agriculture, street vending activities, or other trades. According to many money dealers, they do not need to spend substantial energy working, walking, and crying to attract customers. Practitioners also have the opportunity to acquaint high-ranking officials, government leaders, and other influential people. Moreover, their profits are higher than in other categories of informal business.

In the transaction, suppliers give their foreign or local currencies to street-based traders. The trader employs one or more *schokers* to increase the volume of money transacted.[4] Indeed, money dealing is the only informal activity where practitioners earn well and make high profits. This was borne out by visits to some money dealers' homes, which revealed that the dealers' living standards were superior to those of other households in the area. Trust is the main characteristic of money dealing. For instance, a cabinet minister can hand the equivalent of U.S.$300,000 to his money dealers without asking them to sign a single paper.

We have shown informal activities in Kinshasa to be fluid and dynamic, not employing only illiterate people and not concentrated solely on manual work (Iyenda 2002: 18–21). Personal ties and informal relationships are vital in all activities, especially in money dealing. Reciprocity is central to these relationships as everybody has an obligation to give and to help. However, although its practitioners consider money dealing to be a very desirable informal job, some Kinshasa residents have less esteem and respect for female dealers, considering many to have low morals and to be unfaithful or even prostitutes.

Conclusion and General Explanations

We have shown that the conditions of women in Kinshasa have changed in two ways over recent decades: through top–down intervention of the state by updating the employment law and the family code, and through bottom–up efforts by churches, local communities, development agencies, civil society in general, and women themselves.

Women have become the principal income providers in many Kinshasa households and thus have primary responsibility for the survival of their families. Personal ties allow women to cope with the crisis in different ways. Relationships among women within Kinshasa's informal sector involve mainly simple reciprocity between friends, relatives, colleagues, neighbors, and close members of the community.

To survive in a city where no state support exists, urban dwellers are expanding their circle of relationships since almost nobody in Kinshasa can now rely on salaries alone. Women use their own networks and ties, they trust each other and they have become involved in self-employment and the informal sector as their principal survival strategy. In most cases, women's working conditions in Kinshasa remain very hostile. Many still face police harassment, vandalism, lack of capital, inadequacies in raw material provision and merchandise, and lack of suitable sites from which to sell goods in hygienic conditions in markets and other public areas.

The grassroots-based mechanisms developed by women to tackle poverty show that they are able to plan and design effective and alternative survival strategies and to improve their own welfare and that of their households. As Hannan (1982: 69) pointed out, "altruism dominates families' lives; it drives out selfishness." In its current situation, women's empowerment and enhanced participation in decision-making over the lives of their households have increased, to the benefit of all household members. However, there is scope for further improvement.

In many cases, women also need access to additional resources and to sufficient purchasing power to buy household necessities. Notwithstanding the importance of the informal credit mechanisms examined here, many of our interviewees felt that greater access to credit and technical advice would enable them to improve the quality of their work and of their goods. Increased quality and sales would translate into improved incomes and in turn—as the research reported here has shown—to welfare benefits for their households. This raises a set of policy implications that are beyond the scope of this chapter.

NOTES

1. The research was principally household based and we examined overall livelihood activities, not only the informal sector. Our sample comprised 600 conversational interviews, 120 questionnaires, and 16 extended participant observation case studies. Interviews comprised approximately 90-minute conversations with each informant within households and 45-minute discussions outside households (in workplaces, streets, markets, and shops). These semi-structured interviews combined standardized and nonstandardized question formats and facilitated the collection of extensive information, verified by discussion and probing of problematic areas. In addition to interviews, we used questionnaires with standardized questions to obtain some kinds of information related to interviewees' livelihoods, their income, profit levels, accommodation, food and household goods, education, health, transport and social expenditures, and their survival strategies. Since the questionnaires were anonymous, many people responded with honesty and provided more details than expected. Finally, participant observation was undertaken within 16 households not covered by the questionnaires. Three days were spent in each selected household in order to obtain an insider's view of their daily lived realities, how they organized their lives, earned their livelihoods, and struggled against poverty and destitution. This enabled the triangulation of data collected by the other methods.
2. On the functioning of these markets, read G-M. Kamandji, *Le Phare*, September 27, 2001.

3. MacGaffey and Bezenguissa (2000) have argued in depth on these issues. Our research also revealed that most people in the Congo still believe that women are more honest than men and that it is more difficult for a woman than a man to disappear with large amounts of money.
4. A "schoker" is a young man or boy who cries out and calls out for customers on behalf of a money dealer. He also helps the money dealer to trade money and to organize the business. He is paid daily.

REFERENCES

Banque Centrale du Congo. 2001. *Rapport Annuel.* Kinshasa: Banque Centrale du Congo.

De St Moulin, L. 1976. "Contribution a l'histoire de Kinshasa (I)," *Zaïre Afrique*, Kinshasa.

De St Moulin, L. 1977. "Perspectives de la Croissance Urbaine au Zaïre," *Zaïre Afrique*, Kinshasa.

Economic Intelligence Unit (EIU). 2000. *The DRC: 1999–2000.* London: EIU.

Elson, D. (ed.).1991. *Male Bias in the Development Process.* Manchester University Press.

Evans, A. 1992. "Statistics," in L. Ostergaard (ed.). *Gender and Development. A Practical Guide.* London: Routledge, pp. 11–40.

Fetter, B. 1987. "Decoding and Interpreting African Census data: Vital Evidence from an Unsavoury Witness," *Cahier d'Etudes Africaines* 27 (105–106) (1–2), pp. 85–89.

Hannan, M. 1982. "Families, Markets, and Social Structures: An Essay on Becker's Treatise on the Family," *Journal of Economic Literature* (20): 65–72.

Institut National des Statistiques (INS), République du Zaïre. 1992. *Recensement Scientifique de la Population, juillet 1984, caractéristiques démographiques*, Vol. V. Kinshasa: INS.

Institut National des Statistiques (INS), République du Zaïre. 1993. *Projections démographiques. Zaïre et Régions 1984–2000*, Kinshasa: INS.

Iyenda, G. 2002. "Pauvreté Urbaine et Secteur Informel à Kinshasa," *Développement et Coopération* (September and October): 18–21.

Kamandji, G-M. 2001. *Le Phare*, September 27.

Koda, B. C. and C. K. Omari. 1991. "Crisis in the Tanzania Household Economy: Women's Strategies in Dar es Salaam," in M. Suliman (ed.). *Alternative Strategies for Africa*, London: The Institute for African Alternatives, pp. 117–131.

MacGaffey, J. and G-R. Bazenguissa. 2000. *Congo–Paris. Transnational Traders on the Margins of the Law.* Oxford: James Currey.

Molyneux, M. and S. Razavi (eds.). 2002. *Gender Justice, Development and Rights.* Oxford: Oxford University Press.

Momsen, J. H. 1993. *Women and Development in the Third World.* London and New York: Routledge.

Moser, C. O. N. 1993. *Gender, Planning and Development. Theory, Practice and Training.* London: Routledge.

Mwanza, W-M. 1997. "Le transport urbain a Kinshasa. Un noeud gordien," *Cahiers Africains*, No. 30, Bruxelles.

Nalini, V. et al. (ed.). 1997. *The Women, Gender and Development Reader.* London and New Jersey: Zed Books.

Nzuzi, L. 1992. "Gestion foncière et production de l'habitat urbain au Zaïre," *Bulletin Géographique de Kinshasa-Geokin*, Vol. III, No. 2, Kinshasa.

Ostergaard, L. (ed.). 1992. *Gender and Development. A Practical Guide.* London: Routledge.

Piermay, J-L. 1997. "Kinshasa: A Reprieved Mega-City?" in C. Rakodi (ed.). *The Urban Challenge in Africa: Growth and Management of Its Largest Cities*, Tokyo: United Nations University Press, pp. 223–251.

Potuchek, J. L. 1997. *Who Support the Family? Gender and Breadwinning in Dual Earner Marriages*. Stanford: Stanford University Press.

Rai, S. 2002. *Gender and the Political Economy of Development*. Cambridge/Oxford: Polity in association with Blackwell.

Standing, H. 1992. "Employment," in L. Ostergaard (ed.). *Gender and Development. A Practical Guide*. London: Routledge, pp. 57–74.

Tripp, A. M. 1997. "Reindustrialization and the Growth of Women's Economic Associations and Networks in Urban Tanzania," in V. Nalini, L. Duggan, L. Nisonoff, and N. Wiengersma (eds.). *The Women, Gender and Development Reader*. London and New Jersey: Zed Books, pp. 238–250.

United Nations Economic Commission for Africa. 2005. *The Millennium Development Goals in Africa: Progress and Challenges*. Addis Ababa: UNECA.

Vansina, J. 1973. *The Tio Kingdom of the Middle Congo 1880–1892*. London: Oxford University Press for the International African Institute.

World Bank. 1980. *Zaïre: Current Economic Situation and Constraints*. Washington, DC: World Bank.

III

Urban Planning, Administration, and Governance

While ostensibly a scientific-rational process that is separate from politics, urban planning is never far removed from the exercise of power. Efforts to create and maintain orderly urban landscapes are inextricably linked with the process of boundary-making. Regulatory systems, such as licensing, zoning, code enforcement, health and safety inspections, and so forth, effectively open opportunities for some at the expense of others. Various projects aimed at disciplining the unruly residents always take place within contradictory fields of force, as urban planners, municipal authorities, and city officials operate with different agendas. Depending upon different historical circumstances, sometimes negotiation and compromise dominate the approach to policing the city and at other times repression and violence rule the day. In African cities, the poor have responded to various disciplining efforts by adopting various strategies of enterprise, compromise, and resistance. These multiple practices, simultaneously social and spatial, have ensured that urban planners are never able to shape the urban landscape in accordance with their grand schemes.

With the shift toward entrepreneurial urbanism, new modes of urban governance have replaced conventional "managerial" approaches to administering the city. Historically speaking, cities in Africa have served as staging-areas for large-scale financial and business interests operating out of Europe or North America. At the same time, they have become repositories, or a refuge of last resort, for displaced peoples no longer capable of sustaining a livelihood in the rural areas. In the current historical phase of globalization where the prevailing trajectories of urban development stress capital intensity and technological innovation, cities in Africa are undergoing profound change.

The essays in part 3 focus on questions of urban governance, municipal administration, and city planning under circumstances where requisite resources—financial and otherwise—are either nonexistent or severely limited. In many cities in Africa, urban spaces are put to uses never intended, basic infrastructure has broken down, and vast expanses of the built environment have fallen into disrepair. Without waiting for social assistance from city administrations that lack the capacity to deliver anyway, the urban poor have frequently struck out on their own, improvising and stitching together the kinds of networks, connections, and linkages that they need in order to survive.

In his brief survey of South African urbanism, AbdouMaliq Simone argues that though urban planning initiatives in cities like Johannesburg have sought to heal the spatial wounds engineered under apartheid urban governance, these interventions have inadvertently opened up new lines of cleavage. Borrowing the notion of a "right to the city" from Henri Lefebvre, Simone contends that those marginalized urban residents who have been excluded from the benefits of modern urban living have actively pursued their own aspirations in ways that cut against the grain of urban planning initiatives.

To a large extent, cities in Africa are fragmented and disjointed places that have largely resisted modern urban planning and procedures of rational spatial organization. Yet they are also called upon to service a wide variety of sometimes overlapping and sometimes competing interests. Only rarely did they develop organically, more in response to local needs than to outside pressures. In cities that lack planning guidelines, the spatial patterns of urban growth are haphazard where the urban landscape has become a patchwork of disconnected parts. Without the constraints provided by building codes and city bylaws, the built environment has become a heterodox assemblage of disparate elements lacking coherence and overall design.

Following his whirlwind tour of Lagos, the renowned architect Rem Koolhaas expressed surprise at the capacity of the city to function despite its ostensible lack of planning or coherence. By way of counterpoint, Matthew Gandy takes issue with the somewhat celebratory tone of these remarks, suggesting instead that this self-organization of urban life takes place in the context of persistent hardship and enduring poverty. In his investigation of Lagos, Gandy subjects the conventional usage of the term "governance" to a rigorous analysis and critique. In resisting any reliance upon "exceptionalist" interpretations of cities in Africa, he seeks to link the experience of megacities like Lagos with patterns of urban growth and development elsewhere in the global arena.

In launching "Operation Murambatsvina" to cleanse cities in Zimbabwe of the urban poor, the political regime under the leadership of Robert Mugabe has resorted to physical force to gain the upper hand in the battle over the use of urban space. In her account, Deborah Potts provides a passionate, blow-by-blow analysis of the operation, attempting to understand it in comparison with the tactics of the Apartheid regime in South Africa and as a tactic for repression of Zimbabwe's main opposition party. Ultimately she places the operation within its longer Zimbabwean urban context of the maintenance of the image of urban order, as well, linking her up-to-the-minute analysis of Operation Murambatsvina (or Operation Tsunami, as many of its victims have taken to calling it) with her long-term analysis of urban housing issues in Harare.

Due to the persistence of stagnating economies and lackluster rates of real economic growth, municipal authorities, city officials, and urban planners have found it nearly impossible to respond to the rising demands of urban residents. Without commensurate increases in opportunities for work and income, the urbanization process has placed severe strains on the institutional structures of municipal governance, physical and social infrastructure, and the provision of basic services. The shortage of jobs in the formal economy, inadequate housing, outmoded infrastructure, and under-resourced social services have gone hand-in-hand with widespread poverty, environmental degradation, and the precariousness of everyday life.

Urban politics is played out not only in terms of competition over control of specific sites and institutional resources, but also in terms of extending connections, broadening social fields, and reconfiguring intersections with the aim of forging alliances, fostering collaborations, and "hedging one's bets." The politics of the city is a matter not only of the inequitable distribution of satisfactions and misery, but also struggles around such issues as gender, ethnicity, age, and religion. In looking at popular struggles over the provision of free basic water services for poor families in South African cities like Durban, Johannesburg, and Cape Town, Greg Ruiters argues that the implementation of neoliberal modes of urban governance is rarely a seamless, linear process. In charting the emergence of new modes of urban governance after *apartheid*, he contends that municipalities have combined the carrot and the stick, giving in to popular demands for water as a basic right while at the same time seeking to enforce strict market rules of cost-recovery and pay-as-you-go. In a broader vein, Ruiters suggests that the strategies of local government represent a much more nuanced and sophisticated response to disciplining, regulating, and governing the urban poor than the critiques of neoliberal policymaking typically acknowledge. He argues that the new urban services regime in urban South Africa is one component in a wider state initiative designed to gain control over "unruly" residents and to keep the urban power in their place.

10

South African Urbanism: Between the Modern and the Refugee Camp

AbdouMaliq Simone

The Urban Landscape: Fractured and Fracturing

South African urbanism during the past decade in most respects reflects some of the most innovative policy and institutional narratives and maneuvers applied to cities anywhere. From integrated development planning, cross-subsidization of urban services, the massive overhaul of local authorities to the selective deployment of infrastructure projects to facilitate social integration, interventions have substantially remade the urban landscape with limited capital budgets and enormous challenges embedded in highly fractured and discordant cities. Yet in significant ways, the Apartheid city past is as indicative of general urban futures as the repairs and innovations of the past decade.

Cities everywhere exhibit a capacity to have a smaller percentage of their productive capacities, whereas populations and physical territories generate the significant portion of their economic product—and thus their viability. Cities everywhere are increasingly skewed in terms of spatial development, resource investment, and infrastructural composition. Cities, as domains of publicity, as arenas of socialization for national belonging, and as facilitators of social cohesion among heterogeneities of all kinds are functions that have substantially been eroded during the same decade that South African cities have simultaneously tried to become more coherent as contained urban systems and more connected to regional and global economies.

The intensified divergence of these trajectories—on the one hand more compact and integrated urban systems and on the other hand the greater integrations of those urban systems in multiple networks of decision-making and economic transaction—pose critical dilemmas for South African urban policymakers. For despite local and national frameworks, practices, and interventions, the reorientation of the country's largest urban areas to various facets of region-wide management and service provision generates its own fracturing effects that compel the need to rethink what the right to the city actually is.

Cities everywhere become increasingly articulated and interwoven with cities elsewhere. At the same time, the internal coherence of discrete cities is substantially fractured, in part, by these very articulations and by many unanticipated threats, difficult to detect and track, which can ramify far beyond the administrative border and ecological domains of a given city.

Technological Change and Urban Interactions

Such a notion of the right to the city has to be rethought in terms of three levels of technological change. At the first level, there are technological changes for inducing the capacity of cities to both extend their reach and to consolidate spaces of economic capacity and extensiveness regardless of the histories, livelihoods, and aspirations of the majority or urban residents. At the second level, the fragmentation of cities, and the unbundling of public infrastructure, service delivery systems, and institutional life in general, generates a wide range of local initiatives aimed at low-cost provisioning of essential urban services through the deployment of appropriate technologies. The development of such initiatives almost exclusively takes place within very circumscribed territorial parameters that tend to reinforce notions of urban community in cities largely operating against the sustainability of community life. At the third level, the disarticulation of urban spaces and the increased inability of key state and municipal institutions to engender frameworks of governance applicable to cities as a whole generates a vast array of economies centered on repair, the illicit or unconventional use of built and institutional environments, and piracy driven by specific amalgamations of technology that enable these economies. Though remaining largely within the realms of local survivalist orientations, these economies can also attain significant transnational reach.

These levels of technological change generate specific modulations in the relationships between residents and the urban environment, between the city and cities elsewhere, and among the flows of goods, information, capacities, and powers. They institute their own specific rhythms, speeds, and time frames, reworking the value of urban financial investments, infrastructure, space, and human resources in terms of the various interactions that can be brought together between different markets, production systems, money trains, consumption styles, and media. In its simplest terms, the value of a given property, a given life, or institution and skill can radically change depending on how it is made known in relationship to other sites, structures, and lives in the city, and increasingly everywhere else. Changes can be made without precedence; everything that exists in a city can be potentially an object of speculation. At times it appears that the only options for urban residents are to quickly do whatever they can to normalize themselves to standard levels of middle-class consumption, or to become marginalized and disappear off the radar screen.

Urban environments are increasingly dependent on complex information and communication systems and infrastructure inputs tailored to enabling economic transactions conducted in real time. Yet, this dependency ends up maximizing the potentially countervailing and destructive effects of low technology, readily accessible to the use of most urban residents. In urban environments concentrating investments in privatized premium infrastructure, public grids and reticulation systems fall into increasing disrepair. As municipal institutions find it increasingly difficult to offer and enforce an overarching administration of the urban system, the different populations that make up the city are left to "go their own way." Many compensate for the lack of public infrastructure and production opportunities through economies of repair, privacy, subversion, and "heretical" uses of the urban environment. Prolifically discrepant uses of the urban environment facilitated by the variable intersections of high and low technologies related to communications, transport, repair, and power far exceed the ability of urban government to specify how the city should be used.

The Right to the City: The Right to Pursue Aspirations

South African urban policymakers have tried hard to fill in the gaps engineered by Apartheid: the gap between a modern urban existence for a few and the life of a refugee camp for the majority. As enormous resources were spent to enforce a fractured urban landscape, ten years is hardly sufficient time to redo this architecture. The question is: with limited resources, how does one proceed to remake South African cities in the future? What kinds of speeds are involved? What constitute strategic sites of intervention with maximum multiplier effects? To what extent can and should the infrastructures of connection—between the township, the peri-urban, the downtown, the economic enclave, the high- and low-density residential areas—be specified, and by whom?

Given the extent to which a highly fractured landscape remains and is reproduced in new spatial dimensions, what kinds of connections can take place between different facets of the urban environment and over what period of time? What kind of time is at work in the eastern central business district (CBD) of Johannesburg, where illegal housing in mothballed office buildings meets an emerging regional fashion district meets the fortified enclaving of the ABSA Bank district meets the refashioned muti market meets new social housing developments meets the largely informal appropriation of the former light manufacturing district for artisanal production? As the central business district combines the discrepant speeds of the hemorrhaging of business headquarters to the northern suburbs, the entrenchment of Anglo-American in a particular corner of the western CBD opening up to a reinforced cultural precinct, the continued occupation of commercial office space for residence—how are these divergent trajectories going to meet over time; again, what kind of time is involved?

Like much of Africa, the discernment between night and day, present and past is minimal for many South African urban youth. Without any prospect of employment, there is no platform to signal progression from youth to adulthood; little likelihood of viable social reproduction—of family, cultural value, memory. Their lives are analogous to those of refugee camps—an endless present unavailable to politics, unavailable to the elaboration of institutions and ways of life capable of marking a passage of time, of rendering what one does today in some larger framework of purpose and meaning.

The right to the city is not in the end reduced to the right to be maintained in the city—that is, to be housed and serviced. Rather, these are critical elements of the right to use the city as an arena through which one can realize specific and usually mutable aspirations without necessarily having to recompose the characteristics of those aspirations in terms of other ones at work in the city. Though accommodations are necessarily viewed as spatial ones, the rights to pursue aspirations are, perhaps more fundamentally, matters of time—that people have time to pursue particular ways of living and being that are not judged within specific imposed temporal frameworks as having a definitive value or efficacy.

Critical to this unfolding of different ways of using and being in the city as the means of realizing certain aspirations is the divergent composition of the city itself—its very own movements toward decline and ascendancy, its varied juxtapositions of planning and improvisation, of business and residence, of security and insecurity. Viewing the right to the city as the right to pursue multiple aspirations ensures that no structure of governance can ever really manage the activation of this right. In other words, it can never grant the resources or the platform on which different kinds of residents in the city can equally pursue their aspirations. Though urban government may guarantee as best as it is able that the pursuit of aspirations entailed in acting on the right to the city does not harm, injure, or marginalize specific residents, it can neither be the purveyor of a specific aspiration nor the patron of all aspirations.

Constructing Urban Connectivity in a Disjointed Environment

The pursuit itself again largely depends on what kinds of connections residents can put together between the diverse infrastructures, spaces, populations, institutions, and economic activities of the city. The more governments attempt to specify these connections, attempt to develop a fixed overarching map of just how integration is to take place and how spaces are to be used, the more it tends to contract the possibilities diverse residents have of finding a way to pursue this right. This pursuit stretches over varying time spans, with many changes along the way. When cities specifically ask residents to fix themselves to a long-term commitment to a particular way of living urban life—whether it be by encouraging home ownership with long-term bonds, to not use residential space for commercial activity—a wide range of claims are made on the future, thus depriving it of certain resourceful flexibilities.

Though urban policy, infrastructure, and economic development interventions are important tools to cross the gaps of disarticulated cities, it remains the presence of urban residents themselves and their varied uses of each other as instruments to realize particular aspirations and imaginaries that constitute the most significant form of urban connectivity. Individual urban selves mark both the gap and the connection in interwoven economies—material, symbolic, and spatial. The gap is between what buildings, people, spaces, objects, and gestures can be normatively or customarily used for and how they can be put to task to do more than what is specified. At the same time, selves act as connections among disparate uses and users. Here, urban persons constitute themselves as unavoidable insertions into operations of all kinds—transport, eating and drinking, supplying, or theft, employing a range of specific technologies, from cell phones, to religious media, divination rituals to electronic equipment under a nearly constant state of improvised repair.

Cities everywhere then are a patchwork of increasingly dense infrastructures—optic fiber cables, surveillance systems, bundled packages of diverse services and highways dedicated to private use—and vast expanses of decayed or underutilized built environments. The city in its very physicality has been largely disjoined and deprived of an overarching institutional logic or public discourse capable of tying its heterogeneous residents together in some conviction of common belonging or reference. As such, there is little to deter the proliferation of many different impressions and interpretations concerning what is taking place in the city and, as such, there are a wide range of discrepant imaginaries about the built environment, how it operates, what it looks like, and what takes place within it.

If we take the inner city of Johannesburg, residence often means living in buildings that frequently lack basic amenities and security, or where provisioning of both requires substantial financial and personal investments. In addition, residents have to cope with an incessant preying upon their own vulnerabilities. For the inner city is an environment of trickery and deception, where at the same time the need to forge solid relationships of mutual dependency exists. Because such dependency is often relied upon in order to make ends meet, residents are all the more vulnerable to deception. Fellow residents who otherwise might look out for each other can also give information to thieves about who may not be in their apartments at certain times. Sexual partners are especially held in suspicion as the rights each individual in the couple would normally grant also leave them vulnerable to being taken advantage of. The desperation for jobs has cultivated an enormous industry of fake employment agencies and shakedown schemes. Residents are conscious about displaying any weakness and continuously watch what they say about themselves, what they wear, the routes they travel, and the company they are seen with. Even in cursory relationships with neighbors or associates, a person cannot be construed as having significant relationships in the event that others to whom these associates may owe money or are perceived to have been harmed in some way decide to hold that person as somehow culpable. What will this look like over time? What kind of urban citizen is constructed? How will new forms of sociality be created? What time is required?

Insurgent Practices and the Prospect of Change

In some areas, such as the inner city of Johannesburg, the extent of demographic shifts is certainly unprecedented in contemporary urban history. Also unprecedented is the degree to which social boundaries are marked by spatial arrangements in high-density quarters and the ways in which the physical trappings of wealth and security can be penetrated by "roving bands" of "opportunists" taking whatever they can. The intense levels of contestation over who has the "right" to do what in South African cities produce a situation where things can happen very quickly. Urban dwellers do not, as a result, feel constrained by the sense that specific places and resources belong to only certain kinds of uses or identities. There are constant and often violent arguments in apartment blocks, on streets, in taxis, in schools, and in stores about who can do what where. Such argumentation can open up places to greater flexibility as to their use, but it also can break down the integrity of places and a sense of propriety, which in turn makes them vulnerable to incursions and distortions of all kinds.

Drawing on urban survival strategies used during Apartheid to avoid pass laws and other forms of state surveillance, populations proficient in sending the "wrong" signals can continue to do so in order to "win" spaces of autonomous action. Who is a "real" policeperson, security guard, domestic worker, gardener, deliverer, and who is not is increasingly hard to discern. In any event, in many cases it does not matter as levels of complicity between the real and the "pretender" intensify. At other times, things move slowly, since urban residents know that many people are paying attention to what they do. They then try to conform to some sense of what can pass as conventional in order not to stand out. So in South African cities, spaces can change very quickly and also not at all.

The intersections of low-level computing and telecommunications with the capacity of many urban residents, out of the loop of regularized formal employment, to develop a finely tuned sense about the flows in the city—people coming and going from residences and businesses, changing shifts, loading and unloading trucks, flows of cars from auto parks—give rise to unexpected ways of intervening in urban space. Whatever their legal nature, however fraudulent the intent, the remarkable proliferation of scams and schemes of all kinds across urban South Africa not only point to the desperation of people looking for employment and places to live, but also the capacity of residents to converge in all kinds of combinations and generate money on the basis of almost nothing. Though I am not encouraging the elaboration of such illegality per se, it does point to how generative other kinds of experimentations with minimal technological investment could be in converging different kinds of actors under a variety of circumstances. This is particularly the case as more and more people do not live as conventional families, do not work conventional jobs and see themselves as prepared to be many different kinds of things for many different kinds of people. It is similar to what Franz Fanon talked about in the *Wretched of the Earth*—the notion that the time lost in allowing people to find their own vernaculars and practices for realizing themselves as creators of life (and not just consumers or victims of it) is recuperated in the advent of real collective change.

For all the suffering it generated, for all the ways it ripped off the best years of entire generations and deprived people of having aspirations to pursue, the very fracturing that is the unavoidable legacy of many South African cities may actually be a blessing in disguise.

Note

This chapter was originally presented at the South African Cities Symposium at Wits Institute for Social and Economic Research (WISER), University of the Witwatersrand, Johannesburg, May 20, 2004.

11

Planning, Anti-Planning, and the Infrastructure Crisis Facing Metropolitan Lagos

Matthew Gandy

Introduction

Lagos is a difficult city to study or understand. Its spatial organization has a kinetic quality that allows it to escape conventional methods of analysing cities.

Uche Isichei[1]

If you want to wash, na water you go use
T'o ba fe se'be omi l'o ma'lo
If you want cook soup, na water you go use
T'o ri ba n'gbona o omi l'ero re
If your head dey hot, na water go cool am
T'omo ba n'dagba omi l'o ma'lo
If your child dey grow, na water he go use
T'omi ba p'omo e o omi na la ma'lo
If water kill your child, na water you go use
T'omi ba pomo re o omi na no
Ko s'ohun to'le se k'o ma lo'mi o
Nothing without water

Fela Anikulapo-Kuti[2]

When the Nigerian musician Fela Anikulapo-Kuti recorded his song "Water no get enemy" in 1975 he could not have anticipated that living conditions would continue to worsen in coming decades to the point at which Lagos would garner the dubious accolade by the 1990s of being widely regarded as one of the worst cities in the world.[3] The deteriorating state of the city since the post-independence euphoria of the early 1960s, to reach its current position as a leitmotif for urban poverty and injustice, has occurred in the midst of a global transformation in patterns of urbanization. Lagos is now one of a number of rapidly growing cities in the Global South, which appears to challenge many previously held assumptions about the relationship between economic prosperity and demographic change: unlike the experience of nineteenth-century Europe and North America, for example, we observe a form of urban "involution" marked by vast expansion in combination with economic decline (see Davis 2004; Gandy 2005a; Sala-i-Martin and Subramanian 2003; UN 2003a). The UN has recently predicted that by the year 2015, the population of Lagos—currently estimated at over 10 million—will reach 17 million, making it one of the largest cities in the world (UN 2003b). The sprawling city now extends far beyond its original lagoon setting to encompass a vast expanse of mostly low-rise developments including as many as 200 different slums ranging in size from clusters of shacks underneath highways to entire districts such as Ajegunle and Mushin (see Map 11.1). This urban behemoth has emerged in spite of all efforts to contain the growth of the city and has produced a loose federation of diverse localities whose interaction is perpetually hampered by immense "go slows" that periodically threaten to bring the city to a virtual standstill.

The recent history of Lagos has been marked by a stark deterioration in quality of life. Over the last 20 years, the city has lost much of its street lighting, its dilapidated road system has become extremely congested, there are no longer regular refuse collections, violent crime has become a determining feature of everyday life, and many symbols of civic culture such as libraries and cinemas have largely disappeared. The city's sewerage network is practically nonexistent and at least two-thirds of childhood disease is attributable to inadequate access to safe drinking water. In heavy rains, over half of the city's dwellings suffer from routine flooding and a third of households must contend with knee-deep water within their homes. Average incomes of under one dollar a day are now lower in real terms than in the 1960s and export earnings from manufactured goods have fallen dramatically since the de-industrialization and economic instability of the 1980s. A combination of external debt, currency collapse, and capital flight has contributed toward an investment crisis across virtually every sector of the Nigerian economy complicated by centrifugal tendencies that threaten to tear the country apart along lines of ethnic, religious, and tribal difference.

Cities such as Lagos have become pivotal to recent debates over the need to transform modes of urban governance as a prerequisite for social cohesion and economic development (see, for example, Abiodun 1997; Graham and Marvin 2001; Olukoju 2003; Rakodi 2002). Yet the word "governance" has been used very loosely in an African context to encompass everything from an externally driven concern with the institutional context for economic liberalization to a "grassroots globalization" agenda stemming from ethnographic explorations of civil society and community self-help organizations.[4] The narrowly communitarian, neoliberal or technocratic conceptions of urban governance that predominate in "developmentalist" literature fail to grasp the degree to which power is radically dispersed through a variety of different social institutions and networks. Much of the focus on "good governance" by NGOs and development agencies based in the global North ignores the reasons why rent-seeking, clientelist, and "neo-patrimonial" states have emerged across much of sub-Saharan Africa (see Lockwood 2005). Much academic discourse about Africa has taken on the normative role of "social engineering" rather than the need to

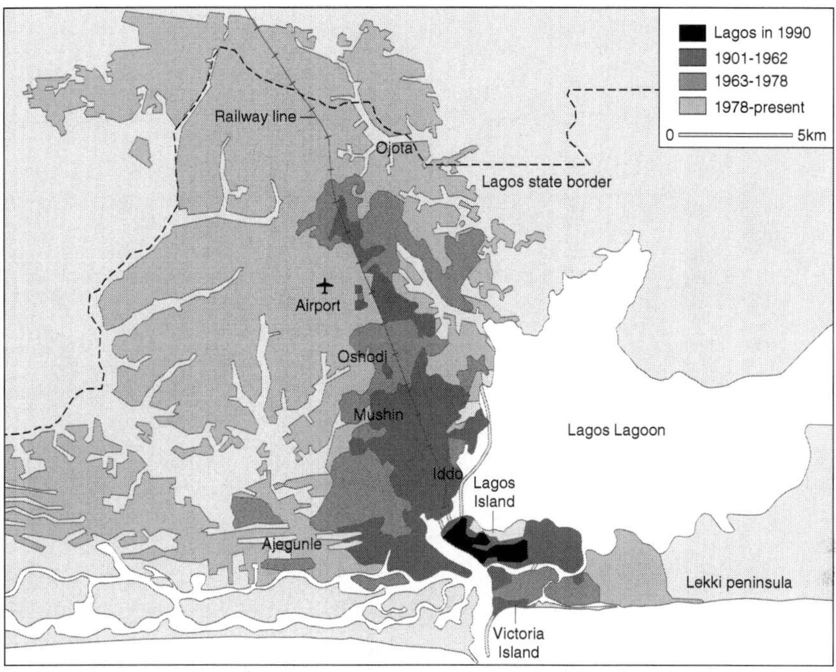

Map 11.1 The growth of modern Lagos.
Source: Gandy (2005b)

provide critical and politically aware insights into actually existing conditions (see Mbembe 2001). The idea of governance, for example, as an expanded role for civil society cannot be disentangled from issues of legitimacy for traditional power structures persisting within the modern African city. Similarly, the innate weakness of the state in Africa—further eroded under structural adjustment programs since the 1980s—has given added impetus to an emphasis on governance as a concept that can incorporate the efforts and capacities of civil society to provide basic services in the wake of various forms of "state failure" (see Hyden and Bratton 1992; McCarney 1996). In colonial Nigeria, for example, the introduction of so-called indirect rule sought to co-opt traditional power structures into the British imperial project deploying regional variations across the newly created state to reflect different types of indigenous political organization (see Mamdani 1996). Any consideration of the exercise of power in contemporary Nigerian society must contend with networks of subjugation that predate yet coexist within the modern yet at the same time intersect with sources of disequilibria and violence that emanate within a wider political and economic arena. In his analysis of postcolonial Nigerian developments, for example, Michael Watts (2003) has deployed Mitchell Dean's neo-Foucauldian term "authoritarian governmentality" to denote the particular conjunction of violence and rent-seeking activity undertaken by the Nigerian state in conjunction with corporate oil interests. In addition to studies of "petro-capitalist development" the concept of governmentality is also well suited to an analysis of the

Photo 11.1 Ebute-Metta, Lagos, 2003. Photograph: Matthew Gandy.

infrastructure crisis facing Nigeria since the construction, planning, and maintenance of the built environment require specific organizational and governmental capacities that fall outside the scope of civil society: the crucial coordinating role of the state is obscured in those accounts of urban politics that consistently emphasize communitarian or small-scale solutions to structural problems that are regional in their manifestation.

Although Lagos may appear to present an ostensibly unfamiliar set of urban developments—principally from the overwhelming scale of poverty and environmental degradation—the argument presented here resists any reliance on "exceptionalist" interpretations of urban change in sub-Saharan Africa and seeks to connect the experience of Lagos with wider developments operating both within the regional and global arena (see Robinson 2002). Recent developments in African research have enabled themes such as power, identity, and rationality to be explored in new ways; and an engagement with the complex realities of everyday life has facilitated a broader conception of social and cultural practice in the contemporary African city (see, for example, Abrahamsen 2003; Ahluwalia 2001; Enwezor et al. 2002; Simone 1998; 2004). The cities of the global South have begun to assume a far more prominent role within urban theory to the extent that these cities do not represent an anomalous category but rather a fundamental dimension to the global experience of urbanization. A focus on a city such as Lagos has the potential to illuminate not just a peculiarly African experience but also raise wider questions about the nature of modernity, urban governance, and the interactions between global capital flows and the material conditions of actually existing cities in the global South.

CENTRIFUGAL GOVERNMENTALITIES

The extraordinary Lagos master plan of 1980, produced before Nigeria's economic collapse and return to military rule, marks one of the most ambitious attempts by a civilian administration to grapple with the complexities of the city's problems. The UN-sponsored plan, initiated in the early 1970s, anticipated that the city would grow from a population of around 4.2 million in 1980 to reach around 13 million in the year 2000. In order to manage the city's vast expansion the plan called for the municipal government to "fully marshal its resources" in order to address "the multitude of physical, social and environmental needs of an area of this size" (UN 1980: 1). As if to underlie this sense of anxiety, the plan also anticipated an emerging stand off between municipal authorities and civil society:

> The Master Plan for Metropolitan Lagos, no matter how logical or technically sound, will fail without adequate levels of enforcement on the part of the government to: (1) protect existing investments and (2) to control future development patterns. Untold millions of nairas have already been lost in equipment, structures, road facilities, and other infrastructure because of undisciplined and/or illegal behavior on the part of the populace of Lagos (UN 1980: 2).

The Lagos plan identified various activities that might threaten its realization such as the spread of illegal structures, nonpayment of income and property taxes, and illegal connections to public utilities. The centralized approach marks the end of a distinctive phase in technocratic policymaking whereby the urban population are regarded as an undisciplined impediment to the rationalization of the city and planning discourse is preoccupied with how the city can be controlled or shaped according to a preconceived set of technical specifications provided by an array of experts (see also Mitchell 2002; Rabinow 1989). Following on from the UN Mar de L'Plata declaration of 1977, for example, which initiated the International Drinking Water Supply and Sanitation Decade, the plan envisaged that within the space of two decades all households would be connected to a water supply and sewerage system.[5] Under the so-called Second Republic, between 1979 and 1983, the Lagos municipal authorities attempted a significant expansion of water supply infrastructure but the program of works was curtailed by a combination of economic crisis, externally imposed structural adjustment policies, and the return of military rule (Olukoju 2003). The failure of the Lagos master plan signaled an effective abandonment of attempts to conceptualize the city's problems in any integrated or strategic way and the rapid urban decline and brutalization of political life experienced from the 1980s onward heralded a retreat of policy discourse into the realm of crisis management.

Since the state has proved unable to improve social and environmental conditions, an intensified divide is emerging between better connected commercial and high-income districts that can take advantage of new modes of service provision and vast areas of the city which may be permanently excluded from this new phase in urban development. The association of the state with force or the threat of violence, as has been the experience of Lagos through most of the colonial and postcolonial period, has denuded the prospects for building a workable relationship

Photo 11.2 Lagos Island, Lagos, 2003.

between state institutions and other social networks originating within civil society. Yet the state brutality that manifests in the urban arena through political repression or the forcible clearance of informal settlements is also an indicator of innate weakness: the seeming inability of the state to improve urban conditions for the poor majority presents not just a crisis of legitimacy for urban government in general but also fosters a fragmentary, refracted, and truncated political discourse within which any putative "public realm" can find only uncertain expression. The intense social polarization and spatial fragmentation since the mid-1980s has led to a scenario in which many households—both rich and poor—attempt to provide their own water supply, power generation, and security services. As night falls the drone of traffic is gradually displaced by the roar of thousands of generators that enable the city to function after dark. Many roads in both rich and poor neighborhoods become closed or subject to a plethora of ad hoc check points and small-scale security arrangements to protect people and property until the morning. In the absence of a subsidized housing sector most households must struggle to contend with expensive private letting arrangements often involving an upfront payment of two years rent and various other fees whereas the richest social strata seek to buy properties outright with vast quantities of cash. A self-service city has emerged in which little is expected from municipal government and much social and economic life is founded on the spontaneous outcome of local negotiations. Deficiencies in water and sanitation provision continue to provide some of the most striking manifestations of the city's worsening infrastructure crisis. We now find that less than five percent of households in Lagos have piped water connections (a fall from around ten percent in the 1960s) and that less than one percent are linked to a closed sewer system (principally hotels and high-income compounds). Even those with piped connections must contend with interruptions due to power supply failures affecting the city's water works. The rest of the city depends on wells, boreholes, water tankers, various illegal connections, street vendors, and in desperation, the "scooping" of water from open drains by the side of the road (Ajanaku and Alao 2002; Expunobi 2001; Sulaimon 2000). Inhabitants of slum settlements often face a stark choice between either polluted wells or expensive tanker water distributed by various intermediaries at high and fluctuating prices making the management of household budgets even more precarious. When municipal authorities do attempt to extend water supply to poorer neighborhoods they are often met with violence and intimidation from water tanker lobbies, "area boys," and other groups who benefit from the unequal distribution of water and the "micro-circuits" of exploitation that characterize slum life: the city's water corporation must consistently confront the so-called "water lords" who intentionally vandalize the network in order to continue charging exorbitant rates to the poor.[6]

People's daily survival is based on careful distinctions between different kinds of water suitable for drinking, cooking, and washing, with much time and expense devoted to securing household water needs. Regulatory authorities also struggle to cope with the proliferation of "pure water" manufacturers producing small plastic sachets of drinking water sold throughout the city, which have been associated with the spread of water-borne disease (Aina 1994; Osumah 2001). The sellers of these "pure water" sachets—thousands of mostly young Lagosians—weave their way between lines of slowly moving or stationery traffic as the need for potable water has become part of the city's burgeoning informal economy.

The politics of infrastructure provision in the post-Abacha era is currently undergoing a subtle yet profound transition in Lagos marked by an extended influence for NGOs and a plethora of interest groups that could not function under military rule. Organizations such as the housing activist network Shelter Rights Initiative, the critical architectural forum Central Intelligence Agency, and the urban environmental group Metamorphosis Nigeria have made demands for an improvement in urban conditions and have become a significant element in new forms of civic mobilization facilitated by the rapid spread of wireless communications, new press freedoms, and the wider dissemination of information. And patriarchal structures, underpinned by political clientelism and military rule, are now being increasingly challenged by a new generation of women activists and public servants committed to improving social and environmental conditions within the city.[7] Yet as the Lagos-based planning consultant Ako Amadi relates, the pervasive problems of corruption, however we choose to define this term, in combination with widespread public indifference have produced a scenario that is peculiarly antithetical to more socially responsive forms of urban policymaking.[8] Despite these formidable barriers, however, some limited changes are discernable in the electoral arena: in the regional elections of 2003, for example, the governor for Lagos State, Bola Ahmed Tinubu, a U.S.-trained accountant, was reelected on a political program that specifically sought to address the city's crisis in the provision of basic services (see Vidal 2005a). The issue of water, for instance, featured prominently within Tinubu's reelection campaign as part of a more technocratic approach to Nigerian politics reflected in the appointment of public administrators with extensive international or private sector experience. In the space of four years, water billing and revenue collection efficiencies in the city have leapt from less than 4 percent in 1999 to reach nearly 30 percent in 2003 leading the recently appointed chief executive of the city's water corporation to quip that "Tinubu was the only governor in the country who could use pipe-borne water supply as a campaign issue" and his campaign slogan "the primary objective of this administration is to provide potable water for all" was prominently displayed on billboards throughout the city.[9] The shifting complexion of urban politics in Lagos remains fragile, however, because Tinubu represents a different political party to that of the federal government based in Abuja, and in the absence of significant borrowing or tax raising powers the city remains dependent on the federal government for its derisory annual budget of less than 400 million dollars.

Yet the current emphasis on more technocratic forms of urban politics threatens to widen disparities in service provision between different parts of the city: rather than a renewed dynamic between the state and civil society, the underlying impetus is toward a business led model for urban regeneration. In 2003, for example, the city transformed the administrative structure of water provision to create 28 water zones and 13 sewerage districts geared toward "strategies specific for the demographics in those areas."[10] Yet the creation of these "governable entities" based on the demographic characteristics of different areas raises important questions: in prosperous parts of the city, for example, water charges will be made directly to individual households whereas in slum areas "community-based markets" will be established utilizing the traditional authority of chiefs as a revenue raising strategy (see Page 2004). This emerging dichotomy in modernization strategies for water provision raises the specter of new forms of "authoritarian governmentality" that combine neoliberal concerns with "full cost recovery" with dependence on nondemocratic sources of power in civil society.

International agencies such as the World Bank have emphasized the privatization of public services as a panacea for the city's infrastructure crisis but the broader implications of legal and institutional reform that might underpin tentative moves toward improved and more accountable modes of public administration have been scarcely addressed.[11] These tensions were exposed in 2003 with the break down of negotiations between the Lagos State Water Corporation and the International Finance Corporation when it became clear that the proposed privatization proposals prepared by external consultants were unworkable and bore little relation to the "social and economic realities on the ground."[12] This represents a significant change from the late 1990s when a number of Lagos newspapers openly embraced the prospect of privatization as an alternative to the municipal control of basic services.[13] We can discern a shift in policy discourse underway in Lagos, which is marked by less reliance on external expertise and a greater commitment to developing local solutions that learn from best practice elsewhere: the impact of failed large-scale divestment programs in cities such as Buenos Aires, Manila, and most recently in Dar-es-Salaam has had a profound impact on policy discourse in the city (Vidal 2005b). The newly emerging African technocrats running public services in Lagos and elsewhere are much better informed about international policy developments than their predecessors and are far more skeptical of the advice of the World Bank and other international agencies.[14] The economic reality is that the urban poor cannot afford to pay high enough charges to make the necessary extensions and improvements in urban water and sanitation systems viable let alone profitable: an argument that now appears to have been widely accepted by the water multinationals themselves since the scale of the need far outreaches the financial and risk-taking capacities of the private sector.

The prohibitive capital costs of improvements in water and sanitation infrastructure help to explain the growing "concrete divide" between the rapid spread of new telecommunications technologies throughout the city in the context of widening inequalities in social and environmental conditions. Nigeria has the fastest growth in mobile-phone use in sub-Saharan Africa with the number of subscriptions having risen from a mere 30,000 in 2000 to over 9 million by 2005—a development that may yet have profound consequences for new forms of social and economic interaction in hitherto isolated or marginalized communities. These spreading digital networks also illustrate new patterns of capital flow within Africa—the South African company MTN being a major player in this process (Vasager 2005). Early twenty-first-century Lagos is undergoing a new phase of development in which poorer parts of the city are subject to a dual process of exclusion and integration into both established and emerging urban technological networks.

A fundamental paradox facing Lagos is that its vast demographic expansion over the last 20 years has taken place in a context of far-reaching economic decline. Whereas city administrations in the past tended to deny that slums had any legitimate presence within the city—exemplified by the clearance of the vast Maroko settlement in 1990—there is now an emerging recognition that the morphology of Lagos is shaped to a significant degree by informal and unplanned settlements (see Agbola 1997b). The upgrading and improvement of slum areas, including institutional innovations over security of tenure, is a precondition for any development strategy that does not exacerbate existing inequalities (see Ahonsi 2002; Aina 1989; Aina et al. 1994; Olanrewaju 2001). The state has played an active role in attempting to control the land market in the face of extensive confusion over communal and private ownership claims and successive city administrations have engaged in "rent-seeking strategies," which are ubiquitous in many African metropolitan areas (Simone 2005: 21). The city's population is currently growing at some 4 percent per annum but in some districts such as the Lekki peninsula annual growth rates have reached nearly 17 percent, driven in part by displaced communities from civil strife elsewhere in the region. The role of conflicts in Liberia, Sierra Leone, and elsewhere, as contributory factors behind the city's growth, is largely overlooked in most recent debates on the city. These developments underline the degree to which the city has always served, both now and in the past, as a kind of "city-state" that can provide safe haven. Eschatological accounts of the city's problems fail to perceive the degree to which urban conditions within the Lagos metropolitan region may afford greater security and opportunity than innumerable other spaces occluded from analysis or discussion.

VIOLENCE, INSECURITY, AND THE FRAGILITY OF THE PUBLIC REALM

The transition of Nigeria to an oil exporting economy served to exacerbate the political and economic weaknesses of the Nigerian state and instituted widening disparities in living standards. In the absence of either a viable public realm or a workable set of institutional mechanisms for urban reconstruction the structural deficiencies within the Lagos urban system significantly worsened. An emerging "oil culture" has worked powerfully against any civic ethos in public life by fostering widespread opportunism on the part of social and political elites and the illusion of unlimited wealth has served to deflect attention from the efficiency or effectiveness of public services.[15] The kind of secular and cosmopolitan ideals promoted at Nigerian independence have become increasingly remote from the lived realities of the city as a fragmentary, polarized, and unstable urban space within which the legitimacy of municipal reform must contend with alternative modes of utopian transcendence offered by new and volatile forms of religiosity and ethnic identification. Given the young demographic profile of Lagos and the high proportion of migrants from elsewhere in West Africa most people have never experienced functional public services so that any political mobilization for change cannot simply be predicated on the memory of Lagos before its rapid deterioration during the 1980s and 1990s. In these circumstances the construction of a viable public realm is doubly difficult because of the fiscal and administrative weaknesses of municipal government in combination with the lack of political salience for any appeal to better urban conditions experienced in the past.

A critical exploration of the infrastructure crisis facing a city such as Lagos cannot be disentangled from an engagement with the complexities and significance of the "public realm" as an organizational, political, and material dimension to the development of the built environment. The emergence of highly fragmentary and clientelistic modes of political discourse in the postcolonial era has had a profound impact on the scope and limitations of public-policy making in the African city. Much recent planning literature has tended to combine a Habermasian ideal of communicative rationality with various forms of philosophical pragmatism as if some kind of consensus could emerge on the basis of mutual understanding alone. In a city such as Lagos, however, where fervent religiosity intersects with politically mobilized forms of ethnic chauvinism it is extremely difficult to establish a viable public sphere—even the post-Habermasian public sphere described by Chantal Mouffe and others where fundamental disagreements are accepted rather than occluded in political discourse (see Mouffe 2000; 2002). Mouffe's "agonistic" public sphere presupposes the existence of a framework for political contestation that does not exist in a context such as Lagos where an ideological vacuum has produced a scenario in which counterposing arguments have yet to find shape, form, or rhetorical clarity. A mix of generalized hopelessness and disenfranchisement under years of military rule has led to a scenario in which political demands and expectations are much lower than in other volatile urban contexts such as Latin America where alternative urban visions have been more widely articulated. The issue at stake is whether a workable concept of the public realm can be established in a context where social and economic relationships are in a constant state of flux and uncertainty (see Obi 2001; Simone 2005). The last 20 years has seen a vast expansion in the informal social and economic networks that serve to sustain everyday life in the city—largely in response to protracted economic crisis—but by far the most dynamic development in civil society has been the vast expansion in religious activity principally represented in Lagos by the spread of charismatic and Pentecostal strands of Christianity (see Adichie 2005; Falola 1998; Marshall-Fratani 1998). The emergence of a "post-secular urbanism," in which a combination of fatalism, religiosity, and profound insecurity infuses everyday life, cannot be adequately captured by an appeal to "multiple rationalities" since a recourse to relativist discourse risks replicating those distinctions between modernity and "nonmodernity" that have pervaded the governmental interventions of both the colonial and postcolonial period.

The tentative moves toward democracy and freedom of expression since the return to civilian rule in 1999 have still not begun to facilitate the emergence of urban "citizens" as opposed to mere "inhabitants" with little stake in the city's future. As a consequence Lagos faces real difficulties in articulating itself as a city in a way that transcends the multiplicity of sectional interests that share urban space. The city's rapid growth and successive waves of migration necessitate a more fluid and less territorialized conception of citizenship (see Holston and Appadurai 1999); yet the experience of citizenship remains essentially passive and unconnected with common political programs or agendas that might directly challenge the state or reshape the politics of entitlement to basic needs such as health care or sanitation. A radical extension of citizenship rights—or in Lefebvrian terms an explicit recognition of "the right to the city"—involves looking beyond the technical discourses of urban management or the humanitarian conception of the city as a place of refuge. It is better understood as a "right to urban life" (Lefebvre 1996: 158) that combines the practical needs of everyday life with a substantive rather than abstract conception of modern citizenship. The dilemma facing cities such as Lagos, however, is that the possibilities for building a functional public realm have been consistently undermined through the combined impacts of economic insecurity and clientelist political regimes within which inequalities have become magnified and deeply entrenched. The interconnections between urban citizenship and any national state-building project have similarly been placed under severe strain since the 1980s as different manifestations of "state failure" have underpinned the deterioration of urban conditions and a growing sense of powerlessness. The transformation of Lagos into a vast metropolitan region has occurred within the context of centrifugal political and economic tendencies that have produced an urban topography of fear and anxiety. The impact of what Pierre Bourdieu (1998: 98) terms "structural violence" emanating from the collapse of the city's economy and the external imposition of sweeping cutbacks in government expenditure has contributed toward a break down in social life. In February 2002, for example, vicious interethnic riots between Yoruba and Hausa gangs in the Mushin district of the city left at least a hundred people dead and many hundreds more injured.

The increasing prevalence of violent crime and disorder since the 1980s has led to the withdrawal of many Lagosians into a private realm that has further denuded the possibilities for rebuilding civil society (see Agbola 1997a). In less dangerous times, notes Tunde Alao, "people flocked to the Rainbow Cinema in Mushin or the Debacco Cinema in Idi-Oro" without fear of harassment from either the police or "hoodlums" (Alao 2002). The lack of trust that pervades every aspect of social and political life also undermines the potential for "fixing" capital in space through the use of bonds or other institutional mechanisms that might facilitate the reconstruction of the city. In many ways the city of Lagos exemplifies a space of "actually existing neo-liberalism" where global economic and political developments underway since the 1970s have resulted in fundamental yet often poorly explored changes in the urban realm (see Brenner and Theodore 2002). Such lacunae in our current knowledge are especially apparent in the cities of the global South where the interactions between different scales of political and economic change are generating profound changes in the urban landscape that extend from the micro-scale of individual household survival strategies to the regional impact of global capital flows and the geopolitical dynamics of trade in primary resources.

Conclusions

Central to any attempt to comprehend the current challenges facing a city such as Lagos is the ambiguous nature of urban planning as an organizational principle behind the modern city. In a European or North American context, the emergence of urban planning, new modes of municipal administration, and the development of integrated technological networks for water, energy, and other services became part of a nexus of institutional reforms associated with the transformation of the industrial metropolis. These developments held at their core a tension between the need to secure a degree of political legitimacy in the service of an ostensible public interest and at the same time a need to coordinate and rationalize the morphology of space in order to facilitate economic activity. The very idea of "planning" denotes the possibility of influencing or directing different sets of developments; however, the periodic aspirations of successive colonial and postcolonial administrations in Lagos to improve the morphology and structure of urban space have had minimal impact: we encounter a metropolitan region that reflects the steady accretion of human decision-making outside of or in contradiction with stated goals and objectives. The modernist ideal in Lagos was in any case little more than a chimera that characterized sketches, plans, and isolated developments but never constituted the majority experience of the city even before the collapse of the Nigerian economy in the 1980s. From a classic planning or architectural vantage point much of the city's topography can be considered "blind" in the sense that most urban vistas do not represent any design conception beyond the ad hoc vernacular of local construction methods or the self-build of individual dwellings or shelters. A largely spontaneous landscape has evolved in which an uncoordinated and incremental assemblage of structures has gradually spread across all available space.

Lagos faces a paradoxical situation within which any tentative steps toward improvement may engender new waves of migration from more precarious locations elsewhere. Yet this is not a city undergoing an economic transformation comparable with Mumbai, Shanghai, or other dramatic examples of a globalized urbanism. Lagos is a city on an uncertain trajectory that differs from recognized patterns of capitalist urbanization because the city is growing rapidly in a context of economic stagnation to produce what one might term a "post-productive" metropolis on account of its degree of dislocation from the global economy. This dilemma is illustrated by the evolving relationship between capital flows and the built space of the city: under the classic model of Western urbanization, flows of capital were fixed in space through a combination of financial and institutional mechanisms ranging from municipal bonds to legislative interventions in the urban land market. In Lagos, by contrast, the colonial state apparatus and its postcolonial successors never succeeded in building a fully functional metropolis through investment in the built environment or the construction of integrated technological networks. Vast quantities of capital that might have been invested in health care, housing, or physical infrastructure were either consumed by political and military elites or transferred to overseas bank accounts with the connivance of Western financial institutions. Lagos, like many other African cities, is characterized by a complex lattice of dilapidated infrastructure projects derived from the post-independence modernization drive of the 1960s and 1970s without which the contemporary city could not function, but in a context whereby the teleological dynamics of the planned metropolis are now systematically marginalized or even thrown into reverse.

The continued poverty and international indebtedness of Nigeria also poses immense obstacles for the containment of HIV, malaria, and other public health threats that may yet engender a further spiral of social and economic decline. The extreme impoverishment and ethnic polarization within Lagos present a continuing threat to rebuilding the social and physical fabric of the city. Though informal networks and settlements have made an enormous contribution to alleviating the most pressing social and economic needs of the poor, these grassroots responses cannot in themselves coordinate the structural dimensions to urban development for which the state must continue to play a pivotal role through its potential to articulate a public interest above either sectional interests or the impetus toward a purely market-driven approach to urban development. The severe and increased flooding experienced throughout the metropolitan area is one clear outcome of the absence of any strategic vision to manage the urban environment in the public interest as uncontrolled developments encroach across all available land and comprehensive drainage schemes under discussion for decades remain at the most rudimentary planning stage. "Infrastructure is government's responsibility," notes the Lagos based architect Koku Konu, "if not to put it in place, then to plan."[16] Critical to any improvement in urban conditions is the need for a panoply of institutional reforms ranging across specific areas of law, tax, and regulatory intervention, which encompass new codes of professional conduct, transparency, and accountability. With the increasing influence of a new generation of technocratic managers, a different kind of governmental paradigm may be emerging in the city but the long-term implications of this shift remain unclear. There is a danger, for example, of perpetuating a dual discourse of governmentality between wealthy enclaves that emulate the commercial zones of other global cities and the mass of the urban poor trapped under the arbitrary largesse of powerful local networks or held in abeyance by chiefs, elders, and other unelected dignitaries.

Many urban spaces and practices in Lagos appear to confound existing bodies of urban thought yet this does not preclude the possibility for rethinking or reworking what we already know about African urbanism or cities more generally. Appeals to various forms of "African exceptionalism" serve to contain the city within a category of ontological difference whilst obscuring the relationship between urban design and any meaningful forms of social or political deliberation. If we perceive Lagos to be a model for the future on account of the city's capacity to function in spite of its ostensible lack of coordination or planning, we risk condemning much of the city's population to continuing hardship.[17] If, on the other hand, we recognize that the city is beginning to articulate its own vision of African urbanization, however tentatively, it might be possible to initiate a genuine dialogue that would extend to the experience of other fast growing cities in the global South and thereby bring the African city to the center of policy deliberation and debate. The city's infrastructure crisis, is clearly a multifaceted phenomenon that links with political and economic factors operating in a global as well as a regional arena. Similarly, the impact of a denuded or fragmentary civil society on modes of political discourse is not a peculiarly African experience. The potential role of infrastructural networks in forging social collectivities through the "binding of space" holds implications for many cities facing similar problems of poverty, social fragmentation, and governmental failure. It is only through the identification of commonalities that transcend emerging patterns of social, ethnic, and religious polarization that Lagos can begin the complex task of reconstruction and the development of new and more legitimate modes of public administration.

NOTES

This is an edited and revised version of an essay originally published in *Urban Studies*. The research was supported by the UK Economic and Social Research Council and facilitated by a range of organizations including the National Archives (Ibaden), Shelter Rights Initiative (Lagos), and the Lagos State Water Corporation.

1. Isichei (2002: 14).
2. Fela Anikulapo-Kuti, "Water no Get Enemy" (1975). Lyrics reproduced courtesy of EMI publishing.
3. In 1991, for example, Lagos was named by the UN as the dirtiest city in the world. For a Lagosian perspective on the city's recent travails see, for example, Alao (2002), Isichei (2002), and Onibokun and Faniran (1995). For a detailed overview of the city's historical development see, for example, Baker (1974), Olukoju (2003), and Peil (1991).
4. Compare, for example, the Word Bank's 1992 publication *Governance and Development* with the more recent writings on "grassroots globalization" by Appadurai (2002). For recent critiques of the limitations to "governance" discourse, see, for example, Beall et al. (2002) and Cleaver (2001).
5. "It has been assumed that all households will be connected to the water supply system by the year 2000 . . . A separate water-borne sewerage system, including adequate sewage treatment facilities, for human and industrial waste should be provided for all properties connected to the water supply system" (UN 1980: 385–386). Further

details on planning history in Lagos derived from Paul Okunlola, environmental correspondent for *The Guardian* (Lagos); interview with the author (April 28, 2003).

6. Interviews with residents on the Ikota Estate, Lekki Peninsula (May 2003). Olumuyima Coker, chief executive officer, Lagos State Water Corporation; interview with the author (May 6, 2003).
7. Bayo Anatola, Shelter Rights Initiative; interview with the author (February 19, 2003); Koku Konu, architect and director of dkr associates; interview with the author (February 21, 2003). See also Uduku (1994); Tostensen et al. (2001), and Järvelä and Rinne-Koistinen (2005).
8. Ako Amadi, executive director, Community Conservation and Development Initiatives; interview with the author (February 17, 2003); and Victor Olusegun Emdin, director of Town Planning Services (Development Matters), Lagos State; interview with the author (May 2, 2003).
9. Olumuyima Coker, chief executive officer, Lagos State Water Corporation; interview with the author (May 6, 2003).
10. Ibid.
11. A consultative forum on policymaking in Lagos hosted by the World Bank at the Sheraton Hotel in Lagos on February 25, 2003, for example, exposed a deep divide between the intricacies and complexities of the city's predicament and their prescriptive agenda for market-based urban governance.
12. Olumuyima Coker, chief executive officer, Lagos State Water Corporation; interview with the author (May 6, 2003).
13. See, for example, the 1998 editorial "Privatising Water Supply" in the *Midweek Concord* (July 1).
14. For further details on the shifting contours of the water privatization debate see, for example, Bakker (2003), Budds and McGranahan (2003), Hall (2004), and K'Akumu (2004).
15. Paul Okunlola, *Guardian* urban and environmental correspondent for Lagos; interview with the author (May 1, 2003).
16. Koku Konu, architect and director of dkr associates; interview with the author (February 21, 2003).
17. Koolhaas (2001; 2002), for example, has emphasized the novel morphological and organizational aspects of the city. For a critique of this approach see Gandy (2005b).

BIBLIOGRAPHY

Abiodun, J. O. 1997. "The Challenges of Growth and Development in Metropolitan Lagos," in C. Rakodi (ed.). *The Urban Challenge in Africa: Growth and Management of Its Large Cities.* Tokyo, New York, and Paris: United Nations University Press, pp. 192–222.

Abrahamsen, R. 2003. "African Studies and the Postcolonial Challenge," *African Affairs* 102: 189–210.

Adichie, C. N. 2005. "Blinded by God's Business," *The Guardian* (London), February 19.

Agbola, T. 1997a. *The Architecture of Fear: Urban Design and the Construction Response to Urban Violence in Lagos.* Ibadan: Institut Français de Recherche en Afrique.

Agbola, T. 1997b. "Forced Eviction and Forced Relocation in Nigeria: The Experience of those Evicted from Maroko in 1990," *Environment and Urbanization* 9: 271–288.

Ahluwalia, P. 2001. *Politics and Post-Colonial Theory: African Inflections.* London: Routledge.

Ahonsi, B. 2002. "Popular Shaping of Metropolitan Forms and Processes in Nigeria: Glimpses and Interpretations from an Informed Lagosian," in O. Enwezor et al. (eds.). *Under Siege: Four African Cities. Freetown, Johannesburg, Kinshasa, Lagos. Dokumenta 11, Platform 4.* Ostfildern-Ruit: Hatje Cantz, pp. 129–151.

Aina, D. 1994. "The Water Merchants: Killers on the Loose," *Daily Times* (Lagos), February 5.

Aina, T. A. 1989. "Popular Settlements in Metropolitan Lagos, Nigeria: A Socio-Economic and Structural Survey of the Habitat of the Urban Poor," *Third World Planning Review* 11 (4) (November): 393–415.

Aina, T. A., F. E. Etta, and C. I. Obi. 1994. "The Search for Sustainable Urban Development in Metropolitan Lagos, Nigeria: Prospects and Problems," *Third World Planning Review* 16 (2) (May): 201–219.

Ajanaku, I. and T. Alao. 2002. "Population Boom Puts Lagos in Distress: As Inadequate Infrastructure Come under Severe Strain," *The Guardian* (Lagos), March 13.

Alao, T. 2002. "Many Travails of Lagosians: Accommodation, Security and Transportation Issues Make Life a Burden," *The Guardian* (Lagos), March 8.

Alao, T., R. Akpabio, and A. Olise. 2002 "Touts, Thugs . . . 'Kings' of Lagos Streets," *The Guardian* (Lagos), 23 January.

Appadurai, A. 2002. "Deep Democracy: Urban Governmentality and the Horizon of Politics," *Public Culture* 14: 21–47.

Baker, P. H. 1974. *Urbanization and Political Change: The Politics of Lagos 1917–1967.* Berkeley, CA: University of California Press.

Bakker, K. 2003. "Archipelagos and Networks: Urbanisation and Water Privatisation in the South," *Geographical Journal* 169 (4): 328–341.

Beall, J., O. Crankshaw, and S. Parnell. 2002. *United a Divided City: Governance and Social Exclusion in Johannesburg.* London: Earthscan.

Bourdieu, P. 1998. "Neo-Liberalism, the Utopia (Becoming a Reality) of Unlimited Exploitation," in *Acts or Resistance: Against the New Myths of Our Time.* Trans. R. Nice. Cambridge: Polity, pp. 94–105.

Brenner, N. and N. Theodore. 2002. "Cities and the Geographies of 'Actually Existing Neoliberalism,' " *Antipode* 34: 349–379.

Budds, J. and G. McGranahan. 2003. "Are the Debates on Water Privatization Missing the Point? Experiences from Africa, Asia and Latin America," *Environment & Urbanization* 15 (2): 87–113.

Cleaver, F. 2001. "Institutions, Agency and the Limitations of Participatory Approaches to Development," in B. Cooke and U. Kothari (eds.). *Participation: The New Tyranny.* London: Zed Books, pp. 36–55.

Davis, M. 2004. "Planet of Slums: Urban Involution and the Informal Proletariat," *New Left Review* 26: 5–34.

Enwezor, O., C. Basualdo, U. M. Bauer, S. Ghez, S. Maharaj, M. Nash, and O. Zaya (eds.). 2002. *Documenta 11, Platform 4. Under Siege: Four African Cities. Freetown, Johannesburg, Kinshasa, Lagos.* Ostfildern-Ruit: Hatje Cantz.

Expunobi, B. 2001. "Poor or Pure Water," *Daily Champion* (Lagos), 22 March.

Falola, T. 1998. *Violence in Nigeria: The Crisis of Religious Politics and Secular Ideologies.* Rochester: University of Rochester Press.

Gandy, M. 2005a. "Cyborg Urbanization: Complexity and Monstrosity in the Contemporary City," *International Journal of Urban and Regional Research* 29: 26–49.

Gandy, M. 2005b. "Learning from Lagos," *New Left Review* 33: 37–53.

Graham, S. and S. Marvin. 2001. *Splintering Urbanism: Networked Infrastuctures, Technological Mobilities and the Urban Condition.* London and New York: Routledge.

Hall, D. 2004. *Water Finance: A Discussion Note.* Paper commissioned by Public Services International (PSI) for the World Social Forum. Delhi/Mumbai, January 2004.

Holston, J. and A. Appadurai. 1999. "Cities and Citizenship," in J. Holston (ed.). *Cities and Citizenship.* Durham, NC: Duke University Press, pp. 1–18.

Hyden, G. and M. Bratton (eds.). 1992. *Governance and Politics in Africa.* Boulder, CO: Lynne Reinner.

Isichei, U. 2002. "From and for Lagos," *Archis* 1 (January): 11–15.

Järvelä, M. and E.-M. Rinne-Koistinen. 2005. "Purity and Dirt as Social Constructions: Environmental Health in an Urban Shantytown of Lagos," *International Journal of Urban and Regional Research* 29 (2): 375–388.

K'Akumu, O. A. 2004. "Privatization of the Urban Water Supply in Kenya: Policy Options for the Poor," *Environment & Urbanization* 16 (2): 213–222.

Koolhaas, R. (Harvard Project on the City). 2001. "Lagos," in F. Fort, and M. Jacques (eds.). *Mutations.* Barcelona: ACTAR, pp. 650–720.

Koolhaas, R. 2002. "Fragments for a Lecture on Lagos," in O. Enwezor et al. (eds.). *Documenta 11, Platform 4. Under Siege: Four African Cities. Freetown, Johannesburg, Kinshasa, Lagos.* Ostfildern-Ruit: Hatje Cantz, pp. 173–184.

Lefebvre, H. 1996 [1967]. "The Right to the City," in Eleonore Kofman and Elizabeth Lebas (eds. and trans.). *Henri Lefebvre: Writings on Cities.* Oxford: Blackwell, pp. 147–159.

Lockwood, M. 2005. *The State They're in: An Agenda for International Action on Poverty in Africa.* Schumacher Centre for Technology and Development: ITDG Publishing.

Mamdani, M. 1996. *Citizen and Subject: Contemporary Africa and the Legacy of Late Colonialism.* Princeton, NJ: Princeton University Press.

Marshall-Fratani, R. 1998. "Mediating the Global and the Local in Nigerian Pentecostalism," *Journal of Religion in Africa* 28: 278–315.

Mbembe, A. 2001. *On the Postcolony.* Berkeley, CA: University of California Press.

McCarney, P. L. 1996. "Considerations on the Notion of 'Governance'—New Directions for Cities in the Developing World," in P. L. McCarney (ed.). *Cities and Governance: New Directions in Latin America, Asia and Africa.* University of Toronto: Centre for Urban and Community Studies, pp. 3–20.

Mitchell, T. 2002. *Rule of Experts: Egypt, Techno-Politics and Modernity.* Berkeley, CA: University of California Press.

Mouffe, C. 2000. *The Democratic Paradox.* London: Verso.

Mouffe, C. 2002. "For an Agonistic Public Sphere," in O. Enwezor et al. (eds.). *Documenta 11, Platform 1. Democracy Unrealised.* Ostfildern-Ruit: Hatje Cantz, pp. 87–96.

Obi, C. 2001. *The Changing Forms of Identity Politics in Nigeria.* Uppsala: Africa Institute.

Olanrewaju, D. O. 2001. "Urban Infrastructure: A Critique of Urban Renewal Process in Ijora Badia, Lagos," *Habitat International* 25: 373–384.

Olukoju, A. 2003. *Infrastructure Development and Urban Facilities in Lagos, 1861–2000.* Occasional publication No. 15. Ibadan: Institut Français de Recherche en Afrique.

Onibokun, Adepoju and Adetoye Faniran (eds.). 1995. *Governance and Urban Poverty in Anglophone West Africa.* Ibadan, Nigeria: Centre for African Settlement Studies and Development (CASSAD).

Osumah, A. 2001. "How Lagosians Search for Potable Water," *Post Express*, February 14.

Page, B. 2004. "Cyborg Apartheid and the Metabolic Pathways of Water in Lagos." Paper presented to the conference *Techno-Natures* held at the University of Oxford, June 25.

Peil, M. 1991. *Lagos: The City Is the People.* London: Belhaven.

Rabinow, P. 1989. *French Modern: Norms and Forms of the Social Environment.* Chicago: Chicago University Press.

Rakodi, C. 2002. "Order and Disorder in African Cities: Governance, Politics, and Urban Land Development Pressures," in O. Enwezor et al. (eds.). *Dokumenta 11, Platform 4. Under Siege: Four African Cities. Freetown, Johannesburg, Kinshasa, Lagos.* Ostfildern-Ruit: Hatje Cantz, pp. 45–80.

Robinson, J. 2002. "Global and World Cities: A View from Off the Map," *International Journal of Urban and Regional Research* 26: 531–554.

Sala-i-Martin, X. and A. Subramanian. 2003. *Addressing the Natural Resource Curse: An Illustration from Nigeria.* IMF Working Paper WP/03/139.

Simone, A. 1998. *Urban Processes and Change in Africa.* Working Papers 3/97. Dakar: CODESRIA.

Simone, A. 2004. *For the City yet to Come: Changing Life in Four Cities.* Durham, NC and London: Duke University Press.

Simone, A. 2005. "Introduction: Urban Processes and Change," in A. Simone and A. Abouhani (eds.). *Urban Africa: Changing Contours of Survival in the City.* Dakar: CODESRIA; London and New York: Zed Books; Pretoria: University of South Africa Press, pp. 1–26.

Sulaimon, O. 2000. "War against Water Scarcity," *Daily Times* (Lagos), May 15.

Tostensen, A., I. Tvedten, and M. Vaa (eds.). 2001. *Associational Life in African Cities: Popular Responses to the Urban Crisis.* Uppsala: Nordiska Afrikainstitutet.

Uduku, N. O. 1994. "Promoting Community Based Approaches to Social Infrastructure Provision in Urban Areas in Nigeria," *Environment and Urbanization* 6: 57–78.

UN (Wilbur Smith Associates). Ca. 1980. *Master Plan for Metropolitan Lagos*, 2 vols. *Vol. I: Existing Conditions and Needs. Vol. II: Short Range (1985) and Long-Range (2000) Development Programme.* Prepared by UN subcontractor Wilbur Smith and Associates in collaboration with the UNDP Project Staff and the Lagos State Government.

UN Human Settlements Programme (Habitat). 2003a. *The Challenge of Slums: Global Report on Human Settlements 2003.* London: Earthscan.

UN Department of Economic and Social Affairs. 2003b. *Urban Agglomerations.* United Nations: Population Division of the Department of Economic and Social Affairs <http://www.un.org/esa/population/publications/wup2003/2003urban_agglo.htm> accessed June 25, 2005.

Vasager, J. 2005. "Talk Is Cheap, and Getting Cheaper," *The Guardian* (London), September 14.

Vidal, J. 2005a. " 'People Wake Up Angry at Being Alive in a Society Like This,' " *The Guardian* (London), March 5.

Vidal, J. 2005b. "Flagship Water Privatisation Fails in Tanzania," *The Guardian* (London), May 25.

Watts M. 2003. "Development and Governmentality," *Singapore Journal of Tropical Geography* 24: 6–34.

World Bank 1992. *Governance and Development.* Washington, DC: World Bank.

12

City Life in Zimbabwe at a Time of Fear and Loathing: Urban Planning, Urban Poverty, and Operation Murambatsvina

Deborah Potts

Introduction: Operation Murambatsvina

In May 2005 the recently reelected ZANU (PF) government of Zimbabwe began a concerted, well-planned, and prolonged attack on its urban poor and their precarious livelihoods. Toward the end of June it was estimated that 300,000 people had been physically displaced (Solidarity Peace Trust 2005). International condemnation was forthcoming but, for a country already so deeply unpopular with international agencies and Western governments that were already operating a variety of sanctions against it, this was simply ignored. A UN (Habitat) mission to Zimbabwe in late June/early July, by which time the government appeared to have largely achieved its objectives, reported, on the basis of official government figures and average household size, that about 570,000 urban people had lost their homes and around 98,000 their informal sector livelihoods. These estimates were evidently likely to be conservative although there would also be some overlap in the categories. Using other information gathered during the mission, the UN suggested that probably 650,000–700,000 people falling into these two categories had been directly affected and a further 1.7 million indirectly affected by, for instance, knock-on economic impacts: a total of 2.4 million representing around a fifth of the total population (Tibaijuka 2005).

The targets chosen were wide-ranging. They included informal sector operations and sites where informal sector workers gathered to market their wares, as well as formal markets some of which had been in operation for decades. In Harare alone it was estimated that 75,000 vendors were unable to work from late May, 2005. Urban agriculture was banned—although always illegal this time it was clear that the ban would be enforced. In the housing sector, free-standing areas of informal housing suffered but so also did many backyard shacks—small lodging rooms found around the edges of housing plots that are ubiquitous in southern Africa within formal, legal, and planned housing areas some of which are original "townships" dating back to the early years of Apartheid and racist city planning. Also some legal, planned housing was destroyed including sites, many in peri-urban areas, where housing cooperatives had been recently developed to provide permanent low-income housing, or people removed from other sites had been given rights to build.[1] In many cases, however, although planned, even these houses contravened various bylaws and could therefore be deemed "illegal." A particular problem was that urban planning regulations forbade houses being developed on unserviced sites and the municipalities had not serviced some of these sites, despite having been instructed by the government to allocate them (Tibaijuka 2005).

POLITICS, POVERTY, AND IMAGE: PERSPECTIVES ON CAUSES OF THE CAMPAIGN

How can this unprecedented campaign against the urban poor be understood? This essay offers three perspectives relating to national politics, urban planning traditions, and the depth of urban poverty and economic crisis in the country. Undoubtedly the issue of the fear (and loathing) of political pressures from urban dwellers is relevant. Since 2000 the urban electorate in Zimbabwe has, on every available occasion, voted overwhelmingly against the ruling party and in favor of the opposition party, the Movement for Democratic Change (MDC). President Mugabe has since developed a notorious anti-urban dweller rhetoric, including insulting them as "totemless" people without "proper" cultural roots. One analysis of the government's attack on the urban poor characterized it as "a measure of collective punishment and repression of potential uprising against the people who voted for the opposition party in the recent elections" (Habitat International 2005). Some comparison might be made with other sub-Saharan African countries where a combination of SAPs and political conditionality leading to multiparty democracies has seen many elected governments faced with, and evidently exasperated by, active urban opposition. The key difference with Zimbabwe is that the government has acted so savagely, confident (correctly) that the previous five years of brutal repressiveness against the opposition would prevent any meaningful, coordinated response. It was also relevant that the operations began shortly before massive food price rises. As one analyst noted: "Mugabe's paramilitary invasions are designed to disorganize and discourage any resistance to May 28–29 price increases for maize meal (up 51 percent) and bread (up 29 percent). In the past, such increases have triggered massive urban rebellions in Harare" (Dixon 2005).

Yet, it is self-evident that the operations cannot have targeted only MDC supporters. Many caught up must have been ZANU (PF) voters, for the depth of the housing and employment crisis is such that most non-elite households will have some involvement with informal solutions. Furthermore, the destruction of informal sector services and trade activities and many markets will have been disastrous for everyone for this is where the majority source their food and services.

As noted at the time:

> [i]n Mbare, the wholesale vegetable market closed when the vendors who were their main customers were swept off the streets. This destroyed the livelihood of tomato and vegetable growers, whose produce used to be seen daily in lorries and on top of buses coming to the town market. Many of them were considered strong supporters of Mugabe's party . . . but they too were disposable. (McGarry 2005)

The destruction of backyard shacks also removed a hugely significant source of income for many formal plotholders/houseowners in high density areas, most of whom would have also been poor, although not amongst the poorest. Whether they would have had a higher or lower propensity to vote for ZANU (PF) is a moot point, but it seems unlikely they would have been uniformally MDC supporters.

In relation to the urban poor, although they were the main targets of the campaign, those directly affected were only a proportion of the poor and the distinctions between those affected and those not was scarcely clear-cut. The vast majority of people in the formal high density houses of Zimbabwe's cities and towns are now poor—poverty is not confined to those living in an illegal backyard shack or an impermanent structure on an informal site. Nor would those engaged in informal activities, who were also targeted, correlate neatly with the informally/illegally housed. Many would be from formal, legal, high density housing as the decline of the formal economy in Zimbabwe's urban areas has driven many formerly formally employed people into the informal sector, as well as pushing many other members of their households into informal employment.

Another perspective relates to the "image" of the city and this issue is developed in further detail in the following section.

The Maintenance of Urban "Orderliness": Outside and Inside the Houses

The government's program was called "Operation Murambatsvina"—meaning literally "drive out the rubbish" or, more euphemistically, "restore order" (Dixon 2005). Locally it soon became known as Operation Tsunami because of the suddenness and ferocity of the campaign. The continuities in official attitudes to what constitutes "proper" urban economic activity and housing between the former settler government and the post-Independence government in Zimbabwe have often been noted (Bourdillon 1991; Dewar 1991; Drakakis-Smith et al. 1995; Potts 1994; Rakodi 1995; Teedon and Drakakis-Smith 1986). One noteworthy element in this has been the attempt to maintain very high building standards in the cities' site and service settlements, which has caused serious affordability problems (Bourdillon 1991; Potts and Mutambirwa 1991; Rakodi 1995). In addition, the policing and eradication of illegal, squatter dwellings has been pursued with great vigor and general "success" for most of the post-Independence era. This set Zimbabwe apart from other sub-Saharan African countries in that the vast majority of its low-income housing in the cities has been *in* formal and planned settlements. However, a proportion of the actual dwelling units within these settlements have been *illegal*, in that they have been backyard shacks built within the boundaries of legal plots, which contravene a host of planning laws. The proportion of people housed within such shacks varies enormously from High Density Area (HDA) to HDA and between urban areas, however. For example, Mbare, Harare's oldest township, was full of them and many plots had several such shacks. Some townships, such as those in Kadoma, have very few such shacks however (Smith 2004, personal communication).

The government's efforts to maintain "order" and a modern city image in Zimbabwe meant that the visual difference between Harare or Bulawayo and most other sub-Saharan African, let alone Asian or Latin American, cities in the 1980s and 1990s, and even into the early twenty-first century, was remarkable. The central business districts (CBDs) retained a faintly 1950s/1960s feel to them for many years, with outdated shopfronts and other commercial buildings, old colonial hotels, and tidy open spaces. In Harare, in particular, new commercial building gradually injected a more modern style, and the traffic built up a little. Informal sector activities and begging were present on the street in the city centers, but these were very contained and on a minor scale *in comparison with* the bustle and competitive selling of goods and services so typical of cities from Luanda to Kinshasa to Lagos to Dakar. The traffic chaos of Nairobi was unimaginable in Harare, although residents (both white and black) who were unfamiliar with African cities further north were complaining by the 1990s of traffic "jams" when they failed to pass through a junction with two changes of the lights at the "robots" (traffic lights). The almost eerie orderliness of the low density residential areas (the former white suburbs) was a hangover from the cities' segregated past, but has largely been maintained even if the roads are now potholed. Even if this was to be "expected," the formal high density townships and new, postcolonial site-and-service areas, such as Warren Park, Glen Norah C, Dziveresekwa, Budiriro, and the vast and ever-expanding Kuwadzana in Harare, largely also remained generally clearly "suburban" and tidy in character (at least, again, to anyone with experience of low-income urban areas in developing countries elsewhere). An important element of this was the fact that all formal residential plots had on-site sanitation and potable water, so the worst environmental and health issues characteristic of low-income urban settlements in other developing countries were largely avoided. The newer phases of site-and-service settlements had piles of formal, permanent building materials (such as sand for mortar, or bricks) besides many plots, and many had incomplete houses, including some made of impermanent materials, as plot beneficiaries struggled to save enough to build something that would comply with the draconian, Western, building standards. Also, "tuckshops" (informal shops built generally of impermanent materials) were tolerated at times, especially if formal, zoned, and planned shops remained undeveloped. They might, however, be removed when the planned shops eventually appeared.

None of this is to say that the informal sector, the *shebeens*, and the buzz of African town life, were absent from Zimbabwe's HDAs. Indeed, again from a comparative perspective, it was something of a relief to find that there *was* "town life" within the cities, in the HDAs, given the utter sterility of somewhere like central Bulawayo once night fell. Nonetheless, the "image" presented during the day in these residential areas was "orderly" and, generally, clean. Indeed, a remarkable aspect of many phases of Kuwadzana, for example, was the bizarre resemblance between the streets of four-roomed bungalows there and those along the Costa Geriatriaca (a ribbon of retirement homes near the sea along the Sussex, Hampshire, and Dorset coasts, United Kingdom).

Image is, of course, merely the surface impression. Behind the doors of these bungalows this simplistic, if emblematic, resemblance disappeared. Forced compliance with building standards did not extend to internal finishes and occupation rates. The differences between the interiors of Harare's high density, planned housing and those of low-income houses elsewhere in urban Africa were far less than the outside "image" would suggest. Occupancy rates of a household to a room are common, as throughout Africa. The ethos of owner-occupation that has guided housing policy so strongly throughout the region in recent decades (Mutizwa-Mangiza 1985; Potts 1998; Rakodi 1995), despite being contradicted by many of the realities of urban people's incomes, is honored more in the breach than the observance, given the ubiquity of rented rooms within these houses. Furnishings could be very simple or even virtually non-existent. Nonetheless, it is worth stressing again that the availability of water and sanitation on such housing plots (and electricity) did give their urban residents access to particularly critical elements of urban "modernity." Some of these might be cut off with today's privatizing and cost-recovering service delivery models but arrangements might still be made with neighbors, and so forth. Landlords and landladies might limit, in humiliating and burdensome ways, access to these services—and the sheer numbers on a plot needing to use them may be far from ideal, but this is a far remove from having no access at all. A nationwide urban survey in 2003 found that 92 percent of the urban poor had access to piped water either in their houses or just outside on the plot (ZNVAC 2004). Water and electricity cutoffs throughout all urban areas, including wealthy suburbs, however became increasingly common in the twenty-first century as the economy teetered toward collapse.

Backyard Shacks and Building Standards in Zimbabwean Cities

Backyard shacks on plots in HDAs evidently undermine the *outward* image of "orderliness" and "modernity." As already noted, their frequency within HDAs is variable. Mbare had so many because it was the nearest HDA to Harare's industrial areas and CBD. As in all cities, for the poor, access to workplaces (particularly if this means transport costs can be avoided) is a key factor when searching for somewhere to live. A good location is worth a fortune in time and stress and/or money. In recent years, foreign exchange shortages have made fuel supplies, and transport in general, highly erratic in Zimbabwe and rendered outlying HDAs terribly difficult places to work from.

The comparative advantage of Mbare's location meant the demand for accommodation there has been very high. This explains why so many plotholders, many of whom would have obtained owner-occupation status after

Independence from being legal renters of family housing there during the colonial period and Unilateral Declaration of Independence (UDI), built and rented backyard shacks.[2] In Mbare these could be arranged around the entire perimeter of the plot and even be squeezed between the house and the front of the plot (leaving virtually no light for front rooms in the main house).[3] Such "shacks" were undoubtedly illegal, contravening a host of planning laws, but they were ubiquitous by the 1990s. On the other hand, in Kuwadzana, Harare's largest area of postcolonial site-and-service housing, backyard shacks were strongly discouraged and essentially prevented throughout the 1980s and much of the 1990s. During this period therefore the balance between demand and officialdom tilted toward the latter. Nevertheless, by the 2000s, the district office (DO) in Kuwadzana explained that the demand for low-income housing had become so extreme in Harare that such housing options were beginning to be tolerated there.

In earlier writings on housing in Lilongwe, Malawi, with some comparative reference to Harare, the author of this chapter discussed how, despite a highly realistic approach to building standards in the city's Traditional Housing Areas (roughly equivalent to Harare's HDAs), which attracted praise for the affordable, and legally secure, outcomes (Pennant 1990), abject failure to keep up with demand for serviced, planned land for housing (in a city well endowed with land, all of which is owned by the City Council!) was bound to lead to illegal, unplanned housing, despite a politically inspired determination to maintain that city's image, which rivaled that in Zimbabwe (Myers 2003; Potts 1989; Potts 1994). This is precisely what happened, leading to plans (albeit very reluctant) to upgrade and legalize these settlements by the mid-1980s. There are parallels with Zimbabwe's experience in that the Malawian authorities were determined to keep Lilongwe "orderly"— the ordained image by President Banda was that of a "garden city." However their efforts could be likened to keeping their finger in the dyke; eventually the pressure build up was too high and "leaks" could no longer be controlled and plugged. Similar things have happened in Zimbabwe—for most of the post-Independence period, despite mismatches between housing supply and demand, the planners managed to keep their fingers in the dyke, supported by a government prepared to back strong interventions against unplanned housing. Although urban poverty, which correlates strongly with the demand for informal housing solutions, deepened sharply in Zimbabwe after structural adjustment was introduced (Kanji 1995; Mupedziswa and Gumbo 1998; Potts and Mutambirwa 1998; Rakodi 1994; Tevera 1995), it was still far less than in Malawi. However, the economic shocks of the 2000s in Zimbabwe reduced people's living standards and incomes much further and thus the pressure for informal housing became increasingly irresistible. So settlements such as Hatfield on the northwestern edge of Harare were spreading and these were devastated by Operation Murambvatsina (OM).

Similar analysis can be made for the informal sector. By the late 1990s informal market sites for a host of traded items, including the relatively profitable secondhand clothes, were developing and expanding. All were demolished under OM.[4] These were simply an essential part of the supply networks of the city as people's incomes drove them from the formal retail sector to the secondhand, recycled market products. It was clear however that the government was extremely uncomfortable with these developments.

Urban Politics, Urban Planning, and Policy Shifts: 1980s–2000s

It is necessary to recognize that the recent operations against the urban poor are not a sudden change of direction for the Zimbabwean government. It has maintained an almost unyielding battle against informal housing since 1980. In and around Harare this was largely "successful" (for the planners), when compared with the situation in other parts of Africa. A fairly well-known example was when a small squatter settlement in Mbare was cleared before the Commonwealth Heads of Government meeting in Harare in 1990. Along with other evictees from areas in and around Harare, including Borrowdale and Epworth, they were moved to Porta Farm on Harare's outskirts (Zimbabwe Human Rights NGO Forum 2004). Some came from the VID (Vehicle Inspection Department) area in Eastlea in Harare and had previously been evicted from the Railway Station in 1989 where they had been living on the streets (Bourdillon 1991). People at Porta Farm subsequently suffered further periodical evictions, for example, in September 2004, and it was demolished under OM in 2005. Similarly in 1984, just before Harare hosted the Non-Aligned Movement, beggars had been taken from the city to "empty land over a hundred kilometers from the city" (Bourdillon 1991: 99). Broader campaigns included "single" women being rounded up and taken from the city on the grounds that they were prostitutes during the early 1980s. These specific incidents were emblematic ones but they were part of a wider campaign; essentially the government and the city authorities maintained a watching brief on informal housing (beyond the backyard shacks) and usually removed those that appeared swiftly. As a result, the poor who could not get site-and-service housing for which there was a vast waiting list and difficult financial conditions to be met, tended to squeeze themselves into lodging rooms within the formal housing stock (which was legal) or into backyard shacks (which were not).

The antipathy of the Harare authorities to both the informal sector and backyard shacks remained a recurrent issue throughout the 1980s, 1990s, and into the twenty-first century. By the end of the 1980s it was evident that major "contradictions and conflicts [were arising] . . . between the needs of the urban poor and the desire and commitment of local urban authorities to maintain an aesthetically pleasing and 'modern' urban environment, which conforms to planned land-use schemes" (Potts 1989: 332). Threats to the existence of backyard shacks by urban authorities were frequently aired in the newspapers over the years (see Potts and Mutambirwa 1991). In the late 1980s:

> [a] newspaper report on the housing shortage stated that 'one of the fast emerging features of suburban Harare is the backyard timber or tin shack to accommodate the desperate,' and went on to describe how lodgers were paying 25 Zimbabwean dollars [hereafter Z$] to Z$55 per month for one-roomed units which frequently had no windows. One Mbare lodger was said to be paying Z$45 for such a room, when the owner of the main house paid only Z$25 rent to the council. In Epworth rents of Z$20 per month are common for mud brick rooms. The proliferation of rented rooms has led to multiple sub-lettings (i.e. sub-lettings of sub-lettings) so that some people are both lodger and landlord/lady. In line with policies on minimum housing standards and squatting the authorities are

> strongly opposed to the backyard dwellings, although they tend to be more pragmatic about lodgers in the main house. Backyard rooms are often demolished, and a program of demolition in Chitungwiza was announced in July 1989. (Potts and Mutambirwa 20–21)

Full-scale demolition did not, however, proceed although local plot owners were sensitive to fluctuations in the authorities' attitudes to the shacks and were less likely to develop them if they deemed the time not to be right due to a surge of restrictive feelings among urban planners. For example, a case study of one Chitungwiza plot owner by Schlyter (2005) describes how she refrained from building backyard shacks in the early 1990s because the Council was intervening in this respect. She also stopped her *shebeen* operations then as she had been arrested twice. Instead she set up a small welding operation within her plot boundaries. This, too, was illegal but she judged correctly that the Council would not bother her about it. As the 1990s progressed she also judged that the official attitude toward backyard shacks was changing as urban poverty, which had been lessening in the 1980s (Potts 2000), began to increase again. This led to a progressive relaxation of constraints on backyards shacks, and similar responses to urban poverty (Kamete 1999) and this in turn led to further development of these strategies. Building standards were also relaxed (Kamete 2001), although not enough to make a really significant difference, and small and medium enterprises were allowed to be developed on plots, yet were still subject to planning permission (Tibaijuka 2005). By 2000 the plot owner in this case study had six backyard shacks around the perimeter of her plot, although as Schlyter notes, within Chitungwiza, "levels of control have differed considerably between different areas and were often still strict during the 1990s."

This change in the government's attitudes toward informal housing and trading was also evident in conflicts that were played out in the 1990s in Bulawayo between the City Council and the government. In this city the Council's determination to maintain an "orderly" city and prevent illegal / unplanned structures out-rivaled Harare's, and far fewer backyard shacks and tuckshops therefore developed. As the 1990s progressed, however, as elsewhere in the country, the pressure surged for such developments to ease the growing plight of the urban poor as structural adjustment measures transformed the nature of urban employment and incomes. The Council's opposition, however, continued until the *central* government (in other words ZANU (PF)) intervened and put pressure on the Bulawayo authorities to become more lenient (Solidarity Peace Trust 2005). Perhaps this could be constructed as a party political stance against a city felt to be "Ndebele"/ ZAPU,[5] despite the merger of ZAPU with ZANU (PF) at the time of Zimbabwe's Unity Accord in 1987 and the fact that Bulawayo was, at that time, under ZANU (PF) control. However, given that the government's increasing (if fluctuating) leniency toward the urban poor was simultaneously developing within Harare and Chitungwiza where such political point scoring was unnecessary, such an analysis seems to hold little water, even if the government did *additionally* relish interfering with Bulawayo's affairs.

Such a political analysis of the government's shifting ground on informal housing and employment might make more sense had it coincided with the rise of the opposition Movement for Democratic Change (MDC) and the iconic moment when ZANU (PF) lost its referendum on constitutional change at the beginning of 2000. In the same year all urban parliamentary constituencies came under MDC control, although Harare City Council remained under a government-appointed Commission, which had taken over when the elected Council was suspended in 1999 for corruption and mismanagement. However, it is clear that the shift began much earlier and the evidence points to it being a response, albeit reluctant and halting, to pressures related to new types of poverty building up within the urban areas. This is further supported by the government's intervention in Harare in 2001 when the Chanakira Commission threatened to launch its own purge of backyard shacks and tuckshops. This began on March 10, with demolition of tuckshops in Mbare Musika (the main, official city market) and continued in other HDAs, particularly Warren Park. Backyard shacks were threatened en masse and contemporary reports stated that at least 145,000 illegal outbuildings in the HDAs were to be demolished within a fortnight, rendering over 500,000 homeless, a total that would have exceeded those evicted under the 2005 OM.[6] Yet, this time ZANU (PF) stepped in *to prevent* the evictions and further demolitions, thus directly opposing the decisions of its own appointed Commission. The headlines of the time summed up the situation: on March 14 the government's *Herald* ran the headline, "Harare demolishes illegal tuckshops" and the next day ran, "State to stop demolition of tuckshops." The role of the state here was accepted by the opposition newspaper, the *Daily News*, which agreed that "the government stepped in to the Council's plans."[7] The ambiguities and conflicts in official attitudes to the strategies necessitated by urban poverty at this time are evident: the ruling party, faced with an increasingly impoverished city electorate, which had recently routed it and replaced it with the much hated opposition party, and an urban local government body that was theoretically on its side, sided with the former against the latter. It is horribly ironic that the justifications given by the central government for its opposition to the demolitions and its criticisms of the Commission in 2001 were precisely those used in 2005 to condemn the government for OM. For example, it was argued in 2001 by a government official that "it is not the residents who are at fault but a system of by-laws which criminalize the enterprise" and that "the commission should have looked for a more humane way of handling the problem." The government also criticized the Commission for not providing tuckshop owners with an alternative before demolishing their structures.[8]

It is a commonplace to point out that no party, or institution, has a single, unified stance on any topic. The negative attitudes of the city authorities toward informal activities in Harare in 2001 were evident in an interview undertaken by the author with one ward councilor representing part of Kuwadzana. Not only was he very negative about tuckshops, associating them directly with prostitution and *shebeens*, he also attacked the minibuses that had dominated the city's public transport since economic liberalization. It was clear that his own electorate also had major concerns about the minibuses, which, throughout sub-Saharan African cities, are frequently a nerve-wracking way to travel. Overcrowding, speed, and abusive drivers' assistants are often cause for complaint, although bad "kombis" are usually preferable to virtually nonexistent public buses. This councilor was ZANU (PF) and represented the general attitudes evident in the Commission's 2001 attack on the informal sector. More importantly, the newspapers in March 2001 also reported deeply ambiguous and, in retrospect, highly portentous, statements by the Minister of Local Government, Public Works and National Housing, Ignatius Chombo, who was to be one of the key instigators of OM in 2005. He pointed to the unsanitary nature of many of the demolished tuckshops and that many were being used as residences as well as shops. He also said that "the Government will in future consult with the municipality and the Zimbabwe Tuckshop Owners' Association *before demolishing* illegal structures of small traders" and that "we cannot have a situation where one street has up to 40 or 50 tuckshops and where anyone can erect structures where they want. *We cannot run a city that way.*"[9] It seems clear, therefore, that the 1990s trend toward leniency and, apparently, greater sensitivity toward the needs of the urban poor, though real enough as judged by the changes allowed within the cities, was still countered within the government by many whose sentiments remained against informality and in favor of "order" and planning.

It is worth noting that contradictions and ironic reactions toward city planning are not the preserve of ZANU (PF). OM was opposed in Bulawayo by the MDC City Council and Mayor in 2005, who made efforts to explain to the people that it was not of their making but a central government move. Yet the same report that emphasized this important difference (Solidarity Peace Trust 2005), presumably in an attempt to support Bulawayo, further went on to *praise* Bulawayo City Council for its history of opposition to unplanned structures, and the way in which it had to be forced by the central government to relax this stance in the 1990s, as discussed above. This was counter-posed to Harare's more lax approach, which was seen as being evidence of corruption. Thus, in 2005, it was being argued that:

> The Bulawayo city council has had a reputation of being efficient and generally not corrupt since colonial days, in sharp contrast to the Harare city council. For this reason the number of illegal structures—and therefore the current displacement—has been significantly lower in Bulawayo than in Harare. (Solidarity Peace Trust 2005: 17)

The Mayor of this "efficient" council was also quoted as noting, presumably with some surprise, that:

> many of these [illegal structures] are very well constructed, and not makeshift buildings: once people perceived that unofficial structures were now being ignored, they invested a lot of money in building brick cottages and extensions. (Solidarity Peace Trust 2005: 17)

This analysis obviously misses the point that "efficient" Councils are rarely the friends of the urban poor, the very people who have been attacked by OM and whose plight and rights are elsewhere strongly upheld in this report. The fact that Bulawayo had allowed far fewer tuckshops and backyard shacks aligns it with the current government position on the needs of the urban poor, not against it! Indeed, had the government, in its 1990s and early 2000s stance on these issues, not pushed Bulawayo to be more lenient, there would have been hardly any demolitions there because it would have so successfully maintained "order" that it would have been scarcely necessary to restore it. Further irony emerges from the mayor's sudden alignment with the "John Turner" position on the advantages of improving security of tenure for the poor![10]

Informal Settlements: Epworth and Hatcliffe Extension

There were exceptions to this generalized picture of informal housing being concentrated in the backyard shack sector. In and around Harare, for example, there was Epworth settlement, just beyond the city's borders to the southeast. This had been allowed to develop on mission land in the 1970s, before independence, and was therefore not illegal and was not cleared. By 1984 this was estimated to have a population of 25,000. Attempts were then made to "freeze" the settlement's population and it was upgraded, starting in 1985. By 1988 safe water sources had been provided for most residents, and many Blair toilets (ventilated improved pit latrines or VIPs) had been built with government assistance (Potts 1998). However the "freezing" failed; the 1992 census enumerated about 63,000 people in its two urban wards, then within Harare. In the 2002 census it was designated, for the first time, as a *separate* urban settlement under a Local Board with an enumerated population of 114,000. Many of the potential "squatters" of Harare "proper" therefore were setting up homes in Epworth but as this was beyond the authority of the city itself, and not particularly "visible" (except to visitors to the nearby Balancing Rocks), it largely, though not entirely, escaped the war of attrition against informal housing. Despite its formal acceptance as a separately enumerated urban settlement with its own administration in the census, it was reported that 100,000 were made homeless by OM on June 20 (McGarry 2005). Other, later, reports suggested more partial demolition with specific structures, deemed illegal, being pinpointed (Manangazira 2005). This settlement, which was the single largest area of urban housing in the country that had developed in a way which was not, originally, planned and zoned by urban authorities, appears, perhaps inevitably, to have been the source of a large number of those evicted under OM.

The other important exception, this time within Harare's boundaries, is Hatcliffe Extension on the northwest edge of the city. Hatcliffe itself was originally set up in 1984 as a formal housing scheme for male gardeners from Borrowdale, a low density area. Hatcliffe *Extension* was officially established in 1990 on about 60 acres as a "holding camp" for squatters from various areas including Porta Farm, the pre-1991 CHOGM evictions from the squatter settlement in Mbare, and Epworth. In 1993 the Department of Physical Planning designed a high density site-and-service layout next to the extension but this was not implemented and people were not moved into this more secure situation. Further evictions to Hatcliffe Extension during the 1990s swelled the population so that by 2001 it was estimated to cover about 120 acres. Estimates of its population by then were extremely varied. The residents numbered themselves at around 15,000 but there were also other estimates of 9,000 to as high as

25,000. A number of NGOs were involved in the area by then, including World Vision and Dialogues on Shelter (Nyamvura 2001). According to Dixon (2005), in 2002 some new evictees from other settlements were supporters of ZANU (PF). Tragically, Hatcliffe Extension was singled out for wholesale demolition during OM, despite the fact that many of its residents had been *officially* moved there over the years, had been allocated plots, and had documents to prove this. Furthermore, in the run up to OM, the status of the residents seemed to have improved with a move to "formalization" and the allocation of many more plots of land. It was reported that people had paid Z$300,000 per stand and again had lease documents (Solidarity Peace Trust 2005). Nonetheless, much of the housing, if not all, was "illegal" in that it was not properly serviced by the municipality, and this was beyond the residents' control. Many would also not have complied with Zimbabwe's strict building standards, even were they built of "permanent" materials like brick.[11] Many people from other settlements were also forced to move to Hatcliffe Extension shortly before OM. Its subsequent demolition received major press coverage because the MDC MP for that area, Trudy Stevenson, publicized it. She reported that 30,000 people had their homes demolished and were evicted, although other, probably more realistic reports, put it at 10,000 (Dixon 2005; Solidarity Peace Trust 2005).[12]

Forced Urban–Rural Migration

Phineas Chihota, Deputy Minister of Industry and International Trade said in Parliament, on June 25, 2005: "It is common cause that the definition of an indigenous person is one who has a rural home allocated to him by virtue of being indigenous, and a home that one has acquired in an urban area because it has been bought or it has been allocated to him by the State" (Solidarity Peace Trust 2005). Habitat International (2005; emphasis added) made it clear that "the vast majority of evicted residents [of Hatcliffe Extension] have not been offered any alternative place to settle and *have been told to go back to the rural areas they originally come from.*" Indeed, "tens of thousands of people being displaced in urban areas have had to comply with the Government's declared intention of the exercise, and return to rural areas" (Solidarity Peace Trust 2005). Walter Nzembi, ZANU (PF) MP for Masvingo South said in Parliament, on June 23, 2005: "this exercise . . . has been one of the biggest reversals of rural-urban migration" (Solidarity Peace Trust 2005). The implications of this attempt to force urban people out of the cities is analysed below, and will be returned to in the conclusions.

In 1985 a major survey of migrants who had come to live in Harare HDAs since independence found that a significant proportion of them did not plan to remain in town permanently, although there was a tendency toward long-term stay with most of the immediate family for much of the time (see Potts and Mutambirwa 1990). Subsequent surveys in 1988, 1994, and 2001 uncovered a clear upswing of uncertainty among new migrants (recent incomers before each survey date) in the declining economic circumstances of the post-structural adjustment economy of 1994 and the post-fast track land reform economy of 2001. The proportion who think they will probably leave town in the future has increased significantly (Potts 2006). Many migrants were choosing to maintain a portfolio of rural assets and planned to go to communal areas when (and the feeling was increasingly "when" and not "if") the going got tough in town. Such patterns are common enough in Africa; net urban–rural migration has even been dominant in Zambia for over 20 years (Potts 2005a).

When reporting such patterns, and their implications of the importance of *migrants'* landholdings and rural assets for their economic security in Africa (Potts 1997; Potts and Mutambirwa 1990), care has been taken to note that, although in-migrants from rural areas are an important element of many African cities' populations, they are a declining fraction and the city born are increasingly dominant, both overall and in annual population increase. This important distinction is helpful when analyzing contemporary urban growth and livelihood options for urban dwellers in the typically straitened economic circumstances of contemporary Africa (Potts 2005b). Policy implications about the possibilities of a rural option that are relevant to *some* rural–urban migrants are evidently not true for the rest of the city population or for some migrants who have lived in town for, say, over 20 years, or for those who have no land to farm. The latter issue is, of course, one of the underlying reasons why people have to turn to towns in the first place, in countries with long histories of land alienation such as Zimbabwe. Even *migrants* who would *like* to try and exercise a rural option may find it impossible: the case study already discussed above of a plot holder in Chitungwiza provides an illustrative example, for she did seek land on several occasions but could not find a sufficiently sympathetic headman (Schlyter 2005). Women are particularly likely to have this problem, given the nature of land tenure in patriarchal Zimbabwe.

All these points have taken on a terrible poignancy in relation to OM. As evident from the quotes in the first paragraph of this section, the Zimbabwe government has been forcing evicted people to leave the towns and "return" to rural areas. There is a tie-up between this policy and the earlier mentioned cultural insults of urban people by the government, since their siding with the political opposition became clear, as "having no totem" and therefore not being "proper" Zimbabweans or truly "indigenous." From the first quote, which is presumed to relate to urban people, there seems to be a message that if you are not a proper Zimbabwean with rural roots and a place to go, then you do not deserve a livelihood or place to live. On the other hand, the statement is ambiguous in that it suggests that you are "indigenous" if you also have a legally acquired urban residence. In reality, seeking to deconstruct such remarks is largely pointless, since it assumes a degree of logical consistency in the policy of OM that is not really there. For example, it is obvious that there is no reason why people living in backyard shacks or trading from informal market sites are less likely to have a "totem" or be truly "indigenous" than those living in formal houses. Indeed, were it argued that they might be more recent rural–urban migrants as they are not in formal housing and jobs (a dubious assumption but frequently made), they are arguably closer to their rural roots, "better" Zimbabweans than those with longer urban histories, and less in need of cultural re-education. Similarly, any assumption that OM was specifically directed against the MDC, and was a party political move, fails on the grounds that supporters of both the government and the opposition will have been living in backyard shacks and working in the informal sector. The government must have known this.

The rural "return" option, conveniently assumed by the government, can easily be disproved for large sections of the urban population. A survey conducted among former residents of Killarney, a long-established informal settlement in Bulawayo, after OM had demolished the area, found that only 17 percent of the household heads identified a rural destination they felt they could go to (see table 12.1). This does not mean that none of the rest could find some rural place to go. Having lived in town for many years, for example, is not necessarily a ban to retirement in rural areas, as is evident from across Africa. The survey report points out that the 25 percent who did not elaborate on why they felt they had "nowhere to go" may simply have not wanted to go elsewhere; the importance of having to earn a living which is often easier in town, if one has no land, was also significant. The key finding of the research is perhaps that, even *in extremis*, most people from Killarney were choosing, or desperately clinging to the wish, to stay within Bulawayo. It would have been interesting to see how length of stay in town affected these decisions, since more recent in-migrants may have found it easier to resurrect, even if temporarily, a rural livelihood of sorts. People who have lost touch with their rural relatives, on the other hand, may find a hostile reception should they "return," as indicated by the results of Ferguson's (1999) research in urban Zambia.

A useful, if crude, index of potential connections to rural areas in African cities is the proportion of the urban population born in town as opposed to rural areas. This is falling over time. Unfortunately disaggregated data of this type for Zimbabwe's 1992 and 2002 censuses are not available. However in 1982, 33 percent of Harare's, and 35 percent of Bulawayo's populations were born within their respective provinces (and a few more would have been born in other towns). It can be safely assumed that, by 2002, over half of the urban population will have been born in town, many of these being children.[13] An indication of the increasing propensity for adults to have their roots in towns can also be derived, however, from the longitudinal surveys of Harare's migrant population. As shown in table 12.2, over time the share of new migrants coming to live in Harare who were born in another town has greatly increased. In 1985, only 6 percent of the recent migrants sampled, all of whom were adults, had been born in towns. By 2001 this had quadrupled to 22 percent. The proportion whose residence immediately prior to their move to Harare was another town had also increased compared to 1985, although it was slightly less than it had been in 1994. The reasons for this can only be speculated upon but it does fit with recent evidence of increased urban–urban migration *down* the urban hierarchy within Zimbabwe presented by Andersson (2002). Her research, based in the small town of Rusape near Mutare in eastern Zimbabwe, suggests that the reason for these new flows is that living costs in small towns are significantly lower and both formal and informal job markets somewhat less saturated. Given the evidence presented above of the dire poverty experienced in contemporary Harare, and the extreme problems created by ever-inflating living costs, the attractions of smaller towns in these respects can be understood. Almost half of the migrants she surveyed had lived in centers classified as cities in the past. Their motives for moving out combined both the increasing dis-benefits of life for the urban poor in Harare, in particular, with the relative ease and lower costs

Table 12.1 Reported possible destinations: The displaced in Killarney, Bulawayo

Possible Destination	Percent of Those Interviewed
Rural destination	17
Urban destination	13
"Nowhere to go" because:	
Lived in Killarney all life/many years	15
Descended from foreign national	15
Relatives all dead/lost touch	15
Did not elaborate/must look for work in town	25

Source: Derived from data reported in Solidarity Peace Trust 2005.

of life in Rusape. Factors included very high food and transport costs, high rents for lodgers and the sheer lack of both rental accommodation and houses or stands to buy in the cities. The depredations of OM may have made Rusape's advantages less notable as it was also badly affected.

As stated above, most of Zimbabwe's urban people by 2005 would have been *born* in towns. Many of these would have lived in backyard shacks, housing cooperatives, peri-urban areas, and squatter areas and been amongst those evicted in OM. Even a fifth of recent in-migrants to the capital are urban born. Many of the urban born would, however, have parents who had previously migrated from rural areas. Depending on their parents' desire and capacity to maintain their rural links, they may or may not have a potential place to go to in rural areas. The likelihood of obtaining land to support themselves there, in any case, is much diminished, if not negligible, because of the land shortage in the communal areas; those most likely to have an active and potentially fruitful economic link are rural born migrants with some land. These people are an important fraction of the population, but a minority even of recent migrants. On the other hand, the majority of migrants surveyed over the years in Harare do not expect or definitely plan to stay there permanently. The proportion with such definite intentions has been decreasing as urban poverty has increased and by 2001 was only 13 percent. Thus most recent migrants were keeping an open mind about *where* their future livelihoods lay and were very unsure or pessimistic about it being in Harare.

In many ways, however, the analyses about whether people have rural places "to go" to or, as the government terminology states, to "return" to,[14] are far less important than the question of whether people *want* or, perhaps more realistically, *are prepared* to go to rural areas. The evidence of the migrant surveys in Harare is clear that many migrants with recent rural backgrounds are keen to keep their rural options open—they are prepared for the possibility that this might become a necessity, even if they do not really *want* to exercise it for many years. The evidence from reports on OM and the demographics of Zimbabwe's cities is that this is, unsurprisingly, not the case for the majority of those evicted. They neither want to leave town, nor are they prepared for this. In the final analysis, OM was a flagrant breach of Zimbabwean urban dwellers' human rights.

Table 12.2 Place of birth and previous residence of recent migrants to Harare in 1985, 1994, and 2001

Year of Survey	Previous Residence			Place of Birth			
	Another Town	Communal Land	Commercial Farming Area	Another Town	Zimbabwe Rural	Malawi/ Mozambique	Other
1985	20	77	2	6	88	4	2
1994	33	67	<1	10	88	1	1
2001	29	70	<1	22	77	<1	<1

Source: Migrant surveys conducted by Potts and Mutambirwa (1990; 1991; 1998), (Potts 2000; 2006).

Many displaced people will have been temporarily accommodated by relatives, as reported by a Jesuit priest who recorded the plight of people in Mbare during and after OM (Mbare Report 2005a). Others moved to urban sites where they hoped they might escape the demolitions and rebuild; however, often the Operation followed them within weeks or days, as reported in Epworth where some displaced people from Harare had moved "as a last resort" (Zimbabwe Human Rights NGO Forum 2005). Some evictees were forcibly removed, however. Most reports focused on the camp set up by the government at New Caledonia Farm, on the outskirts of Harare toward Ruwa, near Tafara HDA. People from a number of Harare settlements, including Porta Farm, which had supplied many of those who had gone to Hatcliffe Extension, believed government promises that their stay there would be legalized and secure. The conditions at Caledonia Farm were reported to be appalling. By mid-July there were about 4,000 people there and a South African church delegation reported that "they could find no words to describe the shocking situation that confronted them" and that "people are dying" (swradio.com 2005).

Two months after OM began, in mid-July 2003, there began to be more reports, however, of displaced people who had been living on the streets, seeking to make their way to rural areas. As reported by the Jesuits in Mbare (Mbare Report 2005a):

> This week we start to transport people to their rural homes. Only those who really want to go. Some people say we should not do this, we were doing the dirty work for government. I think we have to do what the people ask us to do. Those who have no longer strong roots at home should not attempt to go.

There were also by this time reports of people being forced back to the urban areas as the predictions made by many that the communal areas were too short of food to sustain the urban–rural migrants proved disturbingly true. According to one newspaper report, "those with money have left for villages but many have no family to go to and the country's fuel shortage means buses are few and far between. Others have returned to Harare, claiming village chiefs are refusing to accept them because there is not enough food."[15]

Another report stated:

> Not all who escaped the chaos in Mbare to the rural areas have been lucky. A woman who has a history of being harassed as a opposition party supporter, who had her house burnt and was beaten up, came back from a remote area to look for food: there is nothing where she went; she has been feeding her family on vegetables only. (Mbare Report 2005b)

Conclusions

At the time of writing, in mid-July 2005, it was announced that OM had been ended, under pressure from the South African government, using the threat of withholding a U.S.$1 billion loan from the Zimbabwean government, which was desperately needed for fuel and food. Nonetheless only three days later more buildings were destroyed, this time an industrial and office block in the central Kopje area (Zim Online 2005). This happened even as the world awaited the UN special envoy's report on OM. During her visit the demolitions had continued and deaths had occurred at Porta Farm when people had been crushed by falling walls and a pregnant woman had died due to violent police action. Other such deaths also occurred but probably the final death toll from OM will be indirect and harder to measure because of significantly increased death rates among those evicted, due to cold and general lack of means to sustain themselves.

Zimbabwe's government also announced during the Operation that it was to embark on a major rebuilding program, named Operation Garikai (Rebuilding/Reconstruction), costing Z$3 trillion (U.S.$300,000), to address the housing backlog and the new needs caused by OM, and to provide new infrastructure for informal marketing and production. However, given the parlous state of the nation's finances, this was clearly largely meaningless. Its most likely purpose was a public relations exercise for international purposes and to some extent this seemed to work. The new program was impressed upon the UN envoy, whose report noted the need to mobilize international aid to support it, albeit simultaneously making some stringent criticisms of the plan and advising many improvements, based on UN Habitat's long experience in best practice in low-income housing, to which Garikai did not generally conform. There was some evidence that the building standards' obstacle to affordable legal housing for the urban poor might be addressed within Zimbabwe in that Chombo announced that new regulations would be devised, allowing house costs to be cut by 68 percent (Tibaijuka 2005).

The significance of the "illegality," on some grounds or another, of most of the housing and informal enterprises destroyed was evident in this report. First, this muted its tone and recommendations with respect to possible legal redress through international courts. Second, though the report called on the government to pay reparations to those who lost property illegally under OM—which would be most of those affected since there was a general failure to warn people in advance, for example—it recommended a UN Trust Fund be set up to compensate the mainly white commercial farmers who had lost their land, without payments, when the fast-track phase of land reform began in 2000. Whether either sets of compensation will ever become reality remains to be seen, but the property *rights* of the farmers were clearly being favored.

Urban "planning" operations such as Murambatsvina are not unique to Zimbabwe within Africa. As discussed in the introduction, there are disturbing similarities with Apartheid policies, but these are not sufficient to understand an attack on "informality" on the scale described here within an independent African nation. There have been sporadic drives against the informal sector in other African countries. A notorious example was Operation Production, in Mozambique in 1985, when urban people without the required identity cards were rounded up and airlifted to remote Niassa Province. Up to 50,000 were removed from Maputo. Many died due to the difficult conditions and lack of means of sustenance and livelihood in Niassa (Jenkins 2005). Low-level harassment of informal traders and parallel market operators has occurred in a vast array of cities, with the levels fluctuating according to various local political and economic factors. Nonetheless, as described over ten years ago for Zaire (now the DRC) by MacGaffey (1991), in many African cities the informal economy is the *real* economy. It does not contribute the most to GDP, but it keeps the cities "working." Similarly, unplanned housing has become so important in many cities that it seems inconceivable that it will be cleared away, given the current lack of alternatives.

The sheer scale and depth of the contemporary informal economy thus protects it to some extent. So how does this fit with what happened in Zimbabwe in mid-2005? There are many theories put forward to explain the government's sudden, astonishing, wholesale attack on informal housing and economic activities. Many of these can be largely dismissed on the basis that the advantages yielded to the government are insufficiently significant or long term to justify such an extraordinary degree of upheaval. For example, the idea that it was done to stamp out parallel market trading in foreign exchange and fuel scarcely holds as the amounts seized could make no possible long-term difference to the desperate shortages. Forex dealing will not stop but simply become less visible. Furthermore, although governments worldwide like to demonize petty dealers for cashing in on shortages in any such situation, in order to shift the blame, the underlying structural causes of the forex crisis in Zimbabwe (and thus the fuel crisis) are the general collapse of economic production, with GDP in 2004 estimated to be around U.S.$4.8 billion compared to U.S.$8.4 billion in 1997, and the country's cutoff from international loans and aid, as the government is well aware. There has been much demonizing too of the Chinese, with whom Zimbabwe has been building economic links, with rumors flying that vacated niches in the informal trading economy would be filled by Chinese beneficiaries. Again this makes little real sense—Zimbabwe is small beer for China, the informal sector was frequently trading in Chinese goods and thus benefiting China already (the formal manufacturing sector has been far more adversely affected by Chinese competition), and anyway none of these theories explain the main thrust of OM in the housing sector. The same theorizing is made in relation to ZANU (PF) supporters being given licenses to fill the new trading opportunities—though this makes more sense, as with so many theories about African politics and conflict it falls down as a fundamental *cause* of the policy, even if it is clearly a potentially convenient *outcome*. There are always people who benefit economically from wars, conflict, and the destruction of livelihoods—but it is often a mistake to conclude that their interests dictated that such conflicts should start.

More compelling are the arguments about the party political nature of OM—that it was a revenge attack by ZANU (PF) against the MDC, which dominates in the urban areas. Though real anger against, and a desire to punish, urban people because of their voting habits does seem to be an important element of the decision to embark on the immensely destructive campaign, it is felt that this alone is insufficient explanation. As already mentioned, OM was far too broad in its sweep to avoid affecting government supporters too.

There are two other key factors suggested here that have played a part. One has been spelt out in this chapter—a long-standing identification with planned, orderly, "modern" urbanity. As outlined by Bourdillon (1991: 2), "[i]n the post-colonial era, government and city council alike try to present Harare as a modern, well-governed capital city. Crowds of uncontrolled 'squatters' living under plastic spoil such an image. There is a natural tendency to continue the old policy, and to regard such people as a problem." Despite the relaxation of this stance somewhat during the 1990s and the first few years of the twenty-first century, the evidence is clear that this was more of an accommodation to new types of urban poverty than a true ideological shift toward long-term acceptance of urban informalization in Zimbabwe. This is not to say that the reluctant relaxation was not proof of some sort of political recognition of the needs of the urban poor at that time. However, within ZANU (PF), as evidenced by the stance of Ignatius Chombo, adherence to the ideology of planned and orderly cities remained a core belief for many. The shift to an operation such as Murambatsvina was thus not just a knee-jerk reflex to urban opposition, but needs to be understood against this ideological background. In a party full of unrighteous anger against its mainly poor urban electorate, it becomes more understandable how the views of those who always desired urban "order" could gain ground again, and become both more convincing and more attractive. Thus the campaign was characterized by comments such as those made by Harare's government-appointed Mayor Sekesai Makwavara who said in a statement, "[t]he attitude of the members of the public as well as some city officials has led to the point whereby Harare has lost its glow. We are determined to get it back." Arguably, the very fact that Zimbabwe was different from the rest of sub-Saharan Africa in that it had maintained, despite some policy changes in the 1990s and the very significant expansion of informal market trading, a *comparatively* "orderly" urban milieu, without large numbers of very extensive squatter or otherwise informal freestanding settlements, allowed the government to entertain the idea of "getting the glow back." In many cities an operation such as OM would be truly impossible, either politically or economically.[16]

The final major factor that, in combination with the points above, provides sufficient critical mass for a campaign on the vast scale of OM is urban food and fuel shortages. Up to the last elections in March 2005, the government somehow managed to maintain some supplies of both, albeit fluctuating and insufficient for demand, and even improved the situation just before the polls. Almost immediately after, it became clear that even this unsatisfactory situation was no longer possible and supplies plummeted.[17] The far-flung HDAs of Harare are impossible locations without transport; without maize the urban population will starve. In most African cities, including those in Zimbabwe until then, the major food problem since structural adjustment is not supply but *monetary demand*. There is usually food to buy if only people could afford it, although many cannot *afford* enough of the right sorts of food to remain healthy. This was essentially what was being measured by the urban vulnerability assessment in Zimbabwe in 2003. By mid-2005 there was increasing evidence that urban food *supply* itself was reaching a true crisis. In this situation a campaign that removes poor urban dwellers out of town and into the much less-visible countryside would seem politically attractive. The strong evidence that OM intended not only to "restore order" to the towns, but also to physically displace many people *from* the towns, then makes better sense. The Solidarity Peace Trust (2005) emphasizes that statements by the government, police, and Harare City Council officials were clear that the major intention of OM was to "displace the urban poor to rural areas." It is not here believed that the Zimbabwean government believed that urban people always have a rural home to go to or that the rural areas are food self-sufficient. They would have had to have been born and brought up somewhere else to believe this; it is merely justificatory rhetoric. The government's lack of concern for the people's welfare is now well established and sadly suggests that OM was partly "designed to simply shunt the most vulnerable people out of sight to die of hunger or the biting cold" (McGarry 2005).[18]

NOTES

1. On the question of urban agriculture, see "Urban Farming Burned," Herald, June 22, 2005. The rise of housing co-operatives in the 1990s as a means of accessing legal, low-income housing plots and their promotion by the government has been charted by Kamete (2001). After fast-track land reform began in 2000, some peri-urban farms were taken over and urban housing plots were sometimes then allocated to such cooperatives. Indeed, the "overriding motivation for land occupations and fast track in urban and peri-urban areas was the desire to access land for residential development" (Marongwe 2003: 22). Many of these cooperatives were associated with the war veterans who had spearheaded the occupations of commercial farms. They would normally be ZANU (PF) but could also be deeply critical of the government. An example was White Cliff Farm, where the settlement Tongogara Park (named after a famous liberation war leader) was demolished under OM. This farm formed part of a new urban constituency, Manyame, before the 2005 election and voted ZANU (PF). After OM, new stands were being pegged and reportedly allocated to the army and police (Solidarity Peace Trust 2005).
2. A massive transfer of state assets to private ownership occurred after 1980 when the government decided to transfer the rental township stock (representing the vast majority of housing available for urban Africans, apart from hostels) to those renting them. Legal rental occupation of 30 years meant the house was obtained for free; there was a sliding scale of affordable payment over a period for shorter previous rental terms.

3. This precise arrangement, built from breeze blocks, was built upon the plot belonging to one of my research assistants and friends, who lived in the front room of her father-in-law's Mbare house, with her husband and young son. Every other room in the main house was similarly occupied by related households, and the perimeter of the side and back of the plot contained an L-shaped row of rental rooms made of corrugated iron. The estimated occupancy rate of this plot, originally designed for one township family of, say, 6 people, was over 30 in 1994. The father-in-law lived in the communal areas.
4. In Harare the market sites demolished included the retail vegetable market; Mupedzanhamo, which was the main market for secondhand clothes and traditional medicines; and Siyaso, a site where hardware and building materials were sold (McGarry 2005).
5. ZAPU, the Zimbabwe African People's Union, was the other liberation movement party in Zimbabwe. It is associated with the Ndebele (and southern Zimbabwe/Matabeleland and Bulawayo), and ZANU (PF) with the Shona, although these simplifications hide a much more complex history and reality.
6. See "Harare to Demolish Illegal Outbuildings, over 500,000 to be made Homeless," *Herald*, March 10, 2001; "Harare Demolishes Illegal Tuckshops," *Herald*, March 14, 2001; "State to Stop Demolitions of Tuckshops," *Herald*, March 15, 2001; and "Callous move against Tuckshops Suspicious," *Daily News*, March 16, 2001.
7. This MDC paper, unsurprisingly, tried hard to both support the urban poor, and to castigate the central government. This required some convoluted logic whereby the demolitions were postulated to have been agreed by the central government, allowing it to step in and appear as the savior of the urban poor, thereby improving its urban support. However, the position taken was, more simply, consistent with the trend established during the 1990s. See "Callous move against Tuckshops Suspicious," *Daily News*, March 16, 2001.
8. The author is grateful to Kathryn Ewing for drawing her attention to the Harare Commission's attack on the informal sector in 2001. See also "State to Stop Demolition of Tuckshops," *Herald*, March 15, 2001.
9. See "State, Council to Consult over Illegal Structures," *Herald*, March 16, 2001.
10. An architect working in Latin America, John Turner's name is associated with a shift in urban planning circles to recognition of the potentially positive contribution of "informal" housing, which could become decent, "consolidated" shelter if secure tenure was allowed, encouraging greater investment by the inhabitants.
11. Television pictures of such "permanent" structures being demolished shocked many people outside Zimbabwe, as was evident from the focus on this aspect from media reports on OM. An interesting, if unstated, attitude appeared to be that removing flimsier houses would have been understandable, despite the fact that people living in both types of housing are entitled to shelter and livelihoods.
12. See "Mugabe Policy Branded 'New aparthcid,'" *Sunday Times* (UK), June 12, 2005.
13. In Zambia's Copperbelt Province in 2000, the proportion born within the Province, the vast majority of whom would have been born in town, was 78 percent (Potts 2005a).
14. The significance of the terminology is evident. Nonetheless even sympathetic reports emphasizing that not all urban people, in the twenty-first century, still have rural roots, can fall into the trap, as evidenced by the authoritative STP report on OM, which stated: "Tens of thousands of people being displaced in urban areas have

had to comply with the Government's declared intention of the exercise, and return to rural areas."

15. See "Zimbabwe: Priests Told, 'Don't Aid Filth,' " *Sunday Times* (UK), June 19, 2005.
16. The UN envoy's report, for example, detailed a number of other recent demolitions of squatter housing in sub-Saharan African cities, particularly in Nigeria where 30,000 households (probably about 150,000 people) are estimated to have been evicted in various towns in 2004 (Tibaijuka 2005). However, Nigeria's population is well over ten times Zimbabwe's, so the proportionate impact on the total population would be minute in comparison (i.e., representing less than 0.2% of the total Nigerian population). Small-scale evictions in Kibera, Africa's largest squatter settlement in Nairobi, in 2004 were halted by the president.
17. See "Fuel Crisis Thrusts Zim into Despair," *Zimbabwe* Independent, July 1, 2005 <http://allafrica. com/stories/200507050217.html>.
18. See S. Njanji, "Zimbabwe Demolition Well Planned—Mugabe," *Agence France Presse*, June 30, 2005 [accessed from http://iafrica.com/news/specialreport/ zimbabwe/456439.htm].

REFERENCES

Andersson, A. 2002. *The Bright Lights Grow Fainter: Livelihoods, Migration and a Small Town in Zimbabwe.* Stockholm: Department of Geography, Stockholm University; Almqvist & Wiksell International.

Bourdillon, M. 1991. *Poor, Harassed but Very Much Alive: An Account of Street People and Their Organizations.* Gweru, Zimbabwe: Mambo Press.

Dewar, N. 1991. "Harare," in A. Lemon (ed.). *Homes Apart: South Africa's Segregated Cities.* London: Paul Chapman.

Dixon, N. 2005. "Zimbabwe: Mugabe's Terror Campaign against Workers, Urban Poor," *Green Left Weekly*, June 8 <http://www.greenleft.org.au/back/2005/629/629p20.htm>.

Drakakis-Smith, D., T. Bowyer-Bower, and D. Tevera. 1995. "Urban Poverty and Urban Agriculture in Harare: An Overview of the Linkages," *Habitat International* 19 (2): 183–193.

Ferguson, J. 1999. *Expectations of Modernity: Myths and Meanings of Urban Life on the Zambian Copperbelt.* Berkeley and Los Angeles: University of California Press.

Habitat International. 2005. Habitat International Coalition Housing and Land Rights Network Urgent Action Appeal: 200,000 People Evicted in Two Weeks and another Million Threatened in Zimbabwe: Case ZIM100605 [Action Appeal launched June 2005].

Jenkins, P. 2005. "Image of the City in Mozambique: Civilization, Parasite, Engine of Growth or Place of Opportunity?" in D. Bryceson and D. Potts. *African Urban Economies: Viability, Vitality or Vitiation of Major Cities in East and Southern Africa?* New York: Palgrave, pp. 107–130.

Kamete, A. 1999. "Restructure Control of High Density Housing in Zimbabwe: Deregulation, challenges and complications for Urban Design," *Housing Theory, and Society* 16 (3): 136–151.

Kamete, A. 2001a. "Civil Society, Housing and Urban Governance: The Case of Urban Housing Co-Operatives in Zimbabwe," in A. Tostensen, I. Tvedten, and M. Vaa (eds.). *Associational Life in African Cities: Popular Responses to the Urban Crisis.* Uppsala, Sweden: Nordiska Afrikainstitutet, pp. 162–179.

Kanji, N. 1995. "Gender, Poverty and Structural Adjustment in Harare, Zimbabwe," *Environment and Urbanization* 7 (1): 37–55.

MacGaffey, J. 1991. *The Real Economy of Zaire: The Contribution of Smuggling and Other Unofficial Activities to National Wealth*. London: James Currey.

Manangazira, T. 2005. "Update on Operation Murambatsvina, Epsworth," *New Hope Zimbabwe*, July 7 <http://www.sarpn.org.za/documents/d0001377/index.php>.

Marongwe, N. 2003. "The Fast Track Resettlement and Urban Development Nexus: The Case for Harare." Paper presented at the Symposium on Delivering Land and Securing Rural Livelihoods: Post Independence Land Reform and Resettlement in Zimbabwe. Mont Clair, Nyanga, Zimbabwe, March 26–28.

Mbare Report. 2005a. "Discarded People," *Mbare Report* 12, June 27.

Mbare Report. 2005b. "We Cannot Live without Truth," *Mbare Report* 15, July 13.

McGarry, B. 2005. "Wreckage of the Tsunami" <mandebusvnews@yahoogroups. com> June 30.

Mupedziswa. R. and P. Gumbo. 1998. *Structural Adjustment and Women Informal Sector Traders in Harare, Zimbabwe*. Uppsala, Sweden: Nordiska Afrikainstitutet.

Mutizwa-Mangiza, N. 1985. "Post-Independence Urban Low-Income Shelter Policies in Zimbabwe: A Preliminary Appraisal of Affordability." Paper presented at Third World Planning Seminar, University of Wales.

Myers, G. 2003. *Verandahs of Power: Colonialism and Space in Urban Africa*. Syracuse, NY: Syracuse University Press.

Nyamvura, T. 2001. "Hatcliffe Extension (Holding Camp): A Case for Integrated Development Planning: Brief for Field Trip." Unpublished paper. University of Zimbabwe.

Pennant, T. 1990. "The Growth of Small-Scale Renting in Low-Income Urban Housing in Malawi," in P. Amis and P. Lloyd (eds.). *Housing Africa's Urban Poor*. Manchester: Manchester University Press.

Potts, D. 1989. "Urban Environmental Control in Southern Africa with Special Reference to Lilongwe," *Resource Management and Optimization* 6 (4): 321–334.

Potts, D. 1994. "Urban Environmental Controls and Low-Income Housing in Southern Africa," in H. Main and S. Williams (eds.). *Environment and Housing in Third World Cities*. Chichester: John Wiley, pp. 207–223.

Potts, D. 1997. "Urban Lives: Adopting New Strategies and Adapting Rural Links," in C. Rakodi (ed.). *The Urban Challenge in Africa: Growth and Management of Its Large Cities*. Tokyo: United Nations University Press, pp. 447–494.

Potts, D. 1998. "Housing Policies in Southern Africa [Politiques du logement en Afrique australe]," in P. Gervais-Lambony, S. Jaglin, and A. Mabin (eds.). *La Question Urbaine en Afrique Australe: Perspectives de Recherches*. Paris: Karthala, pp. 185–213.

Potts, D. 2000. "Urban Unemployment and Migrants in Africa: Evidence from Harare, 1985–94," *Development and Change* 31 (4): 879–910.

Potts, D. 2005a. "Counter-Urbanization on the Zambian Copperbelt? Interpretations and Implications," *Urban Studies* 42 (4): 583–609.

Potts, D. 2005b. "Urban Growth and Urban Economies in Eastern and Southern Africa: Trends and Prospects," in D. Bryceson and D. Potts (eds.). *African Urban Economies: Viability, Vitality or Vitiation?* New York: Palgrave, pp. 67–106.

Potts, D. 2006. "All My Hopes and Dreams Are Shattered": Urbanization and Migrancy in an Imploding Economy—Zimbabwe in the Twenty-First Century," *Geoforum* 37 (4) (July): 536–551.

Potts, D. and C. C. Mutambirwa. 1990. "Rural-Urban Linkages in Contemporary Harare: Why Migrants Need Their Land," *Journal of Southern African Studies* 16 (4): 676–696.

Potts, D. and C. C. Mutambirwa. 1991. "High-Density Housing in Harare: Commodification and Overcrowding," *Third World Planning Review* 13 (1): 1–26.

Potts, D. and C. C. Mutambirwa. 1998. "Basics Are now a Luxury: Perceptions of ESAP's Impact on Rural and Urban Areas in Zimbabwe," *Environment and Urbanization*, 10 (1): 55–76.

Rakodi, C. 1994. "Urban Poverty in Zimbabwe: Post-Independence Efforts, Household Strategies and the Short-Term Impact of Structural Adjustment," *Journal of International Development* 6 (5): 656–663.

Rakodi, C. 1995. *Harare: Inheriting a Settler-Colonial City: Change or Continuity?* Chichester: John Wiley.

Schlyter, A. 2005. "Esther's house: one woman's 'home economics'" in Chitungwiza, Zimbabwe, in D. Bryceson and D. Potts (eds.), *African Urban Economies: Viability, Vitality or Vitiation of Major Cities in East and Southern Africa?* New York: Palgrave, pp. 254–277.

Smith, R. 2004. Personal communication. November 18.

Solidarity Peace Trust. 2005. "Discarding the Filth: Operation Murambatsvina: Interim Report on the Zimbabwean Government's Urban Cleansing and Forced Eviction Campaign," May/June 2005.

swradioafrica.com. 2005. "SA Cardinal Says Mugabe's Conduct in Zimbabwe Undermining the Whole of Africa," July 15 <http://www.swradioafrica.com/news150705/cardinal150705.htm>.

Teedon, P. and D. Drakakis-Smith. 1986. "Urbanization and Socialism in Zimbabwe: The Case of Low-Cost Housing," *Geoforum* 17 (2): 309–324.

Tevera, D. 1995. "The Medicine that Might Kill the Patient: Structural Adjustment and Urban Poverty in Zimbabwe," in D. Simon, W. v. Spengen, C. Dixon, and A. Närman (eds.). *Structurally Adjusted Africa: Poverty, Debt and Basic Needs.* London and Boulder: Pluto Press.

Tibaijuka, A. 2005. "Report of the Fact-Finding Mission to Zimbabwe to Assess the Scope and Impact of Operation Murambatsvina by the UN Special Envoy on Human Settlements Issues in Zimbabwe" <http://www.un.org/News/dh/ infocus/zimbabwe/zimbabwe_rpt.pdf>.

Zim Online. 2005. "Harare presses on with demolitions," July 19 <http:// www.zimbabwesituation.com/jul19a_2005.html>.

Zimbabwe Human Rights NGO Forum. 2004. "Political Violence Report," September 2004 <http://www.hrforumzim.com/monthly/september_04.htm>.

Zimbabwe Human Rights NGO Forum. 2005. "Order out of Chaos, or Chaos out of Order? A Preliminary Report on Operation Murambatsvina," June 2005.

Zimbabwe National Vulnerability Assessment Committee (ZNVAC) (in collaboration with the SADC FANR Vulnerability Assessment Committee). 2004. "Zimbabwe: Urban Areas Food Security and Vulnerability Assessment." September 2003, Harare, Urban Report no. 1 (www.reliefweb.int/library/documents/2003/govzim-zim-30sep.pdf).

13

Social Control and Social Welfare under Neoliberalism in South African Cities: Contradictions in Free Basic Water Services

Greg Ruiters

> The organization of social relations demands mapping so that people know their place . . . the power to map the world in one way or another is a crucial tool in political struggles.
>
> (Harvey 1996: 112)

> The party leaders behave like common sergeant majors, frequently reminding the people of the need for "silence in the ranks." This party that used to call itself the servant of the people's will, as soon as the colonial power puts the country into its control, hastens to send the people back to their caves.
>
> (Fanon 1967: 183)

Introduction

Urban services have been a central concern in recent writings about the future of Africa's fast growing city populations (Davis 2004; UN 2003). Among the sub-Saharan Africa population, only 24 percent have in-house water; 36 percent have no access to safe water; only 5 percent have access to the electricity network. There is a common misconception that water access is not as much an urban issue but primarily a rural one. Yet, using an expanded definition of "lack of access" up to 50 percent of the urban population lack adequate water supplies, and 60 percent lack adequate sanitation (UN 2003). Contrary to official statistics, sub-Saharan Africa's urban population probably has the world's worst provision of water and sanitation services. In Accra, in early 1990, only 35 percent had piped water in their houses, and in Addis Ababa, 30 percent used open fields as toilets. Half of Nairobi's three million residents access water from standpipe vendors; 70 percent are not connected to the city's network.[1] In recent times, South Africa has served as a model for Africa. More advanced in physical and social infrastructure than most on the continent, South Africa's state-funded provision of infrastructure, and since 2001, free basic services, have mitigated the absolute forms of service inequalities. The ANC government has pioneered new techniques of service delivery linked to managing resources and people. New "smart" technologies in prepaid water and electricity meters, flow limiters, and free *basic* water (FBW) have made South Africa a "pioneer," one that was also more than willing to export its innovative forms of delivering services to the poor. FBW was meant to speed up social development, to "alleviate poverty, improve community health and free women from drudgery" (DWAF 2001). By 2002, the state claimed that 59 percent of the population of 43 million were receiving FBW (25 liters per person per day, or pppd), and that cut-offs would no longer happen, although the state's claims have been vigorously disputed (Greenberg 2005). Hemson and Owusu-Ampomah (2005) argue, "while there has been progress in life-sustaining services" this has been offset by rising unemployment, falling earnings and "generally by real difficulties in, ensuring the continuation of services over time."[2]

This essay does *not* seek to evaluate whether the overall standard of living of the urban poor has improved. Instead, this chapter explores three themes: the political ambiguities of progress in social welfare in post-Apartheid South Africa, using FBW as a lens in the context of the state trying to maintain the rule of law and consolidate urban "governability." The second focus is to identify who are the objects of social welfare/control, and what are the various strategic-political techniques that have emerged in social programs such as FBW, and how these are resisted. A third aim is to explore how welfare concessions relate to the ruling party's strong commitment to capitalist social norms.

FBW, although having noble aims, needs to be situated within broad social control perspectives[3] and the ANC's problems in constituting the state in urban areas, particularly the black townships.[4] Specifically, I argue FBW has been designed to extend the state's control over municipal resources and over different target populations. The intended and unintended effects of state policies and their real outcomes need to be distinguished (Ferguson 1990; Scott 1998). Social control often fails and it conjures up the wrong image of the state as a singular, omnipotent, and coherent actor (Migdal 2001). The reality is more complex. Probing beyond the stated intentions also captures the variability and tactical character of social welfare/control within a single country and *within different cities.* The *local state* (and its quasi-private proxies) plays a special role in social management: for being closest to "the people" they have to negotiate and strategize in a tactical interplay between social movements and other local forces.

I begin with a background to contemporary urban social and water issues in neoliberal contexts. Then we look at the South African water policy since 1994. The bulk of what follows in this essay is organized under the following themes in social control: Partitioning and separating the "can" and "can't pays;" right-sizing via a discriminatory infrastructures and planning for poor areas; control of popular illegalities and revanchist local management; welfare as social re-education in responsible water usage, customer identity and household budgeting; and finally the massive use prepayment technology as "self-disconnections."

SOCIAL CONTROL UNDER URBAN NEOLIBERALISM

> To stabilise neoliberalism, intervention at the urban scale is . . . essential, because this is where neoliberalism has its most significant economic, political and social impacts on everyday life.
>
> (Jessop 2002: 470)

At the Third World Forum on Water, South Africa was hailed as a country "pioneering" free water and basic sanitation.[5] Very few countries today have FBW. The trade unions and social movements welcomed free basic water as a step toward meeting the social demands of the national democratic struggle. Left critics like Patrick Bond (2002: 238–239), for example, have argued, "the effort was genuine, but it was not backed up by thoughtful, detailed provisions." Bond points to flaws in FBW: the state should have made bigger amounts free on a per capita, not on a household basis (about 50 liters per person per day, available on site, not at communal taps). The Left believe the state has merely "tweaked" neoliberalism, whereas mainstream scholars accept the South African state as fundamentally "developmental" and "solidly pro-poor," even if it has serious capacity problems and there is inadequate participation from civil society (Beall et al. 2000: 119; Laurence 2004).

On the other hand with FBW, and increased grants, alarmists suggested that South Africa was becoming an unsustainable welfare state.[6] Some pro-market analysts argue that people should get jobs first before services. According to John Kane Berman, people should not "be provided with services they cannot afford, or which they can no longer afford."[7] Telkom, for example, blames unemployment as the reason for 2.09 million disconnections that outnumbered its 1.97 million—a net line shrinkage. In South Africa, pro-poor policies are explained by the state as a necessary part of increasing social citizenship and democracy, but the state needs to be aware of the risk of a "dependency" syndrome and paternalism (Mbeki 2004). Giving in to "populist" demands is a cheap form of politics that is unsustainable because it will encourage the poor to make more demands on an "overburdened" and overstretched welfare state, resulting in an "inappropriate politicization" of services and unfulfilled expectations leading to a legitimacy crisis and ungovernability (see Offe 1983: 67–69 for general exposition of these themes; see Mbeki 2004 for an ANC version of this argument).

The neoliberal track is to market services and reduce expectations and claims on the state. But less explored in this literature is a basic "tension" in social wel fare between the state's caring role and social control. Efforts to help the poor may be entangled, if not compromised, by efforts to control claimants and their behavior (Ferguson 1990). The state also imposes concepts of needs, and "resources" creating struggles with communities about what these are and whose standards of needs and justice are being used (Harvey 1996: 147). A stress on defining the "needy" and weeding out unworthy or fraudulent recipients deeply affects the way welfare is experienced by recipients and perceived by the public at large (Walker 1993: 146–147).

Less generous is a view that sees welfare as social control, as a quid pro quo for social peace, as co-opting social movements, as insurance for the safety of the rich, as a way of cementing social inequality, and as a method for expanding state legitimacy and the state's reach (Elster 1988; Painter 1995; Piven and Cloward 1977). In South Africa, new social movements have criticized welfare for its strict requirements, the need to prove poverty and eligibility and means testing. The Left has also noted that certain welfare regimes often require, implicitly perhaps, a "submissive recognition" by claimants of the superior morality of the capitalist order that created these needs (see Desai 2002; Offe 1983: 154–156). The welfare dispensed by the state becomes an "exchange transaction" that harms the politico-ideological dignity of claimants. Curiously these arguments are harnessed by both the Right and the Left although for different ends.

However, detailed studies of different welfare systems paint a more complex picture. Social welfare often is addressed to "women's issues" making it especially germane to the position of women in society. Welfare benefits the middle class disproportionately, where there is higher uptake; the redistribution of income and cross-subsidies that help to fund welfare are often *within* the working class. Implementing and administering welfare can be complex and expensive, and welfare regimes (conservative, liberal, social democratic) differ considerably (Esping-Anderson 1990).[8]

A vital geographical perspective of social control as "spatio-temporal ordering" is explored by David Harvey (1996: 230). "The fixing of spatiality through material building creates solidly constructed spaces that instantiate negotiated or imposed social values." Spatial stigmatization and spatial control of unwanted groups (vagrants, homeless, the poor) constitute a normative ordering of the urban landscape. But state welfare and social infrastructure are as much about constructing needs of the poor as they are about keeping people "in place" (Harvey 1996). Critical geographers stress a socio-spatial dialectic driven by capitalist uneven development that helps to situate welfare as part of the built environment of class reproduction. Housing, sidewalks, water supply are social infrastructures that define residential property markets and place. As Harvey (1996: 312) argues, "Place functions as a closed terrain of social control that becomes extremely hard to break (or break out of) once it achieves a particular permanence."

Social control is not an end in itself for it functions within a particular regime of accumulation. Neoliberal states follow macro-policies that seek to attract global capital, they aim to sell off state assets and outsource or market services and introduce ostensibly cheaper, more businesslike organizational forms in the public domain (Jessop 2002: 454). One result of this shift is a more direct focus on production and finance capital at the expense of social reproduction. The other is increasing social marginality, and increased fear of the "dangerous classes" intensifies state authoritarianism. For Smith (2002), with the neglect of social reproduction comes greater "activism" in social control.

Neoliberalism's accumulation regime also has an internal focus that seeks to redraw the boundaries of state–society relationships, putting individual responsibility and ownership at the center. Looking to create a new social order, with the market a form of sociality, of morality, and civilization, disciplinary neoliberalism (Gill 2003: 120) has had a micro-focus on individuals.[9] Moreover, the downloading of social reproduction functions onto women has become a defining feature, despite official anti-sexism (Deakin and Walsh 1996; Wolch and Dear 1989). Customer charters define new "enabling" rights and procedures that "aimed" to dislodge notions of entitlement; buyers and sellers are cast as bargain-seeking antagonists (Dean 1991: 18). Power in market society is "not enforced in an immediate fashion" or with extra-economic coercion, or bureaucratic rules, but through the free will (see Arthur 1978: 17). Market subjects do not, however, arise within the confines of institutions (schools, prisons, factories—the locus of Foucault's disciplinary subjects) but in the arena of free will, of choice (see Bagguley 1994: 88). These then are the ambitions of neoliberalism as social control, but renamed "governance."

Finally, it is vital also to stress as Jessop does that neoliberalism is a project and has often been accorded far more coherence and success than is warranted (Forrest 1991; Jessop 2002). Neoliberalism, as a political project, has had to fight for its own successes (Jessop 2002: 467). "Its success depends on promoting new ways of representing the world, new subjectivities that establish the legitimacy of the market economy, the disciplinary state and enterprise culture" (Jessop 2002: 470). Most analysts now agree that neoliberalism's claims are largely rhetorical, its freedoms illusory, its successes mixed. The question of "success," however, requires detailed examination of practices, techniques developed in the concrete conditions and various popular reactions to it.[10] Self-evident failures of neoliberal urban governance, however, can be seen in the corrosion of civic values and altruism, the emerging crisis of urban control (Harvey 2004; Jessop 2002: 458; Taylor-Gooby 2000), and the rise of anti-neoliberal social movements. Eviscerated citizenship erodes people's sense of obligation to the state. In Third World countries, the social devastation of structural adjustment resulted in large-scale informalization, illegality, economic insecurity (Jega 2000: 24; Osaghae 2001).

In South Africa, neoliberalism has been contradictory, experimental; it was arguably not the "organic" ideology of the mass of ANC members, but rather more compatible with the ideology of South Africa's liberals.[11] As it unfolded in practice it was hybridized to fit into national liberation discourse. It sought a popular resonance by claiming the market as a sphere of nondiscrimination and equal treatment. Social control took both subtle form—market culture—and also an explicit infrastructural form, to which we now turn.

Urban Water in South Africa since 1994: From Generalized Cut-Offs to "Humane" FBW

The newly liberated South Africa inherited a backlog of 14 million people without safe water and 21 million people without access to toilets. The new constitution (Section 27: 1) uniquely makes access to "sufficient water" a constitutional right and makes municipalities responsible for water services. The Reconstruction and Development Program (RDP), the ANC's popular manifesto for the first democratic election, promised access to water within 200 meters of a person's dwelling. But this was understood as the state covering capital costs only. People would still pay for water (even from standpipes).

The apogee of neoliberal influence in local government services arrived with the 1998 White Paper.[12] "engineering services are better provided by public–private partnerships. This would free municipalities to focus on integrating the activities of different service providers . . . To do this we need . . . government structures that are customer orientated." The 1998 White Paper warned of tough measures: "Where residents fail to meet their obligations in terms of service payments and rates, they will be cut off and prosecuted. Only in this way can we build a local democracy that works."[13] Between 1998 and 2000 the local state did indeed implement confrontational "credit control" measures. By its own figures, millions of families had water cut-offs (McDonald and Pape 2002; DPLG 2002) nullifying to some extent the boast of rolling out services. By 2000, threats to law and order through illegal reconnections (theft of water and electricity) were managed by the state often using private security companies to whom law and order actions such as cutting water, removing infrastructure, and carrying out evictions were outsourced. At this time of turmoil, social movements sprang up in big cities (Johannesburg, Durban, and Cape Town).

But in December 2000 in South Africa, after six years of unsuccessful cost recovery in urban services, and just before municipal elections, the South African government backed down from its hardnosed neoliberal scheme. Mbeki announced that government was giving all households a free ration of basic services (starting with free basic water and then electricity and sanitation). Those using more than the basic amount (six kiloliters of water per month) would pay more. Cholera outbreaks, worsening consumer nonpayment, rising economic hardship, fears of political disaffection, and widespread illegal connections were aspects of turmoil that explain the decision. Clearly, the state was afraid of losing its grip on the population and concessions had to be made. The adoption of FBW can be seen as a recognition that the blunt cost-recovery track had proved socially and politically unworkable (DoF 2003) and a shift to a skeletal welfare system was needed. As Hart (2005) puts it, Mbeki's shift should be seen as

> part of an effort to contain the pressures emanating from the rise of oppositional movements protesting the inadequacies of service provision, the snail's pace of land redistribution, failures to provide anti-retrovirals, and the absence of secure jobs-as well as pressures from within the Alliance . . . What is significant about this discourse is the way it defines a segment of society that is superfluous to the "modern" economy, and in need of paternal guidance . . . they are deserving of a modicum of social security, but on tightly disciplined and conditional terms.

First devised in Durban in 1996, FBW was adopted as a simpler, pragmatic route to deal with the poor. Here we cite the state's justification for extending the Durban "model" of FBW:

> The City of Durban has taken the logical—and socially just and equitable step—of making the first lifeline amount of water (6 000 liters per household per month) free-of-charge. Thereafter, the more you use, the more you pay. This constitutes a significant saving in administrative and postage costs. It is a win-win situation for all. . . . In poor rural areas, . . . we can simply provide water supplies without charging for them which will be undoubtedly simpler. For this to be effective will require

> only discipline to avoid waste at taps and to prevent unauthorized and unmetered connections to the system. (DWAF 2000)

Six kiloliters of water just about equaled the administrative costs of billing (R7.00 or $1.00 at the time). FBW became a channel for achieving several goals at once: formalizing a specific state–society interaction, improving controls over resources, regulating the poor, and creating a culture of payment among the urban poor. Thus FBW looked like a quick "win-win" for the state. But much would depend on how ordinary people would respond to the conditions attached to FBW.

Of special interest are the administrative, financial, and legal *conditions* attached to FBW. The FBW policy stipulated a free monthly supply of at least six kiloliters of water per property (not family). Unmetered communal standpipe supply in informal settlements was free (distance and drudgery instead of meters imposed limits and discipline users). Households with in-house taps had to be metered and desist from meter tampering in order to get the free water ration. Urban households had to pay for any extra water used over the six-kiloliter limit. Illegal connections disqualified the household, and failure to pay incurred being moved onto a restricted service, instead of total cut-off (as in previous years). Residents could also request a prepaid meter. In many big cities residents on the network were not charged for the first six kiloliter, favoring smaller middle-class households compared to multiple families on single plots in townships. Some urban households without metered supply (e.g., Soweto) could *not* get free water because they were still billed on a flat rate basis (i.e., "deemed" consumption). As from 2004, to get free water, Sowetans had to get a prepaid meter.

In September 2003, the Strategic Framework for Water Services document, adopted by Cabinet fearing that FBW would be misunderstood as free water in general warned that: "with the right to free basic water, comes responsibility to pay for services over and above the basic service." The document reflected a duality: "prices of water and sanitation services reflect the fact that they are both social and economic goods."[14]

FBW in Durban: A "Partitioning" Strategy Creating Controllable Populations

Foucault noted that "discipline proceeds from the distribution of individuals in space." "The art of distributions of populations" he goes on to say, requires "partitioning"—techniques inherent in the spatial organization of barracks, schools, walled towns, and the factory—which have as their aim the prevention of "dangerous coagulation" (Foucault 1995: 141–143). How might these insights fit with FBW? Included in the state's reform package, as we have seen, was the creation of new categories of consumers, separated as the "can't pays" and the won't pays. The can't pays were the households with under R1, 500 per month incomes; they would receive enough free water to sustain "basic" life. This ration would be supplied through a prepaid meter, or standpipe or a reduced flow service (e.g., yard tanks or flow-limiters). Prepaid consumers got six kiloliters per month free, but would have to purchase prepaid units for additional water or face an automatic shutoff. Harsher cost recovery and disconnections would be reserved only for the can-pays.

We need to note that in 2001, after FBW was announced it was explicitly rebaptized as a "strategy" and as "an innovative approach to enable us to separate the can't pays from the won't pays" (Muller 2001: 14). Two years later, Director General of Water Muller again clarified: "While the free basic water policy is heresy in some circles, its implementation is already helping to promote good financial management in local government. The distinction between the 'can't pays' and the 'won't pays' is clarified and 'free-riders' with higher than basic levels of service more easily identified" (Muller 2003). Municipalities improved their statistics developing detailed knowledges of different subject populations (e.g., can and can't pays). Registers of can't pays or indigents and means tests administered by well-paid consultants, ward committees, and councilors have become a big part of good management.

In 2003, the state also called for credit control to be exercised with compassion in face of highly publicized public criticisms of frequent, arbitrary cut-offs. Moreover the state sought to prevent problems. "Policies and procedures should seek to avoid the accumulation of bad debts and high costs associated with restrictions or disconnections and reconnections" (see DWAF 2003: 37). The water minister, Kasrils, insisted against councils that were cutting off residential water:

> Users (are) entitled to their quota regardless of the state of their accounts. In no way have we ever indicated that [they can cut water supply] . . . But my hands are tied because I do not have the powers to enforce that, given the constitutional provisions on the role of local government.[15]

Local policy became focused on giving the poor their free water rations, and then capping it so they would not get themselves into debt. They would be restricted by infrastructural means: washers inserted into yard taps that allowed six kiloliters to drip out (for graphic descriptions of tricklers, see Loftus 2005: 194) or by the prepaid meter. As Neil Macleod, Durban's water manager, explained:

> People who feel they are unable to pay us what they owe may agree to the installation of a device which will limit the water supply to 6,000 liters every 30 days. Then the amount owed will be frozen and no further interest will be charged on this amount. The device is removed only to allow a normal supply of water, if the amount outstanding is paid in full, plus R100 to cover the cost of removing the device.[16]

"Rightsizing" in this way was not confined to Durban. In Queenstown, "after disconnecting some residents up to three consecutive times, the municipality has had to resort to removing infrastructure and cables."[17] In Cape Town, entire streets were reduced to using communal water standpipes.[18] A danger of Macleod's restrictors is both that they became generalized and there was a quick move from voluntary to coerced "choice" of restrictors. By 2004–2005 a more aggressive stance to promoting drips developed. For example, the municipality's Water Department in 2005 deployed community service agents to go to households rather than wait for them to visit council offices. These agents:

> Educate people about paying for water. Agents in 20 prioritized wards discussed errant customer's statements urging them to pay up or choose one of several options available to them. The community service agents are managed by an external company, but are controlled by council. Poor customers who have no hope of paying their debts are helped by the fitting of flow limiters, which allow for a lifeline water supply only, and their debts are frozen.[19]

In the South African water (un)governability context, installing the right level of infrastructure for the right socioeconomic class of people has been partly legitimized as "sustainable" service delivery.[20] For many this approach seems reasonable. But the danger, as I have hinted earlier, is that a FBW trap emerges: without the cash to have the device removed, households may be trapped by the tariff structure and by flow-limiters in the six-kiloliter-per-month group (much like Third World countries in a debt trap). "Basic" supply bears little resemblance to actual consumption in most black townships and poor areas of well over 20 kiloliter per month[21] and would require households to actively lower their living standards. As a consumer in Harrismith, a small Free State town, put it:

> Water is a necessity. Really we try and save water and use as little as possible. But with seven people in the house, it's not easy to cope with what we get. We often run short. And this thing (the trickler) plays havoc with the sewerage. It takes long for the toilet to fill up. So if someone uses the toilet, you will have to wait for very long before it can be used again. What is the sense of having this (infrastructure) when you can't use it when you need it?[22]

A councilor from the Harrismith area has criticized the "tricklers" saying that they "should only be used for those people who can afford to pay for water but who don't. What purpose does it serve when applied to poor people, apart from just giving them less water?" Harrismith has an 80 percent indigence rate in its two townships; 75 percent of indigents do not pay when billed for services.[23]

Basic water, to the extent that it is targeted via service levels (i.e., provided through communal taps, restrictors, etc.) reinscribes the differentiated services on a spatial basis—a haunting similarity with Apartheid and an outcome not necessarily intended by policymakers. Instead of squeezing the poor for payment, FBW is a pragmatic recognition that maintaining the "surplus" population at bare levels of existence is better than allowing them to become a bigger political problem. This is ultimately the real meaning of "sustainability."

FBW Reinforcing the Morality of Payment as a Strategy for Cost Recovery

The water director general forthrightly stated that free basic water was the state's cost recovery strategy. This was repeated in the 2003 Strategic

Framework Paper, approved by Cabinet:

> The adoption of free basic water policy has not negated . . . the principle of user pays. On the contrary, the free basic water policy strengthens the principle in that it clearly requires consumption in excess of the free water supply service to be paid for . . . . (DWAF 2003: 29)

As the department of finance put it, "Once municipalities are able to *target* poor households, they will be free to pursue more vigorously higher income households and businesses refusing to pay" (DoF 2003: 44). Free basic services strategy therefore would allow the state to concentrate on improving billing and cost-recovery in middle-class areas and among the working poor who could be forced to pay.

Stressing the cost-recovery aspect above other aspects, the authoritative department of finance suggested: "To make it (FBW) work only the really proven poor should get these while anyone else should be forced to pay even at higher tariffs" (DoF 2001: 132). However, the water minister stressed (even though his hands were tied):

> In the first instance, and after following due process, domestic water connections must first be restricted and not disconnected, ensuring that at least a basic supply of water is available. Domestic consumers may only be disconnected if the system is tampered with or the integrity of the system and therefore public health is compromised.

Thus, FBW gave the state room to pursue other punitive strategies directed at the poor (such as prepaid meters, restricted service, or full cut-offs of those who were stealing services). The state argued, "competing pressures exist on local government to both extend basic services coverage to the poor and keep up high quality services to the 'non-poor' the economic base of a municipality (and) declining service is likely to undermine both local economic development and payment morality" (DoF 2001: 124). Disconnections have continued especially for those in big cities, deemed to be can pays. According to the government, in the *three* largest metros, about 53,400 (17,800 a month) households were disconnected in the *first three months* of 2003.[24]

However, the big problem was that poor urban households needed much more than six kiloliters, as was later recognized. "There is some evidence to suggest that poor households using more than 6 kl per month are adversely affected due to the steep increase in tariffs after the free 6 kl" (DoF 2003: 222).

The consequence of this is best appreciated by looking at tariff structures that have changed. After FBW, most urban municipalities shifted to stepped-up tariffs to recover the cost of providing free water (Still 2001: 17). In Durban, once households used above the free limit, an extra fixed charge (R29 per month) was levied plus volume charges. Johannesburg similarly charged R5.81 per kiloliter in the 20–40 kiloliter range (compared to R2.49 per kiloliter in the 7–10 kiloliter range) but without fixed charges as in Durban (DoF 2003: 223). The 20–30 kiloliter is acknowledged as the average for black townships (DoF 2003). The Durban municipality also accepted that most "normal" households were expected to use 30 kiloliter per month, or just over R200 ($30) per month.[25] The implication is that the poor and low-income working households were not deemed normal consumers and would have to be approached differently.

"Some for All": How Much Is Enough? Johannesburg's Education Campaign on Needs

The state set the tone by arguing that "while government can provide 'some for all' we cannot provide unlimited supplies. We understand that 6,000 liters per month is less than many people aspire to" (Kasrils 2003). The United States, on the other hand, regards 6,000 gallons a month as a minimum lifeline amount. Inevitably, a key issue that affected FBW's credibility would be whether six kiloliter was enough.[26] By making water expensive at the 7–30 kiloliter consumption tier, the local state has tried to force the poor and the working poor to use much less. If this failed, then the next step was the trickler.

FBW, on this basis it can be argued, was self-negating. To indicate this (and the incoherence and self-negating nature of state welfare policies), consider Johannesburg Water. The Johannesburg Water Company's "customer services" division has conducted a campaign to teach the poor that six kiloliter was enough in an urban setting. A family (of unspecified size) could choose five body washes; six toilet flushes, two kettles of water, one sink of water for dishes (per day), and one clothes wash every second day.[27] Expected to count their toilet flushes, those who do not achieve this were assumed to have knowingly exceeded their free limit and thus blamed for fecklessness. Thus FBW have become weapons used against the poor. The conservative, neo-Malthusian use of water scarcity combined with market environmentalism became a powerful cocktail (see Harvey 1996 for a brilliant critique of eco-scarcity arguments).

In reality (as the state has recognized), most poor urban families normally used 20–30 kiloliters of water per month. But water needs are also varied over different seasons and between different regions and there are health, age, and cultural components to mention only a few factors. Many townships have more than a single family per plot, some have several backyard structures; and there are special needs and occasions that require extra water. The struggle over defining needs is political.

Depoliticized Governance and "Actually Existing" Consumers

The fictional water customer plays a central role in official discourse and practices in the effort to present urban services as ordinary, depoliticized commodities. As early as 1997, the state introduced a shift to a customer discourse in public services: "Customer . . . embraces certain principles which are as fundamental to public service delivery as they are to the provision of services for commercial gain" (DPSA 1997). Transnational French water companies had also put pressure on the ANC to depoliticize local services arguing, "it is essential that the management of the service is not influenced by the politics of the day" (WSSA 1995a: 20). These firms have also taken a more prominent role in southern Africa and beyond with many having contracts and offices in Angola, Tanzania, Zambia, Zimbabwe, Namibia, and South Africa (McDonald and Ruiters 2005). WSSA (Water and Sanitation Services South Africa) a subsidiary of Suez, manages Johannesburg Water. It boasts almost five million people served but the state often seeks to underplay the extent of private sector reach and influence for fear of public criticism.[28]

It was also stated that privatization would develop state capacity by relieving local government from having to handle "difficult" communities and unionized workers (WSSA 1995). The World Bank's experts similarly argued for services to be handed over to business because "the principal source of benefits from privatizing is the arms length relationship between the infrastructure provider and short-term political pressures . . ." (Kerf and Smith 1996: 6). Supporting this thrust toward commercialism, the Municipal Systems Act of 2000 (sect 95) obliges municipalities to have "sound customer management," "customer charters," and "customer service centers." Johannesburg Metro adopted these ideas one step further. Customers would be differentiated by area. As Johannesburg Metro explained: a "customer orientation" in local services meant different ways of "owning" services by geographically distinct areas:

> . . . the needs in a high-income commercial centre such as the Sandton CBD area, will be very different to the needs of a low-income area such as Orange Farm. The regional administration must change the way services are delivered to suit these needs . . . increased local ownership of processes within each region could lead to the development of a unique identity for each region. (Johannesburg Metro 2001)

"Customer" discourses and institutions presumed an atomistic individualism but also required regional or area-based class differentials, separate "communities of consumption" (see Murray 2004: 145–146 on gated communities). Christopher (2005) adds, "the extremely high White segregation levels, attained under the previous dispensation, have changed comparatively little. . . . the rate of integration has declined after an initial rush in the early 1990s. The post-apartheid city continues to look remarkably like its predecessor, the apartheid city." The new architecture of depoliticized, outsourced, and geographically distinct services sought to reconstitute the political relationships in services from elected councils and citizen voters to one between would-be customers and service providers (a formula often captured by the term public–private partnership). Customer identities aimed to change what might be called the "socio-political relations" of public services.

Neoliberal utopianism in practice has fallen short of its own ambitions and instead provoked a massive crisis of control, forcing its sponsors to find new paths to implement it. "Neoliberal-ization" as Peck and Tickell (2002) argue, captures the reality that neoliberalism is not an actualized program, but an internally contradictory and ongoing process. As recently noted, eviscerated, and demoralized, at least 136 municipalities lost the ability to send out correct bills, do routine maintenance, and even spend capital budgets. By 2004–2005 local riots were spreading across South Africa. Despite free services, widespread illegal connections continued as municipal consumer debt spiraled into tens of billions.[29]

EXPORTING SOCIAL CONTROL; "FREE-PAY" METERS AND SELF-DISCONNECTIONS

> The conventional metering, in the absence of proper social attitudes to electricity, became a system demanding very high maintenance. Prepaid metering reduced this cost tremendously.
>
> (McGibbon, Eskom "Group Customer Service Manager" 2002)

Dubbed a "paradigm shift," town planners, leading local politicians and municipal experts see prepayment as "the way of the future" (Imiesa 2000). Nonpayment of municipal bills would become a thing of the past with upfront prepayment. By 2000, some 3.2 million prepaid meters in the electricity service went to new customers, most in black townships (Tewari and Shah 2003: 25–26).

Conlog, an ANC-linked firm, boasted of a customer base of two million prepaid meters, undoubtedly one of the largest in the world. In 2002, Conlog won a R100 million contract to supply 80 percent of all Eskom electricity prepaid meters "into predominant low-cost and rural housing."[30] Ronnie Kasrils called prepaid water meters "an example of how South Africa is harnessing home grown technology for development."[31] After 2002 all RDP houses with in-house or yard taps were meant to be fitted with prepayment water. In 2003, large townships like Orange Farm and much older ones like Soweto were targeted. Conlog, by 2004, had made six million prepaid meters for South Africa.[32] and won a contract to install 300,000 prepaid meters in Khartoum in the Sudan. This served as a "reference site" for planned contracts in Ethiopia, Egypt, and Saudi Arabia.[33] In Sudan, unlike South Africa, the market in prepaid electricity meters is in businesses and high-income groups, as these are the largest consumers.[34] Prepaid meters have also been tried in Swakopmund (Namibia). The rhetoric used to justify this is remarkably similar to South Africa (see LaRRI 2005).

Prepaid meters, a silent form of social control taken alongside FBW, became a weapon in local political "management." The "technical" literature on prepayment (DWAF, September 2000; DBSA 2001; and WRC 2003) note the political "benefits" of prepaid water, in particular its value for "conflict avoidance." Minister of Water Ronnie Kasrils noted: "The pre-paid meters are in fact designed and programmed to provide the basic amount for free. They have the added advantage of allowing households to monitor and control their water consumption . . . households appreciate this facility" (Kasrils 2003). Ideally the consumer "takes ownership" of the service (Johannesburg Metro 2001). Concealing the penalty itself, as Foucault (1995: 10) would put it, the PPM puts the onus of control on the users. Prepaid meters reduce the political dilemmas of "loud" punishments that arise with disconnections.

They are also part of a wider project by the new state to fashion new subjects. To borrow from Foucault (1995: 23), these are "political tactics." As technologies they educate and they create "modern" rational patterns of behavior suitable for marketized social life. As Foucault insisted, modern forms of power such as those evident in the FBW and prepaid meters are not prohibitions but "go right down to the depths of society" as "fields of knowledge." An "out of sight, out of mind" technique, these meters can be checked remotely and physically inspected every few months. Prepaid meters as "smart technology" appears to render township services legible, simple, and governable. The opportunities for contestation, that is, payment boycotts—made popular by the ANC and UDF in the 1980s—are denied.

But prepayment technology has reduced, not necessarily solved, the problem of pilferage; revenue losses from pilferage are still high.[35] A recent national survey of municipalities revealed that municipal managers overstate the extent of community support for PPM and "there is a tendency by water services providers to assume that technology will solve problems which are in fact social ones" (14). PPM may also encourage consumers to steal water, they may force people back to streams or informal water sources, and desperate residents may reuse dirty water, with dire health consequences. The social and political costs of this form of social control may be high. Consumers' perceive prepayment as an instrument to control communities; they complain of inconvenience and high costs of transport to purchase prepaid units from distance shops and garages, especially in small towns and rural areas. Highly politicized communities such as Soweto in Johannesburg also have perceived prepaid meters as racially discriminatory.[36] Angry Soweto residents have repeatedly ripped out electricity prepaid meters and dumped them at local council or Eskom offices.

Since 2000, several dozen groups, fiercely critical of the ANC's neoliberal water policies gained mass support by encouraging popular illegalities and civic disengagement from official politics and more recently launching electoral challenges to the ANC. Although openly advocating direct action and civil disobedience (destroying bills, meters, and reconnecting electricity illegally) these groups have won considerable sympathy given the widespread frustration with the ANC corruption, and mismanagement of housing, service delivery, HIV/AIDS, mass unemployment). Nevertheless, as argued earlier in this essay, the agenda for universalizing prepaid meters from electricity to water seems set as it has become a big business and much money has already been spent on installing them.[37]

CONCLUSIONS

The chapter demonstrates the different ways in which something apparently progressive like FBW can be subverted to serve bureaucratic, financial, and state management imperatives (a win-win for the state) at the same time as reducing the living standards of urban township residents. In this chapter, the paradoxical logics of FBW and the links with a broader neoliberal governability project were outlined. The chapter sought to move the analysis of service delivery beyond quantifying backlogs, capacity constraints, as well as beyond the idea that the ANC simply follows a neoliberal blueprint without strategically calculating the political costs. I argued that service delivery and sociopolitical control are in general inseparable.

The extension of basic infrastructure and FBW in South Africa has been as much about constituting the state, what "needs" ought to be, as it has been about meeting the targets for poverty alleviation. It is also significant that government's change of heart *predated* a later shift in the United Nations Water framework, which also accepted that water should be allocated through market-like processes *except* for water needed for drinking and basic needs (UN 2003: 31). Rather than "blindly" following neoliberal prescriptions, the state has had to concede ground to powerful urban social forces, navigating concessions such as FBW in order to win legitimacy, and then to open up new fields of strategic possibilities such as free-pay meters. Technocrats, I argue, also helped to diminish concessions, translating them into grounded strategies for managing unruly citizens and for clawing back social control. In the end, the tension between caring for the people and putting them in their place (social control) has been resolved largely in the latter's favor.

Soon after FBW was introduced in June 2001, some communities very quickly were forced or cajoled into accepting restrictors and prepaid meters as a quid pro quo for the free water ration. These new tools extended the state's control over water flows at an everyday level but had several consequences (intended and unintended). One of these was a rash of illegal reconnections (a huge problem in 2004 but especially so in Durban and Soweto, and in 2005 in many small towns where riots occurred). The state's partial concessions (free services for the poor) have also allowed it to be more "legitimately coercive" in recovering costs from the can pays (a category that includes a large strata of working poor). FBW has created new social exclusions through "right-sizing" thereby cementing inequality. By combining basic amounts of free services (partial decommodification) with intensified cost recovery, the mass of poor and working people have been under pressure to accept significant restrictions in their water consumption. Partially decommodified services with higher tariffs have helped to trap the poor within narrow consumption limits.

I have shown that the new tools involve a special kind of "disciplinary commodification" that relies on individuals and households internalizing the market (and their own effective demand) through acquiring a customer identity and through learning to experience services consumption as if it were any other commodity. I showed how prepayment has become a very widespread political technology in South Africa.

To this extent, Fanon is right. South Africa's new urban services regime is part of a wider state effort for gaining and sustaining state control over unruly populations and keeping the poor in their place while being seen to meet electoral promises (a strong theme in ANC public statements). Remarkably free basic services have not translated in greater popularity for the ruling party as the widespread rioting in South Africa's cities suggest.

Considered broadly, the FBW concession by the state also showed that urban township populations in South Africa cities still wield considerable bargaining power (using collective bargaining by riot and disruption has become common in South Africa). This is a big part of what the local state (meant to be close to the people) has to take into account when crafting the implementation of national policies. The state has had to fight hard to partly implement neoliberalism. Hence the projected depoliticization of services has *not* happened even if customer discourse has been vigorously introduced.

A significant rise in popular illegalities and the widespread intensity of service delivery riots suggests that the stricter formalization and re-commodification of urban services implied in FBW has failed. The widening socioeconomic gaps in South Africa, the social decline, slow growth in employment, and long wait for change has driven many households into partial disengagement from the state (Olukojo 2004; Osaghae 2001). The failures of the local state and the poverty of state delivery have produced both cynicism and reactivation of grassroots township activism. In the end, urban stability may be elusive as the rash of service delivery riots since 2004 has already shown. Trying to "roll out" market society and impose remote, depoliticized forms of governance to the mass of people under South African conditions (mass unemployment, poverty, and HIV/AIDS) has been easier said than done.

NOTES

1. See *Panapress*, Nairobi, November 22, 2004.
2. Five years after the government restructured municipalities, "most local governments are still struggling to integrate staff, structures, systems, and tariffs and have debt estimated at almost R40 bn for last year. Apart from organisational disarray and non-functioning systems, they have massive skills shortages, with 61% of all senior management posts in provincial and local government vacant" (*Business Day*, August 15, 2005).
3. Social control is an overburdened concept with a long history. I use it, but not in a functionalist way.
4. What some scholars call the "native question" (see Mamdani 1996) arises in the new South African context as explained by President Mbeki (2004). " 'We should not cultivate a culture of dehumanizing dependency on these masses' through increasing welfare . . . the objective is that we should increase the number of people in society who depend for their livelihood, not on social grants, but on normal participation in the economy. During the Second Decade of Liberation, we will have to pay particular attention to this question, to ensure that our policies and Budgets increase the possibility for our people to depend AQ: Not given in the List less on social grants and more on normal participation in the economy."
5. See <http://www.peopleandplanet.net/doc.php?id=1911>.
6. Those getting social grants (including pensions, disability grants, and child support) will total 10 million people by 2006–2007, up from 2.9 million 10 years ago (*Business Day*, March 9, 2004).
7. See John Kane Berman, *Business Day*, December 2, 2003.
8. The conservative argument (sometimes expressed by the Democratic Alliance and even in the ANC) is that welfare (or the wrong kind and amount of welfare) will discourage the unemployed from looking for work and encourage dependency and discourage an entrepreneurial culture (see Trevor Manuel, minister of finance, in *Business Day*, February 2004).
9. As Thatcher argued, all forms of society need to dissolve in favor of the individual. "Economics is the method but the object is to change the soul" (cited in Harvey 2005).

10. Most commentators tend to see neoliberalism as an ideology or script adopted with religious zeal by governments and implemented with singular determination (see Bond 2002; McDonald and Pape 2002).
11. It is often forgotten that neoliberal austerity is less a political choice of the state, or a grand plan of the state, than a necessity reflecting a crisis condition (see Meszaros 1995). This may explain why many ideologically different parties in different parts of the world end up as *de facto* if not reluctant neoliberals.
12. See Lorrain and Stoker (1997) for a succinct account of neoliberal shifts in local government services.
13. Chippy Olver, Director General of the Department of Constitutional Development, quoted in *Business Day*, March 13, 1998.
14. Regarding urban water, the World Bank specifically rejected the ANC's "water welfare." It held that water is best managed as a scarce resource. It argued, "overseas companies would fail to invest in South Africa if rich consumers cut down on their water usage" because they cross-subsidized the poor (*Observer*, August 18, 2002). Households must pay for the full cost of what they use (Bauman et al. 1998).
15. See *Sunday Times*, May 12, 2002.
16. See *Daily News*, March 1, 2001.
17. See *Daily News*, March 18, 2001.
18. See *Cape Times*, September 27, 2001.
19. See City Manager News, *eThekwini Online*, July 8, 2005.
20. Harvey (1996: 182) notes that "sustainability" discourse is easily corrupted into covert forms of control and political projects by appeal to the authority of "nature imposed necessity" and crisis.
21. See *Sowetan*, January 21, 2003.
22. This consumer is quoted in Smith and Fakir (2003).
23. This councilor from Harrismith is quoted in Smith and Fakir (2003).
24. See *Business Day*, June 9, 2003.
25. <www.durban.gov.za/eThekwini/Services/water_an . . . /Water_Tariffs>.
26. For monitoring purposes, the World Health Organization/United Nations Children's Fund (WHO/UNICEF: *Global Water Supply and Sanitation Assessment 2000 Report)* specifies reasonable access to water as at least 20 liters per person per day, from an improved source within 1 kilometer of a user's dwelling. This does not, however, represent a definition of adequacy of access, but rather a benchmark for monitoring purposes. For example, in a densely populated squatter community with 100,000 inhabitants, it certainly is not reasonable (United Nations 2004).
27. See www.johannesburgwater.co.za.
28. Data taken from *Water Sewage and Effluent* 21 (4) (August/September): 7.
29. According the IGFR 2003, the City of Johannesburg was unable to account for 42% of the water it paid for in 2001. eThekwini (Durban) could not account for 32% (85 billion liters) of its water; Tshwane (Pretoria) 24% (29 billion liters); Nelson Mandela (Port Elizabeth) 20% (14 billion liters); and Cape Town 12% (36 billion liters). The problem was exacerbated by illegal connections (Mike Muller, May 19, 2003, new24.com). One index of the number of illegal connection is water losses. Durban recently estimated that as much of 26% of its circulated water is consumed via illegal connections (eThekwini 2004: 47). In 2004, the municipality lost a whopping R30 million in revenue due to water losses in Umlazi alone (eThekwini On-line, November 29, 2005).
30. See www.conlog.co/za/PressRelease/pressr/2002/5.htm.
31. See *New York Times*, June 5, 2003.

32. See *Business Roport*, March 4, 2004.
33. See www.conlog.co/za/PressRelease/pressr/2003/htm.
34. See *Business Report*, March 4, 2002.
35. See *Business Day*, March 23, 2003.
36. See *Business Day*, March 16, 2004, and November 17, 2004.
37. See *Business Roport*, May 14, 2004.

BIBLIOGRAPHY

Arthur, C. 1978. "Introduction to Pashukanis," in E. Pashukanis (ed.). *Law and Marxism*. London: Ink Links, pp. 9–32.

Bagguley, P. 1994. "Prisoners of the Beveridge Dream? The Political Mobilization of the Poor against Contemporary Welfare Regimes," in R. Burrows and B. Loader (eds.). *Towards a Post-Fordist Welfare State?* London: Routledge, pp. 74–93.

Bauman, D., J. Boland, M. Hanemann. 1998. *Urban Water Demand Management*. New York: McGraw Hill.

Beall, J., Crankshaw, O., and S. Parnell, 2000. "Local Government, Poverty Reduction and Inequality in Johannesburg," *Environment and Urbanization* 12 (1): 107–122.

Bond, P., 2002. *Unsustainable South Africa*. London: Merlin Press.

Christopher, A. J. 2005. "The Slow Pace of Desegregation in South African Cities, 1996–2001," *Urban Studies* 42 (12): 2305–2320.

Clarke, J. and J. Newman. 1997. *The Managerial State*. London: Sage.

Dandeker, C., 1990. *Surveillance, Power and Modernity*. Oxford: Polity Press,.

Davis, M. 2004. "Planet of Slums," *New Left Review* [NS] 26 (March–April): 5–34.

Deakin, N. and K. Walsh. 1996. "The Enabling State: The Role of Markets and Contracts," *Public Administration* 74: 33–48.

Dean, H. 1991. *Social Security and Social Control*. London: Routledge.

Desai, A. 2002. *We are the Poors*. New York: Monthly Review Press.

Development Bank of South Africa, 2001. *The Role of Prepayment Water Meters for Sustainable Delivery of Water Services, Discussion Document*. Midrand.

DoF (Department of Finance). 2001. *Intergovernmental Fiscal Review 2001*. Pretoria.

DoF (Department of Finance). 2003. *Intergovernmental Fiscal Review 2003*. Pretoria.

DPLG. 2002. *Quarterly Monitoring of Municipal Finances and Related Activities, Summary of Questionnaires for Quarter Ended, 31 December*.

DPSA (Department of Public Services and Administration). 1997. *Batho Pele*. Pretoria.

DWAF (Department of Water and Forestry). 2000. Kasrils statement on logic of Durban.

DWAF (Department of Water and Forestry). 2003. *Strategic Framework for Water Services*. Pretoria.

DWAF (Department of Water and Forestry). 2001. *Free Basic Water Implementation Strategy. Case Study: Durban Unicity*. Prepared by Palmer Development Group <http://www.DWAF.gov.za/FreeBasicWater/Docs/casestud/ >.

Elster, J. 1988. "Should there Be a Right to Work?" in A. Gutman (ed.). *Democracy and Welfare State*. Princeton: Princeton University Press.

Esping-Anderson, G. 1990. *Three Worlds of Welfare*. Princeton: Princeton University Press.

eThekwini. 2004. *Water Services Developmet Plan, Vol 2* <http://www.durban.gov.za/eThekwini/Services/water_and_sanitation/policies_and_guidelines/WSDP/>.

Fanon, F, 1967. *The Wretched of the Earth*. Middlesex: Penguin.

Ferguson, J. 1990. *The Anti-Politics Machine: "Development," Depoliticization, and Bureaucratic Power in Lesotho*. Cape Town: David Phillip.

Forrest, R. 1991. "The Privatization of Collective Consumption," in M. Gottdiener (ed.), *Urban Life in Transition*. Thousand Oaks, CA: Sage, pp. 169–195.

Foucault, M., 1995. *Discipline and Punish.* New York: Vintage Books.

Greenburg, S. 2005. "The Rise and Fall of Water Privatisation in Rural South Africa," in D. McDonald and G. Ruiters (eds.). *The Age of Commodity. Water Privatization in Southern Africa.* London: Earthscan, pp. 206–222.

Gill, S. 2003. *Power and Resistance in the New World Order.* New York: Palgrave.

Hart, G. 2005. "Beyond Neoliberalism? Post-Apartheid Developments in Historical & Comparative Perspective," in V. Padayachee (ed.). *The Development Decade? Social and Economic Change in South Africa 1994–2004.* Pretoria: HSRC, pp. 13–32.

Harvey, D. 1996. *Justice, Nature and the Geography of Difference.* Oxford: Basil Blackwell.

Harvey, D. 2005. *A Brief History of Neoliberalism.* London: Oxford University Press.

Hemson, D. and Owusu-Ampomah. 2005. "A Better Life for All? Service Delivery and Poverty Alleviation," in J. Daniel, R. Southall, and J. Lutchman (eds.). *State of the Nation 2004–2005.* South Africa: Human Sciences Research Council Press, pp. 515–516.

Imiesa. 2000. "Prepayment Meters: The Way of the Future," *editorial* 25 (9).

Jega, A. 2000. *State and Identity Transformations under Structural Adjustment in Nigeria.* Uppsala: Nordiska Afrikaininstitutet.

Jessop, B., 2002. "Liberalism, Neoliberalism, and Urban Governance: A State-Theoretic Perspective," *Antipode* 34 (3): 451–472.

Johannesburg Metro. 2001. *City Development Plan 2001/2002* <www.johannesburgnews.co.za/budget_2001/develop_plan.html>.

Kasrills. 2003. www.dwaf.gov.za/Communications/PressReleases/2003/ Prepaid%20right%20to%20water%20campaign%20reply1_.doc [accessed August 6, 2004].

Kerf, M. and W. Smith. 1996. *Privatising Africa's Infrastructure: Promise and Challenge.* World Bank Technical Paper No 337. Washington, DC.

LaRRI.2005. "Water Privatization in Namibia: Creating a New apartheid," in D. McDonald and G. Ruiters (eds.), *The age of Commodity, Water Privatization in Southern Africa.* London: Earthscan, pp. 148–165.

Laurence, P. 2004. "Albatrosses Hanging around Mbeki's Neck," *Focus* 34.

Loftus, A., 2005. "Free Water as a Commodity: The Paradoxes of Durban's Water Services Transformation," in D. McDonald and G. Ruiters (eds.). *The Age of Commodity, Water Privatization in Southern Africa.* London: Earthscan, pp. 189–203.

Lorrain, D. and G. Stoker. 1997. *The Privatisation of Urban Services in Europe.* London: Pinter.

Mamdani. M. 1996. *Citizen and Subject.* Princeton: Princeton University Press.

Mbeki, T. 2004. *The ANC Today* 4 (7) (February): 20–26.

McDonald, D. and J. Pape. 2002. *Cost Recovery and the Crisis of Service Delivery in South Africa.* Cape Town: HSRC Publishers.

McDonald, D. and G. Ruiters. 2005. *The Age of Commodity. Water Privatization in Southern Africa.* London: Earthscan.

McGibbbon, H. 2002. "Prepaid Vending Lessons Learnt by Eskom." Updea Conference, June.

McInnes, P. 2005. "Entrenching Inequalities: The Impact of Corporatization on Water Injustices in Pretoria," in D. McDonald and G. Ruiters (eds.). *The Age of Commodity, WaterPrivatization in Southern Africa.* London: Earthscan, pp. 99–117.

Meszaros, I. 1995. *Beyond Capital.* New York: Monthly Review Press.

Migdal, J. 2001. *State in Society: Studying How States and Societies Transform and Constitute one Another.* Cambridge: Cambridge University Press.

Muller, M. 2001. "Free Basic Water, Challenge, Sustaining Free Basic Water," *Water, Sewage and Effluent* 21 (4): 14.

Muller, M. 2003. "Presentation to Bonn Water Conference, December 2003" <www.dwaf.gov.za>.

Murray, M. 2004. "The Spatial Dynamics of Postmodern Urbanism: Social Polarisation and Fragmentation in São Paulo and Johannesburg," *Journal of Contemporary African Studies* 22 (2): 139–164.

Offe, C. 1983. *Contradictions of the Welfare State*. London: Hutchinson.

Olukoju, A. 2004. "Never Expect Power Always: Electricity Consumers' Response to Monopoly, Corruption and Inefficient Services in Nigeria," *African Affairs* 103: 51–71.

Osaghae, E. 2001. "Exiting from the Existing State in Nigeria," in S. Bekker, M. Dodds, and M. Khosa (eds.). *Shifting African Identities*. Pretoria: HSRC, pp. 21–42.

Painter, J. 1995. *Politics, Geography and Political Geography*. London: Arnold.

Palmer Development Group. 2001. "Free Basic Water: Tswane." A case study prepared for DWAF <http://www.DWAF.gov.za/ FreeBasicWater/Docs/casestud/>.

Peck, J and A. Tickell 2002. "Neoliberalising Space," *Antipode* 34 (3): 380–404.

Piven, F and F. Cloward. 1977. *Poor People's Movements, How They Succeed and How They Fail*. New York: Pantheon.

Ruiters, G. 2002. "Debt, Disconnection and Privatisation," in D. McDonald and J. Pape (eds.). *Cost Recovery and the Crisis of Service Delivery in South Africa*. Cape Town: HSRC Publishers, pp. 41–60.

Scott, J. 1998. *Seeing like a State*. New Haven: Yale University Press.

Smith, L. and Fakir, E. 2003. "The Struggle to Deliver Water Services to the Indigent: A Case Study on the Public–Public Partnership in Harrismith with Rand Water." Centre for Policy Studies, Johannesburg.

Smith, N. 2002. "New Globalism, New Urbanism and Genrificationas Global urban Strategey." *Antipode* 34 (3): 427–450.

South Africa Cities Network. 2004, *State of the Cities Report*. South African Cities Network, Johannesburg.

Still, A. 2001. "Free Basic Water, Who Pains, Who Gains," *Water, Sewage and Effluent* 21 (4): 17.

Taylor-Gooby, P. 2000. *Risk, Trust and Welfare*. Houndsmill: Macmillan.

Tewari, D. and T. Shah. 2003. "An Assessment of South African Prepaid Electricity Experiment, Lessons Learned, and Their Policy Implications for Developing Countries," *Energy Policy* (31): 911–927.

United Nations (UN). 2003. *World Water Development Report*. New York.

United Nations (UN). 2004. *Water for People, Water for Life*. New York. <http:www.un.org/esa/sustdev/publications/WWDR-english-129556e.pdf>.

United Nations Human Settlements Program. 2003. *Water and Sanitation in the World's Cities*. London: Earthscan.

Walker, C. 1993. *Managing Poverty, the Limits of Social Assistance*. London: Routledge.

Water and Sanitation Services South Africa. 1995. *The Delegated Management Concept*. Annexure 5, Fort Beaufort Proposal, April. Fort Beaufort Municipality.

Water Research Commission (WRC). 2003. Institutional and Socioeconomic Review of the Use/Application of Electronic Pre-paid Meter Technology in the Provision of Water Supply Services, Project No. K5/1206/0/1. Johannesburg.

Wolch, J. and M. Dear (eds.). 1989. *The Power of Geography*. Boston: Unwin Hyman.

Notes on Contributors

Elizabeth H. Campbell completed her Ph.D. in Sociology at the State University of New York, Binghamton, in 2005 and is currently employed by the Bureau of Population, Refugees, and Migration at the U.S. Department of State.

Matthew Gandy is Reader in Geography at the Department of Geography, University College London.

Aubrey Graham is a major in Sociology/Anthropology and French Language at Colgate University.

Miriam Grant is Associate Professor in the Geography Department of the University of Calgary.

Guillaume Iyenda holds a Ph.D. from Royal Holloway, University of London, and is a freelance researcher based in the United Kingdom.

Dominique Malaquais is Professor of Art History and Africana Studies at Sarah Lawrence College in New York and Director of Research and Concept Development for the Africa Centre in Cape Town.

Darlene Miller is Senior Lecturer in the Department of Sociology at Rhodes University in Grahamstown, South Africa.

Martin J. Murray is Professor of Sociology, State University of New York, Binghamton.

Garth A. Myers is Associate Professor in the departments of Geography and African/African-American Studies at the University of Kansas, and I am now Director of the Kansas African Studies Center.

Basile Ndjio was most recently Lecturer at the School of Social Science Research, University of Amsterdam, The Netherlands.

Joyce Nyairo is Senior Lecturer, Department of Literature, Theatre, and Film Studies, Moi University (Eldoret, Kenya).

M. Anne Pitcher is Professor of Political Science and Director of the Center for Ethics and World Societies at Colgate University, Hamilton, New York.

Deborah Potts is Senior Lecturer in Geography at King's College, London.

Greg Ruiters is Matthew Goniwe Chair in Development and Society Institute for Social and Economic Research (ISER) at Rhodes University in South Africa.

David Simon is currently Professor of Development Geography at Royal Holloway, University of London.

AbdouMaliq Simone is Senior Lecturer at Goldsmith's College, University of London.

Daniel Jordan Smith is Assistant Professor of Anthropology, Brown University, Providence, Rhode Island.

Index

Aba, Nigeria 62–63, 65
Abbas, Ackbar 188
Abdoul, Mohamadou 2
Abrahamsen, Rita 19
Abuja, Nigeria 254
Accra, Ghana 13, 289
Addis Ababa, Ethiopia 289
Africa xiii, 1–2, 36, 248, 277
  cities in xiii, 1–3, 5–9, 11–13, 19, 119, 121, 124, 174, 237–238
  diversity of 7
  states in 249
  stereotypes of 2
  sub-Saharan 1, 5, 11, 56, 58–59, 103, 151, 225, 231, 248, 255, 266, 289
African Continent 13
African National Congress (ANC) 290, 293, 299, 301
  Reconstruction and Development Program of 293–294, 301–302
African Renaissance 150, 159, 162, 167
Afropessimism 2, 151, 158
Agriculture 56
  cash-crop 128
  urban 265
AIDS 123, 151, 202, 210, 215
Akam, Melvin 107
Alao, Tunde 258
Amadi, Ako 253
American cities 35, 155
Anglo-American Corporation 157, 243
Angola 173–191, 195–199
  blood diamonds in 180, 191
  economy of 175
  Marxism-Leninism in 175–178
  oil resources of 175–177, 180, 191
  war in 175–176, 180, 190–191, 199
Anikulapo-Keti, Fela 247
Apartheid 28, 36, 95–96, 122, 128, 238, 241, 246, 266, 282, 297
  end of 150
  post- 28, 150, 290
Appadurai, Arjun 105
Arabs (in East Africa) 128
Architecture 7, 27, 39, 41–45, 57, 77, 180, 195
Arrighi, Giovanni 155
Asian cities 268
Asians (in East Africa) 134
Awori, Moody 130

Bakassi Boys (of Nigeria) 64–65
Banda, Hastings Kamuzu 270
Barth, John 54
Bayart, Jean-Francois 44
Bazenguissa-Ganga, Remy 17
Belgian Congo 224
Benjamin, Walter 27, 105, 116
Berman, John Kane 291
Berry, Sara 56
Biafra, see under Nigeria
Biya, Paul 43, 104
Black market 15
Botswana 202
Bourdieu, Pierre 257
Boyer, Christine 175
Brazzaville, Congo 37
British, see under colonialism
Buenos Aires, Argentina 254
Built environment 7, 15, 121, 174–175, 180, 237–238, 245
Bulawayo, Zimbabwe 123–124, 201–218, 268, 272, 274, 278
  City Council of 204, 272, 274
  Killarney neighborhood in 278

Cameroon 29, 31–47, 103–116, 181
Cameroon Tribune 108

Campbell, Elizabeth 121
Cape Town, South Africa 8, 37, 95, 173, 188, 239, 294, 296
  Lansdowne area of 150
  Wynberg area of 150
Capital, finance 20
Central Africa 31, 121, 125
Centro Commercial (Maputo) 151, 158–160
Chad Basin 33
Chicago, USA 39, 41
Chombo, Ignatius 274, 283
Christians 11
  Catholic 56
  conflict with Muslims 11, 27, 59–65
  Protestant 56
Churchill, Winston 127
Cities xiii, 27, 31, 66, 122, 242
  African 1, 7–9, 16–19, 27, 31, 36, 42, 73, 103, 121, 154, 249, 260, 268
  CBDs of 268
  rights to 242–244
  South African 289–304
  as texts 28
  walking in 74, 82
City management 1
City-ness 8, 29
Cityscape 45, 191
Civil society 18, 65, 250
Class difference 174, 187–190
Class formation 88
Colonial administration 8, 225
Colonial cities 8, 12
Colonial era 28
Colonialism in Africa 4, 7, 12, 75, 89, 127, 173, 195, 199
  Belgian 222
  British 19, 59, 127–128, 131, 152, 249
  European 4, 7, 121
  Portuguese 177, 180–181
  Segregation policies of 75
Commandement operationnel (Cameroon) 43–44, 107
Congress of South African Trade Unions 166
Consumer culture 174
Consumerism 175
Cooper, Frederick 152
Copperbelt, Zambian 8, 157
Core (of world economy) 9
Cosmopolitanism 16, 45, 87, 164, 173, 256
Couto, Mia 187
Crime 1, 65, 173, 183, 248
Crisp, Jeff 126
Cultural difference 11
Cultural geography 11, 74
Cultural theory 71
Cultural turn 11
Culture 2, 10–12, 16, 27
  -making 11
  popular 28

Dakar, Senegal 268
Dar es Salaam, Tanzania 222, 231, 254
Davis, Mike 4
Dean, Mitchell 249
Dear, Michael 45, 113
de Boeck, Filip 46, 103–104, 115
de Certeau, Michel 28, 72, 74, 89, 116
deindustrialization 157
Democratic Republic of Congo (DRC) 132, 173, 176, 221–235
de Soto, Hernando 14
Deregulation 14
Derrida, Jacques 39–40
Developmentalism 10, 173
Diaspora 13, 120
dos Santos, Aguiar 187
Douala, Cameroon 27, 29, 31–47, 103–116
  Bonanjo neighborhood in 31, 36–38
  Chinese business people of 110
  New Bell neighborhood in 36–38, 105, 115
  Nylon neighborhood in 31, 36–38
Dubai, UAE 135, 138
Durban, South Africa 8, 239, 294–298

East Africa 121, 125
East European cities 38
Eastleigh Business Community (Nairobi) 139
Economic growth 4, 126, 164
Economic liberalization 273
Embedded resources 201–218
Enclave economies 151
Entrepreneurship 16
Entreprenialism 6, 14, 18
Environmental degradation 1, 250

Equatorial Guinea 37
Ethiopia 132, 140, 301
Ethnic identity 5, 16, 54, 67
Ethnic strife 1, 11, 27
Ethnic violence 1, 62–64
Euro-American cities 31
Europe 248, 258
Europeans 128, 132

Fanon, Franz 246, 303
Feld, Steven 74
Ferguson, James 154, 278
First World 3, 9, 31, 38, 158
Formal economy 1, 6, 14–16
Formality 14, 16
Formal sector 14–16, 163, 186, 216, 226
Foucault, Michel 28, 72–74, 79, 301–302
French Africa 152
Freud, Sigmund 39–40
Furedi, Frank 79

Gabarone, Botswana 8
Gabon 37
Gandy, Matthew 238
Gated communities 5, 98, 179
Gbadolite, Democratic Republic of Congo 42
Gender 201–218, 221–235
Ghettopolis 104, 106
Gikandi, Simon 71
Gleeson, Brendan 104
Global, intersection with local 27
Global cities 9, 31–32, 259
Globalization 3–6, 12, 32–33, 38, 116, 121, 151, 237, 248
  economic 126, 130–131
Global networks 3, 174
Global North 4, 32, 248
Global South 3–4, 33, 247, 250, 258, 260
Goldenberg Scandal (Kenya) 137
Governance 17, 238, 244, 293, 299
  good 7, 10, 17–19
  local 17
  urban 17
Governmentality 244, 259
Graham, Aubrey 122–123
Grant, Miriam 123

Habitat International 276
Harare, Zimbabwe 179, 265–286
  Chitungwiza suburb of 272, 277
  City Council of 272–274
  Epworth area of 271, 275
  High Density Areas of 268–269, 273, 276, 284
  Kuwadzana township of 268–270, 273
  Mbare township of 268–271, 275, 280–281
  Porta Farm suburb of 271, 275
  Warren Park area of 268, 273
Harrismith, South Africa 297
Hart, Gillian 294
Hart, Keith 13
Harvey, David 292
Hausa 53–67, 257
  migrants 62–64
Hawala money transfer 138
Hedonopolis 29, 104, 113
Hirschman, Albert 161, 168
HIV/AIDS 123, 151, 202–203, 215–217
Hodges, Tony 180
Homelessness 273
Hometown associations 6
Hong Kong 188
Horn of Africa 125
Households 201–202, 205, 209, 217, 221, 226, 230, 252, 301
Housing 1, 18–19, 31, 56, 119, 184, 225, 243, 266, 268–275
Houston, USA 188
Human capital 201–218
Hybrid city 7–8
Hybridity 45

Igbo 53–67
Imaginaire 34, 41–45, 47
Imagination 11, 27
Indians 128
Inequality 1, 67, 129–130, 175, 190
Informal economy 4, 13–16, 120, 123, 126, 139, 178–179, 222
Informal financial networks 138, 230–233
Informality 13, 14, 16, 88
Informal sector 13, 18, 135, 174, 183, 186, 227–230, 265, 268
Informal settlements 4, 275–276

Infrastructure 1–2, 7, 10, 20, 31, 224–225, 241, 244–245, 247–261, 290
  collapse of 6, 18, 247–261
International Financial Institutions 18
Internet cafes 188
Islam 57
Iyenda, Guillaume 123

Jessop, Bob 293
Johannesburg, South Africa 8, 27–29, 95–101, 238, 294, 298–300
  Alexandra township of 96
  Central Business District of 243
  Chinese migrants in 97
  Hillbrow neighborhood in 36, 96, 101
  Sandton neighborhood in 95, 97
  Soweto area of 301–302
  Water Company of 299
Jua kali ((under) the hot sun) businesses 134, 138

Kaduna, Nigeria 65
Kagwanja, Peter 130
Kano, Nigeria 27, 53–66
  Sabon Gari neighborhood of 55–57, 62–65
Kasrils, Ronnie 301
Kenya 71–92, 125–142
  Building Society of 77
  corruption in 136–137
  Mount Kenya region of 139–140
  Music Copyright Society of 84
  popular music of 71–92
  refugee camps of 125, 138
  Revenue Authority of 137
Khartoum, Sudan 301
Kikuyu 128, 132–133
King, Kenneth 77
Kinshasa, Democratic Republic of Congo 27, 32, 42, 46, 103–104, 123–124, 221–235, 268
  history of 222–223
  industrial sector of 225
  Kasa-Vubu district of 223, 232
  Lebanese business people of 123, 228
  Masina district of 224, 230
  Pakistani business people of 123, 228
  population of 224
Konu, Koku 259
Koolhaas, Rem 122, 238
Kribi, Cameroon 106
Kristeva, Julia 71
Kurtz, Roger 79
Kuwaits (DRC street markets) 228

Lagos, Nigeria 8, 27, 32, 45, 56, 64, 122, 238, 247–261, 268
  Ajegunle district of 248
  Master Plan for 251
  Mushin district of 248, 257–258
  State Water Corporation of 254
  water supply infrastructure for 251–255
Land markets 255
Land transfer 133
Land use 18–19, 119, 226
Latin American cities 268
Lefebvre, Henri 238, 257
Leopoldville, see under Kinshasa
Libreville, Gabon 37
Lilongwe, Malawi 8, 270
  Traditional Housing Areas in 270
Little, Peter 138
Livelihoods 10, 13, 126, 242
Local, intersection with global 27
Localities 3, 18
Localization 6, 38
London, England 27, 32, 128
Luanda, Angola 8, 37, 122–124, 173–191, 195–199, 268
  automobiles in 173–191
  Boavista neighborhood in 178, 190
  Chinese traders in 178, 183
  Cidade Alta neighborhood in 179
  Congolese traders in 185
  Malian traders in 178, 185
  Senegalese traders in 178
Lusaka, Zambia 8, 153, 160–168, 181
  George compound in 210
  Manda Hill shopping area in 151

MacGaffey, Janet 17, 282
Macleod, Neil 296
Makwavara, Sekesai 283
Malan, Juanita 28
Malaquais, Dominique 27, 181
Malawi 270
Malthusianism 4, 299

Maputo, Mozambique 8, 122–124, 149, 158–168, 181
Central Business District of 158
Matatu transport 135
Mbeki, Thabo 150, 294
Mbembe, Achille 105, 109
Mbogol, Kon 114
Megacities 4, 8, 56, 238
Mentoring 202, 213–218
Mexicali, Mexico 46
Micro-enterprises 2, 14–15
Middle Eastern cities 38
Migrants 53, 56–57, 276
Migration 13, 36, 54, 257
circuitry of 55, 60–62, 64–66
rural-to-urban 128, 224
urban-to-rural 276–281
urban-to-urban 278
Millennium Development Goals 221–222
Miller, Daniel 189–190
Miller, Darlene 122
Mobutu Sese Seko 42–43, 232
Modern 10, 154
Modernism 103, 173, 195, 258
Modernity 5, 11, 16, 27, 121, 173, 250, 269
expectations of 164
Western 5
Modernization 2
Mombasa, Kenya 8
Momsen, Janet 230
Money changing 232
Mouffe, Chantal 256
Movement for Democratic Change (MDC) in Zimbabwe 266–267, 273
Mozambique 149, 154, 158–160, 162, 282
MPLA (Popular Movement for the Liberation of Angola) 176–178, 186
Mugabe, Robert 179, 238, 266
Multinational corporations 155
Mumbai, India 105, 259
Municipalities 1, 19, 266, 298
Murray, Martin 28
Muslims, Nigerian 61
Musyemi, Iddi 133
Nairobi, Kenya 8, 28, 71–92, 121, 125–142, 268, 289
Buru Buru neighborhood of 72, 78–79
Central Business District of 85–86, 132
City Council of 76–77, 128–129, 131, 133
Eastlands neighborhood of 77, 79, 81–82, 129
Eastleigh neighborhood of 75, 121, 125, 130–133
Embakasi constituency of 75–77
Garissa Lodge in 134–135
Githurai neighborhood of 82–84
Kayole neighborhood of 76
Komarock neighborhood of 76–77
Pumwani neighborhood of 129
refugees in 121, 125–142
Somalis in 75, 121, 125–142
Nairobi River 129
Ndarlin P (Kenyan rapper) 75–76, 79, 81
Ndebele 272
Ndjio, Basile 29
Necropolis 29, 103, 106
Nelspruit, South Africa 159
Neoliberal economic policy 126, 141, 153, 175, 239
Neoliberal governance 18, 248
Neoliberal ideology 14
Neoliberalism 14–15, 258, 289–304
urban 291–293
Neoliberal reform 17
New York City, USA 27, 32–35, 41
Manhattan island of 35
Nigeria 53–66, 241–255
Abia State in 55–56
Biafra war in 27, 58–60
cities of 27, 53–66
colonial era in 249
Igboland of 28
press of 61
Second Republic in 251
southeastern region of 55
Non-Governmental Organizations (NGOs) 18, 253, 276
transnational 184
Noor, Mahmoud 134
North Africa 57
North America 17, 32, 237, 248, 258

Nouakchott, Mauritania 8
Nyairo, Joyce 28
Nzembi, Walter 276

Odhiambo, Atieno 87
O'odua People's Congress (Nigeria) 64
Operation *Murambatsvina* (Zimbabwe) 238, 265–286
Outsourcing 17–18
Owerri, Nigeria 62–63, 65

Paris, France 27, 32, 188
Patronage 2, 16, 18
Peck, Jamie 300
Peripheral urbanization 9
Periphery (of world economy) 9, 20
Peri-urban areas 178, 189, 243, 266
Perrot, Michelle 152
Phimister, Ian 154
Pitcher, Anne 122
Place 10–12, 27, 32, 87, 292
  sense of 71, 74
Political economy 10, 13
Political parties 18
Port Harcourt, Nigeria 56
Post-border city 45
Postcolonial cities 12, 103
Postcolonial regimes 12
Postmodern geographies 46
Potts, Deborah 238
Poverty 1–2, 6, 13, 125, 129–130, 191, 201, 221, 234, 238, 250, 265–286
Power 6, 55, 187, 191, 237, 250
  and the city 175–179
Privatization 5, 15, 104, 119, 164
  of housing markets 19
Protectionism 5
Public-private partnerships 17

Queenstown, South Africa 296

Racism 157, 203, 266
Refugee camps 243
Refugees 126–127
Religions 11, 16, 56, 60
Religious identity 67
Religious violence 62–64
Rental markets 184–185
Ross, Kristin 187
Ruiters, Greg 239

Said, Edward 28, 72–74
  Orientalism idea of 72
Samper, David 76
Sassen, Saskia 32
Saul, John 155
Schlyter, Ann 210, 272
Segregation 127–128
  racial 149, 300
Service delivery 17
Service provision 13, 77
Services, public 132
Services, social 2, 5–6
Shantytowns 4, 178
Sharia law 60–61, 64
Sheller, Mimi 180
Shock cities 4
Shoprite stores 122, 149–168
Silver, Beverly 152
Simon, David 123
Simone, AbdouMaliq 6, 32, 36, 45, 238
Smith, Daniel 27–28
Smith, Ian 203
Smith, Neil 103, 292
Social capital 202, 205, 207, 213–216
Social control 289–304
Social exchange theory 202
Social geography 188
Social movements 18, 292
Social welfare 289–304
Soja, Edward 72–74
Somalia 130, 132, 138
Somali diaspora 140
Sonangol oil company 176–177, 186
South Africa 37, 122, 128, 151, 205, 281, 289–304
  cities in 289–304
  investors from in rest of Africa 149–153, 156–158, 166–167, 255
  regional hegemony of 150
  retail sector in 155–156
  sub-imperialism of 168
  Truth and Reconciliation Commission of 60
Southern Africa 151
  post-Apartheid 152, 166, 168
Southern African Development Community 166

Space(s) 10–12, 27, 183
of consumption 153
of death 109
of hope 165
of life 109
production of 72
public 20, 32, 179
sense of 39
theories of 72–74
Spatial fragmentation 6, 252
Spatial segregation 127
Squatter settlements 18, 104, 119, 253, 275
Stanley, Henry Morton 222
Structural adjustment programs 5, 155, 201, 266
Sudan 130, 132
Sustainable cities 4

Tanzania 231
Technological change 242, 302
Third World 3, 9, 33, 104, 158, 293, 297
Tickell, Adam 300
Timbuktu, Mali 39, 41
Tinubu, Bola Ahmed 253–254
Tourism 5, 157
Trade 16, 59, 126, 135–137, 226
liberalization of 2, 5, 119
networks 127
small-scale 56
unions 157
Tradition 11
invented 12
Traffic jams 34, 175, 181, 268
accidents 180
Transnational city 127
Transnational division of labor 4
Transnationalism 13, 126
Transnationality 13, 16
Transnational migration 126
Transnational traders 174
Transparency International 136
Transportation 10, 132, 135, 173–191, 225
public 182, 225
Tribalism 2
Triulzi, Alessandro 89
Trotsky, Leon 154

Ubakala, Nigeria 53–66
Improvement Union of 58
Uganda 173
Uganda Railway 127
Uige, Angola 181
Umuahia, Nigeria 56
Unemployment 4, 136, 201, 227
Uneven regional development 155
Unilateral Declaration of Independence (UDI), see under Zimbabwe
UNITA (Union for the Total Independence of Angola) 176, 180
United Nations Economic Commission for Africa 222
United Nations Habitat 265
Urban Africa 195
Urban agglomeration 4, 103–104, 121
Urban crisis 1–3
Urban development xiii, 8, 10, 18, 154, 164
conflation with urban growth 10
Urban environments 5, 242–243
Urban experience 3, 10, 11
Urban governance 10, 17, 237, 248, 250
neoliberal 293
Urban growth 1, 10, 119, 178
conflation with urban development 10
Urban hierarchy 4
Urban image 27, 267–269
Urbanism xiii 2, 6–9, 175, 223, 237
South African 238, 241–246
Urbanization xiii, 2–5, 8, 10, 223
Urban landscapes 5, 11, 15, 174–175, 237, 241, 243
Urban life xiii, 2, 13, 28
Urban planning 10–11, 17, 175, 237–239, 247–261, 265–286, 289–304
Urban politics 239, 271–275
Urban poor 119–120, 266, 269, 271, 283
Urban population 4, 289
Urban primacy 225
Urban refugees 126
Urban services 1, 5, 239, 289–304
Urban space 71, 119, 258
Urban theory xiii, 3, 10
Urry, John 180

Venturi, Robert 27
Vigilantism 64–66
Violence 1–2, 53, 65, 256–258

Water 251–255, 289–304
  free basic provision of 289–304
  policy 290
Watts, Michael 249
Wealth 6, 179, 191, 256
West Africa 31, 39, 256
Western cities 10
Western influences 18, 59, 116, 232, 265
Wolch, Jennifer 113
Women 221, 226, 234
Work 10, 13, 205, 207
Workers 152–153, 161–166, 226
  strike by Zambian retail 165–166
World Bank 254, 300
World Summit on Social Development 221

Yaounde, Cameroon 43, 108, 111–112
  Central Hospital of 111
Yoruba 257
Youth 12, 201–218, 243

Zaire (see Democratic Republic of Congo)
Zambia 151, 154, 156–157, 160, 162, 277
ZANU-PF (Zimbabwe African National Union-Patriotic Front) 265–267, 272, 274, 283
Zimbabwe 37, 123, 156, 179, 201–218, 238, 265–286
  Chinese interests in 282–283
  economic crisis in 201
  Unilateral Declaration of Independence (UDI) in 270
  Unity Accord of 272
Zimbabwe African People's Union (ZAPU) 272